KT-228-160

HANDS-ON HOLIDAYS

Charitable trips
Rewarding adventures
Volunteer breaks

The Carey Centre
Canterbury College
New Dover Road
Canterbury, Kent CT1 3AJ

CLASS No. F.R.T...3.......

BOOK No. 097177

LOAN PERIOD 3W.........

SHELF Careers/Connexions

Guy Hobbs

This edition first published in Great Britain in 2007 by
Crimson Publishing
Westminster House
Kew Road
Richmond
Surrey
TW9 2ND

© Guy Hobbs 2007

The right of Guy Hobbs to be identified as the author of this work has been asserted by him in accordance with the Copyright, Designs and Patents Act, 1988.

All rights reserved. No part of this publication may be reproduced, transmitted in any form or by any means, or stored in a retrieval system without either the prior written permission of the publisher, or in the case of reprographic reproduction a licence issued in accordance with the terms and licences issued by the CLA Ltd.

A catalogue record for this book is available from the British library.

ISBN 978 1 85458 373 4

Designed and Typeset by Nicki Averill Design and Illustration

Printed and bound in Italy by Legoprint SpA, Trento

CONTENTS

GETTING STARTED	**9**

What is a Hands-On Holiday? – Journeys with a Purpose – Mini Gaps 11
Types of Hands-On Holiday – Make a Difference: Voluntourism – What Kind of
  Volunteer Work is Available on Short Breaks? - What to Expect –
  How Much Will it Cost? – A Word of Caution – Do Something Different –
  Personal and Professional Development – Paid Work – Individual Interests 16
Who Takes a Hands-On Holiday and Why? – Students and Young People –
  Young Professionals: Twenties and Thirties – Taking the Family –
  Life Begins At… – Mature Travellers 26
Choosing a Hands-On Holiday – Using an Agency v. Independent
  Hands-On Holidays – Evaluating an Agency 32
Practicalities and Red Tape – Getting There – Passports and Visas – Travel
  Insurance – Travel Safety – Travellers' Health – Theft 35

CONSERVATION AND WILDLIFE	**45**

Holidays that Save the World – Practicalities 47
The Holidays
  Worldwide 50
  UK and Ireland 66
  Europe 73
  North America 80
  South/Central America and the Caribbean 88
  Africa 97
  Asia 105
  Australia and New Zealand 109

COMMUNITY AND DEVELOPMENT PROJECTS	**113**

Giving Something Back 115
Responsible Tourism 117
The Holidays
  Worldwide 118
  Europe 138
  North America 139
  South/Central America and the Caribbean 139
  Africa 147
  Asia 153

INTERNATIONAL WORKCAMPS	**159**

Temporary International Communities – What is a Workcamp? – What to Expect –
  Further Information 161
The Holidays
  UK-Based Organisations 165
  Organisations Worldwide 167

ARCHAEOLOGY AND HERITAGE 181

Working on a Dig – What to Expect – What to Bring – Finding a Dig 183
Cultural Heritage and Historical Restoration 187
The Holidays
    UK and Ireland 188
    Europe 200
    Archaeological Digs in Israel 209
    Worldwide 215

CHARITY CHALLENGES 227

Fundraising Adventures – How Does it Work? – Saving the World or a Free Holiday? –
    Who Takes a Charity Challenge? – How to Choose a Challenge – Fundraising 229
The Challenges 234
    Charities 235
    Charity Challenge Operators 242

AGRICULTURE 251

Getting Back to the Land 253
Voluntary Agricultural Work – Agritourism – Sustainable Agriculture Projects – 254
Communities 263
WWOOF: Worldwide Opportunities on Organic Farms – How to WWOOF –
    Contact Details and Membership Fees 264
Paid Agricultural Work – What to Expect – Finding Fruit Picking Jobs 268
    Fruit Picking in the UK – Wages – The Farms 270
    Fruit Picking Worldwide – Vineyard Vacations – Useful Organisations – The Farms 277

TEACHING AND SUMMER CAMPS 285

Volunteer Teaching Holidays 287
Working at Summer Camps 289
Short-Term English Teaching Worldwide 290
Summer Camps
    UK and Ireland 302
    Europe 307
    Worldwide 313

SPORTS, HOLIDAYS AND FESTIVALS 315

Sports and Activities – Trekking and Cycling – Winter Sports –
    Adventure Sports – Volunteer Sports Coaching Worldwide 317
Assisting Groups on Holiday – Paid Holiday Work – Holiday Volunteers 328
Working for Your Ticket at Summer Festivals – Music Festivals in the UK –
    Paid Festival Work – UK Folk Festivals – Literary Festivals – Music Festivals Worldwide 336

WORK EXPERIENCE ABROAD 351

Find Your True Calling on Holiday – Language Ability 353
Work Experience Worldwide 355

INDEX OF ORGANISATIONS 371
INDEX BY LOCATION 376

PREFACE

Let's face it, we could all do with longer holidays. But with the pressures of work, study and everyday commitments we are unlikely to find the time. The only answer is to make sure that we cram the most satisfying, rewarding and refreshing adventures into what little time we do have available.

In the last five years, the number of package holidays booked through mainstream operators has dropped by almost 10%, with travellers turning to experience-based breaks that give them a taste of something completely new. Today's travellers are more sophisticated and confident. They care about the world around them and are actively seeking authentic travel experiences. Today's travellers are not tourists and sightseers; they want to get involved and really understand new cultures. Today's travellers need this book.

There are hundreds of life-changing experiences profiled within these pages: from monitoring pandas in China to working with orphans in Argentina; from diving and surveying marine populations in the Bahamas, to helping to restore tsunami stricken houses and schools in Sri Lanka; from joining a cave archaeology expedition in Belize, to earning money as a short-term ski rep or expedition leader worldwide.

Hands-on holidays are journeys with a purpose. They allow you to get stuck in, to make a difference to the lives of others, to contribute to a better world, to indulge a long-held interest, and to broaden your horizons. They are the kind of adventures that gap year students have been enjoying for years. But these experiences are too important to be the preserve of the young and the time-rich.

During the research for this book we met a woman who spent her 64th birthday at the peak of Kilimanjaro, a school-teacher who monitored white rhinos in South Africa, a student who spent her holiday helping to rebuild New Orleans, a magistrate who races through Italy in a Mini for her annual holiday, a 37-year-old single mum who spent two weeks working with elephant mahouts in Thailand, and a 69-year-old woman who travelled through rural India delivering aid on horseback.

The message is clear: absolutely everybody can take a hands-on holiday. There are holidays to suit every age and every budget, and the fact that they are all short-term means you won't have to put your life on hold. So why follow the crowd? Why spend every holiday lazing around? No matter how little time you have, *Hands-On Holidays* is crammed with intense and rewarding adventures that will allow you to do so much more with your holiday.

Guy Hobbs
London
June 2007

ACKNOWLEDGEMENTS

This first edition of *Hands-On Holidays* owes a substantial debt to all the enthusiastic travellers who have found increasingly innovative ways to combine the most rewarding travel adventures with the hectic commitments of their ordinary lives. Hopefully their intrepid and often inspirational tales will save many a backpack from gathering dust at the back of the wardrobe. In particular, I would like to thank: Martyn Roberts, Jane Reddaway, Lucy Misch, Kirsty Sharratt, Thoger Krogh, Rachel Gibson, Lorraine Flanigan, Mark Weston, Rhiannon Mercer, Caroline Gosney, Gail Carbanier, Nicholas Sean, Barney Robertson, Catherine Johnson, Elena Bridgens, Lorna Allen, Jill Ingoglia, Trinidad Rodriguez, Gillian Meek, Martin Nielsen, Amy Wopat, Sean Crawford, Shirley Campbell, Angelica Leone, Lindsey Moss, Linda Vonken, Federico Spinucci, Linda Handiak, John Gowans, Sonya Grist, Paul Keyland, Simon Ball, Liz Eaton, Julie Russell, Danielle Thomas, Alice Wonnacott, Rachael Muirhead, Danica Mullarkey, Geoffroy Groleau, Lianne Slavin, Vishna Shah, Diana Hannant and Michele Moody.

I am also grateful to the many directors and staff of specialist organisations who have put me in touch with hands-on holiday-makers from around the world, and given me the benefit of their experience. These include Ian Birbeck, Andy Jefferies, Zoe Gamble, Gina Lee, Karen Foerstel, Andrew Birley, Craig Priestly, Helen Stoddart, Katie Fewings, Carol Ellick, Judith Broeker, and Nikki Bond.

Photographs used for the cover and internal pages were very kindly provided courtesy of BTCV (Richard Wadely), classictours.co.uk; Earthwatch (John Rollino, Guy Stockton, Paul Harris), Go Differently, Hands Up Holidays, Bev Wildeboer (Italian Job), Original Volunteers, Projects Abroad, Oxfam (Ade Steward 2006), Real Gap, Relief Riders International, Shumba Experience, Vindolanda, Vitalise, WWOOF, and Youth Action for Peace (SEEDS Iceland).

Thanks to Nicki Averill for design and typesettling, and to mccdesign ltd for the cover.

Special thanks go to Dana Stevens, to Susan Griffith for ideas and contributions, and to Deborah Penrith for her invaluable help with the Community and Teaching chapters.

While every effort has been made to ensure that the information contained in this book was accurate at the time of going to press, some details are bound to change within the lifetime of this edition. If you do take a hands-on holiday or come across something which might be of interest to readers of the next edition, please write to Guy Hobbs at Vacation Work Publications, 2nd Floor, Westminster House, Kew Road, Richmond, Surrey TW9 2ND or email him at guy@vacationwork.co.uk. Substantial contributions will be rewarded with a free copy of the next edition or any other Vacation Work or Crimson Publishing title.

Telephone Numbers: Please note that the telephone numbers in this book are written as needed to call that number from outside the country (eg. +1 for the USA, +34 for Spain). The only exception is UK numbers which are written as needed to call from within the UK. To call a UK number from outside the UK drop the first zero and add the international dialling code of +44.

Currency: All prices/wages are given in the currency that the agency or organisation deals in. For up-to-the-minute currency conversion visit www.xe.com

Getting Started

WHAT IS A HANDS-ON HOLIDAY?

Journeys With a Purpose

Our holiday time is precious. The modern world is hectic, fast-paced and competitive and if we don't stop to take stock, it can grind us down. In moments of fatigue, the sheer routine, the sameness of our daily lives can get on top of us and we all experience the need to escape. Our dreams, interests and ambitions somehow get lost among the overwhelming demands upon us and sometimes we just need to take a step back and put our lives in perspective or re-evaluate our goals. Often a few weeks lying on a beach are perfectly sufficient to recharge the batteries but that too can easily become routine, and when we return, nothing has changed. Sometimes we all need to try something completely different, to pursue a new agenda that applies and develops our skills in a novel way, rekindles a passion or interest, and leaves us feeling totally refreshed. Whether you want to make a difference, or just do something different, a hands-on holiday could be the answer.

Hands-on holidays are all about getting involved, and getting to understand a place and its people in a more profound way than you might as a tourist. Inevitably this will involve getting your hands dirty with a little voluntary or paid work. On the face of it, a 'working holiday' may seem a fairly peculiar notion. Surely 'work' is one of the main irritations of daily life that we seek to escape when we pack our bags and head off into the sun? Surely a 'holiday' should be restorative, filled with fun, relaxation and all of the things that we associate as standing in stark contrast to 'work'? Well this is all true, but 'work' as defined within the pages of this book is quite different to that which many of us have to do in order to put bread on the table. If you take advantage of one of the opportunities presented here, you will be pursuing a dream or interest, immersed in an intriguingly different culture, surrounded by interesting people from diverse walks of life, learning new skills and challenging yourself every day. If that sounds anything like a normal day at work, you are extremely fortunate.

This is not to say that it won't be hard work. Helping to rebuild homes that were destroyed in the tsunami, trekking through a Costa Rican rainforest for charity, teaching children in a Tanzanian village school, picking cherries under the strong Australian sun, helping to restore a 300-year-old monastery in Nepal, monitoring the movements of elephants in a Kenyan wildlife sanctuary, these are all examples of extremely challenging work, both mentally and physically. But every day you will be able to see the tangible results of what you have achieved, and that in itself can engender an enormous feeling of satisfaction. Stretching yourself beyond the ordinary and accomplishing results you never thought possible will not only leave you feeling rejuvenated, it will also allow you to look at the world in a completely new light. The working element of a hands-on holiday will not necessarily be paid, in fact participants may have to make a personal contribution to costs, but it will certainly be rewarding.

Whilst a fly and flop holiday is all well and good, how much benefit do we really gain from it? Invariably, as you are heading to the airport on the way home, somebody will point out that it only seems like yesterday that you were setting off on your holidays. But time stretches when you apply yourself to something really out of the ordinary. You will pack so much into a hands-on holiday that the experience will inevitably be more beneficial, more memorable and will seem much longer.

Another advantage of this type of holiday is that it offers the individual a far more authentic experience. Those on a conventional holiday pass through rapidly; they see the sights and they eat the food, but they very rarely leave feeling that they have completely satisfied their curiosity about a place and its culture. In contrast, those on a hands-on holiday work at close quarters with local inhabitants, they sometimes even lodge with local families, they discuss local issues and they build lasting friendships. They may have to learn fast and think on their feet, but they will certainly satisfy their desire to get under the skin of a different culture.

Hands-on holidays then, are all about taking a journey with a purpose. They are for everyone who has uttered the words 'How I'd love to be a….' or 'I'd give anything to see….' Too many people hide behind an assumption that something they dream of doing is beyond their reach because of the pressures of work and home life. But as this book shows, anyone can pursue a dream without breaking the bank or putting their life on hold. What that dream entails is entirely up to you. You may feel that you want to make a difference to the world, to give something back and help those less fortunate than yourself, or you may want to concentrate on yourself for a change, learn new skills, broaden your horizons and gain new experiences. It's up to you.

Mini Gaps

Hands-on or otherwise, a holiday generally implies a short break. Whilst many of us would love to take a gap year, the reality is that those of us with work, study and family responsibilities can only hope to escape for a few weeks. Traditionally, going on an adventure with a purpose, whether that purpose is self-serving or altruistic, has meant taking a sabbatical, perhaps renting out the house and putting your life on hold. Well no more. The holidays in this book are all designed for people with anything from a few days to a month to spare. These are trips which fit as neatly into the student's easter or summer break as the worker's annual leave. These are trips which can be taken by those with a mortgage, pets, aged parents, or children who can't be taken out of school for too long. They can be taken without fear of bankrupting yourself or having to find a new job upon your return. Not all of us can take a year off, but what we can do is cram as rewarding an experience as possible into the short time that we have available.

The idea of taking a life break without the need to break your life, and of building up a lifetime's worth of memories in just a short trip is one that has been gaining currency over the last few years. As the gap year industry, still in its infancy, develops and matures, the tour operators and organisations have been forced to acknowledge new demands. When the gap year first appeared, it was the school-leavers who were at the front line, demanding a range of experiences that were both enjoyable and bolstered their CVs. As the idea gained legitimacy, and was even encouraged by universities and employers as helping to create more rounded individuals, people of all ages wanted their piece of the action. Until then the career break was still fairly unusual and even looked down upon in some circles. Suddenly, it was re-branded as the 'gap year for grown-ups' and everybody from high-flying businessmen to young-at-heart grandparents were getting in on the act. With the idea now so mainstream, it was only a matter of time before people, fired up with a passion for new cultural experiences, realised that there must be a way to incorporate the gap experience into their everyday lives.

And the gap organisations realised it too. Established gap year companies such as Shumba Experience, Quest and Personal Development Overseas, to name but a few, have begun to promote a series of new 'mini-adventures' or 'mini-gaps'. Even those organisations that were set up specifically to provide gap years are now offering one, two, three and four week projects. For example, Real Gap has around a hundred different projects for 30 days or less, including a two-week seal rehabilitation programme in South Africa and a four-week Moldovan orphanage volunteer programme. In 2006 the volunteer tourism company, i-to-i, reported an increase of 122% in bookings for one to three-week trips, stating in an article in *The Observer* that *'There is a definite shift towards people wanting to help overseas, but also wanting to incorporate the trip into their annual leave'.*

It is not just the gap organisations that have recognised this new trend however. Mainstream tour operators now run a range of gap-style holidays, and several new operators have been set up as a response to the demand, especially for volunteer tourism (or *voluntourism* as it is now known – see below).

While some people have questioned how much can actually be achieved in just a short space of time, *The Independent*'s travel editor, Simon Calder has defended the short-term gap experience. In 2007 he set off on a self-designed Gap Month as *'a reaction to the profligacy of travellers who have plenty of time to revel in the best the world can offer, but lack the funds or forethought to make the most of it'.* He was greeted with cynicism from fellow travellers along the way and cries of *'You can't get to know a place properly if you only spend a day or two there'.* Yet Calder himself found the experience to be an inspiring and gratifying form of tourism stating: *'The quicker your trip, the more intense and rewarding the experience – because it has to be'.* Many of the hands-on holiday participants interviewed in this book agree – because you know your trip is short, you make the most of every moment.

Tessa Le Plar is a single working mum juggling a hectic life. For Tessa, a gap year was out of the question and a hands-on holiday was the only way she could realise her dreams to have a real travel 'experience'. She spent two weeks in Thailand working with elephants and in that short space of time she found that her eyes were opened to a whole new world. Her story shows just how much can be achieved during a hands-on holiday:

I have been bounced around on the back of elephants, the backs of various motorbikes and atop a 5-foot pile of pineapple leaves on a flatbed truck. I have been showered with biting ants, had a lizard up my shirt, and befriended by more dogs than I have ever seen in my life. I have seen sunsets and sunrises like never before. I have misunderstood, been misunderstood, mimed, waved, pointed and danced my way around a language that I can't wait to hear again. I have witnessed elephants misbehaving, playing to cameras, kicking footballs (and dogs), and, most impressively, undoing their chains with their trunks. I have seen temples and Thai boxing. I have drunk alcohol to make my hair stand on end, and food which was so hot as to give me instant hiccups and a dead face. I was looking for an experience and I got absolutely everything I wanted and so much more. It may only have been two weeks' worth but I feel like a better person and it has given me a bug to do some more exploring. You don't need to go with lots of friends, or be a particular age – there is no 'best before' date on a hands-on holiday. There were times when I felt like a fraud because I was purely there for two weeks and not returning from a jaunt up Everest, but now I know that everyone is entitled to do these things. You CAN have an experience without it interrupting your life. Not every holiday has to be about lying on a beach and complaining about life back home. I spent two weeks constantly pinching myself and saying – 'I'm having an adventure!'

CANADA
Minke whale and
marine research p85

COLORADO
Rebuilding and clearing
the Colorado Trail p83

ICELAND
Icecap trek for
charity p250

CORNWALL
Working with woolley
monkeys p69

ITALY
Short-term paid work
as a ski rep p319

WASSAW ISLAND, GEORGIA
Monitoring loggerhead sea
turtles p82

THE BAHAMAS
Snorkelling and
surveying coral reef p56

CANARY ISLANDS
Crewing island-hopping
tall ships p323

BELIZE
Cave archaeology
expedition p225

GHANA
Sports work for
underprivileged
children p326

COSTA RICA
Shark-tagging
expedition p95

ZAMBIA
Journalism work
experience p368

BOLIVIA
Helping to rehabilitate
animals rescued from
abuse p90

BRAZIL
Working with street
children p146

ARGENTINA
Working in an
orphanage p123

SOUTH AFRICA
Game Ranger
Guide Course p97

A WORLD OF POSSIBILITIES

POLAND
Teaching English at summer camps p308

NEPAL
Restoring a 300-year-old monastery p217

CHINA
Monitoring wild pandas p53

THAILAND
Elephant Mahout project p106

INDONESIA
Monitoring wild orangutans and helping preserve their habitat p108

INDIA
Horseback journey delivering supplies to rural ares p156

SRI LANKA
Post-Tsunami volunteering p121

FIJI
Building homes in poor communities p128

AUSTRALIA
Coaching sports to refugee children p328

NEW ZEALAND
Historic Building Restoration p221

MALAWI
Providing food and shelter for orphans p135

TYPES OF HANDS-ON HOLIDAY

Make a Difference: 'Voluntourism'

Volunteering overseas, once the domain of only the most intrepid cultural tourists, has become extremely popular. Over the last decade there has been a subtle shift in the perception of voluntary work, from a pursuit practised only by the most dedicated philanthropists with two years to spare and little regard for their personal safety, to an arena that welcomes anybody with the desire to make a difference.

The increased popularity of volunteering is a result of two factors. Partly, in an age when the old jobs-for-life contract between employer and employee is breaking down, individuals are increasingly looking for rewarding experiences outside work that will add value to their lives. They want to find activities that can bestow pride and a sense of achievement. Work may provide an outlet for some of these yearnings, but many individuals prefer to search elsewhere and the voluntary sector at home and abroad is a major beneficiary. Serial short-term volunteer, Jane Reddaway, is a firm believer in the benefits of voluntourism projects for the participant:

On my many trips, I have found that voluntourism is a great way to get to know a country from the inside rather than the tourist 'shop-front'. Volunteering activities bring you closer to the people of the country you are visiting. Also, if you travel on your own, volunteering is a great way to meet up with like-minded people and it also gives your trip some structure. I also believe it is a good way to keep perspective on life. In the UK, we are so used to high levels of opportunity and security that we often take it for granted, and it's good to be reminded of this sometimes. Short-term volunteering has allowed me to keep a career and yet experience some amazing places.

But mainly the shift is altruistic. Devastating natural disasters and an increasing global awareness of the discrepancy between rich and poor, created by the *Make Poverty History* campaign, among others, added to a sense of helplessness felt by ordinary people. When the tsunami hit South-East Asia on Boxing Day 2004, charities and NGOs were inundated with requests from people wanting to give up their time to help. So much so in fact, that the organisational infrastructure simply was not in place to accommodate them and people were advised to stay at home. This engendered an enormous sense of frustration. People had the desire and the resources to help, but were at a loss as to how best to channel them. Nevertheless, for many this was the first time they had considered volunteering overseas, and while they could be of little use in the immediate aftermath, in the long-term there would be a range of projects to get involved in. As a reaction to this newfound social conscience amongst travellers, many tour operators and organisations set about improving the accessibility of community projects around the world. There is a wide variety of choices now available to the philanthropic traveller and the media has branded this new mainstream combination of travel and good deeds, 'voluntourism'.

Voluntourism offers a unique way to see the world, learn about new cultures and benefit a local community, and its popularity is on the rise. According to a recent *Daily Telegraph* article more than 40,000 Britons took a voluntourism holiday in 2006. Demand is high, but

Projects Abroad volunteer at The Lighthouse Orphanage, Phnom Penh, Cambodia.

unlike many long-term volunteer projects, most organisations are not looking for a particular skill set. They simply want their participants to be enthusiastic and willing to work hard as part of a team. The downside is that the majority of the short-term volunteer holidays come at a price. A month in Africa or Asia can cost upwards of £2,000, plus air fares (although this guide contains a number of low-cost options).

Nevertheless, the benefits of getting involved can be enormous. Very few of us can be entirely unmoved by news reports of disasters, or by appeals from local and international charities on behalf of the struggling and the suffering – abandoned children, needlessly blind farmers, performing bears and so on. And whilst we can't all give up our jobs and dedicate our lives to the needs of the less fortunate, as we might like to, a volunteer hands-on holiday allows us to become usefully involved. Trinidad Rodriguez took time out in 2006 to help with the clear-up operation after New Orleans was levelled by hurricane Katrina. Even though the task seemed insurmountable and she was only able to help rebuild one house in a neighbourhood of many that were destroyed, by working with the community, she felt part of a much larger movement that would eventually restore the Big Easy to its former glory:

The last two days we spent working on Stacy's house, the skies over the Ninth Ward were full of government helicopters. Our national leaders were being given an aerial tour of the devastation. From our vantage point on the ground, surrounded by ruined homes and lost histories, covered in drywall dust and insulation, these helicopters felt like the enemy overseer. They contained the mysterious architects of New Orleans' future, the ones making vital decisions from a position of untouched safety. As an outsider, I felt overwhelmed. What good was the work I was doing? Was I helping wax the floors of a sinking ship?

But as the helicopters hovered overhead, Stacy hung up a sign that had been distributed at the neighbourhood meeting: 'We're coming home'. That was all the affirmation I needed.

Trinidad was welcomed by the local community, and left feeling not only that in her own small way she had helped them towards their goals, but also that she had gained an affinity for and deeper understanding of the poverty-stricken residents of New Orleans' Ninth Ward.

Voluntourists frequently rhapsodise about their experiences and regard their time as a volunteer as an extraordinary episode in their lives. And it is clear that working to help others can also benefit the participants themselves. The need to get away is frequently a desire to challenge yourself in new directions, to move outside your comfort zone, to experience different ways of life and to work in a new geographical location. In addition to an energising break in routine, participants can also gain practical experience in the fields of construction, conservation, archaeology and social welfare; they may improve their language skills, and they will certainly learn something of the customs of the society in which they are volunteering. In fact, undertaking a challenge of this kind can often do wonders for career development. New skills are learned very quickly. Teaching in a small school in India, for example, when one has never taught before, provides daily practice in planning and rapidly hones communication skills.

What Kind of Volunteer Work is Available on Short Breaks?

Most of the volunteer tourism agencies and organisations concentrate on one of two broad areas – development and conservation. Development volunteer work can encompass anything that aims to help people, from teaching and healthcare, to rebuilding communities. Conservation projects focus on monitoring wildlife and environmental education. However, this book covers a range of opportunities for willing volunteers with only a little time to spare:

Conservation and Wildlife: Many environmental charities and NGOs have openings for volunteers. Animal lovers will find a wealth of opportunities. Global Vision International, for example, can arrange for people to work with vervet monkeys in South Africa, turtles in Panama, orangutans in Sumatra and collecting species data in the Galapagos Islands.

Community Projects: This is a vast field, but the emphasis is on helping local communities. The work may include working with street children, working in orphanages, building homes in areas ravaged by war and natural disasters, HIV awareness and human rights work.

Workcamps: The ideal setting for a volunteer with no previous experience, who does not want to commit too much time. Workcamps last from one to four weeks and are often the cheapest form of short-term foreign travel, yet they are an enriching life experience shared with people from around the world. The work undertaken at workcamps varies hugely, depending on the organisation, but can include conservation, community development projects and heritage preservation.

Archaeology and Heritage: Those with an interest in the past are spoiled for choice. There are archaeological digs in desperate need of short-term volunteers across the globe, and those with diving qualifications can also try their hand at underwater excavation. Heritage projects require skilled and unskilled workers to help restore historic buildings and monuments from Chester to the Caribbean.

Charity Challenges: Not strictly volunteering, but still taking a holiday for the benefit of good causes. Charity challenges allow you to visit new places, improve your fitness and realise your dreams whilst raising money for charity. The kind of sponsored challenges available include treks, bike rides, mountain climbs, rafting and horse-riding expeditions.

WWOOFing: Willing Workers on Organic Farms is a worldwide organisation that offers volunteers bed and board in exchange for agricultural labour. This is an extremely cheap way to take a holiday and offers a true grassroots experience.

Short-term English Teaching: Both paid and unpaid short-term teaching opportunities are detailed within this book. English skills are in great demand in developing countries and volunteering with children and communities offers an extremely gratifying volunteer holiday.

What to Expect

For the most part, volunteering hands-on holidays are nothing like conventional holidays. Even volunteers for organisations with glossy seductive brochures often find the tasks that they are assigned to be more physically and emotionally demanding than they anticipated. Teaching English to a group of smiling eight-year-olds in a West African village sounds fun and exotic when contemplated at home, but can land you in a very testing situation which might involve few creature comforts and demand a measure of stoicism. Raleigh International stresses that attitude of the mind, not age, is the crucial factor in coping with the tough conditions of the Chilean Andes or the Mongolian Steppes. If you have any concerns about physical endurance, it is best to consult your GP for a full medical. Explain the conditions you are likely to face and ask for advice.

However, the popularity of voluntourism has prompted a number of tour operators to offer packages for those looking for a little more holiday and a little less work. These operators, including Different Travel, Hands Up Holidays and Go Differently, offer holidays that combine sightseeing, relaxation and appealing but ethical accommodation with opportunities to work alongside local people on development and environmental projects.

Real Gap volunteer helping to build houses on a hands-on holiday in Guatemala.

Usually the split between work and relaxation is around fifty-fifty, but it is up to the tourist how much time they spend on the project. To give an example, The Imaginative Traveller offers an 18–day trip combining house-building in Mongolia with a camping trip on the Ongi River and Great White Lake, and a visit to the ancient capital of Kharkorin, for £425.

The amount of work you will have to do and the conditions in which you will do it varies enormously according to the organisation you go with or the project that you choose. This guide allows you to see at a glance the type of work that each project entails and key details such as the type of accommodation available. Nevertheless, it is always wise to do as much research as you can on the organisation and preferably speak to former volunteers.

How Much Will it Cost?

Paying to volunteer is a relatively new concept and one with which potential voluntourists will have to grapple. Large agencies usually offer an all-inclusive package with insurance, training and local support, plus a raft of optional leisure activities. Just as an example, two weeks of eco-volunteering with Pink River Dolphins in Brazil with the organisation Global Vision International, will cost around £1,195. Some companies are far more commercial than others and it is usually easy to tell from their style and literature. Specialist tour operators charge according to the infrastructure they provide. If, for example, you choose to travel with one of the operators that combines volunteer work with sightseeing, or adventure travel, often with fairly luxury accommodation, you can expect to pay far more. Always ask for a breakdown of the contribution you are being asked to pay. That way you can make an informed decision as to whether the service offered justifies the fee.

Using a large agency is of course the most expensive way to volunteer your time on a short break. But even if you approach a small agency or an individual project you should still consider the financial burden that the volunteer is placing on the host organisation or community. Food, accommodation and local transport all cost money and many projects ask for a donation to cover their costs. Those who find a project without participation fees must still budget for flights, visas, travel insurance and spending money.

Fortunately for those on a tight budget, this guide covers a range of far cheaper and even free voluntourism options. Workcamps, charity challenges and working on organic farms in return for bed and board (covered in *Agriculture*) are all particularly cost-effective ways to travel and make a difference.

A Word of Caution

Volunteering overseas has become big business. The fact that so many more people are expressing a desire to give their time is, of course, a positive development. However there are some negative side-effects and voluntourism has been the subject of a media backlash. Vicky Baker, in an article entitled 'Saving the World in a Weekend' in *The Observer*, asked '*Is* [voluntourism] *just a quick fix for tourists looking to appease their consciences and travel companies looking for a new gimmick?*'. It is clearly a concern that unethical companies may offer a trip that focuses more on providing a rewarding experience for volunteers than on improving life for people overseas. And *The Guardian* has even described volunteering as the new colonialism, with armies of well-meaning idealists forcing their worldview onto developing communities across the planet. Much of this is media hysteria and should not be taken to heart, as it does little more than quash the impulse to help others. Nevertheless it does present a number of important issues that need to be addressed.

Firstly, potential voluntourists should choose very carefully when selecting a project or organisation. Privately-run projects are particularly susceptible to causing disappointment, especially if the individuals in charge fail to maintain high standards. For example, volunteers have travelled to remote corners of the world to work on eco-projects only to find that the managers run them for profit. Occasionally voluntourists are forced to conclude that the voluntary organisation under whose auspices they are working charge volunteers well in excess of essential running costs. Nowadays the large number of voluntary organisations competing with one another for paying volunteers means that it is wise to investigate the proportion of your fee that goes to the needy project and how much goes towards administration, and in some cases, profit. The process of finding an ethical organisation is discussed later (*Choosing a Hands-On Holiday*). A good agency or organisation will promote worthwhile programmes that grow out of local input, while avoiding local rip-off merchants.

Secondly, participants should not raise their expectations regarding what they hope to achieve to unrealistic levels. Participants who travel with Different Travel are advised at their initial briefing: *'Don't expect to save the world'*. Clearly it takes longer than a few weeks before the tangible benefits of a project can start to take effect. It is undoubtedly the case that some of the promotional literature distributed by profit-making companies out to enlist paying volunteers shamelessly tries to exploit people's altruistic urges. Nevertheless, if you are happy to accept that the difference you can make in such a short time may be miniscule in comparison to the problems that a particular community faces, then you will still take a lot away from the experience. Participants should bear in mind that just by visiting they are benefiting the economy, and what little they achieve on top of that can only be a bonus.

It is probably true that the individual volunteer on a short voluntourism holiday will gain more from the experience than they can necessarily give back, but this is certainly not a criticism of the voluntourism model. Many projects are ongoing for months or years at a time, and although the individual's involvement may only be for a few weeks, the sum of the parts will eventually add up to a very worthwhile whole. Additionally, the insights gained by short-term volunteers can in themselves have a positive long-term effect. Even a voluntourist who gave the matter little thought before signing up may end up having their eyes opened to the difficulties of delivering aid across cultural divides and, at the very least, they are sure to go home with a heightened sensitivity to cultural differences.

Useful Web Resources

www.volunteersouthamerica.net: Non-commercial directory of free and low-cost volunteer programmes in South America.

www.truetravellers.org: Canadian based not-for-profit organisation providing free information to help independent travellers make the most of their experiences.

www.go-mad.org: Low-cost volunteer placements in developing countries around the world. Run by volunteers.

www.independentvolunteer.org: Set up by a group that met while involved in volunteer work abroad. Aims to provide no or low-cost volunteer opportunities.

www.idealist.org: Lists thousands of volunteer opportunities around the world.

www.voluntourism.org: Information for travellers about combining travel with voluntary service, including how to select a project that is right for you.

www.ethicalvolunteering.org: Offers advice and information regarding the ethical issues involved with international voluntary work.

www.workingabroad.com: Information on voluntary work abroad including organisations currently looking for volunteers and personalised reports on grassroots projects.
www.worldwidevolunteering.org: Search and match database with over 1300 volunteering organisations in the UK and worldwide.
www.volunteering.org.uk: Volunteering England works to support an increase in the quality, quantity, impact and accessibility of volunteering throughout England.
www.volunteeringoptions.org: Information on volunteering and development worldwide.

Do Something Different: Personal Development, Paid Work and Individual Interest

The point of taking a hands-on holiday is to do something different with your holiday time. When the routine of the daily grind becomes onerous, stressful or dull and begins to swamp other interests, it is certainly time to reclaim your life by taking a break and focusing on your own personal interests, dreams and ambitions. A hands-on holiday does not have to have a higher altruistic purpose. Volunteer work is just one way of doing something different, and while everyone can gain an enormous amount from good works, it still amounts to putting the needs of others before your own. A short amount of time out can be the ideal opportunity to stretch yourself or to act on a long-held ambition. Big dreams and long-range goals give people something to aim for, and the bigger the dreams, the more the dreamer achieves. Of course, in just a few weeks, it would be unrealistic to expect to change your life permanently. But by changing it just momentarily, a hands-on holiday can open your eyes to a world of new possibilities. A hands-on holiday can be a unique opportunity to step back and examine your life and lifestyle and to enrich and broaden interests and experiences.

Perhaps you have always dreamed of trying out an alternative career such as farming llamas, working on a newspaper, or working as a ranger on a wildlife reserve. Perhaps you want to be able to make a little money and combine it with the opportunity to travel and experience new cultures. Perhaps you simply want a free holiday that allows you to indulge

Projects Abroad volunteer helps train local English language teachers in Sivakasi, India

a personal interest such as musical events around the world. Within the pages of this book are hundreds of opportunities and contacts that will help you to act upon whatever your personal ambition or desire might be.

Personal and Professional Development

Almost all of the opportunities detailed in this book offer participants the chance to learn some new life skill, which may either push you in the direction of a new career or simply complement your formal professional training. Whilst the major motivation for voluntourism is not usually to improve career prospects, there is no doubt that indirectly it will do so (see above). Yet there are more focused ways to explore new opportunities. Whether you are a student carefully considering the path that you would like your life to take, or somebody already ensconced in a career, a hands-on holiday can certainly help. The final chapter of this book details a range of opportunities for short-term work experience and internships abroad, all of which combine a holiday with a stepping stone towards longer-term goals.

Students and young people agonising over how best to spend the next 40 or so years of their life are in a very difficult position. While juggling full-time study with part-time and summer jobs to ease the financial burden of tuition fees, they are also expected to somehow find the time to contemplate momentous career decisions. Unpaid work experience at home is one option, but all of this can leave them with very little free time to enjoy holidays and live their life. The solution may well be to combine valuable work experience with a break overseas. A number of organisations have recognised this possibility and have put together a variety of options that allow participants to develop a particular skill in just a short period, while being immersed in another culture. For example, the established gap year agency, Projects Abroad, offers a range of two-week specials for young people in full-time education that mix lectures with hands-on and observational work and weekend excursions. The work experience available includes a law placement in China, journalism in Romania, physiotherapy in Nepal, cookery in India and medicine in Mongolia. Whilst a two-week placement can only scratch the surface of an industry, it can certainly give participants an insight that will allow them to decide whether or not this is how they intend to spend the rest of their lives.

Those who are already in work can use internships and work experience to gain new skills. Onlookers may doubt the value of a break. They may view it as a self-indulgent opportunity to ease the pressure of working life. But that view should be resisted. A hands-on holiday can be regarded as an empowering move in the contemporary workplace and it can also be interpreted positively by employers as a sign of self-sufficiency and initiative.

Alternatively they can use a hands-on holiday to broaden their horizons outside of their chosen field, and try something completely different. The government's championing of lifelong learning is underpinned by an appreciation that the nature of work has become flexible and this meshes nicely with the idea of a hands-on holiday. In the modern economy we are less tied to a career in one field or to employment with one company for the duration of our working lives. Trying out a completely new career can provide an extremely refreshing break. Just to take one example, African Conservation Experience offers a two-week theory and practical Game Ranger Guide course in the African Bush. It is an intensive course set in a 'big 5' Game Reserve and covering animal identification, botany, animal behaviour and geology, as well as rangering skills such as 4x4 driving, dealing with dangerous game, snake identification and tracking. According to ACE's founder Rob Harris, this course has been particularly popular amongst working people on annual leave. While most people attend out of a love for, and deep interest in, South African wildlife, a few have gone on to pursue careers in conservation. As Harris says, *'Spending a few weeks under the stars, out in the wilds of South Africa certainly helps you to gain new perspective on your lifestyle.'*

Paid Work

The rewards of a hands-on holiday are many, but they are not generally financial. In order to combine travel with a paying job it is usually necessary to commit a much larger chunk of time than this book deals with. Those who have a few months to spare and want to earn money in a foreign setting, would be better off consulting the book *Summer Jobs Abroad* (Vacation Work Publications). Equally, it is beyond the remit of this book to provide working opportunities for those funding themselves on long-term travelling expeditions. This topic is covered in some detail in another Vacation Work guide, *Work Your Way Around the World.* As Susan Griffith points out in *Work Your Way*, *'though travelling itself is never dull, a job which can help out your finances along the way may well be....Jobs are jobs wherever you do them'.* In contrast, this book aims to present exciting and rewarding holidays and short breaks, and the opportunities to combine this with financial remuneration are fairly limited.

Having said that, they do exist and are detailed within the pages of this book. One such activity that pays fairly well, offers free or subsidised accommodation, is limited in duration and at the same time will expand your cultural horizons, is fruit harvesting work (detailed in *Agriculture*). Fruit picking has always been a staple of the working traveller due to its flexibility. Seasons tend not to run on too long (the grape-picking season in France tends to last around 10 days) and farms are fairly accommodating to the availability of workers. As a working holiday, fruit picking is particularly appealing because it offers participants a truly authentic experience of alien culture from the grassroots. And while the money won't make you a millionaire, saving is fairly easy as there are few opportunities to spend what you earn on an isolated farm. Dutch student, Danielle Thomas, spent a hands-on holiday grape picking in France:

I went primarily to make some money and keep myself busy. In 11 days I made approximately 650 euros, though with tax subtracted and a contribution to the farming family for food and board, I had 550 euros when I left. I was very pleased as I was able to fund further travels with that money.

Danielle found the work hard, but extremely rewarding because of the people she met, which included locals and workers from around the world. Her story appears in the *Agriculture* chapter.

Other opportunities for paid short-term work include teaching English at summer schools, accompanying British school children on skiing trips and other excursions, and leading holidays. Teaching English as a foreign language is so sought after that many people take voluntary rather than paid positions, often in deprived areas where schools simply cannot afford to pay. Nonetheless there are plenty of paid short-term positions available for all levels of experience and these, along with the voluntary positions, are detailed in *Teaching and Summer Camps*. ACLE, based in Italy and recognised by the Italian Ministry of Education presents one such opportunity. ACLE sends English-speaking counsellors to around 50 camps throughout Italy in August and September each year. Qualified TEFL teachers and unqualified activity leaders are required to combine English lessons with games, songs, sport and drama. While the pay is not huge, approximately £130 per week, participants are provided with transport, accommodation, meals and insurance free of charge.

While you will never make a fortune from a hands-on holiday, the opportunities do exist to make a worthwhile experience fund itself, and perhaps even provide you with a little spending money.

Individual Interests

Personal passions and interests are the first things to go by the wayside when the burdens of everyday life get on top of you. We all lack the time to do what we want to do, simply because that which we absolutely *have* to do gets in the way. Your holiday time should not just be about escaping the trivialities that fill your life by lazing on a beach, but about rediscovering and making time for the passions and enthusiasms that drive you outside of your career.

Some particularly fortunate people have forged careers from their overriding interests and so may not be in need of a hands-on holiday. But for the majority of people it is far better to indulge an enthusiasm that bears no relation to their normal lives. It is only when you apply yourself to something totally alien to your established routine that you are fully able to relax and enjoy yourself on a hands-on holiday. For example, David Forster, a 54–year-old operations manager who builds and tests spacecraft mechanisms by day, spends his holiday time each year digging up Roman remains on an archaeological excavation in Northumberland. It is hard to think of two activities less connected, but David thoroughly enjoys the simplicity of working outdoors on a worthwhile project, and balks at the idea of over-complicating his holiday: *'There is little point in the supervisors training me in more complex techniques such as planning and mapping. All I want to do is dig and find stuff!'*

Those of a sporting bent will find a range of working holidays that may take their interest, from taking a short break helping to crew a tall ship, to volunteering as a football coach, to paid short-term work as a watersports instructor or ski rep (all covered in *Sports, Holidays and Festivals*). Those who are interested in music and the arts will also find appealing work in *Sports, Holidays and Festivals*. Demand for entry to summer music festivals around the world increases year on year and so, for that matter, does the price of tickets. One route to free entry is to volunteer with one of the charities that organises wardens and litter pickers, or to gain entry as paid support staff. While the work may be laborious, a free ticket, space for your tent, and a guaranteed number of hours off are enough to attract hundreds of people each year.

Conservation, wildlife, history, construction, agriculture, adventure sports, arts and crafts and literature are just a few of the other interests catered for here. If you don't already have a pastime that you are passionate about, we hope that you will find one within the pages of this book.

Shumba Experience volunteer spends the weekend looking after lion cubs on a hands-on holiday in South Africa.

WHO TAKES A HANDS-ON HOLIDAY AND WHY?

The short answer to this is everyone. Just as gap years have transcended the generational boundaries so too has the hands-on holiday. While 16 or 18 is usually quoted as the minimum age, an upper age limit is seldom specified. Even if an agency specifies 30 or 40, these upper limits tend to be flexible and an energetic candidate may have little trouble being accepted. Most of the programmes detailed in this book are open to anyone with an adventurous spirit, good health, reasonable fitness, sometimes a willingness to rough it, and enough money to pay for it.

Due to its short duration, the hands-on holiday is often more suitable than a gap year for people in work, and retirees with too many commitments to spend an extended period away from home. As more and more people take up these opportunities, the profile of participants you are likely to meet on a hands-on holiday has become increasingly varied. Sharing the experience with people of all ages and from many different walks of life is likely to enhance your enjoyment of the project and expand your worldview. Stereotypes of carefree youth versus cautious middle age are often overturned when thrown together in a hard-working environment. However, there is always a chance that older participants may find themselves in a minority amongst energetic 18-year-olds, or vice versa. Workcamps for example, almost always attract a younger participant. Anyone who is concerned about this possibility should simply enquire what the average age and full age range will be on the project.

Students and Young People

The benefits of a hands-on holiday are similar to those of the gap year. One of the most vaunted benefits of travel, work and experience of foreign cultures is that it will enhance your CV, make you stand out from the crowd and genuinely make you a more appealing proposition for potential employers. In a career market place that is becoming increasingly competitive, these considerations cannot be emphasised enough. The placement agency, Madventurer, sums it up nicely on the website www.careerbreaker.com:

> As businesses become globally focused, an understanding of cultures different from our own is considered a huge asset. Not only that, you become more interesting. How many interviews are conducted in which the candidates can barely be distinguished from one another? Everybody looks the same, everybody has the same qualifications and everybody has the same experience. How many built an orphanage or taught in a school in Africa? Employers are looking for evidence of experience beyond the workplace, for the ability to be innovative and creative.

Once you are settled into a university placement or period of training for a career, it is very unlikely that you will have the time, let alone the money to take a full year out. University degrees are becoming increasingly expensive, and the average student completes their higher education with debts of up to £20,000. The hands-on holiday is an affordable option that can boost your CV in just a few weeks and offer you an enjoyable travel experience.

Of course, CV points are just one reason for young people to take a hands-on holiday. There are countless others, such as making new friends from around the world, applying energy and enthusiasm to a worthwhile project, opening your eyes to different cultures, earning some money and simply trying something different.

An Earthwatch volunteer on patrol; monitoring wildlife at a reserve in Kenya.

Young Professionals – Twenties and Thirties

Today's young professionals, those in the early stages of their careers, can sometimes find the unfamiliar world of the nine-to-five, and the lack of freedom that it entails, unbearable. These are the gap year generation and they have been spoiled. They probably took a year out before university to *'see the world and find themselves'*. They may even have taken another gap year post-university, using the excuse that they needed to discover their calling. Yet suddenly they are staring down the barrel of 40 years at work (or more if the government has its way), safe in the knowledge that their gapping days are over and they may never again travel for a longer period than the statutory twenty days annual leave. Holidays become their only sanctuary from the daily grind and the pressure to do something exciting, different and rewarding becomes all the more acute.

The quarter life crisis is now an accepted phenomenon. Young professionals often feel caught in a career trap, with no way out before retirement. They also feel pressure from various sources (parents, peers, society in general) to get onto the property ladder, settle down, find a spouse and reproduce. Often this can engender panic and young professionals are forced to drastic measures. Many throw in the towel, withdraw their savings, and leave their jobs in order to set off for their last fling with youth. The hands-on holiday can offer an effective antidote to the nostalgic calling of the gap year. Spending a few weeks on a project that is completely different from their working lives, be it tracking dolphins and whales on a marine research ship, teaching English to underprivileged Brazilian children, or working on an organic farm in the outback, will certainly help to recharge the batteries.

It is not uncommon to use the hands-on holiday as a chance to re-evaluate your options. In the early stages of their career, many people panic that they have set themselves hurtling along a path that, it turns out, is entirely unsuitable. The American company Vocation Vacations has been inundated with applicants since setting up its Dream Job Holidays operation in 2004. The premise is simple: test drive your dream job without having to leave your current position, or even tell the boss. Participants can choose from a range of careers and then spend a week working one-on-one with a mentor, to see what it really entails. This is just one of a range of options detailed in *Work Experience*. A potential change of direction at this stage in your career will almost always entail a pay cut and an entry level job, but then again it is far better to find yourself on the bottom rung of an exciting career ladder than half way up a ladder leading nowhere.

Even those in their first job are prone to a rising concern that the career path they have chosen may not be the right one. Those who have not taken a gap year are particularly likely to suffer from this anxiety and this was certainly the case for Rachael Muirhead, who left her first job in book marketing to take a journalism work experience placement in India with i-to-i:

> I had been in my job for almost two years. I felt I had got everything that I could out of it and there was nowhere else for me to go within the company. The prospect of moving on immediately to another job was rather depressing because I had gone from school to university, and straight into a job at the end of it.
>
> I really wanted to give journalism a try, but it was never going to be an easy move to make. Everywhere I asked, people were banging on about building up my portfolio and I decided that if I was seriously considering doing it, work experience was the only sensible way to go. But placements in the UK are very hard to come by and because I was working full time I didn't have the time to apply myself fully to looking for one. Also, after earning money for two years, I really didn't want to take on an unpaid placement in the UK. Doing it abroad had less of a stigma. I also wanted to travel but wanted to have some kind of structure to it. The i-to-i placement offered me an interesting experience, immersed in a foreign culture and the opportunity to prove that I had a demonstrable interest in journalism.

Rachael thoroughly enjoyed her experience, coming away with a bulging portfolio and some great experiences. However, her placement taught her that the grass isn't always greener and although journalism appealed to her, she realised that working in marketing offered just as much creativity and excitement. Upon her return she found a job as a marketing executive with a high-profile publishing company, and is now far happier in her role. Rachael's story appears in the *Work Experience* chapter and helps to illustrate that by taking some time out and gaining a little perspective, we can all avoid making a rash life decision that we may ultimately regret.

Those in their thirties often find themselves tied down by an ever-increasing onslaught of commitments, and the opportunity to take time out seems depressingly distant. Yet anybody can take a hands-on holiday, and increasingly they are doing so. Secretary and single mum in her thirties, Tessa La Plar, surprised herself when she took a two-week break to Thailand to work on an elephant mahout project:

> I'm not a gap year student or a hippy explorer, or a campaigner for world peace. I'm not particularly brave either! I'm just a single City secretary mum with a four to five hour daily commute, an eight-year-old, little spare cash or time for adventures and a pretty hectic life which I am constantly juggling. Travelling after you left school wasn't something that happened when I left; it was something I associated with the younger

generation, and something I thought I'd never get a chance to do. Yet I did it and in a very short space of time I have been completely enlightened in so many ways and to so many things!

Taking the Family

One of the main reasons for taking holidays is to spend more time with the family. A hands-on holiday, more than any other type of holiday, allows the chance for a collection of individuals, sometimes with widely differing interests to operate as a single unit, working towards a collective goal. It also affords a rare unbroken opportunity to experience unadulterated family life, undistracted by phones, meetings, deadlines, work and the demands of a social calendar.

Nevertheless, children will undoubtedly make a hands-on holiday more complicated and will certainly limit the kind of trip you can take. The majority of holidays detailed within this book will not be suitable for young children. Companies that place volunteers abroad for example are seldom equipped to find housing for families. On the other hand, some of the tour operators that offer voluntourism packages will happily cater for children. According to a spokesman for Hands Up Holidays, the family-oriented holiday that offers a taste of volunteering is increasing in popularity: *'Not all of our projects are suitable, nor are our more physically demanding tours. But children can benefit enormously from trips that focus on orphanages or teaching, as it allows the youngsters to interact with children from other cultures while their parents are volunteering'.*

Equally, many WWOOF farms are children friendly, although prior arrangement with the host is always required. The short-term volunteer work overseas agency, AidCamps International offers special family camps. Children of any age can participate but once they reach the age of 12 they are considered capable of being actively involved in the placement, and 16–17-year-olds are treated exactly the same as adults. Another family-friendly organisation is i-to-i, which offers family volunteering experiences at community development and conservation projects in Bolivia, Costa Rica, Guatemala, Honduras, India, Kenya and Sri Lanka. The minimum age for children to attend ranges from three to 15 and the minimum age for participation in the project ranges from 10 to 15. The opportunities are there for family hands-on holidays, they will just take a little more planning.

Life Begins At...

There are of course professional benefits to taking a hands-on holiday at a later stage in your career. Large companies spend thousands on team-building exercises and leadership courses for middle managers, which in many cases are aiming for the same things as a hands-on holiday. The potential benefits include a refreshed attitude, new skills outside your skill set, improvement of communication and teamwork skills, a newfound respect for community values and an appreciation for the privileges that are often taken for granted.

However, for most people taking a hands-on holiday in their forties and fifties, professional considerations are the last thing on their mind. Mid-life crises, like failing eyesight and greying hair, can strike at any point between the ages of about 40 and 60, but frequently it is the half-century that acts as a prompt to appraising the direction and priorities of life. People coming up to 50 begin to panic that they have embarked on the gentle slope to retirement and they want something to wake them up and reinvigorate their lives.

Another trigger for taking a hands-on holiday among this age group is the sudden freedom from responsibilities that hits when the last child leaves home. For many parents this is the first time in years that they are able to contemplate ambitious travel that takes into account their own desires and interests. No longer do they have to consider the children's propensity for travel sickness, or their dislike of hotels without swimming pools, or of remote villages with no nightlife. The sudden lifting of parental obligations is often more keenly felt by mothers than fathers, who for years have borne the burden of anxiety on their children's behalf. According to AidCamps International, the single biggest demographic group among their volunteers is women in their fifties.

Hands-on holidays are too important to be the sole preserve of the young, and the propensity for people in their forties and fifties to take off on exciting and exotic adventures has earned them a new label – 'SKI-ers' (Spending The Kids' Inheritance).

Mature Travellers

While the idea of gaining CV points or earning a bit of holiday money may have little appeal to older people, it seems that they are heading in their droves to short-term volunteer projects around the world. Voluntourism annually attracts hundreds of thousands of older adults who are keen to become part of a short-term labour force, whether that involves unearthing archaeological ruins, helping to rebuild tsunami-affected communities or tracking orangutans in Borneo.

This is hardly a surprise. The baby boomers, the first wave of whom are approaching retirement today, grew up in an era of post-war optimism and new social freedoms. They have spent a lifetime reconstructing social norms and no-one really believed that they would spend their retirement settled in front of the television with an electric fire and a can of soup. Quite the opposite, in fact. Far from being decrepit, today's retirees are leaving the workforce at a younger age, are both fitter and wealthier than their forebears, and are looking forward not to their retirement, but to their 'renaissance'. According to a recent report by the democracy think tank, Demos, the baby boomers are intent on having their time again; of creating a new life phase in which they can revisit their own desire for personal fulfilment free from the pressures of overwork and child rearing. These are the 'Saga-louts', growing old disgracefully, and having an extremely good time doing it. High on their list of demands is the opportunity to travel and seek out new cultural experiences.

According to Alison Gardner in her guidebook, *Travel Unlimited: Uncommon Adventures for the Mature Traveller* (Avalon Travel Publishing), older people generally sign up for short-term volunteer work for the following three reasons. Firstly, because they have a strong interest in a particular cause, project or subject area that is often related to a long-held hobby or an earlier career. This was certainly the case for Ian McHaffie and his wife Averil, both former school-teachers. Ian was a teacher of Classics and had taken school parties to the Vindolanda Roman archaeological dig in Northumberland for years, and his wife had a long-held interest in history. Since retiring, both have taken the opportunity to indulge their interest by volunteering annually at the excavation, and still find it thrilling when important finds are made.

Secondly, older travellers, who may have spent most of their holidays on organised tours often express a desire to visit a region at its 'grassroots' – a feat not easily accomplished by joining an organised tour, or even passing through as an independent traveller. There is certainly no better way to experience a culture than to work day-to-day with local members of the community.

And finally, many retired volunteer tourists express a wish to give something back to a world that has been, by and large, economically kind and physically comfortable to them in their earlier years. This desire to help is gratefully accepted by all sorts of organisations and projects. Anthony Lunch, managing director of the organisation MondoChallenge points out that *'The senior age group has a huge amount to offer, not least life experience. They have a wide variety of skills that can be put to use'*.

With an increasing number of retired people expressing an interest in short-term volunteer work abroad, some organisations have developed programmes specifically for the older traveller. For example, Saga Holidays, the specialist tour operator for the over-fifties, moved into the voluntourism sector as recently as 2006, offering four-week community development programmes throughout South Africa (See *Community and Development Projects*), and the organisation has plans to expand their range of volunteer holidays in the near future. However, many of the retired travellers we talked to highlighted the value of working side-by-side with people of different ages to achieve a common goal. The chance to share experiences and achievements with the younger generation is often a novel and refreshing feature of the experience.

Older travellers are particularly suited to the hands-on holiday, as unlike their younger counterparts, they rarely want to be away from home for long blocks of time; invariably they will have overwhelming commitments and ties at home (the house, children, grandchildren and even their own aged parents). However, as mentioned above, the hands-on holidays in this book all last for anywhere between a few days and a month, and the older traveller will find a huge range of attractive ideas. Equally appealing is the fact that hands-on holidays, as opposed to long-term volunteer projects, sometimes offer a surprising level of privacy and physical comfort, often with air-conditioned private rooms, rather than dormitories or encampments. Short-term volunteer tour operators also tend to offer packages that include fieldtrips to explore surrounding areas or educational lectures and entertainment in the evening. While the emphasis is always on the work required, most operators are also keen to provide an enjoyable holiday experience.

Earthwatch volunteers survey dolphins, manatees and giant river otters in the Peruvian Amazon.

CHOOSING A HANDS-ON HOLIDAY

Before you apply to a project or an agency that sends hands-on holiday-makers abroad, it is best to research the options available to you and try to match them with your objectives. What skills do you have to offer and what can you expect to achieve? Are you prepared to accept a different level of comfort? Are you adaptable to foreign cultures? Can you work alone or in a team? There are thousands of opportunities out there and in order to get the most from your holiday, you need to put effort into choosing who you go with and what you do.

This book is a very good starting point, listing an enormous range of opportunities in a variety of fields. However, before making a choice, potential participants should be aware of the difference between agencies, which generally charge a fee in order to set you up with either paid or voluntary work, and independent projects, for which there may be little or no administration fee. Mediating agencies come in all shapes and sizes. Some are ethical non-profit charities that have links with local grassroots projects; some are bastions of the establishment with long-standing programmes in a range of countries; others are tour operators that either established themselves in the voluntourism sector, or have diversified to that sector to meet the growing demand. Others still are profit-making companies and are always seeking new projects in developing countries to which they can send paying workers. It is not always easy to tell the difference between the various types of sending agency. If you decide to use an agency, evaluate them carefully using the guidelines below.

This book is intended as a resource, not a review guide, and while every attempt has been made to select responsible agencies and projects around the world, they have not all been individually vetted. Every organisation's profile in this book contains extensive contact information. Always research and evaluate potential holidays the same way you would go about making any other decision about how to use your time and money. Where possible we have included the stories of returned participants to give an idea of the type of experience one can expect and to help you to imagine yourself in their place. Once you have taken a hands-on holiday of your own, please do get in touch with us to tell us about your experience (guy@vacationwork.co.uk), so that we can improve this book for future editions.

Using an Agency v. Independent Hands-On Holidays

A plethora of organisations, both charitable and commercial, offers a wide range of packaged possibilities, from conservation and development expeditions, to work experience placements and teaching in Himilayan schools. The agencies do not just deal with volunteering opportunities, they also offer a selection of paid work, such as teaching projects throughout the world. Even those interested in grape picking, traditionally the preserve of the independent working traveller, will find that there are now agencies that can guarantee a place on a farm before you set off, and will transfer you to a different one should it not work out. The appeal of applying to a large organisation is that they offer you a safety net. You can be reasonably sure that your interests will be handled professionally and with attention to the safety and welfare of participants. Accommodation will be arranged, insurance provided and the logistics in place. You will also have the benefit of being put in touch with former participants.

Nevertheless, when you begin to search for hands-on holiday opportunities, you will quickly conclude that the mediating agencies can be expensive. By finding a placement independently, potential hands-on holiday-makers can save themselves hundreds of pounds in agency fees. Individuals have to decide for themselves whether the fees charged by agencies offer value for money, and this can vary hugely according to the organisation in question. Most participants who have gone abroad through one of the sending agencies agree that they could not have had the experience without the backing of the organisation. Indeed, certain grassroots development charities and NGOs in the developing world will not accept foreign visitors unless they are organised through an agency. Where an organisation deals with a very specific style of project, it is quite unlikely that participants would be able to find such a wide range of opportunities by themselves. The Earthwatch Institute for example is an international environmental charity specialising in engaging people worldwide in scientific field research. The chances of an individual having sufficient contacts within the scientific world to provide a variety of potential projects are fairly slim. On the other hand, if you do have those contacts, then it would be fairly pointless to pay hundreds of pounds to a mediating agency.

If you are looking for a voluntourism-style holiday that combines a small amount of work with a more conventional holiday experience, then using an agency will certainly be your best bet. However, older travellers, with experience of working and volunteering abroad may conclude that they do not need the safety net of a sending agency. They may feel that an agency can over-package the experience and it is certainly not impossible to make direct contact with small local organisations which actively look for short-term workers. This was what Steve McElhinney, founder of www.volunteersouthamerica.net, did in 2005. Steve was looking for grassroots, zero-cost volunteer work in Argentina, but finding volunteering opportunities that did not involve paying large sums to a middleman was more difficult than he had anticipated and he spent hours trying to track them down. He then posted his findings onto the above website, and it has now developed into an extremely useful resource. Clearly the internet has made it far easier to connect with local organisations and charities in a way that has never been possible before. Another traveller who found work this way was Geoffroy Groleau, an economist and consultant from Montreal. He stumbled across the website of an Indian NGO and arranged to work for a month with Dakshinayan (listed in *Teaching and Summer Camps*) which works with tribal peoples in the hills of Rajamhal and nearby plains: '*The application process is simple and can be conducted fully over the internet. The registration fee which must be provided before setting out for the project is a primary source of revenues for Dakshinayan*'. Geoffroy thoroughly enjoyed his holiday and clearly felt happier that his fees were going directly to the charity with which he was working, rather than being lost in administration fees.

However, travellers who opt to go it alone do run the risk of massive disappointment. A placement may look spectacular on the web, but once you arrive it could turn out that the NGO has no money and the work you end up doing could be nothing like the work you signed up for. The only way around this is to find a project after you arrive and assess its suitability on the spot. While this can be a useful approach for travellers with more time, for the short-breaker it is a fairly risky and inadvisable course of action. Of course, such issues can arise even when travellers have used an agency. Usually problems are the result of a mismatch of expectations between the aspiring hands-on holiday-maker and the venture itself. However, it is the responsibility of the sending agency that collects the volunteer fee to provide as clear and honest a briefing as possible about what the volunteer should expect. As a general rule, if you are at all nervous about an independent hands-on holiday and feel that you need the structure and support that an agency can provide, it is far better to employ the services of an intermediary.

The Ethics Box – Evaluating an Agency

If you decide to use an agency, you should find out as much as you can about the organisation in order to determine whether it is right for you, and also whether it is completely ethical. Some organisations may exploit both hosts' and travellers' expectations, or may simply operate in a way which does not fit your worldview. Asking the following questions should help you to make a more informed decision about signing up to a project:

What will your exact job responsibilities be? Dissatisfaction often arises when a participant's expectations do not match the reality of a project. A reputable agency will be able to tell you the exact working conditions you should expect. Some of the lesser voluntourism agencies do place unskilled volunteers in skilled positions and this rarely benefits the host organisation.

How much training and orientation will you receive? For placements outside your home country this is particularly important. Even on short breaks, the effects of culture shock can be dramatic. Every participant wants to be as much use to the project as possible and this can only be achieved with an appropriate amount of local training and support.

Where does the money go? Always be suspicious of an organisation that can't or won't tell you exactly how they will be spending your contribution. As long as they are up-front about how the money is spent, you can decide for yourself whether or not they are taking an excessive cut. You should also be aware that often payments for your own food and lodging do not assist the volunteer programme.

What is the time frame for the project? It is particularly important in the voluntourism sector to ensure that your contribution is made to an on-going project. A programme that occurs just once can have negative long-term effects on a community.

What positive or negative experiences have former participants had? An agency that is sure of the quality of its projects will willingly put you in touch with previous participants, so that you can get a firm idea of exactly what a project entails.

How exactly does the agency operate? Responsible agencies build up strong relationships with host organisations and only arrange placements when there is a specific requirement for workers. More profit-oriented agencies will sign up as many travellers as they can and then find them relevant work placements. You should be able to get meticulous details about a project months in advance. Be wary if you can't, it may mean that the programme has been hastily organised, may not meet local needs and will ultimately prove unsatisfactory to both the local community and the traveller.

How many partner organisations does the agency work with? Seek out agencies that work with just a few partner organisations. Those that offer hundreds of placements in several countries are unlikely to have visited and vetted every project.

Does the agency have a demonstrable commitment to ethical tourism? Most of the agencies offering hands-on holidays have a responsible tourism policy and will be able to tell you exactly how it is implemented. Of particular importance in the voluntary sector is whether or not organisations have a long-term commitment to the community they are working with. For example, whether they employ local staff and consult with the local authorities to see exactly what is required.

PRACTICALITIES AND RED TAPE

Getting There

Even if you choose to book your hands-on holiday through a recognised organisation, it is likely that you will still have to organise your travel independently. There follow some general guidelines for finding travel bargains. More detailed information on specific destinations can be found in country-specific travel guides and the amount of travel information on the internet is staggering. There are websites on everything from sleeping in airports (the fabulous www.sleepinginairports.net) to sharing lifts across the USA and Canada (www.erideshare.com). Many sites have pages of intriguing links; to name just one, try www.budgettravel.com.

By Air

For long-haul flights, especially to Asia, Australasia and most recently Latin America, discounted tickets are readily available and there should never be any need to pay the official full fare. Scheduled airfares as laid down by IATA, the airlines' cartel, are primarily designed for airline accountants and businessmen on expense accounts and should be avoided.

The days of the bucket shop are long gone. Now high street travel agents and mainstream internet travel agents can offer exceptional deals. But the very lowest fares are still found by doing some careful shopping around on the telephone and internet. Even if you choose not to book online and want the reassurance of dealing with a human being, the web can still be a great source of information about prices and options.

Discount agents advertise in London weeklies like *TNT* and *Time Out*, as well as in the travel pages of newspapers like the Saturday *Independent*. Phone a few outfits and pick the best price. Those with access to the internet should start by checking relevant websites, for example www.cheapflights.co.uk which has links to other useful sources of travel information. Viewers can log onto their destination and then see a list of prices offered by a variety of airlines and agents. Increasingly it is possible to book tickets on the internet, though this is too impersonal for some, who prefer the personal touch available from face-to-face or at least voice-to-voice contact.

In the US, check the discount flight listings in the back of the travel sections of the *New York Times* and *Los Angeles Times*. Discounted tickets are available online from Air Treks in San Francisco (tel. +1 877 247 8735; www.AirTreks.com)

An unusual way of locating cheap flights is available from Adventurair (tel. 01293 405777; www.rideguide.com) which produces *The Ride Guide* on CD-ROM (£11.99/$16.99) which gives details of companies operating cargo planes, aircraft deliveries and private planes. Any of these may have seats available for bargain prices.

Useful Contacts
Long-haul Travel
Some of the principal agencies specialising in long-haul travel are listed here. Telephone bookings are possible, though these agencies are often so busy that it can be difficult to get through. Although STA specialises in deals for students and under-26s, they can also assist older travellers:

STA Travel (tel. 08701 630026; www.statravel.co.uk) have about 65 branches in the UK and more than 450 worldwide. Offers low-cost flights, accommodation, insurance and car hire.

Trailfinders Ltd (tel. 0845 058 5858; www.trailfinders.com). Also more than a dozen branches in UK cities plus Dublin and five in Australia.

Flight Centre (tel. 0870 499 0040; www.flightcentre.co.uk) – branches around the UK.

Journey Latin America (tel. 020 8747 3108; www.journeylatinamerica.co.uk). A fully-bonded agency which specialises in travel to and around all of Latin America. Consistently offers the lowest fares and the most expertise.

Marco Polo Travel (tel. 0117 929 4123; www.marcopolotravel.co.uk). Discounted airfares worldwide.

North South Travel (tel. 01245 608291; www.northsouthtravel.co.uk). Discount travel agency that donates all its profits to projects in the developing world.

Quest Travel (tel. 0870 444 5552; www.questtravel.com). Kingston, York and Brighton offices.

South American Experience (tel. 020 7976 5511; www.southamericanexperience.co.uk). Latin American specialist with good customer service.

Travelbag (tel. 0870 814 4440; www.travelbag.co.uk). Originally Australia & New Zealand specialist, now owned by ebookers.

Travelmood (tel. 08700 664566; www.travelmood.com). Branches in Islington, Guildford, Leeds, Liverpool and Dundee.

Short-haul Travel

From the UK to Europe it is generally cheaper to fly on an off-peak no-frills flight out of Stansted, Luton or regional airport than it is by rail or bus. Almost all bookings are made online and telephone bookings attract a higher fare. Some of the better-known budget carriers from the UK to Europe and beyond are:

EasyJet (tel. 0905 821 0905; www.easyjet.com)

Ryanair (tel. 0871 246 0000; www.ryanair.com)

BMIbaby (tel. 0871 224 0224; www.bmibaby.com)

Jet2 (tel. 0871 226 1737; www.jet2.com), based at Leeds Airport

Thomsonfly (www.thomsonfly.com)

No-frills flying has been available in North America for some time, especially through Southwest Airlines based in Dallas (www.southwest.com). Meanwhile this style of flying has spread to the continent and discount airlines have proliferated, such as Germanwings (www.germanwings.com) in Germany and Wizz Air in Poland (www.wizzair.com). To check which discount airlines operate to which European destinations, log on to www.flycheapo.com. The idea has also spread to Australia with Richard Branson's Virgin Blue (www.virginblue.com.au) and to Canada with airlines like CanJet (www.canjet.com) and WestJet (www.westjet.com).

By Rail

One of the classic youth travel experiences is to InterRail around Europe (www.interrail.net). However the scheme is readily available to people over 26, albeit at a higher price than it is to young travellers. InterRail may be a useful way to travel to a hands-on project, or possibly to travel between several projects. For the InterRail ticket, you must choose how many zones you intend to cover and bear in mind that seat reservations will cost extra. InterRail offers several types of ticket. Those who wish to travel in just one country will find these tickets to be cheaper than a global pass. Current prices for the global pass are from £159 for five days, £239 for 10 days, £309 for 22 days, and £399 for a month. Tickets bought in Euros whilst on the continent are lower.

Anyone intending to do some concentrated travelling by train should contact a specialist such as Rail Europe (tel. 08705 848848; www.raileurope.co.uk) or Rail Choice (tel. 0870 165 7300; www.railchoice.co.uk) which sells a range of European and international rail passes.

Within Europe, consult the *Thomas Cook European Rail Timetable* whereas the bible for rail travellers outside Europe is the *Thomas Cook Overseas Timetable* (£11.50 each).

By Coach

Eurolines is the group name for 32 independent coach operators serving 500 destinations in all European countries from Ireland to Romania. Promotional prices start at £30 return for London-Amsterdam if booked seven days in advance. Bookings can be made online at www.nationalexpress.com/eurolines or by phoning 08705 808080. For smaller independent coach operators, check advertisements in London magazines like *TNT*.

One of the most interesting revolutions in budget travel has been the explosion of backpackers' bus services which are hop-on hop-off coach services following prescribed routes. These can be found (among others) in New Zealand, Australia, Ireland, Scotland and England. In Europe, Busabout (tel. 020 7950 1661; www.busabout.com) offers flexible routes all over Europe from May to October.

Passports and Visas

A ten-year UK passport costs £66 for 32 pages and £77 for 48 pages, and should be processed by the Identity and Passport Service within three weeks. The one-week fast-track application procedure costs £91 and an existing passport can be renewed in person at a passport office but only if you have made a prior appointment by ringing the Passport Agency on 0870 521 0410 and are willing to pay £108 (£114.50 for 48 pages). Passport office addresses are listed on passport application forms available from main post offices. All relevant information can be found on the website: www.passport.gov.uk. Most countries will want to see that your passport has at least 90 days to run beyond your proposed stay.

With more than 150 nations crammed onto this minor planet, you can't continue in one direction for very long (unless you are a national of the European Union travelling in Europe) before you are impeded by border guards demanding to see your papers. Post 9/11, immigration and security checks are tighter than ever and many countries have imposed visa restrictions, particularly on North Americans in retaliation for all the new restrictions the US has implemented. Embassy websites are the best source of information or you can check online information posted by visa agencies. Getting visas is a headache anywhere, and most travellers feel happier obtaining them in their home country. Set aside a chunk of your travel budget to cover the costs.

It is very important that you establish your immigration status before travelling. The majority of hands-on holidays in this book involve an element of volunteering. However, volunteer visas, where they exist, are usually intended for long-term volunteers. It is therefore almost always necessary to enter the country as a tourist, making no mention of voluntary work, as this could slow down your entry considerably. Always take advice from the group or organisation that you are travelling with.

Some of the holidays included within these pages involve short-term paid work. In these cases, a tourist visa will rarely be enough and you may find yourself in hot water if you attempt to earn money without proper authorisation. Within the EU, the free reciprocity of labour means that the red tape has been simplified, although not removed. Always check with the embassy of the relevant country before travelling. UK citizens will find that many countries offer special schemes for short-term work. For example British and Irish citizens (among others) can obtain a Working-Holiday Visa to work in Australia for up to 12 months. New Zealand and Canada both offer similar visas for short-term work.

Travel Insurance

On any kind of holiday with a purpose, an adequate and appropriate insurance policy is absolutely essential. Increased competition among travel insurers has brought costs down over the past few years, though it will still be necessary to set aside a chunk of your travel fund. Travel policies do not automatically cover certain hands-on holiday activities deemed to be dangerous such as winter sports and manual work (e.g. on a volunteer project). Anyone wanting to engage in adventure or extreme sports should do some comparison shopping. By studying the fine print, you may find a company that will cover your preferred activity without the need of investing in special cover. You are expected to inform your insurer ahead of time if you plan to indulge in any potentially risky activities.

The UK has reciprocal health agreements with more than 40 countries worldwide that entitle you to emergency care, though it is still recommended to have your own comprehensive private cover which will cover extras like loss of baggage and, more importantly, emergency repatriation. Many countries in Africa, Asia, Latin America and the USA do not provide any reciprocal cover. Travelling without travel insurance can literally break the bank. Medical care in an emergency might cost an individual tens of thousands of pounds.

If you're travelling independently, you will find that almost every enterprise in the travel business will be delighted to sell you insurance because of the commission earned. Ring several insurance companies with your specifications and compare prices. Europ-Assistance Ltd (tel. 0870 737 5720; www.europ-assistance.co.uk) is the world's largest assistance organisation with a network of doctors, air ambulances, agents and vehicle rescue services managed by 208 offices worldwide offering (at a price) emergency assistance abroad 24 hours a day.

Many companies charge lower premiums, though you will have to decide whether you are satisfied with their level of cover. Most offer a no-frills rate which covers medical emergencies and a premium rate which covers extras that might be considered non-essential like loss of personal baggage. If you are not planning to visit North America, the premiums will be much less expensive. Some companies to consider are listed below. Expect to pay in the region of £25 for a month of basic cover and £35–£40 for more extensive cover.

Useful Contacts

Alexander Forbes World Service (tel. 020 7933 0000; www.afiaws.com). Provider of specialist travel insurance including travellers on an expedition, expatriates and aid workers, in its key markets of Africa, South America, Asia, the Middle East and Eastern Europe.

Austravel (tel. 0870 166 2020; www.austravel.com). Specialists in travel to Australia and New Zealand selling a range of competitively priced insurance policies for both the family and the budget traveller. Cover for adventure sports is available too.

Club Direct (te. 0800 083 2466; www.clubdirect.com).
Columbus Direct (tel. 020–7375 0011). One of the travel insurance giants chosen by Rough Guides as its partner.
Direct Line Insurance (tel. 0845 246 8910; www.directline.com).
Downunder Worldwide Travel Insurance (tel. 0800 393908; www.duinsure.com).
Endsleigh Insurance (www.endsleigh.co.uk). Offices in most university towns.
Europ-Assistance Ltd (tel. 0870 737 5720; www.europ-assistance.co.uk) .
International SOS Assistance Inc. (www.internationalsos.com). Recommended US insurers for hands-on holidays abroad, used by Peace Corps and designed for people working in remote areas.
MRL Insurance (tel. 0870 876 7677; www.mrlinsurance.co.uk). Offers policies to all travellers up to age 90.
Travel Insurance Agency (tel. 020–8446 5414; www.travelinsurers.com).

Emergency medical claims are normally processed efficiently but if you have to make a claim for lost or stolen baggage, you may be unpleasantly surprised by the amount of the settlement eventually paid, especially if you have opted for a discount insurer. Loss adjusters have ways of making calculations which prove that you are entitled to less than you think. The golden rule is to amass as much documentation as possible to support your application, most importantly medical receipts and a police report in the case of an accident or theft.

Travel Safety

Travel inevitably involves balancing risks and navigating through hazards real or imagined. But with common sense and advice from experts, you can minimise potential problems. The Foreign & Commonwealth Office runs a regular and updated service; you can ring the Travel Advice Unit on 0870 606 0290 or check the website www.fco.gov.uk/travel. This site gives frequently updated and detailed risk assessments of any trouble spots, including civil unrest, terrorism and crime.

General advice on minimising the risks of independent travel is contained in the book *World Wise – Your Passport to Safer Travel* published by Thomas Cook in association with the Suzy Lamplugh Trust and the Foreign Office (www.suzylamplugh.org/worldwise; £6.99 plus £2 postage). Arguably its advice is over-cautious, advising travellers never to ride a motorbike or accept an invitation to a private house. Adult travellers will have to decide for themselves when to follow this advice and when to ignore it. In the US, the State Department publishes warnings and advice on its website www.travel.state.gov.

Travellers' Health

No matter what country you are heading for, you should obtain the Department of Health leaflet *T7.1 Health Advice for Travellers*. This leaflet should be available from any post office or doctor's surgery. Alternatively you can request a free copy on the Health Literature Line 0870 155 5455 or read it online at www.dh.gov.uk, which also has country-by-country details.

The old E111 certificate of entitlement to medical treatment within Europe has been superseded by the European Health Insurance Card (EHIC), which covers health care for short stays within the EU. At present this reciprocal cover is extended only to emergency treatment, so private insurance is also highly recommended, not least to cope with theft.

If you have a pre-existing medical condition it is important to anticipate what you might require in a crisis. Ask your GP or specialist support group for advice before you leave. If you're travelling with a tour operator let the company know about your condition in advance. Under extreme climatic conditions chronic or pre-existing conditions can be aggravated. Try to ascertain how easy it will be to access medicines on your trip, whether you'll be able to carry emergency supplies with you and how far you will be from specialist help. Always carry medications in their original containers and as a precaution you might carry a note from your doctor with an explanation of the drugs you are carrying and the relevant facts of your medical history. This could also include details of any allergies for example an intolerance of penicillin. This might be of use if you are involved in an accident or medical emergency.

In an age of mass communication it is usually possible to manage a medical condition while travelling or erect a safety net. If you plan to travel to an area with poor medical standards and unreliable blood screening, you might want to consider equipping yourself or your group with sterile syringes and needles. The Department of Travel Medicine at the Hospital for Tropical Diseases recommends that you should carry a specially prepared sterile needle kit in case local emergency treatment may require injections; MASTA (see below) sells these for £17–£31.

Any visits beyond the developed world, particularly to tropical climates, require careful preparation. You will face the risk of contracting malaria or water-borne diseases like typhoid and cholera. You will need to provide your medical practitioner with precise details about where you intend to travel. Visit a medical centre at least a month before departure because some immunisations like those for yellow fever must be given well in advance.

Some of the advice given below may seem intimidating. While preparing for travelling in the developing world, you might begin to feel as if you're joining an SAS induction course. Expert medical advice is widely available on how to avoid tropical illness, so you should take advantage of modern medicine to protect yourself. And be prepared to pay for the necessary inoculations which are not normally covered by the NHS.

Increasingly, people are seeking advice via the internet; check for example www.fitfortravel.scot.nhs.uk; www.tmb.ie and www.travelhealth.co.uk. The website of the World Health Organisation www.who.int/ith has some information including a listing of the very few countries in which certain vaccinations are a requirement of entry.

Inoculations: The only disease for which a vaccination certificate may be legally required is yellow fever. Many countries insist on seeing one only if you are arriving from an infected country, though it is a good idea to get protection if you are planning to travel to a yellow fever zone (much of Africa and parts of Latin America).

One of the best sources of health advice for travellers is MASTA (Medical Advisory Service for Travellers Abroad – see below) which was set up in association with the London School of Hygiene and Tropical Medicine to meet the needs of the eight million international visits made every year from the UK.

Americans seeking general travel health advice should ring the Center for Disease Control & Prevention Hotline in Atlanta (1 877 394 8747; www.cdc.gov). CDC issues travel announcements for international travellers rated from mild to extreme.

Malaria: Malaria is undoubtedly the greatest danger posed by visits to many tropical areas. It is important to consult a specialist service like MASTA or the Hospital for Tropical Diseases. The Malaria Prevention Advice Line (tel. 09065 508908) can be dialled 24 hours a day (£1 per minute). You can also become better informed by looking at specialist websites such as www.preventingmalaria.info/prevention/index.htm. You need to obtain the best information available to help you devise the most appropriate strategy for protection in the areas you intend to visit. Research indicates for example that the statistical chance of being bitten by a malarial mosquito in Thailand is once a year, but in Sierra Leone it rises to once a night. Start your research early since some courses of malaria prophylaxis need to be started up to three weeks before departure. It is always a good idea to find out in advance if you are going to suffer any side-effects as well.

In the case of malaria, prevention is vastly preferable to cure. It is a difficult disease to treat, particularly in its advanced stages. If you suffer a fever up to twelve months after returning home from a malarial zone, visit your doctor and mention your travels, even if you suspect it might just be flu.

Food and Water: Tap water throughout the developing world is unsafe for travellers to drink because there is always a chance that it contains disease organisms to which the westerner has had no chance to develop immunities. Do not assume that you can get by with substitute beverages such as cola or tea or even bottled soda water. In hot climates, it is imperative to drink large quantities of water to avoid dehydration, possibly as much as six pints a day. The most effective method of water purification is boiling for at least five minutes.

A more manageable method of water sterilisation is to use chemical purifiers. Simply pick up the appropriate chlorine tablets or tincture of iodine from a chemist before departure, checking how long they take to become effective (ten minutes is preferable to 30 in a hot climate when you're gasping for a cold drink). You can buy a product that neutralises the unpleasant taste of iodine. Remember that ice cubes however tempting should be avoided. Drinking water can also be purified by filtering. MASTA and Nomad market various water purifiers; among the best are the 'Aquapure Traveller' (£40+) and the 'Trekker Travel Well' for £70.

Deciding what food is safe to eat is not always easy. You should aim to eat only freshly cooked food and avoid raw vegetables unless they have been peeled or washed thoroughly in purified water.

Diarrhoea: Up to 50% of travellers will suffer from 'Delhi belly' and a mild case of diarrhoea is virtually inevitable for travellers outside the developed world. Doctors warn that however many precautions with food and water you take, it is simply impossible to guard against it completely. If left to its own devices, most bouts clear up within two or three days, although in an extreme case the fluid loss may leave you weak and tired. You should keep drinking to avoid dehydration. This is particularly important for the young or the elderly. Rehydration tablets, which replace lost salt and sugar in the right proportions, are an important item for your first-aid kit.

Diarrhoea will clear up more quickly if you can get a lot of rest and stop eating altogether. When you begin eating again, stick to as simple a diet as possible, eg boiled rice and tea (without milk).

Useful Contacts
The Foreign and Commonwealth Office maintains a Travel Advice Unit helpline on 0870 606 0290 and posts information and risk assessments at www.fco.gov.uk/travel. **MASTA** (enquiries@masta.org; www.masta.org) has already been recommended. Calls to the Travellers' Health Line (0906 822 4100) are charged at 60p per minute (average cost of call £2). With its database of the latest information on the prevention of tropical and other

diseases, MASTA is one of the most authoritative sources of travellers' health information in Britain. The practical information accessible on its website and helpline is impressive. It can provide personalised advice depending on your destinations, which can be either emailed or posted to you. Here you can find explanations about protection against malaria, guidelines on what to eat and drink, and how to avoid motion sickness, jet lag and sunburn. MASTA's network of travel clinics administer inoculations and, like their online shop, sells medical kits and other specialist equipment like water purifiers and survival tools.

Hospital for Tropical Diseases (www.thehtd.org). Call 020–7388 9600 for appointments at Travel Clinic or the Travellers Healthline Advisory Service (tel. 020 7950 7799).

Travelpharm (tel. 01395 233771; www.travelpharm.com). Extensive range of mosquito nets, anti-malaria drugs, water purification equipment and travel accessories available via online store.

British Airways Travel Clinic (tel. 0845 600 2236). Walk-in service operates Monday to Saturday; consultation charge £15. Its prices are posted on the website www.britishairways.com/travel/healthclinprods/public/en_gb. Prices range from £25 for a combined diphtheria and tetanus shot to £65 for tick-borne encephalitis.

The Royal Free Travel Health Centre (tel. 020 7830 2885; www.travelclinicroyalfree. com). Well-regarded private clinic.

Trailfinders Travel Clinic (tel. 020 7983 3999; www.trailfinders.com/clinic.htm).

Theft

From London to La Paz crooks lurk, ready to pounce upon the unsuspecting traveller. Theft takes many forms, from the highly trained gangs of children who artfully pick pockets all over Europe to violent attacks on the streets of American cities. It is also not unknown to be robbed by fellow travellers from hostels, beaches, etc nor by corrupt airport officials in cahoots with baggage handlers.

How to carry your money and valuables should be given careful consideration. The first rule is not to keep all your wealth in one place. A money belt worn inside your clothing is good for the peace of mind it bestows. Keep large denomination travellers' cheques and any hard currency cash there plus a large note of the local currency. Then if your wallet or purse is stolen, you will not be stranded.

To reduce the possibility of theft, steer clear of seedy or crowded areas and moderate your intake of alcohol. If you are mugged, and have an insurance policy which covers cash, you must obtain a police report (sometimes for a fee) to stand any chance of recouping part of your loss.

If you end up in dire financial straits without a cash or credit card, and you do not have the backing of a tour operator or organisation, you will have to contact someone at home to send you money urgently. You can contact your bank at home (by telephone, fax or online) and ask them to wire money to you. This will be easier if you have set up a telephone or internet bank account before leaving home, since they will then have the correct security checks in place to authorise a transfer without having to receive something from you in writing with your signature. You can request that the necessary sum be transferred from your bank to a named bank in the town you are in – something you have to arrange with your own bank, so you know where to pick the money up.

If a private individual has kindly agreed to bale you out, they can transfer money in several ways. Western Union offers an international money transfer service whereby cash deposited at one branch by your benefactor can be withdrawn by you from any other branch or agency, which the sender need not specify. Western Union agents – there are 245,000 of them in 200 countries – come in all shapes and sizes (eg travel agencies, stationers, chemists). Unfortunately it is not well represented outside of the developed world. In the UK, ring 0800 833833 for further details, a list of outlets and a complete rate schedule. The website www.westernunion.com allows you to search for the nearest outlet.

Thomas Cook, American Express and the UK Post Office offer a similar service called MoneyGram (www.moneygram.com). Cash deposited at one of their foreign exchange counters is available within 10 minutes at the named destination or can be collected up to 45 days later at one of 60,000 co-operating agents in 160 countries. Ring 0845 722 3344 for details or check the Post Office website (www.postoffice.co.uk).

HANDS-ON

Conservation and Wildlife

HOLIDAYS THAT SAVE THE WORLD

Holidays offering the chance to help the environment have been growing in popularity for many years now. We are all becoming increasingly aware of the damage to the environment that travel, especially flying, can do. The tourism industry has reacted by creating a range of 'ethical, 'alternative', and 'responsible' holidays that seek to minimise the negative impacts of tourism and maximise the potential economic benefits to the hosts. Off-setting carbon emissions, carefully choosing your carrier, and even avoiding air travel where possible are all ways that we, as tourists, can reduce the harmful effects of tourism on the planet. But for many, simply reducing the negative impact of their holiday is not enough. There is a way to have an enjoyable holiday, while also making a positive contribution to the environment, helping to preserve the world's endangered habitats and species of wildlife for generations to come. As the issue of 'saving the planet' climbs the international agenda, more and more people are combining their holidays with conservation initiatives worldwide.

As *The Observer* recently put it, *'Go on holiday and save the world may sound like a title of a Ben Elton sketch, but the idea seems to be catching on'*. Some 2,500 volunteers each year pay to go on holidays organised by the UK's largest practical conservation charity BTCV. It is hardly a surprise that so many people are concerned by the issue of conservation. The world is currently facing its greatest biodiversity crisis and over the next few decades many species of flora and fauna are likely to become extinct. Primarily this is due to changes in land use, pollution and the introduction of alien species. In the UK, for example, the increase in intensive agriculture has resulted in the loss of many specialised habitats. Semi-natural habitats such as downlands and hearthlands have declined through the effects of commercial plantation forestry, and the continued growth of the country's population has been matched by the pace of housing, industrial and road development, all of which encroach into the countryside. This process is echoed throughout the world as uncontained urban and industrial sprawl and global warming destroy supplies of once plentiful habitats. Understandably, many people feel overwhelmed by the scale of environmental issues and think that they, as individuals, can't do anything to help. The huge variety of opportunities detailed within this chapter aims to demonstrate that this is simply not true.

So how exactly can ordinary people, with little or no experience, use their holiday time to help? Well there are a number of ways. First of all, included in the cost of a conservation holiday is a donation towards the project itself. Many projects are self-funding and receive little or no support from governments and external sources. Quite simply, without the financial support of ethically-minded travellers, they could not continue their work. The proportion of the cost that goes towards the project or organisation can vary enormously, and this is something to investigate before choosing a conservation holiday. Secondly, volunteers are actually able to make a tangible contribution. It may seem like a few weeks is barely enough to get started on the problems facing the environment and individual species of endangered animals, but in fact short-term volunteers can be extremely useful. Most of the projects listed below are ongoing and don't simply end when the individual voluntourist goes home. Your contribution is therefore of enormous benefit to long-term projects, especially as much of the work involved is labour intensive and requires little training. The organisation Biosphere (see below), gives an example of how volunteers with no previous experience can help a project monitoring bear populations in Slovakia:

A bear track is unmistakable – even with no training you'd probably know when you see one. A local scientist alone can only cover a small area each day, but a whole expedition team can survey a very large area and thereby provide the scientist with a much better picture of bear movements and numbers.

Finally, many of the projects listed below include an element of education. Participants do not just contribute directly to conservation initiatives, they also learn an enormous amount about the individual issues and in many cases are involved in imparting that information to local schools, members of the local community and tourists passing through, so that they too can become involved. Conservation holidays do more than back vital research, they inspire participants and others to understand their global responsibilities as citizens of the world.

Volunteers are involved in all sorts of work from forest clearance, footpath restoration and enclosure maintenance, to observation and scientific monitoring of endangered species. Many of the projects covered in this chapter are concerned with the conservation of natural habitats and of the wildlife that depend on them. These are closely linked issues, and conserving one usually involves conserving the other. The RSPB for example, although primarily involved in the protection of birds, is responsible for the management of more than 140 reserves throughout the UK and therefore for a wide range of different habitats. Effective management of these habitats is essential to ensure the prosperity of the birds themselves. Other conservation initiatives that welcome volunteers aim to protect areas of natural beauty, simply so that they will be available to visit for generations to come. The Great Baikal Project in Russia for example invites volunteers each summer to help build a footpath around the world's largest lake, and a number of organisations in America also put holiday-makers to work preserving the country's great trails.

Animal lovers will find a wealth of opportunities. One of the main conservation organisations, Earthwatch, currently offers projects working with Amazon dolphins, giant river otters, monkeys and birds while living and working on an Amazon riverboat; monitoring and collecting species of butterflies in Vietnam; helping to protect elephants in a Sri Lankan national park and forest reserve; and investigating how monkeys are adapting to human disturbance in Costa Rica. Not only do these holidays (with a scientific focus) help scientists to understand and therefore improve the likelihood of the survival of individual species, they also present a truly unique way for people to connect to the environment around them and explore some of the real challenges that our world is currently facing. Other operators offer conservation holidays that have a more immediate impact. For example a number of the operations listed below are rehabilitation projects, taking animals that have been mistreated, neglected, abused, sold on the black market, or made to perform in circuses and on the street, and preparing them to be released back into the wild. Volunteer work is almost always a two-way street and participants get as much out of the experience as they put in. Without fail, no matter how physically exhausting, or emotionally draining the volunteer work may be, it is always just as rewarding. This was certainly what Catherine Johnson found while working with the Centre for Rehabilitation of Wildlife in South Africa:

During my time there three of us had to empty the giant petrel's swimming pool. It took three hours and the pool was full of dead fish and frog spawn. Not very pleasant. But after a tea break I returned to check on the petrel and found him diving in the clean pool and splashing his feathers, clearly very happy. Those three hours of hard and dirty work were instantly rewarded.

As well as being rewarding, conservation holidays can also be extremely enjoyable, allowing participants to live and work in areas of outstanding natural beauty and there is always ample free time to explore the surroundings. Though the hours can be long, the work itself can also be enjoyable. Take for example the marine conservation organisation Blue Ventures, based in Madagascar. Participants stay in beach cabins with stunning views of the ocean and each day they scuba dive in order to collect data on various marine species. Caroline Gosney describes her experience: *'Soon after arriving in Madagascar, I was swimming among schools of florescent-coloured fish, monitoring octopus populations and exploring underwater caves and coral reefs no-one had ever seen before'*. Now that doesn't sound too bad does it?

Practicalities

Conservation holidays are generally fairly expensive. As an example, three weeks working on Global Crossroads' Gibbon Rehabiliation Project in Phuket costs around £900, excluding the airfare. The more exotic trips overseas will require a fairly large financial outlay. Those on a tight budget should consider a conservation holiday in the UK, which generally offer a low-cost break (the National Trust's Working Holidays cost from £75 per week).

Regardless of which organiser you choose, the price you pay usually covers food, training, supervision and accommodation. The cost of travel to your holiday destination is rarely included in the participation fees, nor are travel insurance and the cost of any kit you may need to buy such as outdoor clothing or a sleeping bag. It is important to budget for these extra costs which may be significant if, for example, your destination includes a long-haul flight.

Accommodation varies in standard from a tent with few or no facilities, through to bunkhouses, shared houses, homestays, B&Bs, hotels and even luxury villas. You should usually expect to share a room with a fellow volunteer, and to muck in with communal duties such as cleaning and preparing food.

The majority of projects do not require previous experience or specific skills from their volunteers. All training is provided onsite. Some of the underwater research expeditions may require scuba diving certification (PADI), but in many cases this can be gained with the organisation as part of your holiday. Nor is it necessary to be super-fit on most conservation holidays. So long as you are reasonably healthy and happy to work outside, typically five to six days a week from 9am to 5pm, most projects will be happy to accept your help.

Age is not usually a barrier. Nevertheless most projects are for adults only and organisers say that they get a large variation in ages from teens to retired, with the majority of volunteers in their 20s and 30s. Most organisations specify a minimum age of 18, but many will accept younger volunteers who are accompanied by an adult or who have a letter of consent from their parents. Many older participants attend conservation holidays, and Biosphere Expeditions claims that the oldest participant they have had was 87 years old.

A Pas de Loup (Volunteers for Nature)

Duration: Min. 3 weeks
Location: Benin, Togo, Costa Rica, Honduras, Greece, Italy, Croatia
Season: Year round
Prerequisites: Min. age 18

☎ +33 (4) 7546 8018
🖰 info@apasdeloup.org
💻 www.apasdeloup.org

Organisation: Independent non-profit making organisation that aims to promote awareness about the importance of safeguarding the environment
Description: The organisation positions itself as a link between volunteers and scientists and conservationists. Volunteers are carefully selected before being assigned to a project. In the field, participants are welcomed and trained by local research and conservation specialists. The work includes physical labour for the management of natural sites, monitoring of protected species, collecting scientific data and guiding local visitors and tourists. Recent projects have included bird migration projects in Israel, working in wildlife health centres in Greece and Honduras, sea turtle monitoring in Greece and Costa Rica, and eagle protection in Portugal
Accommodation: Provided in rudimentary conditions. Volunteers usually share dorm rooms and prepare meals together
Cost: No participation fees, though where the budget for a programme is not big enough, volunteers are asked for a contribution towards food. Participants pay their own travel expenses

Brathay Exploration Group Trust

Duration: 2-4 weeks
Location: Europe, Africa, India
Season: Year round
Prerequisites: Ages 15–25, self-motivation, physically fit. No experience required
Organisation: Charitable voluntary group committed to youth expeditioning and personal development

☎ 01539 433942
🖰 admin@brathayexploration.org.uk
💻 www.brathayexploration.org.uk

Description: The group organises expeditions combining adventure with field study work and voluntary projects. Around 100 volunteers are required each year. Expeditions offer participants the chance to discover new skills and resources and improve team skills and self-confidence. Individual projects change each year, but current conservation expeditions include a three-week trip to Romania trekking, wild-camping, and working on a conservation project in the Danube Delta
Accommodation: Varies according to the expedition. Often participants camp in tents, or stay in youth hostels or people's homes. Food is usually obtained locally
Cost: Varies. Sample: three weeks trekking in Romania and working on a conservation project in the Danube Delta – £880. Price includes all non-air travel, food, accommodation, insurance, and training

Biosphere Expeditions

Duration: 2–10 weeks
Location: Several countries including Oman, Slovakia, Honduras, Namibia, Brazil
Season: Year round
Prerequisites: Any age (under 18s must have parental consent). Expeditions available for all levels of fitness. Some English language required

☎ 0870 4460801
✉ info@biosphere-expeditions.org
🖥 www.biosphere-expeditions.org

Organisation: Award-winning non-profit organisation for hands-on conservation expeditions
Description: Biosphere Expeditions place members of the public on genuine research expeditions alongside scientists who are at the forefront of conservation work. Projects are constantly changing but examples include surveying whales, dolphins and turtles in the Azores, working with cheetahs in Namibia, surveying snow leopards in central Asia, and studying jaguars and pumas in Brazil. All data collected during the expedition is published in a report within a few months of the end of the expedition
Accommodation: Provided in locally owned lodgings that include B&Bs, research centres and tent base camps
Cost: Approx. £990 to £1,390 depending on duration and project. Price includes food, accommodation and all expedition expenses

A POSTCARD FROM Central Asia

Martyn Roberts travelled with Biosphere Expeditions as a member of the first team to take part in a survey of snow leopards in the Altai Republic (Central Asia). He describes the day they found snow leopard tracks:

On the first day, four of us set off up one of the mountains to do our first surveying with our guide Oleg, ironically named Big Oleg because he was far older but much smaller than Little Oleg. We spent most of the morning climbing the mountain. By early afternoon when we reached what appeared to be the top but was another ridge, I was pretty tired but happy to be in these spectacular but desolate and rocky mountains. Just being in this remote part of the world, meeting local people and working with local scientists in this spectacular setting to study one of the rarest and most elusive cats on the planet was the experience of a lifetime, but the Altai had more in store for us that day...

The radio crackled into life. One of the other groups were nearer than we thought and though barely able to speak through excitement told us that they had just discovered fairly fresh snow leopard tracks! On arrival we found the other group silently staring into a gully that was well shaded and filled with snow. A set of very clear paw prints ran from top to bottom. Yuriy, the expedition scientist, confirmed they were snow leopard tracks and a few days to a week old at the most. Staring in awe at them I was overcome with a feeling of complete exhilaration. One of the rarest big cats in the world had passed through where I was standing. They were here and what we were going to do would help them and their habitat to survive.

All the trials and tribulations of the past days fell away as we embarked upon recording and photographing the critical evidence we had only dreamt of finding. The long walk back to base camp that night seemed to go by in seconds.

51

BTCV – Conservation Holidays

Duration: 1–6 weeks
Location: 23 countries worldwide including Albania, Bulgaria, Cameroon, China, Estonia, Germany, Iceland, Italy, Japan, Kenya, Lesotho, Nepal, New Zealand, Portugal, Romania, South Africa, the UK, and the USA
Season: Year round
Prerequisites: Min. age 18. No special skills required
Organisation: The UK's leading practical conservation charity for improving and protecting the environment in countries worldwide
Description: BTCV offers a huge range of short-term volunteer opportunities and conservation holidays around the world. Examples of past projects include turtle monitoring in Thailand, Greece and Grenada, endangered primate surveys in India, footpath construction in Iceland, and wetland management in Hungary. All of the projects they offer allow participants to spend their holiday time contributing to a sustainable future for the planet. Participants work alongside local people and help them to protect their environment. In the UK there are also a range of shorter, often one-day, projects available. Volunteers engage in strenuous physical work but there is plenty of free time to relax, socialise and explore the local area

☎ 01302 388883
✆ information@btcv.org.uk
🖥 www.btcv.org

Accommodation: Included in the project price but varies according to project
Average Cost: £385 to £880 a fortnight on international projects/£150 a week in the UK. Fees for UK projects include food and board. International project fees may also cover local transportation and local leisure activities

BTCV volunteer working on a relocation programme in New Zealand holds a Hutton's Shearwater that has just been fed; Kaikoura, South Island.

A POSTCARD FROM China

Sales manager and serial short-term volunteer, Jane Reddaway's most recent trip was with BTCV to a remote protection station in China, where she was involved in a three–week wild panda monitoring programme:

I have been volunteering for some time now and I find it both a valuable and rewarding way to travel. Being single and travelling can be a bit daunting, but I find that visiting places as part of a structured voluntary placement makes for an extremely memorable holiday. The panda monitoring project was the third international trip I had volunteered on with BTCV (I had previously worked on a nature reserve in Iceland and an elephant monitoring project in Namibia), so I had a reasonable idea what I was letting myself in for!

I was attracted to this particular project because it satisfied both a yearning to see a panda in the wild (while there still are some), and to see China. I really didn't want to visit China or a package trip, being shepherded from one coach to another. Volunteering brings you much closer to the people of the country you are visiting and allows you to get to know a country from the inside.

The project had two different components. Given the remoteness of the protection station we had to stay overnight in Xian and travel into the mountains on the most challenging roads I have ever seen. At the station, we would get up at around 7am for a breakfast of steamed buns and pickled vegetables and then trek into the bamboo forests behind a guide to track the movements of pandas. We walked up to 10km on some days in high humidity, which was quite exhausting and returned late afternoon to base.

The accommodation was rather basic, with horrendous long-drop toilet facilities and only electricity for two hours a night. But I have stayed in worse. Meals were prepared by a cook at the base camp and were a far cry from the kind of Chinese food we are used to in the UK. A lot of the food was grown on site and was very healthy so I managed to lose a bit of weight. The cook did very well considering that the station was 8km from a bad mountain road and everything had to come on the back of a pack pony.

Although eco-tourism has a long way to go in China, and I personally would have preferred to have more to do in terms of constructive activities, I thoroughly enjoyed the experience. The countryside was full of bird and insect life with enormous butterflies everywhere. The experience of seeing pandas in the wild, albeit largely through dense bamboo, was one that I will value for a long time to come. We also had great fun with the guides, who had not met many westerners, so culturally, the trip was an extremely interesting exchange. On our last night at the station, the villagers made a wonderful meal in our honour. I felt extremely privileged as they had clearly gone to great efforts for us.

Working with the local team in a giant panda monitoring station on a BTCV holiday to China.

Coral Cay Conservation – Expeditions and Conservation Holidays

Duration: 1, 2, or 3 weeks (conservation holidays); Min. 1 week (marine expeditions); Min. 4 weeks (forest expeditions)

Location: Tobago, Papua New Guinea, the Red Sea, and the Philippines

Season: Year round

☎ 020 7620 1411

✍ info@coralcay.org

💻 www.coralcay.org

Prerequisites: Min. age 16, team spirit, moderate level of fitness, a keen interest in conservation, a sense of adventure and fun. No experience required

Organisation: Non-profit, non-governmental organisation that trains volunteers to collect scientific data to aid conservation

Description: Hundreds of volunteers join CCC projects each year to assist in conserving fragile tropical marine and terrestrial environments. The aim of CCC expeditions is to help gather scientific data for the protection and sustainable use of tropical environments, and to provide alternative livelihood opportunities for local communities. Participants have the opportunity to do something positive for the environment, learn new skills, meet new people and explore new environments. CCC has run successful one to two month expeditions since 1986. Now, to meet the demand of those who are interested in marine conservation, but due to time constraints cannot commit to a longer expedition, CCC has launched one, two and three week conservation holidays. Current conservation holidays include a seven–day research cruise to survey and dive with whale sharks at Sogod Bay in the Philippines and a reef biology and conservation trip on the Red Sea

Accommodation: Varies according to project. Provided in price

Cost: Programme fees for marine expeditions start at £360 for 1 week and fees for forest expeditions start at £1380 for 4 weeks. Conservation holiday prices start at £600 per week. Fees include food, lodging and training

A POSTCARD FROM Fiji

Lucy Misch, 20, went on a CCC expedition on the Fiji Coral Reef Conservation Project as part of her gap year:

People often ask me which was the best part of my gap year. I tell them that Fiji was the most intense and amazing experience I had because I learnt how to recognise and talk about a vast array of species in the Indo-Pacific. I saw things I had only ever seen on TV. I made friends that I will never lose contact with, and I also began to realise how I could live without my creature comforts. When I think back to the fun we had on the surveys there are too many moments to record. One time we were on our first deep survey dive of the day and were about half way down when a large sting-ray came swooping out of the blue. We just watched in awe as this massive creature moved majestically through the water. It circled us once and then disappeared. It was a stunning moment.

This experience is something you will never repeat, and is an experience that you shouldn't miss out on. Diving for me has become a passion, and now as a fully-fledged instructor I teach throughout my university term. Every holiday I travel and teach diving, educating people about the coral reefs and helping other divers and snorkellers enjoy their holiday and learn fish identification techniques.

Different Travel

Duration: 14 days/13 nights
Location: Galapagos, Tanzania, Kenya, Zimbabwe, Sweden
Season: Year round
Prerequisites: Open to all. Some tours are suitable for accompanied children but not all

☎ 02380 669903
✆ info@different-travel.com
🖥 www.different-travel.com

Organisation: 'Direct Action' tour operator, committed to ethical and responsible travel, offering holidays that include an element of voluntary work
Description: Different Travel holidays combine sightseeing, leisure and relaxation with time spent working on projects. These projects vary but are always run by local people and for local people. Current conservation projects include 13 days in the Galapagos Islands (Ecuador), which includes trekking, snorkelling and a tour of the islands. Three days of the holiday is spent with National Park staff and local people helping to clean the coastline and also helping to preserve a fragile ecosystem. Other conservation projects in the pipeline include a chimpanzee rehabilitation project in Tanzania, a lion project in Zimbabwe, and reindeer migration in Sweden
Accommodation: Provided in 3–star or above hotels, with air conditioning, en-suite bathrooms and western facilities. All hotels are locally owned and ethically run
Cost: Varies between projects. Example cost – Galapagos project (13 days): £2,400. Prices include return flights, donations towards the project, tour escorts, accommodation, meals, and a carbon off-setting component

Ecovolunteer

Duration: 1–4 weeks
Location: 19 countries worldwide
Season: Year round
Prerequisites: Min. age 18, good physical condition, able to speak English, and flexible towards other cultures and lifestyles

☎ 0117 965 8333
✆ info@ecovolunteer.org
🖥 www.ecovolunteer.org

Organisation: Self-supported conservation volunteer placement organisation
Description: The Ecovolunteer Programme organises wildlife conservation projects and wildlife research projects operated by local conservation NGOs worldwide. Over 500 volunteers are recruited each year for such projects as jaguar conservation in Brazil, minke whale research in Canada, monitoring wild horses in Mongolia, and protection of the endangered blue duck in New Zealand. Volunteers participate as hands-on assistants. Work varies from practical fieldwork to production and support jobs in wildlife rescue centres, to visitor education, maintenance work, and household duties, dependent on each individual project. All training in scientific and conservation methods will be provided in the field
Accommodation: Provided in a variety of, usually basic, lodgings including field stations, local houses, a cabin on a research vessel and a tent. Rooms are usually shared with one other volunteer. Food is sometimes included
Cost: Varies hugely. Sample – €1,360 for three weeks of elephant research in Cameroon. Price includes accommodation and sometimes food

Earthwatch Institute

Duration: Most projects are 10–14 days, but 1-week, 3-week and weekend opportunities are available

Location: 50 countries worldwide

Season: Year round

Prerequisites: Min. age 18. Some expeditions require a high level of fitness or scuba diving qualifications. Teen and family trips also available

☎ 01865 318831

🖱 projects@earthwatch.org.uk

💻 www.earthwatch.org/Europe

Organisation: An international environmental charity offering volunteering opportunities on scientific research expeditions around the world. All volunteer contributions go directly towards supporting the scientific research

Description: Earthwatch expeditions are short-term opportunities for participants to work directly in the field on a range of conservation projects and make a personal, hands-on contribution. Current projects include helping to protect Amazon dolphins, giant river otters, monkeys and birds while living and working on an Amazon riverboat, snorkelling in the Bahamas to help researchers survey coral reef health, helping to protect elephants in a Sri Lankan national park, and investigating how monkeys are adapting to human disturbance in Costa Rica

Accommodation: Food and lodging arrangements vary widely and may take the form of camping, dorm rooms, guesthouses, hotels or apartments

Cost: Prices range from £165 to £2,995 excluding flights. Price includes food and board, in-country travel and training

Earthwatch volunteers help find ways to improve sustainable cocoa production in Ghana.

Frontier

Duration: Min. 4 weeks (although a few offer min. 2 weeks)
Location: Worldwide
Season: Year round
Prerequisites: Min. age 17, physically fit. Marine expeditions include free scuba diving training

☎ 020 7613 2422
🖱 info@frontier.ac.uk
💻 www.frontier.ac.uk

Organisation: International not-for-profit conservation organisation dedicated to promoting field research and implementing practical projects contributing to the conservation of natural resources and the development of sustainable livelihoods
Description: Frontier recruits more than 300 volunteers a year to participate in exciting projects in beautiful unexplored parts of the world. The projects address high priority resource management and habitat conservation issues. Volunteers can scuba dive in crystal clear coral waters alongside sharks, rays, dolphins and colourful reef fish, track elephants and lions through the savanna, and search for tigers in the dense jungle. Conservation projects focus on threatened tropical ecosystems (rainforest, savanna, coral reef and mangrove areas) and include a full scientific training by some of the world's top experts
Accommodation: Provided in communal tents or huts. Food preparation is a shared responsibility of the group
Cost: International volunteers raise approx. £1,200–£1,500 for 4 weeks which covers all individual costs, scientific and dive training, visas, insurance, food and accommodation but excludes flights

Global Crossroad – Wildlife Volunteers

Duration: Min. 2 weeks
Location: South Africa, Zimbabwe, Botswana, Kenya, Tanzania, Sri Lanka, Thailand, Guatemala
Season: Year round
Prerequisites: Volunteers under 15 must be accompanied, 16/17-year-olds may volunteer

☎ 0208 263 6095
🖱 info@globalcrossroad.com
💻 www.globalcrossroad.com

unaccompanied with a letter of parental consent. No previous experience required
Organisation: International volunteer organisation committed to providing meaningful volunteer opportunities abroad
Description: The wildlife volunteer programme offers participants a rewarding conservation experience, supporting ongoing wildlife research and preservation efforts while working alongside conservationists, wildlife researchers and park managers. Project fees also contribute to sustainable development and further protection of the land, reserves and wildlife. Current volunteer projects include colubus monkey, olowaru lion and elephant conservation in Kenya, work for orphaned, neglected and abused animals in Namibia, gibbon rehabilitation in Thailand, and rare leopard expeditions in Sri Lanka
Accommodation: Provided with host families, in hostels or lodges. Food is included and usually provided by a host family
Cost: Varies according to project location/duration (average of approx. US$1,500). As an example, three weeks at the Gibbon Rehabilitation Project in Phuket costs US$1,694. Includes board and lodging, transfers and insurance

Global Vision International

Duration: Min. 1 week
Location: Worldwide
Season: Year round
Prerequisites: No experience necessary
Organisation: GVI promotes sustainable development by
supplying volunteers, equipment, funding and training to
governmental groups, charities, NGOs and communities around the world

☎ 0870 608 8898
✉ info@gvi.co.uk
💻 www.gvi.co.uk

Description: GVI works locally with partners to promote sustainable development through environmental research, conservation and education. Current short-term conservation projects include volunteering at an animal sanctuary in Florida, conservation work with turtles in Panama, studying humpback whales in Brazil, researching orangutans in Sumatra, volunteering with vervet monkeys in South Africa, working with desert elephants in Namibia, working with rhinos in Uganda, and volunteering at a primate rehabilitation centre in Thailand

Accommodation: Included in price. Varies according to project
Sample Cost: 2 weeks working with pink river dolphins in Brazil £1,195. All prices include food, accommodation, training, airport pick-up, in-country orientation, back-up and insurance

A POSTCARD FROM South Africa

In 2006, Kirsty Sharratt took part in GVI's Wildlife Research Expedition in South Africa. She describes her most rewarding day on the project, tracking Zero the lion:

It was 5am and I was ready for another day of data duty but as we set off from base the reserve manager called us on the radio, requesting that we urgently locate Zero, one of the male lions, as the reserve vet was on his way to dart and re-collar the lion!

The unexpected news was welcomed by a buzz of excitement and a mad dash to find Zero. We located him by the river; he was with his son Mpho. We contacted the vet and he told us to stay with Zero until he arrived in approximately 20 minutes. I was taking data: location details, GPS points and full-ratings, when the two lions decided it was time for a wander. We followed them as they crossed the river, then panicked as we lost sight of them in the dense vegetation on the bank. A frantic 10 minutes passed as we drove from one side of the river to the other, up and down banks, trying not to get stuck in the sand. Thankfully, both Zero and Mpho soon decided to stop in the riverbed and we were able to direct the vet to them.

We were able to watch the darting from the opposite bank of the river. Our job was to keep an eye out for Mpho, who had run off after Zero was darted. We had to ensure he did not come too close to where the vet was working on Zero. It was amazing to be able to watch the procedure and be involved in our own way. After the vet had changed the collar, we had to use the telemetry equipment to note the new frequency by which we would be able to locate Zero in the future.

We then had to stay in the area for over an hour after the vet had left, just to keep an eye on Zero as the drugs wore off. It was interesting to see how he reacted, and to watch a nervous and very curious Mpho return to Zero's side. By no means a normal day of data duty, but a very exciting and rewarding one.

Global Volunteer Network

Duration: Min. 2/4 weeks
Location: South Africa, Thailand, USA (Alaska), New Zealand, Costa Rica, Ecuador
Season: Year round
Prerequisites: Min. age 18, good physical condition, able to speak English. No special skills or qualifications needed

☎ +64 4 569 9080
✎ info@volunteer.org.nz
💻 www.volunteer.org.nz

Organisation: Private NGO dedicated to supporting the work of local community organisations through the placement of international volunteers
Description: Around 2,500 volunteers are recruited by GVN each year for a variety of placements. Current conservation and wildlife projects, provided in partnership with local organisations include helping to manage and maintain a wildlife sanctuary in South Africa, working with abused and neglected animals at a rescue centre in Thailand, environmental fieldwork in Alaska, helping preserve, monitor and re-establish the natural environment in Wellington, New Zealand, working to protect sea turtles in Costa Rica and working in biological reserves in Ecuador
Accommodation: Provided. Volunteers usually live and work in the same conditions as members of the host community
Cost: US$350 application fee to GVN covers administration, marketing and programme information. Programme fees vary from US$445 per month in Ecuador to US$1,500 a month in Alaska to cover training, accommodation and meals during training and placement, in-country transport and supervision

Greenforce

Duration: Min. 2 weeks
Location: Bahamas, Fiji, Tanzania, Ecuador, South Africa, China
Season: Placements start in January, April, July and October
Prerequisites: Min. age 17. No previous experience or qualifications necessary

☎ 020 7470 8888
✎ greenforce@btinternet.com
💻 www.greenforce.org

Organisation: Non-profit organisation working alongside local people on international conservation, community and sport volunteer projects
Description: Greenforce offers a range of volunteer projects that focus on improving the environment and human interactions with it. All Greenforce projects support the local infrastructure and improve the future of the region. On conservation projects, participants work as fieldwork assistants, carrying out tasks such as tracking animal movements and studying coral reef species. All training is provided. Current projects include working on marine conservation projects in the Bahamas and Fiji and on land conservation projects in Tanzania, Ecuador, South Africa and China
Accommodation: Provided in simple, but clean and safe local housing, which varies between projects
Cost: From £1,500 for 4 weeks. Fees cover training and instruction, food, accommodation, visas and medical insurance but not international flights

WORLDWIDE   CONSERVATION & WILDLIFE

Hands Up Holidays

Duration: 11–17 days (also tailor-made options)
Location: Argentina, Australia, Borneo, Brazil, China, Galapagos, Guatemala, India, Kenya, Mozambique, Namibia, New Zealand, Thailand, Turkey, Vietnam
Season: Year round

☎ 0800 7833554
✉ info@handsupholidays.com
💻 www.handsupholidays.com

Prerequisites: Min. age 18. No specific skills required, just enthusiasm, but any skills you do have are matched with specific projects
Organisation: Leading ethical tour operator working with local suppliers, NGOs, charities and local projects. A minimum of 10% of profits go to further development projects
Description: Hands Up Holidays offers ethically and environmentally responsible holidays that blend sightseeing with fulfilling volunteering experiences. Approx. a third of the holiday is devoted to a meaningful 'taste' of environmental conservation volunteering and the rest of the time is spent sightseeing with local, English-speaking guides. Current projects include coastal cleanup in Galapagos, penguin habitat preservation in New Zealand, coral reef surveying in Mozambique, cleaning panda reserves in China, elephant conservation in Thailand, and bird ringing in Kenya. All flights are carbon neutral
Accommodation: Ranges from home-stays to 5–star hotels and eco-lodges that are locally owned and managed where possible
Cost: From £750 for 11 days in India, through to £2,300 for 15 days in the Galapagos and Ecuador. Average price (excluding flights) for two weeks is £1,600

Imaginative Traveller

Duration: 14–22 days
Location: Kenya, Thailand, China, Ecuador
Season: Year round
Prerequisites: Min. age 18 (but accompanied teenagers aged 16+ are also accepted)

☎ 01473 667337
✉ online@imtrav.net
💻 www.imaginative-traveller.com

Organisation: Tour operator that aims to provide exceptional travel experiences, allowing tourists to relish the diversity of countries and cultures
Description: Imaginative Traveller holidays combine volunteer work with an adventure holiday allowing travellers to immerse themselves in the culture of a country, to interact with local people, and to see the country as it really is. Several days are spent on a rewarding placement, but there is also plenty of time to relax and see the sites. Current conservation and wildlife projects include elephant monitoring in Thailand, preservation of endangered plants and reforestation in Ecuador, and looking after giant pandas in China. Tours use a range of local accommodation, transport and staff, as well as supporting local charities
Accommodation: Tour accommodation ranges from jungle tree houses to basic but comfortable hotels
Cost: The cost is broken down into three payments: tour, local payment and donation. 100% of the donation goes direct to the charities. As an example, the Elephants and Beaches tour in Kenya costs £670 (including accommodation, transport, selected meals and excursions) plus US$270 local payment and a donation of £150

Involvement Volunteers Association Inc

Duration: 2–6 weeks
Location: More than 20 countries including Australia, Bolivia, China, Egypt, Fiji, Korea, Latvia, Mongolia, Namibia, Peru, Samoa, Togo and Venezuela
Season: Year round

☎ +61 3 9646 9392
🖱 ivworldwide@volunteering.org.au
💻 www.volunteering.org.au

Prerequisites: Anyone can volunteer, preferably with knowledge and experience but also possible without. Min. age 18 (unless you have parental agreement)
Organisation: Registered not-for-profit NGO
Description: IVA offers a cost effective way for people of all ages to gain practical experience while helping others as a real volunteer and meeting the local people, and experiencing their culture. Current conservation and wildlife projects include forest conservation in Ecuador, bat research in Panama, reforestation in Samoa, trail-building in Australia, sea turtle protection in Greece, condor research and conservation in the USA and reptile field research in Peru
Accommodation: Provided in basic but clean and safe lodgings. Varies from project to project
Cost: Fees are negotiated with volunteers on an individual basis. On average a 4–week placement costs around £800. Fees include food, accommodation, administration costs and in-country transportation

i-to-i International Projects

Duration: Min. 1 week ('Early Gaps' for 16–19 year olds last 2 weeks)
Location: 23 countries worldwide including Argentina, Sri Lanka, India, Bolivia, Kenya, South Africa, Tanzania, Australia, Thailand and China
Season: Year round

☎ 0870 333 2332;
   toll-free USA 800 985 4864
🖱 uk@i-to-i.com; usca@i-to-i.com
💻 www.i-to-i.com

Prerequisites: Early Gaps min. age 16; all others min. age 18. No previous experience required
Organisation: A founding member of the Year Out Group with Investors in People status, i-to-i is a TEFL training and volunteer travel organisation
Description: i-to-i is a leading global provider of ethical volunteer travel and places more than 5,000 people each year on 500 projects. Their conservation projects allow people to work closely with local people in spectacular locations on worthwhile long-term programmes. There are currently 44 conservation projects on offer including wallaby rehabilitation in Australia, conservation work with golden lion tamarins in Brazil, rainforest preservation in Ecuador, iguana preservation on the Bay Islands, Honduras and conservation on a tropical island in Thailand
Accommodation: Included in price. Varies from project to project
Cost: from £495/€695 (excluding airfares). Sample – 2 weeks of Cloud Forest conservation in Ecuador: £995 (including board and lodging)

Operation Wallacea

Duration: Min. 2 weeks
Location: Honduras, Peru, Cuba, South Africa, Indonesia and Egypt
Season: June – August

☎ 01790 763194
✉ info@opwall.com
💻 www.opwall.com

Prerequisites: Research assistants must be university undergraduates with a keen interest in conservation. General surveyors usually attend as part of a school group
Organisation: Run by a charitable trust dedicated to conservation research
Description: Operation Wallacea is a series of biological and social science expedition projects that operate in remote locations across the world. These expeditions are designed with specific wildlife conservation aims in mind, from identifying areas needing protection, through to implementing and assessing conservation management programmes. More than 1000 volunteers are recruited each year. Volunteers work as general surveyors and research assistants. Medics (doctors, nurses, paramedics and medical elective students) are also needed to provide on-site first aid and medical assistance to volunteers and staff on expeditions
Accommodation: Included in price. Varies according to project
Cost: £950 (2 weeks), £1750 (4 weeks) including all accommodation and food costs, transfers, dive training and participation in research projects

Personal Overseas Development

Duration: Min. 1 week
Location: Nepal, Peru, Tanzania, Thailand
Season: Year round

☎ 01242 250 901
✉ info@thepodsite.co.uk
💻 www.thepodsite.co.uk

Prerequisites: Min. age 18. No specific skills are required, just energy, enthusiasm and a willingness to get involved
Organisation: Volunteer placement agency providing a link between small charities and other organisations in less developed countries and people in the UK wishing to do something worthwhile abroad
Description: Personal Overseas Development coordinates breaks for people wishing to volunteer their time and skills where it is needed, on ongoing voluntary work programmes of support and development in local communities. The organisation offers a range of short-term projects and summer mini-gaps including wildlife rescue, elephant care and marine conservation in Thailand, and the Amazon Jungle Conservation Project in Peru
Accommodation: All programmes include accommodation, the nature of which varies from project to project
Cost: Elephant care: £250 (1 week); wildlife rescue: £445 (2 weeks); Amazon jungle conservation: £945 (1 month). Flights not included

Quest

Duration: Min. 2/4 weeks (projects),
2/3 weeks (escapes)
Location: Southern Africa, East Africa,
Andean South America and Brazil
Season: Year round
Prerequisites: Min. age 18. Average age is 21.
No qualifications needed, just enthusiasm

☎ 01444 474744
🖱 emailus@questoverseas.com
💻 www.questoverseas.com

Organisation: Expedition specialists with projects and adventure travel to suit all ages in South America and Africa
Description: Quest places more than 300 participants each year on holidays with a difference. Quest's projects involve voluntary work on conservation and community projects for a minimum of two or four weeks. Current conservation projects include the Malawi Wildlife Rehabilitation Centre Project, the Chile Conservation Project, the Brazil Coastal Rainforest Project and the Bolivia Animal Sanctuary Project. Marine conservation projects include the Honduras Turtle and Marine Conservation Project. Alternatively, participants can enjoy an 'Escape' which combines a traditional holiday with a chance to spend one or two weeks working on a project, ideal for those who want to combine travel with volunteering but only have a few weeks to spare
Accommodation: Included in price. Varies depending on project, from youth hostels and small hotels, to tents and hammocks in the jungle
Cost: £1,800–£4,920 (South America) and £1,390–£4,240 (Africa)

A POSTCARD FROM Mozambique

Thoger Krogh, a 31-year-old doctor, took part in the Quest Underseas Whale Shark and Manta Ray Preservation Project:

I was particularly attracted to the idea of an expedition because I have always found that working while on vacation gives me a much more intense and enjoyable experience. This project in particular suited me down to the ground, because I have trained as a diving instructor in the past, so I knew I had the skills to really make a difference. Also, as a doctor in the middle of my career and training to be a specialist, an expedition was perfect – nine days was all the time I could get off work.

On a normal working day on the project there were two investigative dives, plus a class where we were taught all about the ecological issues involved. In the afternoons we collated and input the data. It was a satisfying feeling when we came across species that we were monitoring, and being within sight of whale sharks was an awe-inspiring experience. The project was also made special by the other volunteers. We were all able to work together well and we had become good friends by the end. We were staying in excellent accommodation – a forest lodge, and we all mucked in and prepared food together. Spending time with the other volunteers turned out to be a highlight of the expedition.

The best participants are those who are willing to make the project work even when they encounter problems, and those who are able to do it with a smile. My advice to those planning to undertake such a project would be to be open-minded and to expect the unexpected. For me the preservation project really was an adventure, and I was doing something I love far away from home and the pressures of work, but I also knew that some important research might come out of it.

Real Gap Experience

Duration: 2 weeks – 6 months
Location: More than 40 countries worldwide
Organisation: The leading independent gap year specialists, offering the most comprehensive range of gap year opportunities

☎ 01892 516164
🖱 info@realgap.co.uk
💻 www.realgap.co.uk

Description: Real Gap Experience offers an opportunity to volunteer with wildlife in some of the most amazing destinations around the world. There is a huge selection of programmes to choose from. **Conservation** projects involve working in the field, learning essential conservation practices and helping to preserve the planet's precious ecosystems and wildlife. There are programmes in Africa, Latin/Central America and Austaliasia. In Malaysia participants help to protect the endangered orangutans. For a serious qualification participants can also train to become a game warden in Africa. **Wildlife Rehabilitation** projects involve nursing sick and injured animals in some of the most amazing scenery in the world, including the Amazon jungle, Borneo, Costa Rica, Guatemala and Africa. Participants get involved in preserving species and releases back into the wild. For the older traveller, **Gap Year for Grown Ups** (www.gapyearforgrownups.co.uk) is the leading specialist in career breaks and volunteer work, with hundreds of exciting conservation and wildlife projects around the world
Accommodation: Varies depending on programme – ranges from home-stays, volunteer houses, tented camps, huts and hostels
Cost: From £429 including accommodation, meals, airport pick-up, orientation, volunteer placement and tuition

Reef Check

Duration: Min. 1 week
Location: More than 70 countries worldwide
Season: Year round
Prerequisites: Participants must be certified scuba divers, although snorkelling may be sufficient for some surveys. No age or ability limits

☎ +1 310 230 2371
🖱 rcinfo@reefcheck.org
💻 www.reefcheck.org

Organisation: Scientific research project dedicated to creating a global network of volunteer teams trained in Reef Check's scientific methods who regularly monitor and report on reef health, to protect and rehabilitate reefs worldwide
Description: Reef Check aims to educate the public about the coral reef crisis and to monitor reefs worldwide. Volunteers are invited to either join an expedition or to set up their own team in order to participate in coral reef monitoring. There is scope for a team wherever there is coral reef. Reef Check aims to use standard methodology on a global scale and potential volunteers must be trained for an average of three days. In 2007 there were organised expeditions in Thailand, the Maldives, the Red Sea, and Honduras
Accommodation: Depends on the individual project
Cost: No participation fee. May be a small charge for training as required

Responsible Travel

Duration: Min. 2 days
Location: Worldwide
Season: Year round
Prerequisites: Open to all
Organisation: Brighton-based online
eco-travel agent which markets more than
270 tour operators

☎ 01273 600030
🖱 amelia@responsibletravel.com
💻 www.responsibletravel.com

Description: Responsible Travel offers literally hundreds of wildlife, marine and habitat
conservation holidays around the world lasting from just a few days to several months.
The majority last for one or two weeks however. Participants are involved in all sorts of
work, from caring for sick and abused animals, to scientific wildlife monitoring, habitat
preservation and working on a reserve or wildlife park. Volunteers work hard, but also
have plenty of free time to explore the local area. Some of the conservation holidays
currently on offer include: Ecology and Wildlife on Kangaroo Island, Australia; elephant
conservation in Thailand; the Florida Dolphin Expedition; manatee conservation in Belize;
orangutan volunteering in Borneo; reptile conservation in South Africa; a sailing and
conservation holiday in Greece; and Arabian leopard conservation in Oman
Accommodation: Varies according to project but mostly provided in comfortable guest
houses and B&Bs
Cost: Varies according to project. An example cost is 2 weeks chamois, wolf and bear
conservation in Slovakia – £990 excluding flights

Swiss Whale Society

Duration: Min. 2 weeks
Location: Quebec, Canada or the Cape Verde Islands
(off Africa)
Season: June – September (Canada); March – May
(Cape Verde)
Prerequisites: Min. age 18, not easily sea-sick, good
physical condition. No experience or specific skills are
required, but computer, photography and navigation skills are particularly in demand

☎ +41 76 530 91 92
🖱 info@whales.ch
💻 www.whales.ch

Organisation: Scientific research project dedicated to studying marine mammals in their
natural habitat
Description: The Swiss Whale Society carries out biological research on blue, finback,
minke and humpback whales. Volunteers are invited to help with this research both on
the water and back in the lab. At sea volunteers help with species identification, sound
recording and filming, data entry and navigation. On land participants help to collate and
write up the data collected at sea. Participants should not expect to swim with dolphins or
whales
Accommodation: Provided either at the research centre or onboard a research vessel
Cost: US$1,160 (Canada, 2 weeks); US$1,600 (Cape Verde, 2 weeks). Includes room and
board, lectures and all excursions at sea

Canal Camps – Waterway Recovery Group

Duration: 1 week
Location: Throughout Britain
Season: March – August
Prerequisites: Open to anyone aged 18–70. No experience required
Organisation: Voluntary organisation, helping to restore derelict canals in Britain

☎ 01923 711114
🖱 enquiries@wrg.org.uk
💻 www.wrg.org.uk

Description: A Canal Camp is an enjoyable week's outdoor holiday spent working on the canals, meeting new people and doing your bit for Britain's industrial heritage and the environment. Hundreds of volunteers take part in more than 20 camps each summer. Jobs on the camps can include restoring industrial archaeology, demolishing old brickwork, bricklaying and pouring concrete, driving a dumper truck, clearing silt, helping to run a waterways festival, cooking for other volunteers, and clearing vegetation and trees. The working day is roughly 9am to 5pm with evenings free and social activities organised for those who want to take part
Accommodation: Provided in village halls, sports clubs etc. Electricity, showers, toilets and dry, draught-free sleeping areas guaranteed
Cost: £42 per camp. Includes food and accommodation

The Centre for Alternative Technology

Duration: 1 or 2 weeks
Location: Powys, Wales
Season: March – September
Prerequisites: Min. age 18. No experience required
Organisation: Established in 1974, the centre is an internationally renowned display and education centre

☎ 01654 705950
🖱 info@cat.org.uk
💻 www.cat.org.uk

promoting practical ideas and information on technologies, which sustain rather than damage the environment
Description: The centre has working displays of wind, water and solar power, low-energy buildings, organic farming and alternative sewerage systems, receiving around 80,000 visitors per year. Volunteers have the chance to learn about alternative technology for a short period by joining the volunteer programme. Four short-term volunteers are taken on per week and undertake a variety of work tasks. Much of the work involves digging holes and barrowing rocks about, weeding and clearing beds, moving compost, fixing things and painting. Work lasts from Monday to Friday, with weekends free to explore the local area. Demand for these placements is great and the centre is usually fully booked by March of each year.
Accommodation: Basic youth-hostel style accommodation provided, plus food and drinks
Cost: £10 per night contribution towards bed and board

Cetacean Research and Rescue Unit

Duration: 12 days
Location: Moray Firth, Scotland
Season: May – October
Prerequisites: Enthusiasm, the ability to learn and work under difficult field conditions, open-mindedness, a sense of humour, and physical fitness

☎ 01261 851 696
🖰 volunteer@crru.org.uk
💻 www.crru.org.uk

Organisation: CRRU is a small charitable marine research organisation that conducts scientific investigations in Scottish waters and provides professional assistance to injured cetaceans
Description: As many as 22 species of whales and dolphins have been sighted in the Outer Moray Firth. Each year CRRU offers opportunities for volunteers to join in as a part of the research and rescue team. Volunteers learn about whales and dolphins and their marine environment, while receiving training in marine research and marine mammal rescue techniques. Participants work with a team of biologists, receive structured lectures and field tuition and also provide crucial support for the organistion's research programme to improve conservation measures. As well as cataloguing images and recording data, the team may be called upon to help with live whale and dolphin strandings
Accommodation: Teams share a rented cottage with modern facilities and a full kitchen. Participants share cooking and cleaning duties
Cost: £750. This covers full board, equipment and all associated field costs

Groundwork – Irish Wildlife Trust Volunteers

Duration: 1 or 2 weeks
Location: Killarney Valley, Ireland
Season: June – September
Prerequisites: Volunteers should be in good health and aged 18–65

☎ +353 1 860 2839
🖰 info@groundwork.ie
💻 www.groundwork.ie

Organisation: Groundwork is a special section of The Irish Wildlife Trust dedicated to organising voluntary conservation projects
Description: Killarney Valley is world famous for its natural beauty and the volunteer programme was started in 1981 to tackle the rhododendron infestation of the Killarney Oak Woods. The ponticum species of rhododrendron (introduced into Ireland in the nineteenth century) has a tendency to become so dense that it blocks 98% of light reaching the woodland floors thus preventing any regeneration at that level. Volunteers help to tackle this problem, often working in remote areas that can only be accessed by boat and on foot. The work involves clearing rhododendron with hand tools such as bow-saws and mattocks. Work begins and ends on Sundays, with five days spent working in the woods. On Saturdays there is usually an organised boat trip and walk through the red deer range
Accommodation: Provided in a national park hostel on the shores of Lough Leane
Cost: €30 (1 week) or €45 (2 weeks), including food and accommodation

Hebridean Whale & Dolphin Trust – Cetacean Research Project

Duration: 2, 9 or 12 days
Location: Isle of Mull, Scotland
Season: April – September
Prerequisites: Proficient English, patience, fitness, good health, vision and balance, easy-going nature, basic computing skills. Min. age 18

☎ 01688 302620
🖎 info@hwdt.org
🖳 www.hwdt.org

Organisation: HWDT is dedicated to the conservation of Scotland's whales, dolphins, and porpoises and the Hebridean marine environment through education and research
Description: Participants travel the waters surrounding Scotland's Western Isles on a 60–foot, fully equipped yacht ('Silurian'), whilst helping to conduct scientific research. Participants collect data during visual surveys for whales and dolphins. Other work includes conducting acoustic monitoring, data entry and assisting with the day-to-day running of the research vessel. All participants receive onboard training for scientific survey work. There are also short (two day, three night) marine mammal courses available which combine practical discussions on marine mammal biology, ecology and conservation with hands-on fieldwork experience on board the yacht
Accommodation: Onboard for nine or 12-day trips, in bunkhouses for two-day trips
Cost: £150 per person, excluding accommodation (2 day course); £695 (9 days) or £795 (12 days) per person, including food, accommodation and training

A POSTCARD FROM the Isle of Mull

Rachel Gibson spent 10 days on board the 'Silurian' helping to monitor the Hebridean marine environment:

On a cold April morning, thermals and sea sickness bands in hand, I was ready to go aboard Silurian on the first monitoring trip of the year. The aim: to carry out surveys of the Inner Hebrides to quantify the number of cetaceans. None of us volunteers had ever done anything like this before so apprehension and excitement were in the air as we left Tobermory Bay.

We sailed past Duart castle, where five bottlenose dolphins escorted us. The dolphins bow rode for 15 minutes – my first dolphins and they were bow riding! We collected data about the dolphins and entered it into a laptop. We also collected environmental data and listened to the noise in the sea with the hydrophone. We'd hear shrimps, boats and some dolphins.

We would alternate between collecting data and watching the sea, searching for cetaceans for as long as we had daylight. It only took a couple of shifts to grasp the idea, and soon we were all comfortable with the system. Undeniably the best shift you can get is half an hour in the crow's nest. I'll admit I was really scared climbing up, but once you're up there it's great with sea birds flying past you. It gives the best view of the surrounding area and many a porpoise was spotted from this great vantage point.

Towards the end of the 10 days we had the luck of a close encounter with a juvenile minke whale. I rushed out to see a minke spy-hopping behind the boat. We then watched this whale join with its mother and move along the tide line for half an hour. Unforgettable!

After 10 very short days sailing around the Hebrides our trip was over. Were my fears warranted? No, I never did need my sea sickness bands although I did always wear my thermals, the boat was very comfortable and the food was great.

International Otter Survival Fund

Duration: 5–7 days
Location: Hebridean Islands, Scotland
Season: May – September
Prerequisites: Volunteers walk over rough ground or slippery shoreline for 6–8 miles a day, so physical fitness is required. Volunteers under 18 must have written parental consent; senior volunteers are welcomed
Organisation: IOSF is a wildlife charity committed to protecting and ensuring a healthy environment for the 13 species of otters worldwide
Description: IOSF's hands-on holidays are educational and research trips designed to suit almost everyone. There are three types of trip. The Otter Detective trips teach people how to recognise otter signs, observe otters in the wild, and analyse their diet. Wildlife and Heritage holidays offer a more general wildlife watching week, focusing on the geology, history and archaeology of Skye and Raasay. And Survey holidays allow participants to do practical survey work and study otter populations. These holidays are extremely popular among nature lovers and early booking is recommended
Accommodation: Provided at local guesthouses and B&Bs
Cost: £310–£525 depending on the project. All funds from the holidays are put back into practical conservation measures to protect otters

☎ 01471 822487
✆ iosf@otter.org
🖥 www.otter.org

The Monkey Sanctuary

Duration: Min. 2 weeks
Location: Nr. Looe, Cornwall
Season: Year round
Prerequisites: Some English language, good health and a general concern for animals and nature. Min. age 18
Organisation: The Monkey Sanctuary Trust is an environmental charity dedicated to promoting the welfare, conservation and survival of primates and working to end the primate trade and abuse of primates in captivity
Description: The Monkey Sanctuary is home to a colony of woolley and capuchin Monkeys and was started in 1964 as a refuge for ex-pet and ex-zoo monkeys. The sanctuary provides volunteers with a chance to become part of the community and share in a commitment to care for monkeys. Although they cannot help directly with monkey handling, they do help the sanctuary to run smoothly. In the summer, activities range from preparing monkey food and cleaning the enclosures, to helping in the café and talking to visitors. In winter, volunteers help maintain the house and monkey territory and work in the sanctuary gardens. The sanctuary could not function without the help of volunteers
Accommodation: Single-sex dorms
Cost: A £35 per week contribution towards insurance, food and accommodation is requested

☎ 01503 262532
✆ info@monkeysanctuary.org
🖥 www.monkeysanctuary.org

The National Trust – Working Holidays

Duration: 2–7 days
Location: England, Wales and Northern Ireland
Season: Year round
Prerequisites: Min. age 18 (Youth Discovery programme for 16–18 year olds). No specific skills are required

☎ 0870 609 5383
✉ volunteers@nationaltrust.org.uk
💻 www.nationaltrust.org.uk/volunteering

Organisation: Charity, independent of the government, which protects and opens to the public more than 300 historic houses and gardens. Also looks after industrial monuments, mills, forests, beaches, farmland, archaeological remains, castles and nature reserves

Description: Around 450 Working Holidays for the National Trust take place in more than 100 beautiful locations each year, all guaranteed to help participants escape the stresses and strain of everyday life. Participants can get involved in a huge range of conservation and habitat preservation projects, from herding goats to dry-stone walling in the Lake District. Every holiday makes a real difference. There are working holidays specifically for younger, older or disabled volunteers. Other choices include Trust Active Holidays, which combine work with outdoor activities such as sailing canoeing, and walking, and Premium Holidays for those who like to work hard during the day but prefer more luxurious surroundings in the evening

Accommodation: Provided in a National Trust basecamp – farmhouses, cottages or apartments that have been converted into volunteer accommodation. All have cooking facilities, dorms with bunk beds, lounge and toilet and shower facilities. All meals are included

Cost: From £75 per week including food and accommodation

A POSTCARD FROM the North Yorkshire Dales

Retired Canadian Lorraine Flanigan describes her Working Holiday with the National Trust:

Because the Working Holidays programme was new to me, I decided to test the waters by selecting a short-term weekend project. I worked alongside seven other volunteers at the Trust's Nature Reserve at Malham Tarn in the dales of North Yorkshire in England. I was prepared to discover a part of the world that was new to me, to meet people who spoke the same yet a different language, and to have some fun.

A seasoned volunteer advised me to bring along a sense of humour, and laughter certainly got me through the unaccustomed communal living arrangements, the ear-bending Yorkshire accents, and my feeble attempts to wield a hammer and saw.

Our conservation project was to repair the boardwalk that wound through the marsh. We carried a load of oak into the fen and sawed, hammered, and replaced 33 metres of rotted boardwalk. We each took turns at hammering and sawing, taking well-earned tea breaks and stopping for a picnic lunch. While we worked, we tried to identify the wildflowers growing in the fen. We saw carnivorous sundews, valerian and field scabiosa.

Throughout the weekend we were responsible for cooking breakfast and dinner for the group, for preparing our own picnic lunches, and for cleaning up. During the weekend, I worked hard, lived simply and learned a lot about this ruggedly beautiful part of the world from people I would never have met on a packaged tour or car trip.

Royal Society for the Protection of Birds (RSPB)

Duration: Min. 1 week
(Saturday to Saturday)
Location: Throughout the UK
Season: Year round
Prerequisites: Enthusiasm,
the ability to work as part of

☎ 01767 680551
🖰 volunteers@rspb.org.uk
💻 www.rspb.org.uk/volunteering/residential

a team, an interest in conservation and a reasonable level of fitness. Min. age 16 (18 on some reserves)
Organisation: Europe's largest conservation charity
Description: Residential volunteers are taken on 37 reserves throughout the UK to help with practical conservation tasks such as planting trees or clearing paths, assisting with people engagement activities, for survey, protection and monitoring work, and for farm and stock work. Work varies from season to season and from reserve to reserve. Working hours are approx. eight per day, five days a week. Some shift work may be required. There is always free time for bird-watching and other leisure pursuits
Accommodation: Basic, clean self-catering accommodation is provided on, or close to, the reserve
Cost: None. Accommodation is free of charge, but food and travel expenses must be covered by the participant

A POSTCARD FROM Orkney

Mark Weston spent two weeks as an RSPB volunteer warden on Orkney:

It was mid-July when I arrived at Egilsay. My first day was spent exploring the island, with its splendid machairs (fertile plains), lochs, rugged shoreline and amazing beach. There I found two llamas and a goat tucking into the abundant selection of wild plants and flowers that could be seen all over the island. On the rocks, 20 or more grey and common seals were sunbathing, while eider ducks watched over their young along the shore. In the distance was Eday and to the north Westray, just two of the many islands surrounding Egilsay.

I had sent the warden an email before arriving, giving him information about my skills and training and making it easy for him to plan our workload. It did not take long for my practical skills to be put to use fixing doors, windows, taps and fencing. On two occasions we visited Rousay where, after a strenuous but most enjoyable walk, we went looking for red-throated divers and hen harriers to monitor their breeding success, checked the cliffs to survey the kittiwake colonies, and then finished off with a little maintenance to the reserve information signs. At the end of the week we travelled to the Loch of Harray on Mainland Orkney, to help with some swan ringing. Nearly 100 mute swans plus two whooper swans were herded into a pen by a line of canoes and passed to ringers for ringing, weighing, sexing and measuring.

My last night was a true taste of Orkney, an evening of jazz followed by a ceilidh on Wyre. The next day as I left Orkney, I knew I would return as there was still so much to see. The wardens and residents had made me feel so welcome that I did not want to go. As the ship sailed out of Stromness, I reflected on the past two weeks. Then, as we passed The Old Man of Hoy, a pod of five killer whales surfaced in front of me. Perfect.

Trees For Life – Work Weeks

Duration: 8 days (Saturday to Saturday)
Location: Central Northern Highlands of Scotland
Season: Spring (March – May); autumn (September
– November)
Prerequisites: Reasonable physical fitness (though
gentler nursery weeks are an alternative). Min. age 18.
No previous experience required

☎ 01309 691292
✍ trees@findhorn.org
💻 www.treesforlife.org.uk

Organisation: Award-winning Scottish charity working to restore the Caledonian Forest
to 600 square miles of the Highlands
Description: Trees For Life focuses on the natural regeneration of the Caledonian
Forest. Only 1% of the original forest remains and overgrazing prevents most natural
regeneration. TFL helps nature do its work by planting trees and fostering the growth of
naturally regenerating seedlings. Volunteers are invited for work weeks each year to spend
a week among the forests, rivers and mountains of the Scottish Highlands and learn
about ecological restoration. Work includes tree planting, felling non-native trees, wetland
restoration and wildlife and vegetation surveys. Each task begins with an explanation and
demonstration by experienced leaders. Most working days run from 9am to 5pm, with
Wednesdays set aside for relaxation
Accommodation: Various options available, from bunk-rooms to chalets
Cost: A contribution of £45/£55 for unwaged members/non-members and £80/£90 for
waged members/non-members

Thistle Camps

Duration: 1/2 weeks
Location: Throughout Scotland
Season: April or September
Prerequisites: Open to all aged 16/17 (Trailblazer
camps) or 18 or over for all other camps. Overseas
visitors must speak good conversational English

☎ 0131 243 9360
✍ thistlecamps@nts.org.uk
💻 www.thistlecamps.org.uk

Organisation: Thistle Camps are organised by the National Trust for Scotland
– Scotland's leading conservation organisation
Description: Thistle Camps runs a range of residential voluntary projects in locations as
diverse as Fair Isle in Shetland and Grey Mare's Tail in the Borders. The aim of the camps
is to help in the conservation and management of properties and land in the care of the
National Trust for Scotland. Many of these camps are dedicated to animal and habitat
conservation, including woodland regeneration, trailblazing, searching for bats, crofting,
surveying, rhododendron control, drystone dyking and fencing. In addition to outdoor work,
volunteers help with domestic duties such as food preparation and cleaning at the camp
Accommodation: Provided in a range of lodgings, usually a Trust basecamp or outdoor
centre which provides heating, beds and showers. Meals are prepared communally
Cost: From £50–£100 per camp including accommodation, food and transport to/from
the pick-up point

Wildlife Trust of South and West Wales

Duration: 1 or 2 weeks (Saturday to Saturday)
Location: Skomer Island, Wales
Season: March – October
Prerequisites: Min. age 16
Organisation: The Wildlife Trust of south and west
Wales is the fourth largest wildlife trust in the UK,

☎ 01656 724100
🖐 info@welshwildlife.org
💻 www.welshwildlife.org

covering the area from Cardiff to Aberystwyth and south-west to the Pembrokeshire islands
Description: Skomer Island is a national nature reserve off the Pembrokeshire coast.
Resident full-time wardens oversee the running of the island during the months that it is
open to visitors. Six volunteers are taken on each week to assist with conservation work
such as bird and seal surveys, building maintenance, managing day visitors and assisting
with overnight guests. The Trust also has regular non-residential volunteer days across 90
reserves in Wales
Accommodation: Provided in basic bunkhouses with cooking and washing facilities.
There is limited electricity on the island
Cost: None. Volunteers must bring their own food (enough for their stay)

EUROPE

Atlantic Whale Foundation

Duration: Min. 1 week
Location: Arona, Tenerife
Season: Year round
Prerequisites: Ages 18–30
Organisation: The Whale Watching Community
of Tenerife

☎ UK 07847 434440;
　 Spain +34 922 725 736
🖐 edb@whalenation.org
💻 www.whalenation.org

Description: Volunteers are invited to the research
base at Arona where a range of activities takes place, from research on whale-watching
boats, to educational programmes and public relations work. Participants work five days
per week, with three or four spent on the boats and the rest of the time spent in the
resource centre processing data. Weekends are free for participants to enjoy a range of
activities, including surfing courses, Spanish lessons, jet-skiing and marine photography
courses
Accommodation: Provided in shared rooms in the research station or surrounding
properties, with cooking and washing facilities
Cost: £150 per week (discounted rate of £750 for 6 weeks). Includes accommodation,
breakfast and evening meals

Blue World: Adriatic Dolphin Project

Duration: 12 days
Location: Northern Adriatic Sea, Croatia
Season: June – September
Prerequisites: Min. age 18. Must speak English, be in good physical condition and be able to swim
Organisation: Blue World is a not-for-profit NGO based in Croatia

☎ +385 51 520276
🖱 adp@adp.hr
💻 www.blue-world.org

Description: The Project is the longest ongoing study of the ecology and conservation of bottlenose dolphins in the Mediterranean. 30–40 volunteers are accepted annually to join short courses, during which time they are educated in cetacean biology, marine conservation and scientific research techniques by respected authorities. Participants are involved in spotting dolphins, photo-identification, recording data, acoustic sampling using a hydrophone, and analysing data
Accommodation: Provided in a shared house in Rovenska bay, with two bathrooms, a kitchen and lounge
Cost: Approx. €680–€780 (10% discount for students and returning volunteers). Insurance, food and board, lectures and scientific supervision, a certificate of attendance and membership of Blue World is included

Conservation Volunteers Greece (CVG)

Duration: 1–3 weeks
Location: Remote locations in Greece
Season: July – August
Prerequisites: Ages 18–30, fairly good English
Organisation: CVG is a non-profit, non-

☎ +30 10 62 31 120
🖱 cvgpeep@otenet.gr
💻 www.cvgpeep.gr/eng/enindex.htm

governmental organisation promoting conservation work and intercultural exchanges between young people from all over the world
Description: Participating in a CVG volunteer project offers a short-term opportunity to live and work in a group, visit new places and offer your free time for a worthy cause. Under the guidance of experts, volunteers participate in activities such as: working in protected areas, laying footpaths and installing signposts, planting trees and clearing undergrowth. The type of work undertaken depends on the individual project. During free time, local excursions are organised, allowing participants to get to know the area, its history and the surrounding natural environment
Accommodation: Provided by the hosting community in schools, youth centres, gyms or tents. Living conditions are modest but efficient
Cost: Participation fees vary according to the individual project

Delphis Mediterranean Whale and Dolphin Project

Duration: 6 days
Location: Ischia Island, Italy
Season: June – October
Prerequisites: Min. age 18. Participants should be able to speak English or Italian, be comfortable in hot weather and on a boat and be highly adaptable
Organisation: Non-profit organisation dedicated to the welfare and the conservation of cetaceans in Italy through education and research
Description: The research project focuses on conserving groups of cetaceans by examining the degree of residency around Ischia and the social structure of the population, assessing the production of calves, and studying behaviour and habitat use and distribution. Volunteers help with all aspects of the research and also help to sail the boat, as well as mucking in with communal duties. Participants are given a day off during each course, and those who require more spare time need only ask
Accommodation: Provided on board 'Jean Gab', a historic yacht with a kitchen, sleeping quarters (five berth) and a bathroom
Cost: €720–€820 (discounts available for students and returning volunteers). Includes accommodation, food, lectures, scientific supervision, research expenses and port fees. Insurance, travel/personal expenses not included

☎ +39 081 989 578
🖰 info@delphismdc.org
🖥 www.delphismdc.org

Eco-Center Caput Insulae—Beli (ECCIB)

Duration: Min. 1 week
Location: Beli, Croatia
Season: Year round
Prerequisites: Min. age 16. Good physical condition and ability to swim. English, Croatian or Polish language skills and a love of nature required
Organisation: ECCIB is a non-profit, non-governmental organisation established to protect the natural and cultural/historical heritage of the Island of Cres in Croatia
Description: The Eurasian griffon vulture has disappeared from many European countries and its population is declining everywhere. At the Eco-Center, researchers and volunteers aim to determine the critical factors for their survival and to develop new conservation strategies. Volunteers help to record griffon vulture colonies, noting and recording all sightings and behaviour. Other projects include the recovery of freshwater ponds, management of eco-trails, working with tourists, and helping local inhabitants
Accommodation: Provided at the Eco-Center which has 26 beds, two bathrooms, hot showers and a fully equipped kitchen
Cost: £55–£75 per person per week, depending on project

☎ +385 51 840 525
🖰 info@caput-insulae.com
🖥 www.caput-insulae.com

Fiskardo's Nautical and Environmental Club (FNEC)

Duration: Min. 2 weeks
Location: Kefalonia, Greece
Season: Year round
Prerequisites: Min. age 18. Horse patrol volunteers must have riding experience

☎ +30 26740 41081
🖱 info@fnec.gr
💻 www.fnec.gr

Organisation: FNEC is a locally and regionally operating non-profit making organisation focused on environmental research, endangered species and increasing environmental awareness
Description: Fiskardos currently runs the following projects for independent volunteers:
1. Cetacean Observation. The aim of this project is to identify the different species in the area and monitor their populations. It also aims to identify potential threats to their environment. **2. Underwater Research.** Research dives are undertaken to try and locate, identify and observe local seahorse populations and then record the information. Those who do not have a PADI certificate can spend the first week training to scuba dive (for an extra €150). **3.Horse Patrol.** A horse team patrols the island to help prevent fires breaking out. Volunteers are expected to care for the horses, exercise and train them, go out on patrol and investigate opening new routes
Accommodation: Camping space provided in the forest. Volunteers bring their own tents and should expect very basic facilities
Cost: €550 contribution for 3 weeks. Includes basic accommodation. Insurance, food and transport costs not covered

Friends of the Great Baikal Trail

Duration: 2 weeks – 1 month per placement
Location: Lake Baikal, south central Russia
Season: May – September
Prerequisites: Min. age 18, willingness to work hard, good health. No Russian language skills or trail-building experience required

☎ +1 415 788 7324
🖱 baikalwatch@igc.org
💻 www.earthisland.org/baikal/

Organisation: Non-profit project designed to develop a network of international activists to promote sustainable economies in eastern Russia by encouraging the development of eco-tourism in the area
Description: Construction of the Great Baikal Trail in collaboration with national parks and nature reserves is taking place in order to create the first Russian system of trails that will run 1,200 miles around the largest lake in the world. Teams of volunteers work each summer to build new parts of the trail, building bridges, levelling, constructing campsites along the trail, digging, adding signposts and other structures, and replanting trees. The trail leads through lake-shores and beaches, Steppe-land and rolling mountain forests. Local Russians mix with foreign participants in teams of 12–17. Project sites vary from year to year
Accommodation: On-site accommodation on boats and in tents is provided for volunteers. When in towns, home-stays are arranged
Cost: US$250 per week including accommodation, food, training and language interpretation. Volunteers are responsible for their own travel and visa costs

Grupo Lobo – The Iberian Wolf Recovery Centre

Duration: Min. 2 weeks
Location: Malveira, Portugal
Season: Year round
Prerequisites: Min. age 18. No experience required
Organisation: An independent non-profit NGO working
towards the conservation of wolves and their habitats in
Portugal, where the wolf population has been declining for many years

☎ +351 21 750 0073
✆ globo@fc.ul.pt
🖥 http://lobo.fc.ul.pt

Description: Volunteers are invited to work at the recovery centre to help raise
understanding about Iberian wolves and battle against the species' extinction. The work
carried out by participants is varied and depends on specific needs at the time. It will
include: helping to feed the wolves three times a week, checking their water supplies,
maintenance of infrastructures, caring for the grounds (including some reforestation) and
spending at least two hours per day monitoring the health and well-being of the wolves
Accommodation: Provided in a chalet-style guesthouse, fully equipped with all mod
cons. Accommodation costs range from €15.50 to €37 per night
Cost: There are no participation fees, but volunteers must pay for their own food,
accommodation, transport and personal expenses

Hellenic Ornithological Society

Duration: Min. 2 weeks
Location: Greece
Season: March – October
Prerequisites: Depends on project. Min. age 18
Organisation: The only Greek non-governmental body
exclusively concerned with the protection of wild birds
and their habitats in Greece

☎ +30 (1) 822 8704
✆ info@ornithologiki.gr
🖥 www.ornithologiki.gr

Description: HOS monitors and protects all of the important bird habitats in Greece
and acts for the conservation of threatened species. Each year it takes on a number
of volunteers to help with specific projects, which are advertised on its website. Past
projects have included bird ringing on Antikythira Island, an important stopover site for
migration, and a project for the protection of endangered species and the conservation of
Gialova Lagoon in Pylos
Accommodation: Varies according to project. It is either provided by HOS in campsites,
in rooms rented for the projects, or in local guesthouses at a special low-cost deal
Cost: A €60 membership fee is required but thereafter there is no charge to participate.
Travel, food and personal expenses are not covered

Hellenic Wildlife Hospital

Duration: Min. 15 days
Location: Island of Aegina, Greece
Season: Year round
Prerequisites: No qualifications or experience required
Organisation: Non-profit NGO dedicated to the
treatment, rehabilitation and release of all species of
wildlife indigenous to Greece

☎ +30 22970 31338
🖱 ekpaz@ekpaz.gr
💻 www.ekpaz.gr

Description: HWH treats around 4,000 wild animals from all over Greece each year, including many rare and endangered species. Volunteers are invited to gain experience of working in close contact with animals and participating in the rehabilitation process. Work throughout the year includes cleaning of animal treatment areas, food preparation and feeding, maintenance and construction, aid in treatments, and other duties depending on experience
Accommodation: Provided in a dormitory with a fully equipped kitchen, bathroom and a washing machine. Basic food may be provided
Cost: No participation fees. Volunteers pay their own living costs and travel expenses

M.E.E.R. E.V. Whale Behavioural Research Project

Duration: 15 days
Location: La Gomera, Canary Islands
Season: February – June
Prerequisites: Knowledge of English or German
(Spanish also useful), physical fitness and ability to
swim. Min. age 18

☎ +49 (0)30 8507 8755
🖱 meer@infocanarias.com
💻 www.m-e-e-r.org

Organisation: Private organisation dedicated to the conservation of whales and dolphins
Description: The waters off La Gomera provide perfect conditions for cetacean field studies. Sperm, beaked and pilot whales are resident here, as well as bottlenose dolphins. Participants in MEER practical courses gain an insight into the behavioural research conducted from whale-watching boats. The course includes a full training programme including lectures and field instruction. Participants gain experience in sighting data-recording, behavioural sampling and photo identification
Accommodation: Provided in tourist-quality apartments
Cost: €875 (including accommodation, tuition, research expenses, a year's membership of MEER, a donation to MEER, 7 whale-watching research trips and a certificate of attendance of the course

Roman Cat Sanctuary

Duration: Min. 1 week
Location: Rome, Italy
Season: Year round
Prerequisites: Strong motivation, flexibility and a love of cats
Organisation: Charitable organisation run by volunteers

☎ +39 06 687 2133
✎ torreargentina@tiscali.it
💻 www.romancats.com

Description: Located in the centre of Rome, among the archaeological ruins, the Roman Cat Sanctuary is run by an international group of volunteers who work together to care for Rome's abandoned cats. The sanctuary promotes neutering, proper animal care, adoptions and education projects through public relations events. It is entirely funded by the 8,000 tourists who visit each year, allowing them to shelter between 250 and 350 cats at a time. Volunteers are required all year round to help out cleaning cages, distributing food, treating sick cats and with various administrative tasks. Sanctuary tour guides are also required

Accommodation: Volunteers find their own lodging in Rome, although help can be provided. A room in an apartment costs around €400 per month
Cost: No participation fees. Volunteers are responsible for all personal costs

Tethys Research Institute

Duration: 6 days
Location: Greece and Italy
Season: May – October
Prerequisites: Min. age 18. Photography and computer skills helpful
Organisation: Private non-profit organisation

☎ +39 0272 0019 47
✎ tethys@tethys.org
💻 www.tethys.org

dedicated to the study and protection of marine habitats, focusing on Mediterranean cetaceans

Description: The Tethys Research Institute organises whale and dolphin field courses each year led by professional researchers. Participants from all over the world have the opportunity to observe marine mammals in their natural environment and to become actively involved in all activities conducted in the field. This includes whale and dolphin sightings, data collection at sea and informal lectures. There are currently two annual projects: the Cetacean Sanctuary Research Project in the Ligurian Sea, Italy, and the Ionian Dolphin Project in the Ionian Sea, Greece. Further details on both projects are available on the website

Accommodation: Provided either at the research centre or on board the research vessels
Cost: From €500 to €870 inclusive of food and accommodation

American Bear Association

Duration: No minimum or maximum length of stay
Location: Orr, Minnesota, USA
Season: May – September
Prerequisites: Min. age 18. A degree of physical stamina is required
Organisation: Non-profit group promoting the well-being of the black bear

☎ +1 (218) 757 0172
✎ bears@rangenet.com
💻 www.americanbear.org

Description: ABA operates the Vince Shute Wildlife Sanctuary, located in the attractive north woods of Minnesota, and one of the best places to see black bears in their natural habitat. Enthusiastic, hard-working volunteers are required each year to keep the operation running smoothly. Many jobs are available at the sanctuary and ABA works with individuals to find jobs that fit their interests, skills and availability. Work can include cleaning of feeding areas, maintaining the property, preparing bear food, greeting visitors, and educating the public about black bears
Accommodation: On-site lodging may be available. Numerous resorts and campsites nearby
Cost: No participation fees. Travel, accommodation (if necessary) and personal items are at the volunteers' expense

American Hiking Society

Duration: 1 or 2 weeks
Location: USA (29 states)
Season: January – November
Prerequisites: Ages 18–80. Retirees in good physical shape welcomed. No experience required

☎ +1 301 565 6704
✎ volunteer@americanhiking.org
💻 www.americanhiking.org

Organisation: National non-profit organisation dedicated to promoting and protecting America's hiking trails and the natural areas that surround them
Description: AHS offers 'volunteer vacations' that allow participants to visit stunning locations to construct or rebuild footpaths, cabins and shelters and in the process explore canyons, forests and valleys, and meet new people. Each crew consists of six to 15 volunteers accompanied by a crew leader. Tools and supervision are provided by the host agency. Participants work on the trails for six or seven hours a day and return to camp in time to relax and explore the area during the afternoons
Accommodation: Provided in housing or camping space. Campsites range from the fully equipped to primitive 'backcountry' sites
Cost: US$130 per project for non-members ($100 for members). Includes food and lodging

Appalachian Mountain Club

Duration: 1–3 days or 1–3 weeks
Location: USA
Season: March – November
Prerequisites: Min. age 16, good health, willing to work hard, backpacking experience. Open to individuals, families and other groups

☎ +1 603 4662721
🖱 tmrobinson@outdoors.org
💻 www.outdoors.org

Organisation: Non-profit-making recreation and conservation group responsible for more than 1,400 miles of trail in the north-east of the USA, including more than 350 miles of the Appalachian Trail
Description: Every summer the club sponsors Work Parties (1–3 days) and Volunteer Vacations (one to three weeks) in NH, MA and ME. More than 500 volunteers participate annually, working in teams to undertake all types of trail work. Previous projects have included building bridges, rock work on alpine trails, and constructing new trails. Many of the project sites are in remote locations with stunning scenery. Trail crew members can expect to meet interesting people, experience nature, work hard and do something for the greater good
Accommodation: Provided in basic bunkhouses or tents
Cost: Approx. US$150 per week, including food, shelter and leadership costs

Appalachian Trail Conservancy

Duration: 1–6 weeks
Location: Great Smoky Mountains National Park, USA
Season: May – October
Prerequisites: Min. age 18. Good physical fitness and an ability to work hard required. No previous experience necessary

☎ +1 540 953 3571
🖱 crews@appalachiantrail.org
💻 www.appalachiantrail.org

Organisation: ATC coordinates the management and maintenance of the Appalachian National Scenic Trail, a footpath of more than 2,160 miles
Description: Volunteers built the original trail, and volunteers keep it alive and flourishing today. The trail is the longest continuously marked footpath in the world, winding through 14 states from Maine to Georgia in the eastern United States. Each year more than 5,500 volunteers of all ages, and from all over the world help with trail construction and rehabilitation and participants can work anywhere along the trail's length. Trail crews of between six and eight volunteers work under the supervision of an experienced leader and work includes bridge building, shelter construction and trail rehabilitation
Accommodation: Crew set up a basic encampment near to the project site
Cost: There are no participation fees. Food, local transportation, lodging, equipment and training are all provided free of charge

Caretta Research Project

Duration: Min. 1 week
Location: Wassaw Island (Savannah, Georgia), USA
Season: May – September
Prerequisites: Min. age 16, good health, positive attitude and a sense of adventure

☎ +1 912 447 8655
🖱 wassawcrp@aol.com
💻 www.carettaresearchproject.org

Organisation: Non-profit environmental organisation dedicated to monitoring loggerhead sea turtle activity, protecting nests and public education
Description: CRP is a hands-on research and conservation project involving the threatened loggerhead sea turtles that nest on Wassaw National Wildlife Refuge. The work is variable depending on time of season and turtle activity. Mid-May through to mid-August is egg-laying season and participants spend each night patrolling six miles of beach looking for nesting female turtles. The turtles are then tagged, recorded, and the nests are protected either by relocation into a hatchery or by screening. Late-July through to September is hatching season and participants monitor nests and escort emerging hatchlings down the beach and into the surf. The work is hard but rewarding. Participants also have free time to enjoy this pristine island, virtually untouched by mankind
Accommodation: Team members stay in small cabins close to the centre of the island, with a kitchen and bathroom. Housing is rustic but comfortable
Cost: US$675 per week, including food, housing, leadership, transportation on the island and boat transportation to and from the island

Catalina Island Conservancy Volunteer Vacations

Duration: 5 days
Location: Catalina Island, California
Season: May, June, August, September
Prerequisites: Min. age 18, Good physical fitness required

☎ +1 310 510 2595
🖱 volunteers@catalinaconservancy.org
💻 www.catalinaconservancy.org

Organisation: Privately funded organisation that acts as a responsible steward for Catalina Island's resources through conservation
Description: CIC restores and protects the environment on Catalina Island, promoting ecologically sustainable communities. There are a range of projects that volunteers can become involved in, from research projects on flora and fauna, to educational projects for schools. Volunteer work includes assisting with maintenance and construction, transplanting native seeds, building enclosures around sensitive plant species that are unique to the island, and monitoring research projects. Volunteers work alongside staff members to really make a difference to the island's natural environment. Most projects are in remote areas of the island that can only be reached by foot. Trips usually include three days of project work, a half-day of beach cleanup and an activity
Accommodation: Provided in a private camp overlooking the ocean, with permanent tents, a kitchen and bathrooms
Cost: US$175 per person (including accommodation and meals)

The Colorado Trail Foundation

Duration: Weekend and 1–week trips
Location: Colorado, USA
Season: June – August
Prerequisites: Min. age 16, good physical health
Organisation: Non-profit organisation that cares
for the Colorado Trail, a 500 mile trail across the
Rocky Mountains, enjoyed by hikers, cyclists and horse riders

☎ +1 303 384 3729 x 113
🖱 ctf@coloradotrail.org
💻 www.coloradotrail.org

Description: Every summer, volunteer crew members from around the world spend time working outdoors as part of a team to improve the trail. The work varies from project to project but could include rebuilding parts of the trail, clearing vegetation, and dismantling and rebuilding worn bridges. Campsites are reached by vehicle, four–wheel drive, or by hiking, and work takes place at elevations that range from 6,000 to 11,000 feet. One day during the week is left free for hiking, fishing or relaxing. Participants enjoy the camaraderie, sense of accomplishment, and stunning scenery that trail work offers
Accommodation: Provided at basecamps. Participants share meal preparation and cleaning duties
Cost: US$50 registration fee for the week (only paid once per year, regardless of how many trips you take); $25 for weekends. Includes food, camping space, tools, supplies and instruction

A POSTCARD FROM Colorado

American Rhiannon Mercer on getting down and dirty maintaining the Colorado Trail:

I volunteered with a Colorado Trail Foundation backpack crew for a week in the beautiful Collegiate Peaks Wilderness outside of Leadville, Colorado. This turned out to be a fun crew full of laughs and the grunts of hard labour needed to complete a large turnpike and culvert project. We began on Saturday loading up the packhorses and our own backs in intermittent rain. From the parking area, camp was four miles south along the Trail. On reaching the campsite we discovered that the poles for the kitchen tent were 'missing' but with an axe and a handsaw, we got that tent upright in no time. We were not so lucky with the 'missing' dehydrated green beans for which no remedy presented itself. After a tour of the worksite and a tool safety demonstration, the crew scattered into the hills for day hikes. I headed for Rainbow Lake arriving to a terrific hailstorm combined with a gorgeous alpine view.

Starting Monday, the initial work involved clearing out an immense quantity of smelly muck from the waterlogged and damaged trail. Tonnes of dirt were required to replace the tread and build the turnpike. We entertained ourselves with ridiculous stunts, even when there were still hours of work to do; for instance four competitors, of whom I was one, raced to haul two buckets of dirt down to the work site, empty them and race back. The next stage of work involved rocks, needed in all sizes, which had to be rolled to their new home from faraway places. Then logs had to be cut and peeled to act as a stabiliser for the turnpike. In the end, I have to say, the completed project was a beauty to behold.

It's experiences like this one that have kept me returning to volunteer with the Colorado Trail Foundation. A week spent getting dirty, eating heartily and soaking in the wilderness of the Rockies among great company from the USA and overseas is hard to beat.

Kokee Resource Conservation Program

Duration: 1 day – 4 weeks
Location: Kauai Island, Hawaii
Season: Year round
Prerequisites: Volunteers under 18 should be
accompanied by their parents. Anyone who can handle
strenuous work is welcome. No experience required

☎ +1 808 335 0045
🖱 rcp@aloha.net
💻 www.krcp.org

Organisation: KRCP is a volunteer-driven project dedicated to the preservation of the Hawaiian forests
Description: About 100 volunteers are taken on each year to focus on the removal of invasive species from predominantly native forests that will naturally re-seed once threats are removed. Volunteers are taken to the wet montane forests and the mesic montane forests to remove kahili ginger and strawberry guava. Environmental education of youth often runs concurrently with invasive species removal. A small amount of work is done in the nursery in an effort to grow native plants for out-planting at selected locations. Conditions can be muddy and involve hiking through steep terrain
Accommodation: Provided in a large bunkhouse with hot showers and a fully equipped communal kitchen
Cost: No participation fees. Accommodation provided free of charge. Volunteers are responsible for all other costs

Mingan Island Cetacean Research Expeditions

Duration: 7 or 14 days
Location: North-east Quebec, Gaspé Peninsula, St.
Lawrence Estuary (Canada) and Baja California (Mexico)
Season: Winter: February – March; summer: July
– September
Prerequisites: No special knowledge/experience
required

 +1 (418) 949 2845
🖱 mics@globetrotter.net
 www.rorqual.com

Organisation: Non-profit research organisation dedicated to ecological studies of marine mammals
Description: Volunteers join a team of marine biologists as 'research apprentices', to help study blue, fin, humback and minke whales. Participants spend most of their time on the water collecting data, observing researchers, taking photographs and assisting with daily logistics. Research work is not obligatory. Those who simply want to observe and photograph marine life are at liberty to do so
Accommodation: Provided in a private house, motel or B&B
Cost: C$1,590–C$2,090 (1 week); C$2,990–C$3,760 (2 weeks). Includes room and board, all transfers during the session. Group reduction available

The Nature Corps

Duration: 6–8 days
Location: California and Hawaii, USA
Season: May – October
Prerequisites: Min. age 16. No maximum. There
are projects for all abilities and levels of fitness.
Families welcome

info@thenaturecorps.org
www.thenaturecorps.org

Organisation: Non-profit organisation dedicated to engaging volunteers in the
stewardship of America's national parks
Description: The Nature Corps organises volunteer holidays to help bridge the gap
where government resources are unable to meet the growing need for preservation
and rehabilitation of fragile wilderness ecosystems within America's national parks.
Approximately half of the 'volunteer vacation' is devoted to preserving sites such as the
endangered rainforests of Hawaii, alpine meadows in Yosemite and ancient groves of
giant sequoia. For the rest of the trip, participants are guided by naturalists on a range
of recreational activities such as hiking and fishing in the High Sierra. Volunteers on the
Hawaii excursion take a complete tour of the island which includes snorkelling around
spectacular coral reefs and hiking down into active volcanoes
Accommodation: Campsites with hot showers and cooking facilities
Cost: Fees start from US$495 per person. Includes food, accommodation, instruction
and any costs associated with the expedition

Ores Foundation For Marine Environment Research

Duration: 2 weeks
Location: Les Bergeronnes, Canada
Season: July – August
Prerequisites: Min. age 18. No experience required
Organisation: Non-profit organisation dedicated to the
study of whales in order to contribute to their protection

+1 32 623 63 54
utscherter@ores.org
www.ores.org

Description: The foundation offers the opportunity to encounter Minke Whales in their
natural environment while helping with important marine research. During daily outings
with marine biologists, participants help to carry out observations, collect data and
transcribe the information. Regular lectures at the research station and spontaneous
talks on board the boats help deepen volunteers' knowledge about the lives of marine
mammals and the complexity of the ocean's ecosystems. There is also plenty of free time
for participants to enjoy hiking and cycling along the shore of the St. Lawrence Gulf
Accommodation: Provided in shared wooden cabins at the research station.
Participants bring their own sleeping bags and are responsible for food and cooking
Cost: Approx. £700 including accommodation and all costs related to the project

CONSERVATION & WILDLIFE

NORTH AMERICA

Sierra Club Outings

Duration: 1–2 weeks
Location: Throughout the USA and in Puerto Rico, the Virgin Islands and Canada
Season: Year round
Prerequisites: Min. age 18. Most projects can be undertaken by anyone in moderately good shape. Seniors welcome

☎ +1 415 977 5522
✍ national.outings@sierraclub.org
💻 www.sierraclub.org/outings

Organisation: Grassroots environmental organisation providing outdoor adventures for people of all ages, abilities and interests
Description: Sierra Club organises a number of 'Service Trips', volunteer activities focusing on working outdoors. These range from helping with research trips at whale calving grounds in Maui to invasive plant removal. The outings stress the importance of building a strong community as a group and all service trips have at least one day free so that participants may explore the surrounding areas of natural beauty
Accommodation: Varies depending on location of project undertaken
Cost: Approx. US$350–600

Volunteer For Nature

Duration: 1–16 days
Location: Ontario, Canada
Season: April – October
Prerequisites: Min. age 18. No experience required
Organisation: Protects and restores natural habitats through research, education and conservation

☎ +1 416 444 8419
✍ info@ontarionature.org
💻 www.ontarionature.org

Description: The Volunteer for Nature programme gives people the opportunity to learn new conservation skills and participate in hands-on projects including invasive species removal, native seed collection and planting, and endangered species monitoring throughout Ontario. Habitats protected by VFN include limestone alvar, oak savannah, tall grass prairie, Great Lakes shoreline, Carolinian forest and northern boreal forest
Accommodation: Accommodation includes camping, dormitories, lodges, field study centres and B&Bs. All volunteers contribute to cooking and general duties at the accommodation
Cost: Small fee to cover direct expenses

Volunteers for Outdoor Colorado (VOC)

Duration: 1 day – 1 week
Location: Colorado, USA
Season: March – October
Prerequisites: Min. age ranges from 8–16. Families and seniors welcome. Some projects require a good level of fitness. No experience required

☎ +1 303 715 1010
🖰 voc@voc.org
🖥 www.voc.org

Organisation: VOC organises conservation and trail construction projects in a range of urban and natural areas, national parks, national forests and state parks in Colorado
Description: Each year VOC dispatches volunteers throughout the state to build, restore, rehabilitate and plant, while relishing the companionship of other outdoor enthusiasts. These projects offer everyone, regardless of experience, a chance to participate and make a difference. Volunteers move rocks and dirt, cut through brush and trees and dig out plants, working from early morning until around 4pm, followed by social activities and entertainment
Accommodation: Provided in crew encampments set up by volunteers
Cost: No participation fees. Food provided. Volunteers must bring their own tents and provide their own transportation to the camp

Wolf Education and Research Center

Duration: By agreement
Location: North-central region of Idaho, USA
Season: Year round
Prerequisites: Min. age 18, good physical condition, own transportation

☎ +1 208 924 6960
🖰 werced@camasnet.com
🖥 www.wolfcenter.org

Organisation: WERC is dedicated to providing public education and scientific research concerning the grey timber wolf and its habitat in the northern Rocky Mountains
Description: WERC cares for a pack of wolves in partnership with the Nez Perce Tribe. Volunteers are an essential part of the project and are invited to donate their time and effort, in return for which they receive a unique learning experience. Typical duties include clearing and chipping wood for hiking trails, fence repairs, giving presentations to groups of visitors, working in the visitor centre and caring for the pack. Participants agree the length of stay and their duties with WERC in advance and are offered a flexible schedule with at least one day off per week to explore the area
Accommodation: There is no on-site lodging, but there are plenty of campsites, motels and B&Bs in the region
Cost: Max. US$20 per day

SOUTH/CENTRAL AMERICA AND THE CARIBBEAN

Alliance Abroad

Duration: Min 1. week
Location: Costa Rica, Ecuador, Peru
Season: Year round
Prerequisites: Min. age 18. No previous experience required
Organisation: Aims to provide diverse cultural exchange programmes to participants around the world

☎ +1 512 457 8062
🖱 outbound@allianceabroad.com
💻 www.allianceabroad.com

Description: Alliance Abroad offers a range of volunteer projects and hands-on holidays for people of any age, from any country or walk of life. Current conservation programmes include conservation and restoration projects in Peru, working at an animal rescue centre in Ecuador, helping conservation efforts with giant tortoises on the Galapagos Islands, and volunteering at an ecological project in Costa Rica
Accommodation: Provided in a variety of lodgings, but most volunteers are placed in homestays with local families
Cost: Varies according to project. Sample cost: 1 week volunteering in Costa Rica – US$750. Fees include orientation, airport transfer in host country, accommodation, food and insurance

Andean Bear Conservation Project

Duration: Min. 1 week (4 weeks preferred)
Location: Intag region, Ecuador
Season: Year round
Prerequisites: Min. age 18, good level of fitness. No experience required

🖱 volunteer@andeanbear.org
💻 www.andeanbear.org

Organisation: Grassroots operation dedicated to saving the Andean (Spectacled) Bear from extinction through in-field scientific studies and through the rehabilitation and release of captive bears
Description: This is the only project in the world that radio tracks Andean Bears in the wild. Information gleaned by the project will help protect and conserve the bears' habitats and improve future rehabilitation projects throughout South America. Volunteers assist permanent staff in the field, monitoring the movements and activities of bears, following trails and listening for signals from the bears' collars. Volunteers also clear trails, collect samples, record behaviour and help to analyse data. The work is unpredictable and there may be lulls in activity. All volunteers will be required to work some nights
Accommodation: Provided in a dormitory in a traditional Andean house with electricity and running water. Basic, but clean and comfortable
Cost: 1 week US$130; US$420 for 4 weeks. Price includes accommodation, orientation and training, supervision, transport from Quito, 3 meals a day

ARCAS – Asociación de Rescate y Conservación de Vida Silvestre

Duration: Min. 1 week
Location: Wildlife Rescue Centre near the city of Flores, Guatemala
Season: Year round
Prerequisites: Min. age 18. No specific skills required. Basic Spanish is desirable
Organisation: Non-profit NGO created by Guatemalan citizens who are dedicated to conserving their natural heritage, especially wildlife
Description: Since its establishment, the ARCAS Rescue Center has grown into one of the largest of its type in the world. Originally created to provide care and rehabilitation for wild animals that were confiscated on the black market by the Guatemalan Government, it now receives between 300 and 600 of more than 35 species each year. Volunteers are invited to help feed and care for the animals, including parrots, toucans, scarlet macaws, spider monkeys, pacas, jaguars, iguanas, turtles and crocodiles. Other on-going activities include trail maintenance, research, construction of cages and helping to identify appropriate release sites for rehabilitated animals
Accommodation: Provided in a comfortable house with toilet and kitchen facilities and electricity
Cost: US$100 per week (includes food and accommodation)

☎ +502 2478 4096
🖱 arcas@intelnet.net.gt
💻 www.arcasguatemala.com

Caribbean Conservation Corporation

Duration: 1, 2 or 3 weeks
Location: Tortuguero, Costa Rica
Season: March – November
Prerequisites: Min. age 18 (or 15 if travelling with a parent/guardian). Must speak English or Spanish and be in good physical shape
Organisation: Not-for-profit organisation. The oldest and most accomplished sea turtle research and conservation group in the world, founded in 1959
Description: Participants support research efforts financially and work side by side with research staff on the project of their choice. Volunteers assist researchers with scientific field work at a remote field station. There are currently three projects: working with leatherback turtles, with green turtles, and the neotropical bird programme. Duties include helping to tag and measure turtles, counting eggs, marking nests, conducting surveys and recording data. The work is strenuous and requires a lot of walking, but there is lots of unsupervised free time to relax and enjoy the surroundings
Accommodation: Provided at CCC's research station. Dorm-style accommodation with up to six people per room and showers
Cost: US$1,899 (2 weeks leatherback); US$2,149 (2 weeks greenback); US$1,849 (2 weeks tropical birds). Includes all meals, lodging and training, land and boat transport to Tortuguero and return flight to San José. Airfare not included

☎ +1 352 373 6441
🖱 ccc@cccturtle.org
💻 www.cccturtle.org

Centro de Reeducación del Mono Aullador Negro (Black Howler Monkey Project)

Duration: Min. 3 weeks
Location: Cordoba, Argentina
Season: June – September (winter); November – April (summer)
Prerequisites: Min. age 21. Participants must speak Spanish and have a love of animals
Organisation: Part of an NGO. Relies on volunteers, students and independent enthusiasts

carayaproject@yahoo.com.ar
www.refugiodelcaraya.com.ar

Description: The black howler monkey is under threat from illegal hunting and destruction of its natural habitat and this sanctuary, occupying 360 acres of mountains, rivers and forests, in a remote part of the Cordoba province of Argentina, is the first and only centre for the rehabilitation of primates in Argentina. Working with orphaned monkeys, volunteers are required to help out at the centre with duties such as feeding, observation, study, data input, care and attention of the animals, cleaning and maintenance, and assisting with capture and handling. The centre is fairly isolated from civilisation. Visits to the nearest village are made every two to three days. In the area around the centre, volunteers can enjoy mountain biking, trekking and horse-riding
Accommodation: Provided in a bedroom separated from the main house. Conditions are very rustic – no electricity or water in the bedroom, bathing in basins in the Tiu Mayu river
Cost: A €300 donation required for a 3–week stay. Includes daily room and board

Comunidad Inti Wara Yassi

Duration: Min. 15 days
Location: Cochabamba, Bolivia
Season: Year round
Prerequisites: Min. age 18. No experience required
Organisation: Non-profit community project that

 +591 44 136 572
 intiwarayassi@gmail.com
 www.intiwarayassi.org

rescues and rehabilitates native wild animals taken from captive environments
Description: This community project rescues abused wild animals from illegal markets and attempts to rehabilitate them wherever possible so that they can be released back into the wild. Animals cared for at the refuge include wild cats (pumas and ocelots) and monkeys (including capuchins and tamarins), as well as black spiders, tropical birds and reptiles. Volunteers are welcomed and the community could not run without their support. The work is hard and varied. Duties include tending sick monkeys and dealing with newcomers, who need a lot of attention before they can begin to trust humans, daily walks for the big cats, preparing birds for their release into the wild, maintenance, such as building cages and fences, clearing forest areas, and guiding visitors
Accommodation: Provided in basic shared rooms with communal bathroom and kitchen areas
Cost: The first 15 days cost US$90–$100 including accommodation and 3 meals a day. Thereafter the price is $3–$4.50 per night

Conservation Project Utila Iguana (CPUI)

Duration: Min. 3 weeks
Location: Utila Island (off the Caribbean coast of Honduras)
Season: Year round
Prerequisites: Min. age 18, motivation and a willingness to work hard

 volo@utila-iguana.de
www.utila-iguana.de

Organisation: A collaborative project of the Frankfurt Zoological Society, the Senckenberg Nature Research Society and Honduran NGOs, working together for the preservation of the endangered Utila spiny-tailed Iguana
Description: The Utila iguana is a big, black tree-dwelling iguana that can only be found on the tiny island of Utila, a few miles north of Honduras. The iguana is under threat from tourism and the destruction of its habitat. Volunteers help in a variety of ways, from working in public relations and environmental education, to caring for the animals and their habitat, and carrying out ecological research. Other tasks include feeding the animals, facility maintenance and assistance in wildlife rehabilitation
Accommodation: Provided at the research station, in shared rooms
Cost: 4 weeks: €150 (including accommodation and use of the kitchen)

Fundacion Jatun Sacha

Duration: Min. 14 days
Location: 10 biological stations in Ecuador, located in the Amazon, coast and highlands and the Galapagos Islands
Season: Year round
Prerequisites: Min. age 18, some Spanish required

 +593 2 243 2240
 volunteer@jatunsacha.org
www.jatunsacha.org

Organisation: Non-profit operation dedicated to promoting the conservation of forests, aquatic and páramo ecosystems of Ecuador
Description: Jatun Sacha has eight reserves where around 1000 volunteers are accepted annually to participate in activities such as reforestation, environmental education, agroforestry, light construction and organic farming. Volunteers are able to choose their work from a wide range of activities, all carried out under the supervision of residential researchers and environmental education instructors. The stations are located in different areas of Ecuador including the Amazon rainforest, the coast, highlands, and the Galapagos Islands. For those who want to experience more than one area, the organisation offers special volunteer 'packets'
Accommodation: Provided in shared cabins with outside toilets and sometimes electricity. Varies according to the reserve
Cost: US$35 application fee ($50 for Galapagos) plus $395 per month for food and accommodation

Iracambi Atlantic Rainforest Research and Conservation Centre

Duration: Min. 4 weeks
Location: Minas Gerais, Brazil
Season: Year round
Prerequisites: Min. age 18. No experience required

☎ +55 32 3721 1436
🖱 iracambi@iracambi.com
💻 www.iracambi.com

Organisation: Non-profit organisation dedicated to the conservation of the Brazilian rainforest
Description: The research centre is situated on a working farm surrounded by rainforest. The research focuses on land use management, forest restoration, income generating alternatives to the destruction of rainforest and community understanding and engagement. Volunteering at Ircabambi provides participants with the opportunity to get to know a beautiful, little-visited part of Brazil, to live in the way that local people do, among an international community of volunteers and researchers. Volunteer roles include trail maintenance, mapping, environmental education, plant-nursery management, flora and fauna surveys, socioeconomic research, and medical plant work
Accommodation: Provided in shared rooms in a typical rural farmhouse. There will not always be access to electricity and hot showers. Food is delivered to the house weekly and volunteers share meal preparation chores
Cost: US$550 for 1 month including full-board self-catering accommodation

Iyok Ami Eco Reserve

Duration: Min. 1 week
Location: Talamanca mountain range, Costa Rica
Season: Year round
Prerequisites: Min. age 18. No experience required

☎ +506 7720 222
🖱 info@iyokami.com
💻 www.ecotourism.co.cr/iyokami

Organisation: Self-funding private reserve dedicated to protecting the environment through research and promoting eco-tourism
Description: Iyok Ami reserve includes both tropical cloud and rain forests, and an Indian reserve. These wild areas have been set aside to protect flora, fauna and water resources, and also to serve as areas of scientific and research study. Volunteers' help is needed to build and maintain trails and for reforestation, help with labelling and transplantation of flowering plants around the trails, making topographical and pictorial maps of the area, constructing signposts, protecting and stimulating Quetzal bird reproduction. Volunteers also help with the classification of plants, birds and fungi, and other work depending on the volunteer's interest and specialist knowledge. Volunteers are provided with one and a half hours of Spanish tuition per day, plus an optional three-day trek
Accommodation: Provided in a volunteer house set among tropical forest with warm water, communal living rooms, a stereo and phone available. All food is cooked by a local family
Cost: US$180 per week or US$650 for a month (includes board and lodging)

Oceanic Society Expeditions

Duration: Min. 1 week
Location: Belize, Brazil, Costa Rica, Hawaii, Surinam
Season: Year round
Prerequisites: Some projects require PADI qualifications or snorkelling experience. Min. age 18

☎ +1 415 441 1106
✉ office@oceanicsociety.org
💻 www.oceanicsociety.org

Organisation: Non-profit conservation organisation dedicated to protecting marine wildlife through scientific research, environmental education and volunteerism
Description: OSE has researchers stationed all over the world and enables volunteers to work on research programmes alongside biologists conducting on-going vital research in unique sites of significance. Service project members actively contribute to field projects by performing simple but labour-intensive tasks. They receive hands-on experience in the sciences, and often become ambassadors for scientific research and conservation. Activities range from data collection and analysis to taking photographic or collecting acoustic data from marine wildlife and ecology. Current projects include studying sea turtles in Surinam, humpback whales in Costa Rica, and coral reef monitoring in Belize
Accommodation: Provided in two–bed rooms with hot water and electricity. Food is usually prepared locally
Cost: Varies according to project. As an example, the Belize Bottlenose Dolphin project costs US$1,740 (excluding airfares)

Ocean Spirits Leatherback Sea Turtle Research & Education Programme

Duration: 3 weeks
Location: Grenada, Caribbean
Season: March – August
Prerequisites: Min. age 18, good physical condition, enthusiastic. No experience required

✉ volunteer@oceanspirits.org
💻 www.oceanspirits.org

Organisation: A non-profit NGO dedicated to the conservation of marine life and the marine environment through education, research and development
Description: Working together with local communities, government departments and international and regional organisations, Ocean Spirits is working to ensure that the spectacle of a nesting or foraging turtle remains a key component of Grenada's vibrant biodiversity. Volunteers gain hands-on field experience with the world's largest sea turtle, directly help the reduction of illegal egg poaching activities and increase community participation. Duties include night patrols of the main leatherback nesting site, flipper tagging of unmarked females, data collection (egg counts, nest relocation), nest excavations, and assisting with organised turtle watches for schools and tourists
Accommodation: Provided in a three–bedroom house in the picturesque north-east of the island, with two bathrooms and a large balcony with incredible views. Full cooking facilities
Cost: £795, including accommodation, food and airport transfers

Original Volunteers

Duration: Min. 1 week
Location: Bolivia, Costa Rica, Guatemala, Honduras
Season: Year round
Prerequisites: Min. age 18. No experience required

☎ 0800 345 7582
✉ contact@originalvolunteers.co.uk
💻 www.originalvolunteers.co.uk

Organisation: Places volunteers with grassroots organisations around the world. Includes supported volunteer placements and more independent voluntary experiences away from the tourist trail
Description: Original Volunteers was formed in 2006 by a number of former volunteers who came together to provide a network of grassroots organisations willing to take volunteers at a very low cost. Current conservation projects include working in animal shelters, national reserves and zoos in Bolivia, sea turtle conservation in Costa Rica, working at an animal refuge or a coastal ecology project in Guatemala, and working at an iguana conservation centre in Honduras
Accommodation: Varies according to project from homestays to hostels and hotels
Cost: One-off placement fee of £295 plus £20–£50 per week to cover food and accommodation

Pretoma – Sea Turtle Restoration Program of Costa Rica

Duration: Min. 1 week
Location: Punta Blanca/San Miguel – Pacific coast of Costa Rica
Season: July – December
Prerequisites: Min. age 18 (unless with parental consent). Volunteers should be in good health. No experience required

☎ +506 241 52 27
✉ tortugas@tortugamarina.org
💻 www.tortugamarina.org

Organisation: Costa Rican non-profit NGO dedicated to marine conservation and research, working to protect ocean resources and promote sustainable fisheries policies
Description: An opportunity to partake in hands-on sea turtle conservation and experience local Costa Rican culture. Participants search for nesting turtles in shifts. When a turtle is found it is tagged, measured and newly laid eggs are transferred to a nearby hatchery where eggs are reburied and monitored. Hatching success rates are measured and baby turtles are released into the sea. During free time, there are plenty of deserted beaches, jungle trails leading to waterfalls and surfing lessons to enjoy
Accommodation: Provided at the research station, with shared bedrooms and bathrooms and communal areas, or homestays with local families. All food is provided
Cost: 1 week US$310; 4 weeks US$930. Includes lodging (homestay or station) and food. For an extra charge, Pretoma can handle all travel within Costa Rica, plus first and last night hotel accommodation

Pretoma – Shark Tagging Expeditions

Duration: 10 days
Location: Cocos Island National Park, Costa Rica
Season: November
Prerequisites: Intermediate divers with PADI or NAUI membership and personal DiveAssure Insurance

 +506 241 52 27
tortugas@tortugamarina.org
www.tortugamarina.org

Organisation: Costa Rican non-profit NGO dedicated to marine conservation and research, working to protect ocean resources and promote sustainable fisheries policies
Description: In 2004, Pretoma teamed up with the Shark Research Institute to carry out an ongoing census in Cocos Island and study the migratory movements of sharks that live there, specifically scalloped hammerheads. So far 25 sharks have been tagged with acoustic telemetry and five with satellite telemetry. This is a unique opportunity to participate in an expedition, dive among schooling hammerheads, assist researchers and support conservation efforts directly. Each group of volunteers dives under the supervision of an experienced dive master/rescue diver
Accommodation: Provided on board the Undersea Hunter, a vessel with room for 14 passengers
Cost: $4,199 including meals, accommodation, national park entrance fee and nitrox refills

Proyecto Karumbé – Sea Turtle Conservation in Uruguay

Duration: Min. 15 days
Location: Barra de Valizas and Cerro Verde scientific bases, Uruguay
Season: January – March
Prerequisites: Min. age 18, good physical condition

 karumbemail@gmail.com
www.karumbe.org

Organisation: Scientific project, started in 1999. Affiliated to CID/CEUR, an environmental NGO
Description: A high number of juvenile green turtles get tangled in the nets of fisheries that operate off the coast of Uruguay and it is depleting endangered populations. The goal of the project is to investigate habitat needs, uses and movements in order to protect key foraging/developmental habitats for green turtle populations in Uruguayan waters. Volunteers help in a number of ways. Duties include: sighting and capturing juvenile turtles, walk surveys searching for stranded sea turtles, collecting data on fishing activities in the area, rehabilitation of sick or weak turtles, and getting involved in workshops for the community and tourists. Volunteers receive one day off per week
Accommodation: Provided in a house or in tents close to the research station, with indoor bathroom and shower, electricity and drinking water
Cost: US$15 per day (including accommodation and 3 meals a day)

Santa Martha Rescue Centers

Duration: Min. 2 weeks
Location: Tambillo, near Quito, Ecuador
Season: Year round
Prerequisites: Min. age 18. Enthusiastic, hard-working, motivated
Organisation: Volunteer-supported NGO

☎ +593 0 9709 8542
✉ santamartha@mail.com
🖥 www.santamartharescue.org

devoted to rescuing animals from unhealthy and illegal situations, rehabilitating them, and restoring them to their natural habitat
Description: There are two rescue centres, one up in the hills above Tambillo and the other working with an indigenous community of the Amazon rainforest. Both centres take any animal that the authorities confiscate, including monkeys, jaguars, pumas, ocelots, parrots and macaws. Volunteers are always welcomed to help with feeding and cleaning, and to improve the facilities at the centre. For volunteers this is a fantastic opportunity to work extremely closely with, and to directly influence, a large variety of wild animals that really need help. At the Amazon centre, volunteers have the chance to actively contribute to the release of animals into the wild. Participants work Monday to Saturday morning, leaving the rest of the weekend free to travel and relax
Accommodation: Provided in comfortable detached houses with all mod cons (hot showers, TV, stereo, DVD player, fully equipped kitchen). Volunteers live together in dorms and share the household chores
Cost: US$85 per week including accommodation. Volunteers contribute $10–$15 per week for food

The Wild Dolphin Project

Duration: 6/9 days
Location: Northern Bahamas
Season: May – September
Prerequisites: Min. age 18, must be able to swim and snorkel safely
Organisation: Non-profit organisation

☎ +1 561 575 5660
✉ wilddolphinproject@earthlink.net
🖥 www.wilddolphinproject.org

dedicated to research, education and conservation. WDP has been studying a specific pod of Atlantic spotted and bottlenose dolphins since 1985
Description: WDP researches many aspects of dolphin society including behaviour, communication, vocalisations, social structure, genetics and habitat. Volunteers are required to help with this research, and in doing so get the rare opportunity to swim and snorkel with the dolphin in the beautiful waters of the Bahamas sandbanks. Participants on research expeditions carry out routine data collection, galley duties, scheduled dolphin watches, underwater observations and underwater photography. In addition they may also be given the chance to visit other snorkel spots such as coral reefs and shipwrecks
Accommodation: Provided aboard the research vessel, Stenella, with two or four people to a room. All food also provided on board
Cost: US$ 2,495 for 9 days, US$1,745 for 6 days. Includes meals, accommodation, snacks and a professional crew on board

African Conservation Experience

Duration: Min. 2/4 weeks
Location: Throughout southern Africa
Season: Year round
Prerequisites: Min. age 17. No experience required

☎ 0870 241 5816
🖱 info@conservationafrica.net
💻 www.conservationafrica.net

Organisation: Specialises in volunteer placements in, and providing financial support and information exchange for conservation projects in Southern Africa

Description: ACE sends volunteers to game and nature reserves where they have the chance to assist rangers and wardens and to get some first-hand experience of animal and plant conservation, including game capture, monitoring and census, wildlife veterinary work, wildlife rehabilitation, behavioural studies and conservation. About 200 volunteer placements are made annually. Although the website states that four weeks is the minimum duration, due to demand the following projects are also suitable for a two-week break: Moholoholo Wildlife Rehabilitation Centre, Tuli Conservation Project, Shimongwe Wildlife Veterinary Experience and the Ilanchi (horseback) Conservation Project

Accommodation: Varies according to project. Included in price

Cost: Varies, but most participants pay around £2,900 (4 weeks) including international flights, domestic transfers in Africa, full board and lodging, and all training and supervision

A POSTCARD FROM South Africa

David Wright took an unplanned but unforgettable trip to South Africa with ACE:

I opened the envelope and there it was; the final, polite 'no'. Hmm. I now faced a decision; enter UCAS clearing and end up on some bizarre degree course, or take a year out to re-assess my situation. The latter seemed far more sensible.

The most logical place to go, as a born and bred animal lover was, of course, Africa. Somewhere I had dearly longed to go for as long as I could remember. I stumbled across African Conservation Experience, which seemed to fit the bill perfectly.

Before I knew what had happened, I was flying out to begin my adventure, a bag of nerves, excitement and anticipation. I spent a month in South Africa where I had many a wonderful experience. I was involved in physical graft such as road clearing and invasive plant control and spent two weeks on a ranger course learning everything from 4x4 driving skills and firearms handling to dealing with snake venoms and game reserve management. As well as the conservation work, I had the opportunity to camp in the Kruger National Park, to go microlighting and rafting, and to throw myself off a cliff on the world's highest gorge swing (not for the faint-hearted!). The experience really allows you to get a taste of the cultures and societies that are often similar yet often so alien to our own. For me it was a great wake-up call to the fact that there is indeed a world beyond my own four walls.

It is very strange indeed how you set off in life with one particular direction in mind and end up in a completely new and fascinating one! On my return I re-applied to university. My placement with ACE gave me much needed experience in the zoological and ecological fields and I start at the University of Wales, Bangor this September studying a degree in zoology with conservation.

African Impact

Duration: Min. 1/2/3/4 weeks depending on project
Location: Botswana, Kenya, Mozambique, South Africa and Zimbabwe
Season: Year round
Prerequisites: Min. age 18

 impact@africanencounter.org
 www.africanimpact.com

Organisation: Volunteer placement organisation specialising in hands-on holidays in Africa
Description: African Impact aims to facilitate the social development and economic upliftment of Africa and to play a pivotal role in research and conservation of Africa's environment through carefully designed volunteer projects. Current conservation projects include dolphin research in Mozambique, elephant and leopard research shadowing and wildlife conservation in Botswana, African lion/wildlife rehabilitation and 'big 5' wildlife expeditions in Zimbabwe. Participants work closely with scientists and research staff to make a real difference to conservation projects. There is also plenty of time to relax, travel and socialise
Accommodation: Provided in basic but comfortable lodgings. Varies according to project
Cost: Varies according to project and length of stay. As an example, Elephant and Leopard Research Shadowing in Botswana costs £650 (1 week). Prices include a donation to the project, orientation, support and training, daily transfers, full board and lodging

AVIVA

Duration: Min. 2 weeks (depending on project)
Location: In and around Cape Town, South Africa
Season: Year round
Prerequisites: Min. age 16, good level of English. No special skills required

☎ +27 21 557 5996
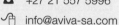 info@aviva-sa.com
💻 www.aviva-sa.com

Organisation: Established volunteering company
Description: AVIVA organises volunteers for a number of wildlife and conservation projects and four of these are suitable for short-term breaks. The Tamboti Conservation Project is set on a private conservation reserve hosting species of antelope, leopard, hyena, baboon, zebra and warthogs. Volunteers undertake biological research and reserve management. The Inkenkwenzi Conservation Initiative offers volunteers the opportunity to experience life on a working game reserve. The Vervet Monkey Rehabilitation Centre offers the chance to care and hand-rear orphaned and rescued vervet monkeys situated on a farm deep within 'Zulu' country. The African Penguin Conservation programme requires volunteers to help catch, feed and care for this endangered species
Accommodation: Varies between projects, from very rustic, through to homestay and hostel-style accommodation. There is also a central AVIVA house in Cape Town where volunteers based locally can stay
Cost: Varies. As an example, four weeks at the Tamboti Project costs £1000

Blue Ventures

Duration: Min. 3 weeks
Location: Andavadoaka, Madagascar
Season: Year round
Prerequisites: Medical certificate of fitness to carry out scuba diving must be obtained prior to departure

☎ 020 8341 9819
✍ volunteer@blueventures.org
💻 www.blueventures.org

Organisation: Not-for-profit, UK registered charity dedicated to working with local communities in Madagascar to protect marine resources
Description: Volunteers are placed in project sites and trained in scuba diving, scientific research, community outreach and on-the-ground conservation. The project site is in the remote village of Andavadoaka, on the south-western coast of Madagascar, where villagers are helped to create community-run marine protected areas. There are never more than 18 volunteers on any one expedition so that volunteers receive the highest standard of scientific training and support. Those who are new to diving begin their stay scuba training. All volunteers receive extensive training in research, identification of marine species and data collection. Once trained, volunteers participate in daily diving and marine research excursions
Accommodation: Provided in beach cabins with private showers. Cabins are located above their own beach with stunning views. All meals provided
Cost: £1,950 (6 weeks). Flights and equipment not included in price

A POSTCARD FROM Madagascar

Student, Caroline Gosney, took part in a Blue Ventures expedition, conducting daily diving and marine research work:

I had never scuba-dived before in my life, and I had certainly never studied marine biology, but soon after arriving in Madagascar I was swimming among schools of flourescent-coloured fish, monitoring octopus populations and exploring underwater caves and coral reefs no one had ever seen before.

I decided to travel to Andavadoaka, a tiny village of just 1,200 people, to have a unique holiday and see the world. But by the end of my adventure, I felt I had done a lot more than just see the world. I felt I had helped improve it.

Our days in Andavadoaka began early and we were already motoring out to sea just as the sun began to peek over the horizon. We were often greeted on these morning outings by dolphins, turtles, sharks, manta rays or flying fish jumping from the water. Once at the dive site, we began conducting surveys of marine life. We lay a 20-metre tape on the ocean floor and then waited for exotic fish to congregate so we could measure their populations. I had never before imagined myself sitting on the bottom of the ocean watching a clown trigger fish with its bright yellow lips and pink fins.

The data collected during our daily ocean surveys was used to develop management plans with local villagers that will ensure the fish, octopus and other ocean resources they rely upon for survival are not depleted by over-fishing or threatened by growing commercial activities.

We arrived back on shore each day by lunch, and spent most of our afternoons teaching English to the local children. The Vezo, as the villagers are known, also regularly challenged us to a friendly game of football – friendly as long as they won or at least tied! The Vezo recently established a new marine reserve based on our marine data – a very satisfying feeling.

Centre for Rehabilitation of Wildlife (CROW)

Duration: Min. 2 weeks
Location: Durban, South Africa
Season: Year round (Peak is November – March)
Prerequisites: Min. age 18. No experience required
Organisation: Non-profit organisation that cares for injured and orphaned indigenous wildlife

 +27 31 462 127
info@crowkzn.co.za
www.crowkzn.co.za

Description: CROW cares for a huge range of species including velvet monkeys, tortoises, bushbuck, garden birds, fish eagles, vultures, crocodiles, lemurs and baboons. The centre has approximately 400 animals in its care at any one time, with the objective of rehabilitating them and releasing them back into the wild. Volunteers are required to help clean cages, feed and care for the animals and assist staff where necessary. Special projects may include observing animals in the rehabilitation area, building cages and helping with release. CROW works in partnership with a tour operator that can provide tours and entertainment for participants' free time
Accommodation: Provided in a furnished house shared with other volunteers, with washing and cooking facilities
Cost: Approx. US$25 per day (including accommodation/three basic meals)

A POSTCARD FROM Durban, South Africa

Catherine Johnson spent a hands-on holiday working at CROW's Wildlife Rehabilitation Centre in Durban:

There is more to CROW than just petting a few tame creatures and if that is your requirement, then CROW is not for you. On a number of occasions I was asked to assist in the surgery. This was an aspect of CROW that I had not been expecting, yet there I was holding a crowned eagle's wings whilst he was force fed, clamping shut the vicious beak of a gannet, or holding an injured monkey.

During my short time there I encountered an extensive range of animals including jackals, crocodiles, baboons, monkeys, goslings, tortoises, goshawks, a crowned eagle and some very noisy barn owls. I also looked after animals I had never even heard of before such as gennets, caracals, canerats and diakers. Some animals become your favourites. I was given the job of looking after a mongoose who had been brought up as a pet and was scared of the other mongoose in the pen next door. He was very lonely and distressed and when I went to check on him, he would scramble up my arm and fall asleep with his nose tucked under my elbow.

Volunteering overseas has been an ambition of mine for a very long time, and at last I have achieved it. CROW enabled me to have a rewarding and meaningful holiday. While my friends stayed in England in the rain I was cuddling a mongoose and feeding a caracal. I could have got bored and sunburnt on some crowded Spanish beach, instead I helped to capture barn owls ready for release. CROW was often hard and messy work, but I have had experiences which I will never forget and I have met some inspirational and dedicated people.

Cheetah Conservation Fund

Duration: Min. 1 week (Kenya); 2/4 weeks (Namibia)
Location: Kenya/Namibia
Season: Year round
Prerequisites: Min. age 18. Volunteers with all kinds of backgrounds needed
Organisation: Namibian non-profit incorporated association dedicated to the long-term survival of the cheetah and its ecosystems

☎ 020 7828 3218;
US +1 513 487 3399
info@cheetah.org
www.cheetah.org or www.cheetah.org.uk

Description: CCF sponsors scientific research and education programmes in areas such as cheetah population biology, ecology, health and reproduction and human impact. Volunteers are expected to be flexible and adapt to whatever work needs attending to. Some administrative work will be required, but participants also get the chance to help with cheetah feeding, raising puppies, assisting in clinical work-ups, observing cheetah behaviour, conducting fieldwork and being involved in outreach and education programmes
Accommodation: Provided in comfortable shared living quarters. May vary during the stay
Cost: Kenya: $300 per week; Namibia $3000 for 2 weeks/$5000 for 4 weeks

Enkosini Eco Experience

Duration: 2, 3 or 4 weeks
Location: North-east and south-west South Africa
Season: Year round
Prerequisites: Min. age 18, open to experiencing new cultures, tolerant, flexible, self-disciplined and proactive. No experience required

☎ +27 82 265 5955
info@enkosiniecoexperience.com
www.enkosiniecoexperience.com

Organisation: Enkosini is a private, non-profit sanctuary dedicated to researching and implementing strategies for wildlife conservation, with a focus on predators, specifically African lions
Description: Enkosini offers participants the opportunity to work at some of South Africa's leading wildlife conservation, rehabilitation and research projects. Volunteers can work in the Enkosini Wildlife Sanctuary, the Makalali Game Reserve, Noah's Ark Wildlife Centre, the Kariega Game Reserve, the Penguin Conservation Centre, the ORCA Marine Foundation, and the Amakhala Game Reserve. Other projects include working with desert elephants, baboons, vervet monkeys, black rhinos and great white sharks. The work involved varies from project to project, but in all cases volunteers are offered complete support from experienced staff and full training where required
Accommodation: Provided in clean, modest chalets, timber cabins, tented camps or homestays depending on each project
Cost: £695 (2 weeks); £895 (3 weeks); £1095 (4 weeks)

GoXplore

Duration: Min. 2 weeks
Location: South Africa, Zimbabwe, Kenya
Season: Year round, but different projects have different start dates
Prerequisites: Min. age 18 (though there are summer projects for 16-year-olds), physical fitness. No special skills required

☎ +27 31 765 1818
🖰 wildlife@goxploreafrica.com
💻 www.goxploreafrica.com

Organisation: Youth travel organisation specialising in Africa that promotes safe, fulfilling opportunities for thousands of travellers from around the world
Description: Around 1,500 volunteers are taken on every year for a variety of wildlife projects that include conservation studies, research, ranger courses, instruction in rehabilitation methods, game counts, work with primates, reptile or cheetah breeding, game farm management, equestrian work and more. All GoXplore staff are born and bred in Africa
Accommodation: Varies according to the project and ranges from lodges to campsites. Check the website for lodging options. Food is provided and prepared either by project leaders or by the volunteers themselves
Cost: Programme fees range from R9,000–R25,000 (in South African Rand) and include food, accommodation, training, in-country transportation and a donation to each project

Munda Wanga Wildlife Park and Sanctuary

Duration: 3 weeks
Location: 15km outside of Lusaka, Zambia
Season: Year round
Prerequisites: Min. age 18. No experience/skills required
Organisation: Non-profit conservation education organisation

☎ +260 1 278 456
🖰 biopark@zamnet.zm
💻 www.mundawanga.com

Description: The park and sanctuary fell into decay in the 1990s due to lack of funds and poor management. Today however, it has been rehabilitated, the gardens reshaped and an education programme developed that addresses environmental education. There are now more than 40 species of mammals and birds in the park and volunteers are invited to help in a variety of ways. Tasks include monitoring animals, cleaning enclosures, helping to hand-rear orphaned animals, construction, fundraising, working with school groups and giving tours. Working days are full, but the hours are irregular. Participants enjoy one day off a week to see the beach and experience the local area
Accommodation: Provided at the park in basic dorm-style rooms with a bathroom and cooking area
Cost: US$750 (3 weeks), including accommodation and a weekly food allowance

Reality Kenya

Duration: Min. 2 weeks
Location: Throughout Kenya
Season: Year round
Prerequisites: Min. age 18. No experience required. For the marine project, a PADI certificate is required but participants can train for this on-site

☎ +254 02 214 088
🖱 simon@realitykenya.com
🖥 www.realitykenya.com

Organisation: RK works in partnership with the Kenya Wildlife Service to create a new form of sustainable development
Description: The Kenya Wildlife Service's objectives include co-ordination of research, ecosystem monitoring, project management, management of wildlife resources and providing security and veterinary services. Volunteers are invited to aid the KWS in a number of projects at Maasai Mara National Reserve, Kisite National Marine Reserve, Abedare National Park and Tsavo National Park. At all of the land-based projects volunteers will be involved with animal surveillance and monitoring, ecosystem upkeep and maintenance, tracking of animals, research projects, educational work with communities and schools, and guiding tourists through the parks. At Kisite marine reserve, volunteers will also be involved in diving, reef checks and marine monitoring
Accommodation: Provided with host families in varying standards of accommodation. All meals provided
Cost: US$1,495 (1 month). Includes food, accommodation, airport pick-up and project administration. 34% of the fee goes to project development

The San Wild Wildlife Trust

Duration: Min. 1 week
Location: South Africa
Season: Year round
Prerequisites: Min. age 18, good physical condition
Organisation: NGO devoted to the rehabilitation of animals rescued from malpractices and released into its own reserve

☎ +27 0 15 318 7900
🖱 sanwild@pixie.co.za
🖥 www.sanwild.org

Description: A wide range of wild animals occupy the reserve, ranging from leopards, white rhinos and giraffes, blue wildebeest to lions and elephants. Working volunteers are invited to join the team, to gain knowledge about ecology and an understanding of the importance of conservation, through active involvement in the daily resource management of the reserve. Volunteer duties range from fixing game fences and building enclosures, to observing emergency rescues of animals, guided bush walks and observing veterinary procedures whenever necessary
Accommodation: Volunteers can choose between tents with no electricity at the Tshokwane Tented Camp, or luxury chalets with TV, communal kitchens and a rock pool
Cost: US$580 per person per week for tent accommodation. US$150 per day for luxury chalets. Prices include all meals

Shumba Experience

Duration: Full experience: Min. 2/4 weeks;
Mini-Adventure 7–14 days
Location: South Africa/Namibia/Kenya
Season: Year round
Prerequisites: Min. age 17. No previous
experience required

☎ 0845 257 3205
✍ info@shumbaexperience.co.uk
💻 www.shumbaexperience.co.uk

Organisation: Gap year company specialising in wildlife projects in Africa
Description: Participants have the chance to work as a volunteer on game reserves, marine placements, wildlife sanctuaries and research projects, working with conservation professionals. The types of full experience available include assisting with game capture, working on a 'big 5' game reserve, learning about conservation and how to manage wildlife in its natural environment. For those who cannot commit to a minimum of two or four weeks, Shumba also offers a range of seven to 14-day Mini-Adventures, including: a bush survival course, a conservation discovery course, game capture and various conservation projects. Participants also enjoy sleep outs under the night sky, nocturnal game drives, and they learn essential bush survival skills
Accommodation: Included in the price. Varies from comfortable lodgings to camping in the bush, depending on the project
Cost: Mini Adventures range from £395 to £995. 4 week experiences range from £1,395 – £1,795. Includes all accommodation, food, training, pre-deaprture information and support, free Lonely Planet, airport pick up and supervision

A POSTCARD FROM Nkombi Reserve, South Africa

Sussex schoolteacher, Diana Hannant, visited the 10,000–acre Nkombi reserve. Here she was actively involved in conservation projects including monitoring the white rhino population:

It's quite hard to write a postcard about my experience because I had such a fantastic time and there is so much to say. Most days started early at about 6am just as the sun was beginning to rise. Some stars were still in the sky and the jackals could still be heard howling over on the ridge. We would check the small mammal traps and after breakfast it could be a game drive or grass survey. Lunch would usually be at the camp and was cooked by team leaders or one of the volunteers. We all got on really well with the team leaders. They were very good teachers and their enthusiasm for the reserve and the project is infectious.

In the afternoons we would often take part in a large mammal survey, spotting rhino. One afternoon, the aim was to trap and collar a hyena for research purposes. This involved dragging a half-eaten impala (medium-sized African antelope) behind the truck to lay a scent, and then placing it in a hyena trap.

In the evening we would usually eat our dinner round the open fire. One evening we had roast wildebeest cooked in an earth oven. I can honestly say it was one of the best meals I have ever eaten. Once or twice we went out on night drives to spot nocturnal animals. It was great to see some different animals and to learn to identify impala by the way their eyes shine. I learnt so much during my mini-adventure, about different antelopes, grasses, and even how to make a drinking bottle out of an ostrich egg. It really was an unforgettable experience, and one I hope to repeat.

Elephant Nature Park

Duration: 1, 2 or 4 weeks
Location: Northern Thailand
Season: Year round – starting every Monday
Prerequisites: Min. age 18 (children may participate with their parents); good physical health

 +66 53 818 754
info@elephantnaturepark.org
www.elephantnaturepark.org

Organisation: Unique long-term project with the aim of providing a sanctuary and rescue centre for distressed elephants from all over Thailand
Description: Thailand's elephant population is struggling for its survival, as mankind encroaches on its natural habitat. This park, established in 1966, currently provides a home for more than 30 elephants. Volunteers are invited to help provide basic care for the elephants. Although professional vets and experienced elephant keepers are required, there are also many positions for those with no previous experience. Volunteer work includes feeding and bathing the elephants, healthcare, visiting elephants working at trekking camps, and learning about elephant communication
Accommodation: Provided in simple bamboo tree huts, with toilet and shower
Cost: US$275 per week (including accommodation, food and local transport)

Global Eco-Spiritual Tours

Duration: 12 days
Location: Himalayan Mountains, India
Season: August
Prerequisites: Min. age 18, good physical condition

+1 561 266 0096
global@paradista.net
www.globalecospiritualtours.org

Organisation: Small non-profit, charitable organisation that uses member contributions to benefit education and healthcare needs of children in developing countries
Description: Annual trips with GEST allow participants to combine eco-tourism with volunteer work and spiritual awareness. Along the way, volunteers undertake ecological volunteer projects such as planting trees, cleaning up mountain trails, locating endangered species for scientists, donating solar panels to remote homes and institutions, and bottling pure mountain spring water for local charities. Volunteers also participate in the religious life of the communities they visit, exploring monasteries and participating in meditation sessions. Participants are free to choose how much of the volunteer work they participate in and go at their own pace
Accommodation: Provided in hotels, guesthouses and tents. Food is provided by local cooks
Cost: US$2,500 (including accommodation and meals but excluding flights)

Go Differently

Duration: Min. 2 weeks (Dusky Langurs); 1–4 weeks (Thai elephants)
Location: Thailand
Season: Year round
Prerequisites: Min. age 18 (unless accompanied by a responsible adult), enthusiastic, willing to work with local people. No experience required

☎ 01799 521950
✉ info@godifferently.com
🖥 www.godifferently.com

Organisation: Tour operator specialising in ethical holidays and volunteering trips based on appreciation and respect of the local environment and people

Description: There are currently two conservation and wildlife voluntourism projects available, the first involves working with the dusky langur, a monkey-like creature facing extinction due to deforestation. This project aims to study the behaviour of the langur in order to gain a better understanding about what can be done to aid its survival. Volunteers will observe langurs in their natural habitat, educate tourists on the issues, and feed and care for the animals where required. The second project involves working with Thai elephants. Participants learn how to ride and care for elephants as part of this conservation project. They become part of the community of mahouts and help feed and clean the elephants, as well as educating tourists. In both projects, evenings and weekends are free

Accommodation: Provided. Various options are available including guesthouses and homestays. Meals are provided

Cost: £320 per week (for the first 2 weeks, £250 p.w. thereafter) including accommodation, meals, guides and supervision

---

A POSTCARD FROM Thailand

Tessa Le Plar, 37, a secretary and single mum went with to Thailand with Go Differently to work on the Elephant Mahout Project:

I had never really thought about taking a working holiday. Holidays for me have always been for one week, somewhere warm, for as cheap as possible. I was looking up flights to Dubai to go and visit my boyfriend when I just happened to click on the 'wrong' button. All of a sudden there was a whole host of holidays with everything from turtles to lions, and orphans to gibbons! I remember thinking – ooh I could never do that....Not long after that I split up with my boyfriend and found out I was to receive some money. It was then I decided that I should do something different, and do it on my own. And I'm so glad I did.

I had no experience whatsoever of elephants, but after two weeks of asking questions and listening to the mahouts' stories, I feel like an expert. On Mondays, Wednesdays and Fridays we would start work at 7am, usually sweeping the area around our elephant, fetching pineapple leaves for their breakfast and maybe having a short ride around the camp. If it was hot, we would take the elephants for a shower (or they would take us for one – you only know who's going to actually get wet at the last minute!). At 6pm we would take the elephants to the forest, riding through residential areas and fields to a place where they could get different food and have a good scratch against the trees. On Tuesdays, Thursdays and Saturdays we would collect the elephants to take them to

continued

the river, where they were bathed by the mahouts. There's nothing like watching a sunrise while you're sitting on top of a soggy elephant! It really is something everyone should try!

In the evenings our time was our own and we spent it in a variety of ways. We took a trip to the Sanctuary of Truth (an enormous temple built out of wood), we went to watch Thai boxing and we had a party on the beach. The mahouts were only too happy to give us lifts dangling from the back of their bikes, and once we got the hang of jumping on taxis, the world was our oyster! Strangely enough though, some of the best nights were just spent playing cards with the mahouts in the moonlight, having a few drinks, laughing and thumbing frantically through the Thai phrase book in a bid to be understood, and just laughing! The mahouts were very passionate about their elephants and their way of life and although I was at first quite shocked about the huts they lived in and their lack of possessions generally, I soon realised that this is just a reaction against the decadent country I come from. Not once, and I mean that, did any of them complain about anything.

One of my favourite moments of all happened when I was by myself. I was leaving my elephant, Docoon, to go to lunch and she had just picked up some pineapple leaves to eat. I said goodbye and she put down her food (unheard of!) and stretched her trunk out to me. This may sound like nothing, but when you've had your commands ignored for most of the day and you are starting to wonder if you will ever get through, it felt amazing!

Go Differently participant hugs her elephant at the Elephant Mahout Project, Pattaya, Thailand.

Naucrates Conservation Project

Duration: Min. 2 weeks
Location: Phra Thong Island, Thailand
Season: January – March
Prerequisites: Min. age 18, physically fit, able to work in a group
Organisation: NGO operation that works in different countries of the world with the aim of contributing to the survival of sea turtles

☎ +39 333 430 6643
🖱 naucrates12@hotmail.com; naucrates12@tiscalinet.it
💻 www.naucrates.org

Description: Much of this island was badly damaged by the 2004 tsunami, including the Naucrates base. Nevertheless research continues and volunteers' contributions are even more welcome. Volunteers are involved in monitoring sea turtle nesting activity, mangrove restoration in the forest, and reef surveying to evaluate the recovery of reef after the tsunami. Volunteers work closely with researchers and full training is given. Periodically visits to the village to assist with the education programme are organised. Other activities such as beach cleaning and vegetation planting also take place. Volunteers have plenty of free time to explore the beauty of the island
Accommodation: Provided in shared rooms in the resort houses. Three meals a day are provided by Thai staff and electricity is available in the evenings
Cost: €550 for 2 weeks (additional weeks €275) including food and accommodation

Orangutan Health

Duration: 13 days
Location: North Sumatra, Indonesia
Season: Year round (one trip per month)
Prerequisites: Min. age 18, good level of fitness, patient, attentive
Organisation: Long-term research project

🖱 orangutanhealth@nusa.net.id
💻 www.orangutan-health.org

investigating the behaviour and ecological conditions necessary to maintain health in wild orangutans
Description: The project protects the habitat of a significant population of wild orangutans in the area, whilst also providing a site for conservation education, summer schools and research. Volunteers split their time between three or four-day treks into the jungle and lab work at base camp. Research tasks in the forest may include nest counting to provide seasonal population estimates, fruit trail transects to record the range of foodstuffs available, locating areas with significant orangutan populations, and observing orangutan behaviour. At the base camp the work mainly involves data entry and analysis. There is no physical contact with orangutans. During free time, river rafting and mountain biking are available. The project provides important work for the local community and employs only local guides
Accommodation: Provided in very basic but clean conditions at the base centre. There is electricity but no shower or hot water for washing. During treks, participants camp in the jungle
Cost: US$1289 (excluding flights, insurance and tourist visa)

Wild Animal Rescue Foundation of Thailand (WAR)

Duration: Min. 2/3 weeks
Location: Thailand
Season: Year round
Prerequisites: Min. age 18, good physical condition and basic command of spoken English. No experience required

 +662 712 9515
 volunteer@warthai.org
 www.warthai.org

Organisation: WAR is a registered charity dedicated to prevention, education and active campaigns against cruelty to wild animals, to rescuing maltreated wild animals and to promoting the conservation of their habitats

Description: WAR recruits 80–100 volunteers annually to help with the work of looking after abused and maltreated wild animals. Projects include the Phuket Gibbon Rehabilitation Project, returning gibbons that have been confiscated from captivity to the wild. Tasks include preparation of food, cage maintenance, observation and data collection. The Wild Animal Rescue and Education Centre in Ranong also requires volunteers to help with similar work. The project also includes the education of local people to help end illegal hunting and abuse of animals by humans. Finally the Sea Turtle Conservation Project runs from December to March only and works in conjunction with WAR to redress the decline in all four species of sea turtle found off the coast of Thailand

Accommodation: Provided in shared rooms in a simple house or local-style hut with toilet, shower and kitchen

Cost: Approx. US$970 (3 weeks) including accommodation, orientation and training

AUSTRALIA AND NEW ZEALAND

Cape Tribulation Tropical Research Station

Duration: Min. 2 weeks
Location: Cape Tribulation, Australia (north Queensland)
Season: Year round
Prerequisites: Min. age 23. No experience required
Organisation: Independent field research station in a

☎ +61 7 4098 0063
✆ austrop@austrop.org.au
💻 www.austrop.org.au

world heritage site, funded through the Australian Tropical Research Foundation

Description: This is the only independent research facility in the coastal lowland seasonally wet tropical rainforests of Australia. The entire region is a World Heritage Site and the research station provides facilities for students, scientists and researchers to study the region. Around 50 volunteers visit the station each year and their efforts are vital to the continuing operation of the station. Volunteers contribute to research, help to look after flying foxes, help with rainforest regeneration projects and maintain station buildings and equipment, with time off to experience the local area and visit the beach

Accommodation: Provided in a bunkhouse at the station
Cost: Small contribution for food and accommodation

Australian Koala Foundation

Duration: 1 or 2 weeks
Location: Near Brisbane, Australia
Season: Year round
Prerequisites: None. Work is available for all ages/fitness levels. No experience required
Organisation: Non-profit, non-government-funded organisation. Its central aim is the conservation of Australia's unique koala and the preservation of its diminishing habitat

☎ +61 7 3229 7233
🖱 research@savethekoala.com
💻 www.savethekoala.com

Description: Research and restoration field trips are for active and adventurous people who want to make a difference to the world and get their hands dirty doing it. Research field trips can be physically demanding. They involve arduous bush walking to gain access to study sites and gain information regarding koala populations and habitats. Participants visit areas seldom visited by people and experience the real Australian bush on foot. Restoration field trips are designed for people who like to play a positive part in conservation. Tasks include preparing ground, weed control, digging holes, planting trees and general cleanup work. Many koala populations are surviving in poor habitats as the most fertile lands have been claimed by farmers and residential areas
Accommodation: Provided in comfortable lodges with warm showers, shared meals and a comfortable bed
Cost: Approx. AUS$1,980 (1 week). Includes accommodation, meals, entry to the wildlife parks, and in-country travel

Conservation Volunteers Australia

Duration: 2/4/6 weeks
Location: 22 locations in Australia
Season: Year round
Prerequisites: Min. age 18 for international volunteers. Senior volunteers welcome, as long as they are reasonably fit and healthy

☎ +61 (3) 5330 2600
🖱 info@conservationvolunteers.com.au
💻 www.conservationvolunteers.com.au

Organisation: Non-profit organisation dedicated to practical conservation projects for the improvement of the Australian environment
Description: CVA completes more than 3,000 individual conservation projects per year. Projects offer a unique opportunity to see off-the-beaten-track areas of Australia and include tree planting, seed collection, construction and maintenance of walking tracks, habitat restoration, flora and fauna surveys, and erosion and salinity control. All volunteer activities are labour intensive and hands-on. Working-Holiday Visas are NOT required for a CVA placement
Accommodation: Varies according to project and location. Types of accommodation include caravans, hostels, bunkhouses and camping
Cost: £399 (2 weeks) including accommodation and meals

New Zealand Trust for Conservation Volunteers (NZTCV)

Duration: 2 days – several months
Location: Throughout New Zealand
Season: Year round
Prerequisites: Min. age 18. No experience required
Organisation: Charitable trust that

☎ +64 (9) 415 9336
🖱 conservol@clear.net.nz
💻 www.conservationvolunteers.org.nz

organises volunteer projects (currently 120 of them) that help to restore New Zealand's ecosystems to their natural beauty by mobilising volunteers for this purpose
Description: This programme offers participants opportunities to visit scenic locations in both the North and South Islands, allowing overseas visitors to share in New Zealand's unique environment and culture. Participants work in national parks and reserves, forests, wetlands and coastal areas throughout the country helping with a variety of work that includes planting, weeding, track maintenance, wildlife, marine and pest management, species monitoring, island revegetation, forest restoration and general maintenance
Accommodation: Varies according to project. Not all projects include accommodation, so check carefully
Cost: No participation fees. Volunteers pay for their own travel and food costs. Many projects offer free accommodation

The Oceania Research Project's Whale Research Expeditions

Duration: 6 days (Sunday – Friday) each week for 1 or more weeks
Location: Hervey Bay/Fraser Island, Queensland, Australia
Season: July – October
Prerequisites: Min. age 18. No experience required

☎ +61 2 668 582128
🖱 trish.wally@oceania.org.au
💻 www.oceania.org.au

Organisation: Not-for-profit operating dedicated to raising awareness about cetacea and the ocean environment through research and education
Description: The research expeditions have provided a dedicated long-term research platform to study humpback whales in Hervey Bay. Participants' duties on board the 'Moon Dancer' include assisting with pod observations, sloughed skin collection, recording GIS spatial data, water quality sampling, environmental readings, or working in the kitchen. Duties are rotated so everyone gets to participate in all the activities involved with a successful expedition. Observation work will include identifying individuals, and observing and recording their behaviour. At the end of each working day, the boat anchors off Fraser Island for dinner and discussion
Accommodation: Provided on board the Moon Dancer, complete with bathroom, shower, kitchen and electricity
Cost: AU$1,750 per person per week, including food and accommodation

Tolga Bat Hospital

Duration: Min. 1 week (Min. 1 month during the busy season October – March)
Location: Atherton, near Cairns, Australia
Season: Year round
Prerequisites: Min. age 21, rabies vaccinated, team players, self-motivated. Wildlife experience helpful

☎ +61 7 4091 2683
🖱 jenny.maclean@iig.com.au
💻 www.tolgabathospital.org

Organisation: Community-based organisation working for the conservation of bats and their habitat
Description: Tolga's main work involves the rescue, rehabilitation and release of all bat species. It also promotes conservation issues, educates and raises public awareness and encourages research into the ecology of bats. Volunteer work is varied. Typically participants help feed, clean, weigh and measure the orphans, clean cages, assist in search or release trips to the rainforest and help with miscellaneous projects around the hospital. Work during the busy tick season (October to March) tends to be more hands-on with the bats, whereas for the rest of the year there will be more building and repair projects and garden work. Working hours are unpredictable. This is a truly unique experience for bat enthusiasts
Accommodation: Provided in a two room self-contained apartment with kitchen, bathroom and verandah
Cost: AUS$30–50 per day for food, accommodation, laundry (sliding scale according to length of stay, experience and accommodation type)

A POSTCARD FROM Atherton, Australia

Australian, Elena Bridgens spent an eventful three weeks working at Tolga Bat Hospital:

Leaving the steaming hot touristy Cairns for Atherton was like arriving at a little piece of paradise, especially as a bat lover! It felt as though not a metre of the property was batless, whether it be manmade or bat made. Nearly everywhere you went you could hear a little flap, cherp, see a little twinkle of an eye belonging to one of the most remarkable, splendid, loveable creatures nature has created and sadly one that faces more than its fair share of problems in its purposeful existence. I was to learn this during my three week volunteering stay at TBH. I was also to learn how to string some apples pretty darn fast!

I arrived just after Christmas, when the babies were coming to terms with 'leaving the nest'. As the days went on, I got more and more attached to the little guys. They gained their independence and were put into the bigger 'houses' to prepare them for their release into the scrub. I honestly think I felt more pride with the release than taking my own child (if I had one) for their first day at school.

As for staying at TBH, we volunteers were right up there with the royal standards too. Great food, comfy beds, our own quarters and lovely surroundings. I would highly recommend being a volunteer!

HANDS-ON Community and Development Projects

GIVING SOMETHING BACK

'Community and Development Projects' encompass a vast field of potential voluntary work covering everything from digging wells and building houses, to providing humanitarian aid and relief, working in orphanages and with street children, healthcare and HIV awareness programmes, human rights education, and helping people to find sustainable ways of making a living. Essentially, whereas the previous chapter focused on everything animal and vegetable, this chapter is solely concerned with the needs of human beings. These projects are about improving the standard of living for people, mainly in developing nations, who, every day, face the difficulties bestowed upon them by war, poverty, natural disasters, lack of education, and a dearth of resources.

Around 20% of the developing world's population lives in extreme poverty, lacking the essentials for a minimum standard of living. These essentials may be material resources such as food, safe drinking water and shelter. Around 850 million men, women and children do not have sufficient daily food, and over half of them are chronically malnourished; and 1.2 billion people live without access to clean drinking water. But the essentials which people in developing countries lack may also be social resources such as access to information, education, healthcare, social status and political power. These issues can be just as life-threatening. For example, due to lack of education and sufficient healthcare, HIV/AIDS kills 6,000 people and another 8,200 become affected every day; and every minute, somewhere in the developing world, a woman will die while giving birth.

For years the ability to help in developing countries was the preserve of providers of long-term humanitarian aid: UN organisations, NGOs and charities such as MSF, VSO, the Peace Corps and the Red Cross. These organisations are staffed by people who have devoted their lives to humanitarian causes abroad, and their commitment is awe-inspiring. In recent years however, a growing desire among ordinary people to help has emerged, even if it is just in some small way, for just a short period of time.

As discussed in the introduction, the emerging social conscience of travellers stems from an increasing global awareness of the plight of others. Every day we are swamped with images of needless suffering, of abandoned children, of the starving, of HIV/AIDS sufferers, of people without access to sanitation, or basic healthcare. And unsurprisingly we want to help. But the event that galvanised the world into action on an unprecedented scale was the Asian tsunami. As the western world awoke on Boxing Day morning, still feeling the effects of Christmas over-indulgence, people were greeted with images of destruction, chaos and suffering throughout Asia. The plight of the many affected people and countries prompted a widespread humanitarian response. In all, the worldwide community donated more than US$7 billion to those affected by the earthquake. But for many, simply donating money seemed insufficient. They wanted to be there offering support wherever they could. They wanted to be doing something tangible. The fact that unskilled volunteers were requested to stay at home led to a feeling of frustration and inadequacy, and in the coming months a whole new generation of people, who had never previously considered volunteering, were looking to offer their services abroad. And a growing number of tour operators and charitable organisations, were keen to tap this new resource.

Several organisations listed below offer projects that include post-tsunami relief, helping to rebuild communities that were cruelly devastated by the ocean. However, although roughly 200,000 people died as a result of the Asian tsunami, around 210,000 children worldwide die from hunger every week. The world's humanitarian crises are ongoing and while the immediacy of the Boxing Day disaster had a visible impact on people, in the long run it has made people more aware of other issues faced by developing nations, and their own potential to offer help and support.

The 21st century voluntourist prefers to make a contribution to overseas relief rather than pursuing hedonism and relaxation. They are not just concerned by issues of third world poverty, they feel moved to do something. Adrian Yalland, co-founder of the Different Travel Company, explains this shifting attitude among travellers: *'The difference between concern and compassion is simple. Concern says "that's wrong and someone should do something". Compassion says "that's wrong, and I must do something".'* Hence, an increasing number of tourists are committing to changing the way they travel and they are signing up with companies that offer them a chance to change the lives of others rather than just sightseeing and lounging on a beach.

Clearly many of the problems faced by communities are deeply engrained in society, and a few weeks of volunteering, however well meaning, will barely scratch the surface. Nobody thinking of taking a hands-on community or development project should set off with the belief that they are going to change the world. Instead they should be happy just to make a small difference, and remember that with a responsible attitude to travel, just by visiting they can support the local economy (see *Responsible Tourism* below). However, it is amazing just what can be accomplished in a few weeks. Lorna Allen visited the south-west coast of Sri Lanka, an area that was left devastated by the Boxing Day tsunami. In just two weeks working at a school for deaf and blind children, she and her team mates:

> *Painted the furniture, walls and ceilings of the rooms, we put in a new water supply and taps in the toilets, and we repaired or replaced the fans and lights in the classrooms. Outside the school was an old playground, which had become dangerous and unusable. We repaired and painted all the equipment and made a new play surface which was filled with coconut shavings.*

When viewed within the context of the region's devastation, their work is a drop in the ocean, but clearly to the children and teachers at the school it had improved the quality of their environment. If your holiday can qualitatively improve the lives of just a few people, it is time and money well spent.

Inevitably a short-term community project will be of huge benefit to the participant. Being confronted with the brutal side of poverty can be overwhelming. Melissa Shulz, writing in *Transitions Abroad* warns: *'Expect feelings of guilt, shock and depression, but don't let these feelings overwhelm you'*. The experience will undoubtedly be rewarding and will broaden your understanding of poverty. As Amy Wopat, who spent time helping to empower women in Bolivia, puts it: *'By the end of the experience, you will most likely have gained much more than you hoped to give'*. Part of the appeal of a project working with people is that it allows you to engage with the country and its culture on a far more profound level. On a package holiday, lengthy conversations with locals are likely to be limited to haggling over some trinket, or complaining that there is no hot water. While working on a community project, you will work together with community leaders and have the chance to really understand the issues that hamper their daily lives, as well as getting a unique insight into what life is really like in that country. More often than not you will also be invited into the homes and hearts of those you are helping. Justine Reilly, writing in *The Guardian*, describes an encounter with a local while on a volunteer holiday in Sri Lanka:

'Before I know it, this new acquaintance is inviting me to his café.

"But I am with a group," I say, "I have to get back".

"Bring them too!" he enthuses as he serves me a delicious roti and pulls the cap off a chilled bottle of coke

"But I have no money on me."

"It's OK!" he says. "You eat."

So here I am, on holiday from a comfortable life in London, and here he is, a man who lives in a town that has seen far more than its fair share of misfortune. Yet it is he who is looking after me.'

The options for short-term community volunteering projects are limited only by your preference, time and budget. You can join the likes of ex-US President Jimmy Carter, and Brad Pitt in building homes for the poor (Habitat for Humanity), deliver aid on horseback to rural communities in India (Relief Riders International), work with orphans in Mongolia (Involvement Volunteers Association), work on construction projects, whilst learning about Cuban culture (Cuba Solidarity Campaign), help with HIV education and at local AIDS drop-in centres in South Africa (GoXplore), and work on irrigation schemes while living and travelling with Bedouin tribes in Egypt (Wind, Sand and Stars). You can choose to rough it, living at the local standards without running water, or sleeping with eight other people on the floor; or you can combine your volunteer work with an element of comparative luxury, staying at three-star hotels with one of the mainstream voluntourism tour operators. You can spend all of your holiday time working on a project, or you can combine volunteer work with more traditional sightseeing and relaxation. The only certainty is that you, as a participant, will throw yourself fully into the task of improving the lives of others, and return home feeling both refreshed and fulfilled.

The Ethics Box: Responsible Tourism

Put simply responsible or ethical tourism is the practice of adding value to and benefiting the societies and communities that you visit, whilst minimising the negative side effects of tourism to both the destination and the global environment. These are issues that you should consider every time you go on holiday, but they are particularly pertinent to a community project. After all, the very point of such a trip is to benefit the community in some way. It would be fairly contradictory to spend time educating locals about sustainable living, while staying at a multinational chain hotel that employs no local staff. The responsible tourist demonstrates both an awareness of, and a respect for, the culture, history, beliefs and practices of the local community, and the economic and social needs of the destination.

What this means in practice, is that before choosing a volunteer organisation or voluntourism tour operator, participants should always investigate their commitment to the destination and the people who live there. If the organisation puts voluntourists up in hotels for example, they should only use hotels with strong links to the local community, and preferably those that are owned and managed by local people. These organisations should also employ local guides, drivers and other staff, and they should ensure that locals receive a fair wage and conditions of employment.

It is also up to you, the voluntourist, to ensure that your visit provides the maximum benefit to the local economy. You can do this in many ways, for example, by purchasing local goods and services, and by eating out at local restaurants. You should also employ local people for any services that you require. All of these fairly small actions will help to boost the impact of your spending on the local economy. Remember that in developing countries, a little can go a very long way.

Aidcamps International

Duration: Min. 1 week
Location: India, Nepal, Sri Lanka or Cameroon
Season: Year round
Prerequisites: Min. age 18. Possibilities for families
Organisation: Registered UK charity. Its primary purpose is to provide grassroots development aid to local communities in developing countries

☎ 020 8291 6181
🖱 info@aidcamps.org
💻 www.aidcamps.org

Description: Volunteers of all ages take part in various projects including renovating a school for disabled children in India, village water projects in Cameroon, working with deaf and blind children in Sri Lanka, and providing assistance at an orphanage in Nepal. Group AidCamps allow you to join a team of volunteers to implement community development aid projects. Independent AidCamps place individuals
Accommodation: Provided in local houses taken over by the organisation for Group AidCamp participants. Weekends in a local hotel on a twin share basis. Accommodation for independent volunteers arranged but at volunteers' expense
Cost: Group participants pay a registration fee of £180 and a minimum donation of £415 for 3 weeks. Flights not included. Independent placements cost £300 for up to 3 weeks, £400 for 4 weeks, plus a £45 registration fee. Travel, food and accommodation are not included

Airline Ambassadors International

Duration: Min. 4 days
Location: Worldwide
Season: Year round
Prerequisites: Min. age 18
Organisation: A non-profit organisation affiliated to the United Nations that promotes 'travelling to make a difference'

☎ +1 (650) 728 7844
🖱 missions@airlineamb.org
💻 www.airlineamb.org

Description: AAI members participate in hands-on relief and development projects around the world, hand-delivering humanitarian aid to children in orphanages, clinics and remote communities and escorting children-in-need to hospitals for donated medical care. Trips take place throughout the year. Some are organised by AAI and others by individual AAI members. Having delivered aid, participants have the opportunity to take part in community projects on the ground, such as building an orphanage or library. There are three types of trip. Class A trips are an introduction to humanitarian missions, are fairly comfortable and include some tourism, Class B trips are more work oriented, and Class C trips have a lower comfort level and involve hard work
Accommodation: Class A: Provided in 4 or 5 star hotels; Class B: provided in boutique hotels; Class C: tents or mattresses
Cost: The basic membership of US$50 per year enables volunteers to participate in AAI programmes. Once on a mission, participants pay all of their own expenses. Class A trips cost around US$100 per day, Class B US$60–80 per day, Class C missions are under US$60 per day

COMMUNITY AND DEVELOPMENT

WORLDWIDE

Amizade

Duration: 1–3 weeks
Location: Bolivia, Brazil, Jamaica, India, Mexico, Northern Ireland, Germany, Poland, Tanzania and the USA
Season: Year round

 volunteer@amizade.org
www.amizade.org

Prerequisites: Min. age 18 if unaccompanied. Senior and disabled volunteers are welcome. No specific skills or experience required
Organisation: Amizade is a non-profit organisation dedicated to promoting volunteerism and providing community service throughout the world. The organisation collaborates with community-based organisations worldwide
Description: Short-term volunteer programmes offer a mix of community service and recreation which provides volunteers with the opportunity to participate first hand in the culture of the region in which they are working. Past projects include a vocational training centre for street children on the Amazon, building additional rooms for a health clinic in the Bolivian Andes, and historic preservation and environmental cleanups in the Greater Yellowstone area
Accommodation: Accommodation and food are always included but vary according to project site from homestays to dorms and hotels. Meals are cooked and served by Amizade staff
Cost: USA projects range from £325 for one week; non-USA projects from £1,430. Price includes lodging, meals, recreational and cultural activities and transport to and from the airport

Community Challenges

Duration: 1 week
Location: China, Cambodia, India, South Africa
Season: Year round
Prerequisites: Energy, enthusiasm and a desire to help. Participants must also raise a

 020 8557 0000
 rufus@charitychallenge.com
www.charitychallenge.com

minimum amount of money for charity. No previous building experience required
Organisation: UK company servicing the charity industry
Description: By taking part in a community challenge, participants not only raise funds for charity but also help to provide positive solutions to the issues of poverty housing. CC organises a series of team challenges that develop and motivate staff, provide assistance to the developing world and provide hands-on help with communities in Africa and Asia, such as the orphans crisis in South Africa and poverty housing in India. Participants help local families to build affordable housing, helping to break the cycle of poverty and hopelessness that inadequate housing creates. The work will involve digging foundations, mixing concrete, moving and laying blocks for walls, roofing, plastering and painting
Accommodation: Provided in a range of hotels
Cost: Prices start from £1295 per person, plus minimum sponsorship

Concordia

Duration: 2–4 weeks
Location: Worldwide
Season: June – September, although there are some spring and autumn projects
Prerequisites: Min. age 18. There are some projects available for 16–17 year olds. Generally, no special skills or experience are required but real motivation and commitment is essential. Some projects require basic foreign language skills
Organisation: Small, not-for-profit charity working in close co-operation with over 80 independent partner organisations which share a common involvement in short-term international volunteer projects
Description: Concordia organises short-term international volunteer projects working on community-based schemes ranging from restoration and construction to more socially based schemes. These initiatives would not be possible without the help of international teams. The website contains a database of more than 1,600 projects including painting an orphanage in Ukraine, participating in human rights workshops in Serbia, and organising activites for street children in India
Accommodation: Provided free of charge. Varies from camping to youth hostels and village hall floors
Cost: Volunteers pay a registration fee of £110 for overseas projects and must fund their own travel and insurance

☎ 01273 422218
✍ info@concordia-iye.org.uk
💻 www.concordia-iye.org.uk

Cross Cultural Solutions

Duration: 1 week (Insight); 2–12 weeks (Volunteer)
Location: Brazil, China, Costa Rica, Ghana, Guatemala, India, Morocco, Peru, Russia, South Africa, Tanzania, Thailand
Season: Year round
Prerequisites: Min. age for unaccompanied volunteers: 18. Senior and disabled volunteers are welcome. Must be proficient in English. No specific skills required
Organisation: Non-profit international volunteer organisation and registered UK charity. CCS is a recognised leader in the international volunteer field, with Special Consultative Status from the UN and working in partnership with CARE
Description: All volunteers work side-by-side with local people on locally designed and driven sustainable projects. These include working with children in orphanages, conducting educational activities for teenagers, working with women's groups, caring for and developing activities for the elderly, and caring for the disabled and people living with HIV/AIDS. Volunteer programmes are designed to facilitate hands-on service and cultural exchange with the aim of fostering cultural understanding
Accommodation: CCS provides a comfortable shared house in a safe location for all participants. The accommodation is clean with basic amenities
Cost: From US$1,595 for a 2–week programme, includes placement, lodging, meals, ground transport and insurance. Airfares, visas and immunisations not included

☎ +1 (914) 632 0022
✍ infouk@crossculturalsolutions.org
💻 www.crossculturalsolutions.org

Different Travel

Duration: 8–17 days
Location: Cambodia, Galapagos, India, Morocco, Laos, Nepal, Peru, Sri Lanka, Tibet, Vietnam, Zambia
Season: Year round
Prerequisites: Open to all. Some, but not all, tours are suitable for accompanied children

☎ 02380 669903
📧 info@different-travel.com
💻 www.different-travel.com

Organisation: 'Direct Action' tour operator, committed to ethical and responsible travel, offering holidays that include an element of voluntary work

Description: Different Travel holidays combine sightseeing, leisure and relaxation with time spent working on projects. These projects vary from country to country, but are always run by local people and for local people. A selection of community projects is available, ranging from refurbishing community buildings, through to working with children and disadvantaged people. Whatever your skill or experience, there is always something you can do on a Different Travel holiday

Accommodation: Provided in 3-star or above hotels, with air conditioning, en-suite bathrooms and western facilities. All hotels are locally owned and ethically run so that local communities benefit from the volunteers' visit

Sample Cost: 13–day Southern India Adventure including helping to renovate a local school – £1,475

A POSTCARD FROM Post-tsunami Sri Lanka

Lorna Allen used her two–week holiday time to help people who had been affected by the Boxing-day tsunami:

I had been to Thailand just months before the tsunami hit and stayed in several of the areas that were devastated, so I felt that I wanted to do something to help, even if it was just in a small way.

We stayed at a 3-star hotel in Unnawatuna and we were working in a school for deaf and blind children, which had been badly damaged. We painted the furniture, walls and ceilings of the rooms, we put in a new water supply and taps in the toilets, and we repaired or replaced the fans and lights in the classrooms. Outside the school was an old playground, which had become dangerous and unusable. We repaired and painted all the equipment and made a new play surface which was filled with coconut shavings.

Our group really gelled from day one and we spent all of our spare time together. When we weren't working we went sightseeing. We visited a turtle farm and a spice island, and we even spent one day on safari. The camaraderie in the group was fantastic and two romances even developed out of a group of 10 people! We had a very special bond which none of us will forget and we are all still in touch.

While talking to a blind music teacher one day, I discovered that they had no instruments at the school so two of us found a music shop and bought a violin, drums and a selection of tambourines, triangles and maracas. The school then had a lovely ceremony to thank us, which was very humbling. Another group took about 15 displaced children to the beach for the first time since the tsunami. This was quite an emotional experience as many of them had been too afraid to go into the water before that.

If you are considering voluntary work abroad, all you need is a love of people and the willingness to get stuck in. Don't hesitate – just do it!

Foundation for Sustainable Development

Duration: Min. 1 week
Location: Kenya, Uganda, India, Argentina, Bolivia, Ecuador, Nicaragua, Peru
Season: Year round
Prerequisites: Min. age 18. A one-week orientation is required. Senior citizens welcome

☎ +1 (415) 283 4873
✆ info@fsdinternational.org
🖥 www.fsdinternational.org

Organisation: A non-profit organisation providing hands-on, service-learning internships and volunteer opportunities for professionals, students and retirees at the grassroots
Description: More than 100 students and professionals each year are placed with NGOs applying sustainable development solutions in environment, health, youth and education, women's empowerment, community development, human rights and micro-enterprise. The participant's knowledge and interests are matched with the organisation that provides the best opportunity to make a contribution. Participants support current projects and initiatives while learning about local development issues
Accommodation: Volunteers typically live individually with host families, ensuring full immersion into the local language and culture
Cost: From US$1,150 covering all in-country expenses including board and lodging, transport, training materials, health insurance and programme support

Global Citizens Network

Duration: 1–3 weeks
Location: Rural villages in Kenya, Nepal, Mexico, Guatemala, Tanzania, Ecuador, Peru, Thailand, USA
Season: Year round
Prerequisites: Under 18s must be accompanied by parent or guardian. Participants need a desire to work

☎ +1 651 644 0960
    or toll-free in US 1 800644 9292
✆ info@globalcitizens.org
🖥 www.globalcitizens.org

cooperatively with others and a willingness to experience new cultures. No special skills required. Seniors are encouraged
Organisation: Secular organisation providing individuals with the opportunity to interact with rural communities around the world
Description: Each volunteer team is partnered with a local grassroots organisation active in meeting local needs. Projects vary but have included the building of health clinics and schools, planting trees to reforest villages and assisting in local classrooms
Accommodation: Provided in homestays or in community centres. Participants sleep in beds, hammocks or on the floor depending on the project
Cost: US$750–US$2,050, includes lodging, local transport, most meals, emergency evacuation travel insurance. Airfare not included

Global Crossroad

Duration: 2 weeks (mini-venture); 4 weeks (summer escape); 2–12 weeks (volunteer project)
Location: Argentina, Bolivia, Brazil, Cambodia, Costa Rica, Ecuador, Guatemala, Honduras, India, Kenya, Mexico, Morocco, Nepal, Peru, Philippines, Sri Lanka, South Africa, Tanzania, Thailand, Tibet, Togo, Vietnam

☎ 020 8263 6095 (UK);
+1 (972) 252 4191 (USA)
🖱 ukinfo@globalcrossroad.com;
info@globalcrossroad.com
💻 www.globalcrossroad.com

Season: Year round
Prerequisites: No skills or qualifications needed. Volunteers must be mature, flexible and willing to help
Organisation: One of the world's fastest growing international volunteer organisations offering placements in 22 countries in Asia, Africa and Latin America that meet the needs of volunteers
Description: Projects match the interests, skills and experience of volunteers with volunteer work. Local coordinators handpick the best programme for each participant. Projects include working in an orphanage or high school in Argentina, with street children in Bolivia, with the elderly in a nursing home in Costa Rica, or with disadvantaged children in Vietnam
Accommodation: Provided with a host family, in a rented house, a hostel, or a cabin depending on project
Cost: Varies depending on project; from $846 in Togo to $1,499 in South Africa

Global Routes

Duration: 3–12 weeks
Location: Africa, Asia, Central and South America
Season: Year round
Prerequisites: All programmes are designed for high school and college students. Gap year students are also accepted. No skills or experience required

☎ +1 (413) 585 8895
🖱 imail@globalroutes.org
💻 www.globalroutes.org

Organisation: A non-profit, NGO committed to strengthening the global community and educating youth through volunteer community service projects in the developing world.
Description: Participants work side-by-side with host families on projects selected by the community, such as constructing a school, health clinic or community centre, reforesting surrounding areas and teaching in schools
Accommodation: Provided in the homes of host families or in group living quarters. All meals are provided
Cost: US$4,000 to US$5,000 depending on programme and destination. All fees include accommodation, food, and all in-country costs. Airfare not included

Global Service Corps

Duration: Min. 2 weeks
Location: Tanzania and Thailand
Season: Year round
Prerequisites: Min. age 18 (Thailand) or 20 (Tanzania)
Organisation: International non-profit service-learning company which cooperates with grassroots organisations in Thailand and Tanzania

 +1 (415) 788 3666
gsc@globalservicecorps.org
www.globalservicecorps.org

Description: GSC's programme offers opportunities for participants from developed countries to work together with citizens of developing countries on village-based sustainable development community projects. Projects in Tanzania involve healthcare, sustainable agriculture, and HIV/AIDS prevention (providing workshops for students, teachers or other community members). In Thailand volunteers work on health, education and Buddhism projects in schools, monasteries, hospitals and orphanages
Accommodation: Provided in local homestay accommodation. All meals are provided by the host family. In Thailand, participants can also stay in a Buddhist temple, a guesthouse or a hostel. GSC can arrange for friends or couples to stay together
Cost: US$2,325 (2 weeks in Thailand or Tanzania). The price includes meals, accommodation, excursions and airport pick-up

Global Volunteer Network

Duration: Min. 2 weeks
Location: Alaska, Cambodia, China, Costa Rica, Ecuador, El Salvador, Ghana, Honduras, India, Kenya, Nepal, New Zealand, Philippines, Romania, Russia, Rwanda, South Africa, Tanzania, Thailand, Uganda, USA (South Dakota), Vietnam
Season: Year round

 +64 (4) 569 9080
info@volunteer.org.nz
www.volunteer.org.nz

Prerequisites: Min. age 18. No special skills or qualifications needed in most cases
Organisation: A private NGO connecting people with communities in need
Description: Around 1,500 volunteers are recruited each year for a variety of educational, environmental and community aid related programmes. Projects include working with children in orphanages, health and sanitation, maintenance and construction, and cultural homestays
Accommodation: Varies from programme to programme from group living with other volunteers to living with a host family. Volunteers generally live and work in the same conditions as members of the host community
Cost: US$350 application fee to GVN covers administration, marketing and programme information. Programme fees vary from US$445 per month in Ecuador to $1,500 a month in Alaska to cover training, accommodation and meals during training and placement, transport for volunteers (but not international airfares) and supervision

Global Vision International

Duration: Min. 1 week
Location: Worldwide
Season: Year round
Prerequisites: No experience necessary
Organisation: GVI promotes sustainable development by supplying international volunteers, equipment, funding and training to governmental groups, charities, NGOs and communities around the world
Description: 150 project partners in more than 30 countries rely on GVI for volunteers, promotion and direct funding. Projects include community development, environment research, conservation and education. Volunteers benefit from support and training. Current short-term community projects include working with children in Latin America, Africa, India or South-East Asia and community construction projects in Guatemala
Accommodation: Provided in basic but comfortable conditions
Cost: Varies according to project. 1 week community construction in Guatemala £595. All prices include food, accommodation, full training, orientation, back-up and insurance

☎ 0870 608 8898
✍ info@gvi.co.uk
💻 www.gvi.co.uk

A POSTCARD FROM Santa Maria, Guatemala

New Yorker, Jill Ingoglia took a week-long break from her fast-paced lifestyle to combine Spanish lessons with a GVI community construction programme, helping some of Guatemala's neediest families:

I was searching for an opportunity to combine a break with an opportunity to give something back to the world. The short-term Guatemala project seemed perfect for me as I only had a week to spare. In that short time, I would build a stove for a family in need and enroll in 20 hours of Spanish lessons.

I had no idea what my accommodation for the week would be like, and I wondered if I would be able to get by on what little Spanish I had. I was also fairly daunted by the prospect of travelling alone, but as soon as I arrived in Guatemala, I knew I had made the right decision. I was lodging with Araceli and her eight-year-old daughter, Gabby. Though the language barrier was significant, understanding each other was relatively simple.

For the indigenous people of Santa Maria, the normal means of cooking is to use a pot over an open flame. This creates a lot of smoke, which blackens the walls and creates health complications for the inhabitants. My task was to work alongside a local mason and the family, to construct a new wood-burning stove that would cut the amount of smoke and carbon dioxide in the home by 70% and add 10-15 years onto the lives of every person in the household.

The actual building was hard work. The iron needed to be cut, dirt sifted, concrete mixed, and bricks set. The entire construction project took just two full days, but the new stove is expected to last more than 20 years. Looking at the finished product gave me a sense of enormous accomplishment. In just a short period of time, I felt like I had achieved so much. I had improved my Spanish, improved the lives of an indigenous family, visited a new and exciting country and met some amazing people.

Global Volunteers

Duration: 1, 2 or 3 weeks
Location: Worldwide
Season: Year round
Prerequisites: No special skills are required. Volunteers must be in reasonably good health and provide three personal references

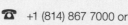 +1 (651) 407 6100
info@globalvolunteers.org
www.globalvolunteers.org

Organisation: Non-profit voluntary organisation that sends paying volunteers to scores of projects worldwide
Description: Around 1,600 volunteers are recruited each year for projects including caring for disabled or orphaned children, building and repairing homes and improving basic health services. Working in cooperation with local people, past volunteers have constructed community centres in Jamaica, provided care to orphans in Southern India, and created special furniture for Ecuadorian children with disabilities. Volunteers work as part of a team, led by experienced leaders who are usually members of the host community
Accommodation: In culturally appropriate hotels, guesthouses, community centres or private homes. Some accommodation is dormitory-style
Cost: For non-US programmes, the cost ranges from $1,595 to $2,595, excluding airfares, depending on project. For US programmes, the fee is $795. Discounts for internet users, students, groups and returning volunteers

Global Works

Duration: 2–4 weeks
Location: Ireland, France, Spain, Argentina, Costa Rica, Ecuador, Peru, Yucatan, Martinique, Mexico, Panama, Puerto Rico, Fiji, New Zealand
Season: June – August
Prerequisites: GW programmes are designed

 +1 (814) 867 7000 or
toll-free 1 800 784 6362
info@globalworkstravel.com
www.globalworkstravel.com

for students aged 14–18. Some programmes may require prior language instruction. Volunteers must have a desire to live, work and travel with others. Training is provided as part of the programme
Organisation: Providers of community service, cultural exchange, adventure travel and language learning programmes for teens and young adults
Description: GW offers community service programmes for high school students that combine a community initiative with language learning and homestays. Examples of past projects include house building in Puerto Rico, work with a daycare centre in Ecuador, and construction projects in Fiji
Accommodation: Provided mainly with a host family, but group housing, B&Bs and environmental centres and sometimes available
Cost: US$2,095–$4,995 depending on programme. Fees include room and board

Globe Aware

Duration: Min. 1 week
Location: Brazil, Cambodia, Costa Rica, Cuba, Laos, Nepal, Peru, Romania, Thailand, Vietnam
Season: Year round (except Thailand: November – May)
Prerequisites: No special skills or experience required. Min. age 16. Senior and disabled volunteers welcome
Organisation: Non-profit charitable organisation offering short-term volunteer programmes to promote cultural awareness and sustainability
Description: Globe Aware projects aim to provide greater independence for local communities. Past community projects include the construction of a community centre in Brazil, building a playground in Vietnam, first aid, language and sanitation training in Nepal, working with deaf orphans in Peru and building adobe stoves in various locations
Accommodation: Provided in lodgings that vary from simple hotels, hostels, shared homes, inns or a base camp, depending on project
Cost: Fees range from approx. US$900–$1,500 including the cost of meals, accommodation, on-site travel, medical insurance and donations to community projects. Airfare is not included

☎ +1 (214) 823 0083 or toll-free 1 877 588 4562
🖰 info@globeaware.org
💻 www.globeaware.org

Habitat For Humanity

Duration: 1–3 weeks
Location: 40 countries worldwide
Season: Year round
Prerequisites: Min. age 18 unless accompanied by a parent or guardian. Participants must be in good health, enthusiastic and motivated. No building experience required
Organisation: Charity dedicated to eliminating poverty housing and homelessness worldwide. Established in 1976, it works with more than 3,000 communities around the world
Description: Volunteers are recruited for short-term house-building projects in rural areas of economically deprived countries. Working alongside local volunteers and home-owners, team members assist people on a low income with construction projects. Volunteers are required at all stages of the construction. While volunteering, participants have the opportunity to learn about poverty housing and development challenges, and to observe and contribute to habitat's long-term work first-hand
Accommodation: Provided in a range of fairly basic lodgings. Food is also provided by local Habitat hosts
Cost: Varies depending on project and location but currently around £1,400 per trip plus donation. A non-refundable deposit of £200 is required on all projects

☎ + 1 295 264240
🖰 enquiries@hfhgb.org
💻 www.habitatforhumanity.org.uk

COMMUNITY AND DEVELOPMENT

WORLDWIDE

Hands Up Holidays

Duration: 4–23 days plus tailor-made options to suit any duration
Location: More than 35 countries worldwide
Season: Year round
Prerequisites: Min. age 18, unless accompanied by a parent or guardian. Generally no special skills are required but medical, dental, teaching, mechanical and horticultural experience will be matched where possible

☎ 0800 7833554
✉ info@handsupholidays.com
🖥 www.handsupholidays.com

Organisation: Leading ethical tour operator working with local suppliers, NGOs and charities such as Tear Fund and Rotary, as well as little-known local projects. A minimum of 10% of profits go to further development projects
Description: Hands Up Holidays offers ethically and environmentally responsible holidays that blend sightseeing with volunteering experiences. About a third of the time is devoted to a meaningful 'taste' of volunteering (teaching, repair and renovation, environmental conservation, house building) and the rest of the time is spent sightseeing around the country with local, English-speaking guides. Current projects include the 15–day Fiji Explorer, which combines a range of activities with a community project helping to build a house for a poor farming family. All flights are carbon neutral

Participant quote:

I had the experience of a lifetime on my trip to Vietnam. On the 'Hanoi & Hilltribes" trip we were able to experience not only the thrill and liveliness of Hanoi city, but also the culture and breathtaking scenery of the Mountain region of Sapa. The highlight for me was interacting with the local people, and being able to experience daily life, especially while volunteering at a local school and during our time spent with victims of Agent Orange at the Friendship Village.

It was a real delight to see the children responding to our time spent with them, and seeing how volunteers can make a real difference in people's lives – even if only for a few days.

We had two fabulous local guides with a real passion for their country. They had a real knowledge of its history and great hopes for its future.

To top it off we were treated to a very high level of service, accommodation and delicious food! I had the best holiday and can't wait to partake in some more adventures with Hands up Holidays!

Accommodation: Mostly provided in four or five-star hotels, eco-lodges, locally owned and managed wherever possible. Meals are provided
Cost: Prices start at £400 for 4 days in Romania, through to £12,000 for 15 luxurious days in New Zealand. Average price (excluding flights) for 2 weeks is £1,600

Heritage Conservation Network

Duration: 1 or 2 weeks
Location: Worldwide
Season: Year round
Prerequisites: Open to all
Organisation: A non-profit organisation
actively promoting the conservation of historic
architecture and sites around the world

☎ +1 (303) 444 0128
✐ info@heritageconservation.net
🖥 www.heritageconservation.net

Description: HCN organises a range of 'workshops' for people whose interest
lies in architecture, art history or historic preservation. Participants with all levels of
experience work side-by-side with community members under the guidance of a building
conservation specialist to restore significant historic structures. HCN receives calls for
assistance on projects around the world. Many of these projects work in collaboration
with the local community, such as the salvage and cleanup project below

Accommodation: Usually at a B&B or small local hotel with sustainable tourism goals.
Cost: Fees range from US$300 to $950 per week, depending on the project

A POSTCARD FROM post-hurricane Katrina New Orleans

**In the wake of hurricane Katrina, HCN volunteers worked on salvage and
cleanup in New Orleans. Trinidad Rodriguez was a participant:**

New Orleans in January [2006] was a ghost town. By some estimates, it had welcomed
back only one fifth of its pre-Katrina population. I was volunteering for a week on the
restoration of a hurricane-damaged home in the Ninth Ward. The entire neighbourhood was
still without electricity and running water, and it was illegal for anyone to stay there
overnight. You'd wonder why anyone would want to. Houses had collapsed in on themselves
and some appeared to have floated away. Cars lay on top of cars on top of mountains of
appliances, furniture, and all the little pieces of a well-established home.

Our project for the week was the home of Stacy, a former elementary-school principal
and a longtime resident. We began each morning on Stacy's front porch. After assessing
our progress from the previous day, we donned safety goggles, gloves and masks and got
to work on deconstruction, a more restorative form of demolition. The house was a swirl
of dust and noise as we tore off peeling wallpaper, hammered through mouldy drywall, and
pulled out wet insulation. When the walls were done, we set to work on the floors. Warped
bathroom and kitchen tiles had to be pried off and the rotting wood underneath replaced,
which meant first removing toilets, sinks and bathtubs. After a full day of this it was
impossible not to feel exhausted, filthy and totally satisfied.

Most days we headed back to the hostel, where the lucky and quick got the only 15
minutes of hot water the plumbing had to offer. On occasion, we put good breeding aside
and headed into town in our work clothes for a drink and a hot meal. The city seemed
to welcome us, showered or not, with open arms, and everywhere we went we listened
to people talk (and sing) about how much they loved New Orleans for its music, food,
culture, and sense of community. I would grow to love it too. It was my first visit to
New Orleans, and thanks to Stacy and her neighbours, and my fellow volunteers, I got to
experience the city with a richness not afforded to a typical tourist.

ICYE (Inter-Cultural Youth Exchange) Short-Term Projects

Duration: Min. 2 weeks
Location: Austria, Belgium, Denmark, Finland, France, Germany, Iceland, Italy, Sweden, Bolivia, Brazil, Colombia, Costa Rica, Honduras, Mexico, Ghana, Nigeria, Kenya, Mozambique, India, Thailand, South Korea, Taiwan, Japan, Nepal, New Zealand

☎ 020 7681 0983
✆ info@icye.co.uk
🖥 www.icye-steps.org; www.icye.co.uk

Season: Year round
Prerequisites: Min. age 18; a commitment to intercultural learning and the principles of ICYE. No formal qualifications necessary, just enthusiasm and open-mindedness
Organisation: Non-profit charity and international exchange organisation
Description: ICYE UK runs short-term exchange programmes worldwide with an emphasis on inter-cultural understanding and integration into local communities. The majority of projects are social and community based, such as working with street children, working in orphanages, HIV awareness, working in disability support, mental health, women's organisations, and construction
Accommodation: Most volunteers live with local host families. A few placements are at live-in projects, or shared lodgings with other volunteers
Cost: Prices vary depending on length of stay and project choice. Volunteers are supported in fundraising efforts and a discount of up to £300 is available for online fundraising

Imaginative Traveller

☎ 01473 667337
✆ ionline@imtrav.net
🖥 www.imaginative-traveller.com

Duration: 14–22 days
Location: Peru, Kenya, India, Thailand
Season: Year round
Prerequisites: Min. age 18 (but accompanied teenagers aged 16+ are also accepted)
Organisation: IT is a tour operator that aims to provide exceptional travel experiences, allowing tourists to relish the diversity of countries and cultures
Description: Imaginative Traveller volunteer trips combine volunteer work with an adventure holiday allowing travellers to immerse themselves in the culture of a country, to interact with local people, and to see the country as it really is. Several days are spent on a rewarding placement, but there is also plenty of time to relax and see the sites. Volunteer duties include supplying water to local families, building work (in conjunction with Habitat for Humanity), as well as a variety of cultural interactions and activities. Tours use a range of local accommodation, transport and staff, as well as supporting local charities
Accommodation: Tour accommodation ranges from jungle tree houses to basic but comfortable hotels. During the volunteer placement, lodgings are in local homes or shared rooms
Cost: The cost is broken down into three payments: tour, local payment and donation. 100% of the donation goes direct to the charities. As an example price, the Thailand Island Insight costs £250 (tour) plus US$100 (local payment) and a donation of £220

i-to-i International Projects

Duration: Min. 1 week. Early Gaps for 16–19-year-olds last 2 weeks

Location: 23 countries worldwide including Argentina, Sri Lanka, India, Bolivia, Kenya, South Africa, Tanzania, Australia, Thailand and China

Season: Year round, with two start dates each month

Prerequisites: Min. age 18. No previous experience required

Organisation: i-to-i is a leading global provider in ethical volunteer travel. It is ABTA bonded and internationally recognised with more than 12 years of experience and support networks across the globe

Description: Participants take part in community development projects that include working with orphans and underprivileged children in Argentina, working with women in Bolivia, working with children in China, working at artisans' cooperatives and on AIDS outreach projects, building homes for the disadvantaged in South Africa, and working at a community health centre for early childhood development in Tanzania

Accommodation: Homestays, hostels, guesthouses or campsites depending on project

Cost: Vary from project to project. As an example, 4 weeks in Argentina costs £1,045 including board and lodging

☎ 0870 333 2332 or toll-free in US 1 800 985 4864

✍ uk@i-to-i.com or usca@i-to-i.com

💻 www.i-to-i.com

COMMUNITY AND DEVELOPMENT

WORLDWIDE

A POSTCARD FROM Ho Chi Minh, Vietnam

Gillian Meek worked with orphans in Ho Chi Minh, Vietnam, through i-to-i:

Within about five minutes of starting work at the orphanage I seemed to have a hundred new friends following me around. It soon became apparent that there was no set structure to my day other than eating and sleeping. Initially, my day consisted of talking to the children, playing games, doing their hair, teaching English, colouring, eating, sleeping and generally giving the children some love and attention. I was given one set class from 3pm to 4pm every day with three girls aged 17 to 22.

Some of the children are very bright and we managed to communicate fine; others were a bit harder. There was one 15-year-old girl who speaks excellent English and I started teaching her to dance. I soon recruited lots of members to my dance class. In between the dancing and teaching, there was generally always something to do. All the kids want cuddles and are very affectionate.

I could go on forever as there are so many things that made me smile and others that brought a tear to my eye. These kids are so kind and happy and some are very talented. It makes me sad to think they may never have the opportunities that many of us do. But at the same time, they live life knowing no different and are very happy doing so. I just hope I gave them a little bit of something that will help them on their way.

International Executive Service Corps

Duration: Min. 1 week
Location: Worldwide
Season: Year round

☎ +1 (202) 589 2600
🖱 iesc@iesc.org
💻 www.iesc.org

Prerequisites: 10 years' experience in a specific field such as tourism, textile/apparel, agribusiness/food processing and NGO development; highly motivated; proficient in using computers. Retirees welcome
Organisation: A not-for-profit economic development company promoting prosperity and stability through private enterprise development
Description: Provides a range of services including technical and managerial assistance, training programmes, workshops, seminars, trade facilitation and grants management to small and medium-sized businesses and to business support organisations in the developing world. Volunteer consultants share their expertise. Participants are required to work six days a week while on a project and to produce a professional report upon completion of an assignment
Accommodation: Provided in quality hotels or clients' guest quarters
Cost: None. Airfare, meals, accommodation and travel-related expenses covered

Involvement Volunteers Association Inc

Duration: 2–6 weeks
Location: Throughout the world, including Australia, Bolivia, China, Egypt, Fiji, Latvia, Mongolia, Nepal, Samoa, Togo, USA, Vietnam and Venezuela
Season: Year round

☎ +61 (3) 9646 5504
🖱 ivworldwide@volunteering.org.au
💻 www.volunteering.org.au

Prerequisites: Min. age 18 (unless they have parental agreement). Knowledge and experience preferred but not essential
Organisation: Registered not-for-profit NGO that seeks to make volunteering readily available to those who wish to assist others anywhere in the world
Description: IVA offers a cost-effective way for people of all ages to gain practical experience while helping others as a volunteer and meeting local people and experiencing their culture. Individual or group placements are available in areas such as assisting with orphans in Mongolia, women's empowerment in Fiji, or helping a community handicraft business in Samoa.
Accommodation: Provided in basic but clean and safe lodgings. Varies from project to project
Cost: Fees are negotiated with volunteers on an individual basis. On average, a placement costs around £600. A contribution for food may be required in some countries

Madventurer

Duration: Min. 2 weeks
Location: Peru, Guatemala, Ghana, Tanzania, Kenya, Uganda, Fiji, India, Thailand
Season: Year round
Prerequisites: No special skills or experience required

☎ 0845 121 1996 or 0191 269 9495
✍ team@madventurer.com
💻 www.madventurer.com;
www.careerbreaker.com

Organisation: Madventurer combines volunteer projects and adventures worldwide with the ethos of assisting rural community development while at the same time enabling adventurous travellers to gain life-changing experiences through cultural integration, challenge and adventure
Description: Madventurer offers rural and urban projects on which volunteers work as part of a team alongside local communities in developing countries. Project options vary from building basic community infrastructure, such as schools and clinics, to teaching English, coaching football or volunteering in a hospital or on a local newspaper. The specially designed career breaker projects are for individuals aged 24 or over who are looking for a unique experience during their time out from work. Specialist projects can be tailored to suit individual interests and level of experience
Accommodation: Provided in local homestays or a shared group house
Cost: From £800 including food, accommodation and support

Mercy Ships

Duration: Min. 2 weeks
Location: Most opportunities in West Africa and Central America
Season: Year round
Prerequisites: Min. age 18, in good health and able

☎ 01438 727800
✍ info@mercyships.org.uk
💻 www.mercyships.org.uk

to cope with a stressful environment. MS offers both skilled and unskilled placements. Medical volunteers must be fully certified
Organisation: International Christian charity with a strong volunteer culture. Many crew and staff pay their own way, often by raising financial support from friends, churches and civic groups
Description: Mercy Ships delivers free world-class healthcare, relief aid and developmental assistance to developing nations. Operating locations include the Africa Mercy as well as land-based operations in Sierra Leone and Honduras. Mobile medical and dental teams establish field clinics to offer vaccination programmes, dental care and minor operations. MS teams also help with community development programmes including the construction of schools and clinics, water and sanitation, agriculture, micro-enterprise training and education on health-related subjects
Accommodation: Shared cabin on board Africa Mercy. Varies with land-based programmes
Cost: About £450 a month, plus flights to the location of the ship. Land-based costs vary

Original Volunteers

Duration: Min. 1 week
Location: Argentina, Brazil, Bolivia, Costa Rica, Ecuador, Ghana, Guatemala, Honduras, India, Mexico, Nepal, Kenya, Peru, Tanzania
Season: Year round

☎ 0800 3457582
✎ contact@originalvolunteers.org.uk
💻 www.originalvolunteers.org.uk

Prerequisites: Min. age 18. No experience required
Organisation: Places volunteers with grassroots organisations around the world. Includes supported placements and more independent experiences away from the tourist trail
Description: Original Volunteers was formed in 2006 by a number of former volunteers who came together to provide a network of grassroots organisations willing to take volunteers at a very low cost. Community and development volunteers are involved in administrative work, construction or organic farming, HIV awareness programmes, teaching English, helping with homework and preparing meals. 24–hour back-up support is provided on-site and from the UK
Accommodation: Varies according to project from homestays to hostels and hotels
Cost: One-off placement fee of £295 plus £15–£36 a week to cover food and accommodation

An Original Volunteer relaxes with children in a Ghanaian orphanage.

People and Places

Duration: Min. 4 weeks
Location: South Africa, Madagascar, India, Pakistan, Nepal, Indonesia, The Gambia
Season: Year round
Prerequisites: Most volunteers are aged

☎ 01795 535718
🖱 info@travel-peopleandplaces.co.uk
💻 www.travel-peopleandplaces.co.uk

35–60. All nationalities accepted. Volunteers' skills and abilities are more important than age and are matched with needs of individual projects, for instance child counselling, education or healthcare training or experience, IT skills, practical and trade skills
Organisation: Volunteer recruitment organisation for skilled volunteers of all ages
Description: People and Places provides various volunteer placements as requested by local communities, liaising with host country project management teams. Examples include: developing and implementing sanitation and hygiene programmes, basic training in small business and employment skills, building social cohesion and cultural preservation, practical help on orphanage projects or offering vocational training for children. No volunteers replace local labour
Accommodation: Provided in community homestays, small hotels or guesthouses
Cost: From £850 for 4 weeks, depending on project. Price includes orientation, half-board accommodation, airport transfers, a project donation, 24–hour support and regular meetings throughout. All volunteer fees are paid direct to the host country, and the company promises that more than 80% stays there

Quest

Duration: Min. 2/4 weeks (projects), 2/3 weeks (escapes)
Location: Southern Africa, East Africa, Andean South America and Brazil
Season: Year round
Prerequisites: Min. age 18. No qualifications

☎ 01444 474744
🖱 emailus@questoverseas.com
💻 www.questoverseas.com

required, just enthusiasm. In-depth interview and full training before departure
Organisation: Expedition specialists with projects and adventure travel to suit all ages in South America and Africa
Description: Quest places more than 300 participants each year on holidays with a difference. Quest's projects involve voluntary work on conservation and community projects for a minimum of two or four weeks. Current community projects include providing food and shelter to orphans in Malawi, and rebuilding centres to be used as clinics and schools. Alternatively, participants can enjoy an 'Escape' which combines a traditional holiday with a chance to spend one or two weeks working on a project, ideal for those who want to combine travel with volunteering but only have a few weeks to spare
Accommodation: Ranges from basic local housing on project sites to comfortable eco-lodges on expeditions
Cost: £1,800–£4,920 (South America) and £1,390–£4,240 (Africa)

WORLDWIDE COMMUNITY AND DEVELOPMENT

Real Gap Experience

Duration: 2 weeks – 6 months
Location: More than 40 countries worldwide
Organisation: The leading independent gap year specialists, offering the most comprehensive range of gap year opportunities

☎ 01892 516164
🖱 info@realgap.co.uk
💻 www.realgap.co.uk

Description: Real Gap Experience offers an opportunity to give something back to underprivileged communities in third world countries around the world. Participants in community volunteering programmes experience the true culture of a country, off the usual tourist route. Participants help within the community through education, conservation and community service work in a wide range of rewarding sustainable development programmes. Popular projects include house building in Guatemala, youth centres for street kids and orphans in South America, Asia and Africa, medical programmes in Malawi and Zambia, and working with tribal communities of Borneo and Venezuela. For the older traveller, Gap Year for Grown Ups (www.gapyearforgrownups.co.uk) is the leading specialist in career breaks and volunteer work, with hundreds of rewarding community and development projects all around the world
Accommodation: Varies depending on programme – ranges from homestays, volunteer houses, tented camps, huts and hostels
Cost: From £449 including accommodation, meals, airport pick-up, orientation, volunteer placement and tuition

Responsible Travel

Duration: Min. 2 days
Location: Worldwide
Season: Year round
Prerequisites: Depends on project but must be a good team worker
Organisation: Brighton-based online

☎ 01273 600030
🖱 amelia@responsibletravel.com
💻 www.responsibletravel.com

responsible travel agent which aims to improve the tourism industry for the benefit of the environment and local people
Description: Responsible Travel offers literally hundreds of community and development holidays around the world lasting from just a few days to several months. The majority last for one or two weeks. Participants are involved in all sorts of work, from improving the lives of disadvantaged people in India, working with children in Ecuador and homeless children in Tanzania, and tsunami volunteering. Volunteers work hard, but also have plenty of free time to explore the local area
Accommodation: Depends on project but ranges from village homestays to group accommodation, comfortable guesthouses and B&Bs
Cost: Varies according to project. As an example, 4 weeks spent on a Kenya water relief project costs £1,495 (not including flights)

Transformational Journeys

Duration: 9–15 days
Location: Brazil, Dominican Republic, Guatemala, Honduras, Kenya (Haiti and Mexico to come)
Season: Mostly in the summer, but some are available year round
Prerequisites: Min. age 15 unless accompanied by a parent or guardian. Senior volunteers welcome
Organisation: Registered non-profit charitable organisation dedicated to overseas travel and humanitarian service
Description: Participants on a transformational journey carry out short-term projects such as helping to build a school, clinic, church or community centre, caring for children, assisting with healthcare services, leading creative music, drama or dance workshops and assisting with religious and festive events. All programmes work with economically disadvantaged communities in developing countries
Accommodation: Depends on project but mostly provided in local hotels with running water and communal bathrooms
Cost: From US$1,600 depending on location. Price includes meals, accommodation, transport, insurance, donation to country partners and airfare from the USA. If you depart from another city, airfares will be adjusted accordingly

☎ +1 (816) 808 3668
🖱 tjourney@sbcglobal.net
💻 www.tjourneys.com

United Planet

Duration: 1–12 weeks
Location: More than 50 countries worldwide
Season: Year round
Prerequisites: All ages (16–18-year-olds required to travel with an adult). No experience or skills required
Organisation: International non-profit educational charity dedicated to fostering cross-cultural understanding, supporting communities in need and promoting prosperity among cultures through volunteer work
Description: Volunteers work directly with the community and the people and activities are designed to meet the specific needs of that community. Projects include working with orphans and disadvantaged children, teaching, healthcare initiatives, HIV/AIDS work, conservation and environmental projects, and sharing/teaching professional skills. In addition, United Planet develops special projects in partnership with local NGOs and seeks skilled volunteers, including healthcare professionals of all types, engineers, business professionals, computer experts, teachers and more
Accommodation: Provided in homestays with local families and some other lodging options
Cost: From US$495. Price includes accommodation, local meals, health insurance, pre-departure and in-country support, language lessons and cultural activities

☎ +1 (617) 267 7763
🖱 quest@unitedplanet.org
💻 www.unitedplanet.org

TOC H

Duration: 2 days – 2 weeks
Location: Throughout the UK
Season: Year round
Prerequisites: Min. age 16, no upper age limit
Organisation: A community-based charity
striving to eliminate social exclusion offering
short residential volunteering opportunities throughout the year in Britain

☎ 01296 642020
✆ info@toch.org.uk
🖥 www.tochparticipation.org.uk

Description: Short-term residential volunteers work on a range of projects including working with people with different disabilities, working with children in need, playschemes and camps, youth mentoring, educational programmes, conservation and manual work. These projects provide those who take part with opportunities to learn more about themselves and the world around them. A full range of volunteering opportunities can be found at the above web address
Accommodation: Usually provided as part of the project. The type and standard of accommodation varies according to the project
Cost: There is usually a minimal administration cost of £15 plus travel expenses. Food and accommodation is generally free of charge

Childaid to Russia & the Republics

Duration: Min. 2 weeks
Location: Belarus, Moldova, Russia, Ukraine
Season: Spring, summer, autumn
Prerequisites: Knowledge of Russian language is
helpful, but not always necessary. Volunteers must
be in good health. Those with skills and qualifications
are placed where they can be of most help

☎ 020 8460 6046
✆ info@childaidrr.org.uk
🖥 www.childaidrr.org.uk

Organisation: UK charity helping street children, orphans and children with disabilities in Russia, Moldova, Ukraine and Belarus
Description: Voluntary opportunities are available for medical professionals (including physiotherapists, occupational therapists and psychologists), social workers, project managers and management consultants to assist and provide training. Help is sometimes needed from carpenters, mechanics and plumbers to work on either vocational training or assist the charity's partners with building works
Accommodation: Provided in basic B&Bs. Hotel provisions can be made but conditions can be difficult
Cost: There is no participation fee. Airfares cost between £200 and £700, depending on location, accommodation from £100 to £300 a month, and an allowance of £100 a month is required for food

Bike Aid

Duration: 2–10 weeks
Location: Seattle, San Francisco, Hawaii, USA
Season: Summer (although Hawaii rides take place in December)

☎ +1 (415) 255 7296
🖱 bikeaid@globalexchange.org
💻 www.globalexchange.org/getinvolved/bikeaid

Prerequisites: Bikers must be in good physical condition, but there are no age restrictions. A medical release form from a doctor is required before the ride. Volunteers with disabilities are encouraged to participate
Organisation: A membership-based international human rights organisation dedicated to promoting social, economic and environmental justice around the world
Description: Bike Aid organises cross-country bike trips that combine a physical challenge with service learning and political education. While cycling across the country, volunteers stop in communities along the route and undertake volunteer projects such as cleaning up parks and painting houses. All projects are undertaken in cooperation with community-based organisations. Local community members frequently supply dinners and community activities
Accommodation: Provided en route in YMCAs, churches, gymnasiums, campgrounds and the homes of individuals
Cost: US$3,800, including accommodation and food

SOUTH/CENTRAL AMERICA AND CARIBBEAN

Alliance Abroad

Duration: Min. 2 weeks
Location: Argentina, Costa Rica, Ecuador, Peru
Season: Year round
Prerequisites: Min. age 18, good health, a desire to contribute. An intermediate level of Spanish may be required. No experience neccessary

☎ +1 (512) 457 8062
🖱 outbound@allianceabroad.com
💻 www.allianceabroad.com

Organisation: AA offers customised volunteer and cultural exchange programmes to participants around the world
Description: AA specialises in providing a variety of programmes to answer every individual need. Current community development programmes include helping children in orphanages, organic farming, teaching English and working in health centres. AA provides 24–hour assistance before, during and after the projects
Accommodation: Provided in a variety of lodgings, but most volunteers are placed in homestays with local families
Cost: 2 weeks volunteering from US$1,300. Fees include orientation, airport transfer in host country, accommodation, food and insurance

Amazon-Africa Aid Organisation

Duration: Min. 2 weeks
Location: Brazilian Amazon
Season: Year round
Prerequisites: Participants must be qualified
dentists. Other medical practitioners are sometimes
required

☎ +1 (734) 769 5778
🖱 info@amazonafrica.org
💻 www.amazonafrica.org

Organisation: A charitable organisation working in partnership with Fundação
Esperança, a Brazilian non-profit organisation providing health and education to the
people of the Amazon
Description: Although Santarém is a tropical paradise, the majority of people live in
abject poverty. Poor health, nutrition and dental hygiene are prevalent. Volunteer dentists
join with local dentists and hygienists to provide general quality care in the local dental
clinic. In addition to the care they provide, volunteers provide a valuable interchange with
local staff
Accommodation: Provided in a 10–room dormitory with shared bathrooms and three
meals provided per day
Cost: Participants need to pay their airfare to Brazil. Food, lodging and airport transfers
are met

Amerispan Unlimited

Duration: Min. 4 weeks
Location: Argentina, Bolivia, Brazil, Costa Rica,
Ecuador, Guatemala, Mexico, Peru
Season: Year round, first Monday of every month
Prerequisites: Min. 18 years. Some Spanish or
Portuguese language requirements depending on
placement. Senior volunteers welcome

☎ +1 (215) 751 1100
🖱 info@amerispan.com
💻 www.amerispan.com

Organisation: Amerispan represents 160 or more local organisations in Latin
America and offers language immersion, volunteer projects, internship placements and
educational programmes
Description: Most of the organisations that Amerispan works with are small, local
non-profit outfits. Volunteer work varies according to the individual organisation but can
include healthcare, education, social work, and student service co-ordinating
Accommodation: Provided in shared homestays with kitchen facilities
Cost: Registration fee of US$350. Prices of programmes vary depending on the country
and the length of stay from US$185–US$195 per week. Volunteers must provide for their
own airfare, in-country transport and meals during the placement

Cuba Solidarity Campaign: International Work Brigades

Duration: 3 weeks
Location: Cuba
Season: September and December
Prerequisites: Min. age 18. All participants must be a member of CSC and attend a preparation day in London about a month before departure
Organisation: British campaign for the defence of Cuba and its people's right to national sovereignty and self-determination
Description: CSC organises and selects volunteers for international work brigades to Cuba. Two brigades take place each year, one in summer and one in winter. Participants spend one third of the time working on either agricultural or construction projects alongside Cubans and people from all across Europe. Another third of the time is spent on a wide range of visits to schools, hospitals and farms in order to experience the Cuban Revolution first hand and show that Cuba is not alone. Entertainment is provided at the camp with live bands and salsa lessons. There are also excursions to beaches and places of interest
Accommodation: Provided in single-sex dormitories on a camp outside of Havana with showers, toilets, washing facilities, a canteen, shop and bar
Cost: £875 September, £950 December, includes all flights, accommodation and food

☎ 020 7263 6452
🖱 office@cuba-solidarity.org.uk
💻 www.cuba-solidarity.org.uk

El Porvenir

Duration: 8–15 days
Location: Nicaragua
Season: January, February, March, June, July, August, September, October and November
Prerequisites: Min. age 18, good health. No experience required as all tasks can be learnt on site
Organisation: Small, non-profit organisation dedicated to sustainable development in Nicaragua
Description: El Porvenir's main priorities are to improve the standard of living for poor people through self-help water, sanitation and reforestation projects and the transferral of skills to villages. More than 40 community-initiated projects a year in three regions of the country are supported by the organisation. Volunteers join local families in the construction of hand-dug wells, spring capture/gravity flow systems and latrines and lavanderos (washing facilities) and reforestation
Accommodation: Provided in modest hotels in nearby towns. Meals are provided with the host communities and in restaurants
Cost: $800–$1,200, includes board and lodging, all in-country transport, guides, health insurance and activity fees

☎ +1 (608) 544 2086
🖱 info@elporvenir.org
💻 www.elporvenir.org

Iko Poran Association

Duration: Min. 3 weeks
Location: Brazil (Rio de Janeiro, Salvador)
Season: Year round
Prerequisites: Min. age 18. Average age range 20–30 but accepts volunteers up to 70. All nationalities welcome. Positive attitude. Basic knowledge of Portuguese or Spanish recommended but not mandatory

☎ +55 (21) 2205 1365
✆ irj@ikoporan.org
💻 www.ikoporan.org

Organisation: A facilitator in the placement, reception, orientation and lodging of volunteers into programmes linked to different NGOs in Brazil
Description: Short-term volunteer placements are created and designed according to each volunteer's skills and interests. Volunteers are therefore able to step in and play a small role within an established organisation. Participants are assigned to various autonomous development projects and Iko Poran is always forging new links with Brazilian NGOs that can use the services of volunteers
Accommodation: Provided in guesthouse with shared rooms
Cost: Programme fee is R$1,500 (US$723/£369) for four weeks which covers lodging, placement, local transport and a donation to the host agency

Mar de Jade

Duration: 3 weeks
Location: Puerto Vallarta, Mexico
Season: Spring, summer, autumn

✆ info@mardejade.com
💻 www.mardejade.com

Prerequisites: No specific skills or experience required. Some Spanish language proficiency is helpful, but not required. Those who assist in the clinic must be qualified healthcare professionals
Organisation: A retreat centre in a fishing village near Puerto Vallarta on the Pacific Coast of Mexico, which offers volunteer opportunities
Description: Mar de Jade is a socially responsible resort on Mexico's Pacific coast. The resort offers its guests volunteering opportunities within the local community. These activities include assisting in a medical clinic, in an after-school children's programme, an organic garden, in cottage industries, or teaching English, computer skills or art. Any home-based skills, such as food canning and preserving, sewing and embroidery and weaving, ceramics and other crafts that volunteers can teach are welcome
Accommodation: Provided in a shared guesthouse
Cost: US$1,400. Price includes accommodation, 3 buffet meals a day and local transport. Airfares and Spanish classes are not included

Nicaragua Solidarity Campaign

Duration: 12 days – 3 weeks
Location: Nicaragua
Season: Summer

☎ 020 7272 9619
✉ nsc@nicaraguasc.org.uk
💻 www.nicaraguasc.org.uk

Prerequisites: No special skills are required but volunteers must be fit, adaptable and prepared to get involved in the work of NSC in Britain on their return from Nicaragua
Organisation: NSC works in partnership with progressive organisations in the UK to promote social and economic justice in Nicaragua. This includes organising study tours and delegations to exchange ideas and experiences with Nicaraguan organisations and fair trade co-operatives
Description: NSC provides opportunities for people to gain first-hand experience of Nicaragua on work brigades. The purpose of these trips is to exchange experiences and skills and to build mutual solidarity with Nicaraguan organisations. Groups live and work with the families of fair-trade coffee farmers for two weeks and spend the third week on a programme of talks and visits to organisations in Managua and other parts of Nicaragua. The programme can be varied according to the interests of the group
Accommodation: Provided with local families and in hotels
Cost: £530. Price includes preparation, accommodation, all meals, transport and an interpreter. Airfares are not included

Orphanage Outreach

Duration: Min. 1 week
Location: Dominican Republic
Season: Year round

☎ +1 (602) 375 2900
💻 www.orphanage-outreach.org

Prerequisites: No special skills or experience are required, just a willingness to help and a love of children
Organisation: Private organisation that provides opportunities to orphaned, abandoned and disadvantaged children in the Dominican Republic
Description: Based within the disadvantaged community of Monte Cristi, the Hope of a Child Orphanage is home to around 40 children. Short-term, hands-on volunteers are required to work in an orphanage in a variety of roles. These include tutoring children (in maths, art, science and reading) who are behind in their studies due to their personal circumstances, to work at camps during the summer in which the children can learn, but also have a great time. There is also volunteer work available on construction projects. Participants are immersed in the culture of the orphanage and the local community during their stay
Accommodation: Provided at the orphanage itself in summer camp-type facilities
Cost: $700 for 1 week. Price includes food, housing, ground transport and emergency travel insurance

Peace Villages Foundation

Duration: Min. 1 week
Location: Venezuela
Season: Year round; June – August is high season
Prerequisites: Min. age 18, enthusiasm, desire to spend time living in a different culture. Senior volunteers welcome. Some Spanish is helpful

☎ +58 (289) 416 0718
✉ email@peacevillages.org
🖳 www.peacevillages.org

Organisation: PVF supports and promotes communities to achieve sustainable development, social justice and peace. It is completely run and financed by volunteer contributions

Description: PVF carries out many types of project including working in the Tucusito school for children with special needs, living with Pemon Indians, teaching English, taking education to children not served by a school system in a mobile school, reforestation of the Gran Sabana, creating conservation education programmes, and carpentry and construction with ecological materials

Accommodation: Four types of accommodation are provided: camping and hammock, guest rooms, co-operative living and host family

Cost: From $718 for one week full-board and $473 self-catering. Price includes accommodation and food. Airfare not included

---

A POSTCARD FROM Venezuela

Martin Nielsen, who is studying social education in Denmark, joined Peace Villages Foundation's social programme in Venezuela. His work at Tucusito, a school for special needs children, proved challenging, but extremely rewarding:

Volunteering has always been something I wanted to do and this project had exactly what I was looking for: the opportunity to work with special needs kids, living among beautiful, isolated surroundings, in a community with other volunteers and since I'm from Denmark, warm weather. I did not have any basic volunteering skills before undertaking this project but I have found that working on a project is a good way to really get under the skin of a small local community.

Each day I walk to town (45 minutes down the mountain) and start the day by working in Tucusito from 8am to midday. Working with special needs kids is very challenging and puts you in many different situations. Lots of the work is centred around looking after the children and keeping an eye on them so that they don't run off and get into trouble. There is also a lot of stimulating work, such as drawing, physical therapy, music, and verbal training. After an afternoon siesta, I go to work either with the mobile school or in the local school and in the evenings I walk back up the mountain and make dinner with the other volunteers.

Getting a smile from one of the Tucusito kids is always heart-warming. I feel like I'm making a difference every day and that is very satisfying. Of course there are also frustrating moments. You need to adapt to the situation, the children need to adapt to you, and you both need to find out what works. From time to time the Tucusito kids can be very hard to deal with, especially when they are sad or rebellious, but all this is part of volunteering.

Peace Villages really is an opportunity for getting into a local community, making lots of friends from Venezuela and from around the world, and spreading your knowledge and skills.

Volunteer Bolivia

Duration: Min. 1 month
Location: Cochabamba, Bolivia
Season: Year round
Prerequisites: Min. age 18. A working knowledge of Spanish required. Those without Spanish language skills can take an optional Spanish course before taking on a volunteer placement
Organisation: VB is a private company offering Spanish language classes, volunteer positions and homestays
Description: VB collaborates with a wide variety of both private and public local organisations that require volunteers. These include orphanages and daycare centres, human rights centres such as women's organisations, local providers of healthcare, and educational institutions. Volunteers are placed upon their arrival, depending on their skills and interests
Accommodation: Provided in homestay accommodation or in independent housing that is shared with other volunteers
Cost: 4 weeks $1,450. Price includes food, accommodation, and the volunteer placements. Airfares are not included

☎ +591 (4) 452 6028
🖰 info@volunteerbolivia.org
💻 www.volunteerbolivia.org

A POSTCARD FROM Cochabamba, Bolivia

Amy Wopat decided that her free time between graduate school and the working world would best be spent by helping others:

The Volunteer Bolivia programme was recommended to me by a colleague and I was extremely keen to get involved. I had previously worked as a teacher with various Latino organisations in the United States that frequently need volunteers to help give them a voice, and during my placement, I was able to help women to empower and educate other women.

Some days we spent meeting with the women in order to plan for fundraising while others were spent helping to quash internal conflict. Some days were spent training the women to manage their time and resources, while others were spent training the women on how to use computers and the internet. I stayed with a host family. Being a vegetarian posed them a huge challenge but my beliefs were graciously respected by my host family.

This experience helped me to better understand certain aspects of the Spanish-speaking world and allowed me to get to know the culture and its people on a more profound level. I enjoyed helping others to help themselves and I equally enjoyed getting to know such great women.

The best advice I can give to anyone considering doing the same thing is to be open-minded, patient and understanding of your host culture. By the end of the experience, you will most likely have gained much more than you hoped to give.

Task Brasil

Duration: Min. 1 month
Location: Brazil
Season: Year round
Prerequisites: Min. age 21; love of children. Any skills in music, computing, TEFL, crafts, sports and lifesaving are particularly useful. Knowledge of Portuguese, Spanish, or Italian is desirable

☎ 020 7735 5545
✆ info@taskbrasil.org.uk
🖥 www.taskbrasil.org.uk

Organisation: UK registered charity set up to operate a network of services for street children in Brazil

Description: Through its Project Daiana for street children, Task Brasil runs the Casa Jimmy home for children up to six years old and pregnant teenage girls. Casa Roger Turner (an overnight shelter and day centre) cares for adolescent boys who previously attended the Street Approach Project, which works with children and adolescents directly on the streets of Rio de Janeiro. The project assesses their immediate needs and refers them to care, shelters or back to their own families. Casa Jimena houses young women between the ages of 18 and 22, acting as a stepping stone to financial independence. All of these projects need assistance from volunteers

Accommodation: Provided in shared apartments adjacent to Casa Jimmy, at Task Brasil's premises, or in the volunteer house

Cost: Each placement's fundraising target ranges from £1,000–£2,500, depending on length of stay including meals and accommodation

COMMUNITY AND DEVELOPMENT

AFRICA

African Impact

☎ 0871 7205439
✏ info@africanimpact.com
💻 www.africanimpact.com

Duration: Min. 1/2/3/4 weeks depending on project
Location: Botswana, Kenya, Malawi, Mozambique, Namibia, South Africa, Swaziland, Tanzania, Uganda, Zambia, Zimbabwe
Season: Year round
Prerequisites: Min. age 17 or 18 depending on project
Organisation: Leaders in the field of African volunteer projects, expeditions and travel. Facilitators of volunteer work.
Description: African Impact aims to facilitate the social development and economic upliftment of Africa through carefully designed volunteer projects, including a huge range of community work and development projects. Current projects include a community programme and medical work in rural community clinics in Zambia, community work in Mozambique, working with street children in South Africa, and AIDS orphan work in Zambia. Although all projects require commitment and responsibility there is also plenty of time to relax, travel and socialise
Accommodation: Provided in comfortable volunteer houses with large living/dining area, bathrooms and a garden
Cost: From £850 to £1,195 depending on project, including accommodation and 3 meals a day

A POSTCARD FROM Kenya

Sean Crawford travelled to the isolated village of Lodongokwe in Kenya where he joined other volunteers to refurbish a building that could be used as a base for a camel mobile health service:

The camel health clinic tours the bush, reaching people who would not otherwise be reached by health services. An innovative programme, possibly the first of its kind, the clinic delivers advice on family planning and carries out HIV testing and individual counselling.

We worked over a period of a couple of weeks, in which time a large and motley crew of paying volunteers, non-paying volunteers and some paid African staff renovated an old building which was originally built as a water-pumping station. We turned it into a base to be used by the mobile camel clinic. Local children arrived to watch – and ended up helping. The work was fascinating.

African Impact organised a brilliant trip and provided us with a rare opportunity to combine living with wonderful Samburu people and working in a wild and remote part of the country. It was the best experience that we could all have hoped for, with not a moment of boredom – and which hopefully gave a lot back to the Samburu community within which we had lived for three weeks.

I'll be back...

Assin Endwa Trust

Duration: 3 weeks
Location: Ghana
Season: August (but other dates can be arranged)
Prerequisites: Open to all, including family groups with children older than 15. No special skills or experience required

☎ 01245 475920
🖐 volunteer@endwa.org.uk
💻 www.endwa.org.uk

Organisation: A small charity based in the UK and Ghana, formed to help the people in the village of Assin Endwa in the central region of Ghana
Description: The trust offers three-week hands-on holidays that are designed to give participants a comprehensive view of life in Ghana. During the holiday, participants work alongside local people helping out with a choice of projects. Previous volunteers have built a garden and an infants' playground at the clinic. Current projects may include working on a playground for children or building a water tower and pump line. The work is broken up by well-earned breaks at some of the best holiday spots in the country
Accommodation: Provided in a range of lodgings including four nights at a beach resort
Cost: £295 including accommodation, excursions and all food and housekeeping expenses while in the village. Flights (about £650) are not included. Participants also need to fundraise £250 to support their work with the charity

GoXplore

Duration: Min. 2 weeks
Location: South Africa, Zambia, Kenya
Season: Southern hemisphere summer
Prerequisites: Candidates should be aged between 18 and 80 (although some projects have an upper limit of 40), as long as they are fit. No special qualifications or skills are required

☎ +27 (31) 765 1818
🖐 info@goxploreafrica.com
💻 www.goxploreafrica.com

Organisation: Youth travel organisation specialising in Africa that promotes safe, fulfilling opportunities for thousands of travellers from around the world
Description: The Kruger Area Humanitarian Project assists local people living in rural communities surrounding this national park. It has a holistic approach to supporting people to stand up against poverty, sickness and death. Volunteers help with HIV education, feeding schemes, as well as working and teaching at a rural school. The KZN Community programme involves working at local AIDS drop-in centres and hospices, rural clinics and building projects in KwaZulu Natal province
Accommodation: Provided in a farmhouse, including three meals, for the Kruger Area project and in a large house, dormitory-style with shared facilities for the KZN project
Cost: Applicants pay a programme fee, which covers food, accommodation, training, local transport and 24–hour support, excludes airfares. Kruger Area costs £160 a week; KZN costs £150 a week

Saga Volunteer Travel Projects

Duration: 4–8 weeks

Location: South Africa, plus new destinations to follow in 2008 (possibilities include Peru, Nepal, Sri Lanka, India and Vietnam)

Season: Throughout the year

Prerequisites: Volunteers must be over 50

☎ 0800 015 6981

✆ volunteer@saga.co.uk

💻 www.saga.co.uk/volunteer

Specific skills and experiences will be considered as part of the detailed process of matching volunteers to projects to provide a mutually beneficial experience, but everyone can make a valid contribution as long as they have an open mind and a willing spirit

Organisation: Saga Volunteer Travel is specifically for the over 50s, who have more skills and experience to offer than younger volunteers. It is linked with the Saga Charitable Trust (projects help to raise funds for the Trust, and some of the volunteers visit projects that are supported by the Trust). The Saga Charitable Trust is a registered charity, which benefits under-privileged communities at destinations in developing countries that host Saga holidaymakers

Description: Saga Volunteer Travel offers the opportunity for participants to give something back of their knowledge, experience and skills, to people economically less fortunate than themselves. For those who crave more than just lounging by a pool, Saga Volunteer Travel offers the opportunity to make a difference where it matters. Current Saga Volunteer Travel projects include life-skills and mentoring for high school students, complementary teaching support, community care support, and a school support programme.

It is made clear what the volunteer price is spent on, and the money is directed to where it is most needed. Only locally owned project management teams are used, providing employment and economic benefit, and a small proportion of the price is used as a contribution to the specific project the volunteer visits. As an example this might be spent on reading books for a volunteer providing English-teaching support. One previous volunteer used this contribution to pay for production of a CD of the school choir, which was sold and generated funds to buy school equipment. Another volunteer paid for a limited internet connection and taught students how to use it.

Participants stay in hotel accommodation with other volunteers and holidaymakers, plus they benefit from a named English-speaking contact person in the area to provide assistance as required. All experiences are covered by ATOL bonding with an ABTA member company, and the flights and accommodation are all included

Participant quote: *'I have come home with a lot more self-belief, self-confidence and self-worth'*

Accommodation: Full-board hotel accommodation is provided, with daily transport to and from the project

Cost: Prices for 4 weeks start at £2,399 for 2007. The cost includes flights, accommodation, transport, in-country orientation and a project contribution

COMMUNITY AND DEVELOPMENT

AFRICA

STAESA – Students Travel And Exposure South Africa

Duration: 2–3 weeks (mini-adventure); min. 2 weeks (volunteer placement)
Location: South Africa, Ghana, Togo, Benin, Nigeria, Cameroon, Mali, Tanzania, Malawi, Senegal, Zambia, Uganda, The Gambia, Lesotho, Botswana, Namibia
Season: Year round
Prerequisites: Min. age 18. No previous experience necessary
Organisation: A registered NGO promoting and enhancing cultural exchanges to more than 50 communities in 15 countries in Africa
Description: STAESA programmes are a great opportunity for students and professionals to gain hands-on experience and to see and understand more about African culture, while making a difference to the lives of many people. Volunteer programmes include teaching, healthcare, working in orphanages, classroom block construction, water and sanitation, HIV/AIDS education and teaching English
Accommodation: Provided in host family lodging, or at independent accommodation if desired
Cost: 3 weeks in The Gambia US$895; 2–week mini adventure US$650

☎ +27 (11) 910 4095
🖱 info@staesa.org
💻 www.staesa.org

Ugunja Community Resource Centre

Duration: Min. 1 week
Location: Kenya
Season: Year round
Prerequisites: Min. age 18. Send CV
Organisation: A community development NGO promoting sustainable development and empowering communities through increasing access to information
Description: UCRC acts as an umbrella organisation for more than 60 local community groups including women, children, farmers and people with disabilities. Programmes are divided into finance and administration, adaptive research and information technology, advocacy and networking and affiliated projects. Activities include sustainable agriculture, preserving indigenous knowledge, women and youth empowerment, health, human rights, food security and technology transfer
Accommodation: Participants can live with a local family (from US$15 a week) or rent their own accommodation (from $40 a week)
Cost: Participants meet their own airfares, local travel, accommodation and food costs. A suggested weekly donation of US$35 is also required

☎ +254 (57) 34131
🖱 iucrckenya@gmail.com
💻 www.ugunja.org

Volunteer Africa

Duration: Min. 4 weeks
Location: Tanzania
Season: May – November
Prerequisites: Min. age 18. Applicants are
interviewed and must undergo police and medical checks before departure. Senior
volunteers welcome

support@volunteerafrica.org
www.volunteerafrica.org

Organisation: International not-for-profit organisation recruiting volunteers to work on
community-initiated projects in developing countries
Description: VA places participants from all over the world to work on community
development projects in Tanzania. These programmes include building school
classrooms and healthcare centres in rural areas. The work is hands-on and includes
rock-breaking, bricklaying and carpentry. Other projects include rural development and
working with orphans and vulnerable children
Accommodation: Provided in specially rented houses or campsites in rural villages with
no electricity or running water
Cost: Participation costs for 4 weeks start at around £899. Price includes food,
accommodation, language training and in-country travel. Insurance and airfare not
included. Approx. 60% of the fee is invested directly into the host community

A POSTCARD FROM Tanzania

**Michele Moody used up all of her annual leave to spend four weeks
working with an NGO to build a dispensary and housing for health workers
in a remote area of Tanzania:**

I was looking for a project that allowed me to get involved with a local community in
Africa and do something useful for those less fortunate. I had been thinking about this for
a long time and after both of my children had left home and were no longer reliant on me,
I decided that the time was right. I am still in work, but this project could be taken on
during my annual holiday, so it seemed like an ideal opportunity.

The project allowed us to work closely with locals to really make a difference to
their lives. It was the locals who showed us the ropes when we arrived and taught us
the skills we would need for the project. The work was physically demanding. Each day
we would start at around 6.30am, we would light the fire and cook breakfast, pack our
lunches and head off for the site (a 45-minute walk). Most of the work involved making
bricks which could then be used for the construction projects. We would break rocks, make
aggregate, or mix cement, then carry the cement in pans to the brick moulds. At the end
of the day, the dried out bricks had to be stacked. The lack of resources made the job
even more tough. Getting enough water with which to mix cement, and stop the bricks from
drying out, was a real physical test.

At night we slept in a large 10-man tent with camp beds. It was reasonably
comfortable, if a little dusty and cold.

During our free time we walked to the surrounding villages to meet the local people
and encourage them to come and get involved with the building project. We also visited a
private hospital and a local school, where we were made to feel incredibly welcome by the
locals. It was this hospitality and gratitude from the local people that made all of our
hard work worthwhile.

Wind Sand & Stars: Summer Expedition

Duration: 4 weeks
Location: Desert and mountain regions of Sinai in Egypt
Season: July – August
Prerequisites: Participants need to be reasonably fit

☎ 020 7359 7551
✉ office@windsandstars.co.uk
💻 www.windsandstars.co.uk

Organisation: Responsible travel tour operator specialising in Sinai
Description: On the Sinai expedition, participants travel and live with the local Bedouin learning about their culture and way of life and working on a number of community-based projects. Desert, camel and mountain trekking are built into the expedition. Projects are chosen in conjunction with the Bedouin and are designed to ensure that they meet a very real need. Work can include clearing garden debris, dry stone walling, animal access prevention, irrigation channelling, well cleaning, and storage construction. Participants will also have the opportunity to learn about leadership and remote survival skills
Accommodation: Participants sleep under the stars, except for the last night which is spent at a hotel by the coast. All food and water is provided
Cost: £1,390 including all costs except return flight to Cairo. Many people raise sponsorship money to fund the expedition

WWISA – Willing Workers in South Africa

Duration: Min. 1 month or 2–4 weeks for group projects
Location: South Africa
Season: Year round
Prerequisites: Min. age 18
Organisation: Community-focused organisation that supports the development of independent sustainable projects for under-privileged communities through the work of volunteers

☎ +27 (44) 534 8958
✉ info@wwisa.co.za
💻 www.wwisa.co.za

Description: WWISA matches the skills and desires of volunteers with the needs of local communities. The majority of community projects are ongoing and include working on community radio, working on farming initiatives, managing the land and transferring skills to cooperative workers, addressing the social development needs of Kurland village through fundraising and arts and crafts projects, working on the community home and allotment centre vegetable-growing projects, and volunteering with women who manufacture and sell hand-crafted textile products
Accommodation: Varies from project to project, but is usually provided in communal venues
Cost: From £640 for a month, including all accommodation and meals

Adarsh Community Development Trust

Duration: Min. 2 weeks
Location: Anatapur District, India
Season: Year round
Prerequisites: Ages 18–40. All volunteers are welcome, but those with experience of small enterprise and alternative livelihoods are particularly sought after

☎ +91 (8554) 274492
✆ info@adarshcommunitydevelopment.org
🖥 www.adarshcommunitydevelopment.org

Organisation: An NGO serving socially disadvantaged children, their families and communities. Affiliated to and funded by the Christian Children Fund
Description: Programmes support the integral growth and development of children stimulating basic learning to support childhood development as well as health and sanitation projects. A Micro Enterprise programme coordinates with village committees to establish a village banking system to help rural families start their own businesses. Previous self-help programmes have helped people with bamboo basket making, cattle rearing, dairying, handlooms and other small businesses
Accommodation: Provided in a variety of locations depending on project
Cost: No participation fees. Participants cover their own travel, insurance and living expenses

Dragonfly

☎ +66 (0) 44 281073
🖥 www.thai-dragonfly.com

Duration: Min. 2 weeks
Location: Thailand
Season: Year round
Prerequisites: A high level of spoken and written English is required. No specific skills; training is provided for all projects. Good physical health
Organisation: A small English camp organisation providing governmental and non-governmental projects with volunteers, financial support and training in rural areas
Description: Dragonfly's Volunteer Thailand Project offers volunteer opportunities for anyone interested in helping local communities in the most rural and traditional areas of Thailand. Community development projects involve helping communities and grassroots organisations by building parts of schools or playgrounds, care-work in orphanages, and teaching English in government-run schools
Accommodation: Depends on placement but includes volunteer houses or homestays
Cost: 4 weeks £585, includes accommodation and meals and airport pick-up but excludes airfares

Go Differently

☎ 01799 521950
🖱 info@godifferently.com
💻 www.godifferently.com

Duration: Min. 1 week
Location: Thailand
Season: Year round
Prerequisites: Min. age 18 (unless accompanied by a responsible adult), enthusiastic, willing to work with local people. No experience required
Organisation: Tour operator specialising in ethical holidays and volunteering trips based on appreciation and respect of the local environment and people
Description: Current community projects include tsunami volunteering; staying with the Karen Hilltribe where participants help teach English to locals, and help out with farming and daily activities; tree planting and running an English camp on the silk roads; and on the Kiriwong Cultural Tour, helping with a range of activities including painting and repairing community buildings, working on waste cleanups and helping to develop English language resources for the Kiriwong Information Centre
Accommodation: Provided in clean, comfortable, locally owned guesthouses or village homestays depending on the project
Cost: Varies according to project. As an example, 2 weeks on the tsunami volunteering project costs £850

The Real Nepal Experience

Duration: Min. 2 weeks
Location: Nepal
Season: Year round

☎ +977 (1) 460 0210
🖱 info@realnepal.org
💻 www.realnepal.org

Prerequisites: Min. age 18. No specific skills or experience required
Organisation: Real Nepal aims to create an opportunity for Nepali youth to work together with international participants so that both can have a better understanding of their respective cultures
Description: Volunteers work on projects that include school construction (painting, plastering and more advanced work), teaching English to Tibetan children, improving health and sanitation, volunteering in medical centres, working in the fields with locals on agricultural projects, and volunteering in orphanages. Volunteers work around three to five hours per day on the project and have the rest of the time free for sightseeing and travel. Excursions are also organised, including rafting, trekking and jungle safaris
Accommodation: Provided in a family home or in a hotel on request
Cost: £400 for 2 weeks or £550 for 4 weeks. Price includes airport transfers, 2 days orientation, accommodation and main meals. Airfare not included

Rural Organisation for Social Elevation

Duration: No minimum or maximum time frame
Location: India
Season: Year round
Prerequisites: None

☎ +91 5963 241081
🖱 ilverma_rosekanda@yahoo.co.in
🖥 www.rosekanda.info

Organisation: A non-profit charitable organisation founded in 1981. Its activities include volunteer tourism, environment and agricultural work, community and healthcare, sanitation and income generation schemes

Description: Provides volunteers with the opportunity of experiencing rural Indian life while providing education and improving local sanitation and healthcare facilities. Volunteers carry out work in rural areas, including teaching English to children, construction, poultry farming, environmental protection, organic farming, agricultural work, recycling paper to make handmade greetings cards, office work, compiling project proposals, reports and healthcare

Accommodation: Provided in a family home

Cost: Application/registration fee of £45. Volunteers pay their own travel costs and about £4.50 (350 Rupees) a day towards board and lodging costs, administration, guide, telephone, internet and school expenses

Relief Riders International

Duration: 15 days
Location: India
Season: October – March
Prerequisites: Open to all
Organisation: A humanitarian-based
adventure travel company that organises
horseback journeys in developing countries

☎ +1 (413) 329 5876
🖱 info@reliefridersinternational.com
💻 www.reliefridersinternational.com

Description: A maximum of 15 riders embark on a 15–day journey on horseback to five remote villages in rural Rajasthan. Riders deliver relief supplies, books, educational information, medicine and goats to villagers, as well as helping a team of medical professionals set up and run a medical and free eye surgery camp. At the beginning of the journey all participants are assigned certain responsibilities based on their skills and experience. The journey passes through areas of great natural beauty with ancient villages and forts. Along the way participants enjoy the region's unique cultural life
Accommodation: Provided in hotels, forts, a traditional villa and, for the majority of the expedition, tents
Cost: US$6,300, includes lodging and meals. Airfares not included

---

A POSTCARD FROM rural Rajasthan

69-year-old Shirley Campbell trekked through India on horseback, delivering essential aid and relief to rural village communities:

I had always admired those who took their vacations doing relief work, and envied riders on long horseback treks, but with my age and infirmities (arthritis, a mild heart condition and a significant hearing loss) had not thought I could handle the inevitable physical challenges. Now here was a trip that combined riding and relief work... perhaps...?

The idea was intriguing. Within a few hours I had signed up, within 24 hours I was in a major panic. What was I doing?

I went for a riding lesson and bumped along like a sack of potatoes over the frozen ground on a horse too wide for me; I ached for days. My anxiety reached gut-wrenching, insomniac, levels. This trip was obviously a crazy idea!... Luckily, at this point Relief Riders telephoned to check on my progress and patiently administered encouragement, suggesting that I take as many riding lessons as possible before departure.

The ride turned out to be the most exhilarating, unforgettable, trip I have ever taken. I discovered that I could ride, and revelled in it, cantering along soft, sandy country lanes between brilliantly green fields, where the wheat flourished in a Rajasthani spring. Everywhere we went we were greeted by villagers who turned out to wave and smile.

Co-sponsored by the Indian Red Cross, the expedition was accompanied by camel carts carrying medicines, as well as notebooks, pencils, crayons etc to be distributed at the poorest schools in the area. Doctors with the Indian Red Cross met us at village centres where we helped to organise clinics, hand out medicines, and assist in registration. Some of our group helped with dental procedures and shots, freeing the doctors to focus on diagnosis and treatment. Eye and ear problems were very common; one boy needed rabies shots his family couldn't afford (we contributed about four dollars each to pay for them), aches and sprains were treated and a gynaecologist, a paediatrician and an ophthalmologist were on hand when possible.

At two stops, we delivered goats to some of the villagers. Most of the recipients were women, many of them remaining veiled before the crowd while accepting their nanny-goat and sometimes a kid. Goat meat and goat milk are staples in this part of the world and the goats would be bred to provide continuous milk for sustenance.

For four of our 12 first nights we stayed in tents, circular yurt-like structures 20 feet in diameter lined with Indian cottons. With only two people to a tent they were spacious, and comfortable. Flat woven rugs, easily swept with the brooms provided, covered the floor and we had camp beds with colourful bed linens, a table, a candle, a mirror and our belongings, all in place and ready for us when we rode into camp. Like Victorian explorers with their retinues of bearers and cooks, we had all our needs taken care of. Meals were cooked and served for us, combinations of mildly flavoured, delicately seasoned vegetables, curries and rice. Every night after dinner we sat around a bonfire. Several evenings the men performed traditional Rajasthani songs and dances for us. The rest of the time, we stayed in forts and Havelis,

Relief Riders hopes that these trips will provide life-changing experiences for the participants; I suspect that this will be true for me, maybe it already is.

Alexander Souri, founder of Relief Riders International, rides alongside volunteers through rural Rajasthan, India.

HANDS-ON
International
Workcamps

TEMPORARY INTERNATIONAL COMMUNITIES

What is a Workcamp?

Volunteer projects known as workcamps offer an attractive alternative to volunteer projects requiring large amounts of time and money. They generally last from two to four weeks, bringing together a temporary international community of 10–20 volunteers from different backgrounds, to work together providing services to local community projects. Workcamps offer an inexpensive (sometimes as little as £50!) and incredibly rewarding way to go abroad, usually during the summer. They enable unskilled volunteers to become involved in useful work for the community, to meet people from many different backgrounds and to increase their awareness of other lifestyles, social problems and their responsibility to society.

The term 'workcamp' is falling out of favour and these days is often replaced by 'project'. However, as part of an established international network of voluntary organisations they are not subject to the irregularities of some privately run projects, and being so cheap, they are less susceptible to being run by profit-motivated and irresponsible organisations.

The workcamp concept has a long and impressive history. The very first workcamp was led by Swiss pacifist and Quaker, Pierre Ceresole, who took a small international team to reconstruct a French village destroyed during the First World War. He hoped that such projects would provide an alternative to military service and his efforts later evolved into Service Civil International (SCI), today one of the largest workcamp organisations with 33 branches worldwide.

During the next 25 years, new workcamp organisations experimented with disaster relief and social, environmental and Third World developmental projects, until the modern workcamp formula was perfected, and gained UN recognition. Since then, the workcamp movement has steadily grown on a global scale adapting to new aims for sustainable development, national independence, racial equality and ecological protection. The movement is now active in more than 90 countries worldwide.

Workcamps are perfect for people who want to get some experience volunteering, either in a specific field, or in general, as participants are not expected to have any qualifications or specific skills. They are also ideal for those who are not skilled enough in the host country's language for more advanced work. Because workcamps are intended as short-term international communities, the communal language is usually English (although for those who wish to improve their language skills, a number of camps operate in French, German or Spanish). Finally workcamps suit those who are looking for something beyond just travelling, but do not have the resources for a long-term stay.

Workcamps should not be seen first as a means of accomplishing individual goals such as travelling in a particular area, improving language skills, gaining CV points or having a cheap holiday. Nevertheless, these are all things that can feasibly be achieved during a short period. More important is that participation in a workcamp makes it possible to experience different areas of countries and cultures not usually accessible to foreigners. It is a unique opportunity for people of different nationalities, ages, abilities, social, cultural and religious backgrounds to live, work and cooperate together. According to journalist

April Thompson, *'Ultimately, volunteers get back much more than the time and tiny amount of money they give. By working with people from a variety of cultures, volunteers transcend a country's tourist façade and transform their own sense of the world'.*

What to Expect

The Work: Volunteers carry out unskilled tasks. Many projects are environmental and involve the conversion/reconstruction of historic buildings and building community facilities. Interesting projects include building adventure playgrounds for children and renovating an open-air museum in Latvia, organising youth concerts in Armenia, constructing boats for sea-cleaning in Japan, looking after a farm-school in Slovakia during the holidays, helping peasant farmers in central France to stay on their land, forest-fire spotting in Italy, plus a whole range of schemes with the disabled and elderly, conservation work and the study of social and political issues. Projects are on-going and although individual participants cannot expect to make a huge difference in just a few weeks, they are part of a larger movement that will. Sometimes just the very act of international cooperation can be a major achievement in itself, as Russell Carlock found when he joined a workcamp in Bosnia:

> *I joined a group of international volunteers to help Serbians and Muslims in Bosnia rebuild bridges and parks destroyed in the war. Bosnians still tended to be segregated along ethnic lines and tensions were running high, but in Bosanska Krupa I watched Serbians work together with Muslims to rebuild their country. 'Working together shows that Serbians and Muslims don't have to hate each other', said the camp leader, 'We can work together for common goals. We can learn to live with each other'.*

Participants can expect to give around 30–40 hours of unskilled work per week and to become closely involved with the local community, who will provide the expertise. Participants should not consider themselves tourists, or development workers. They are providing a service that otherwise would not be available (the work of the project should not replace work that could be undertaken by paid workers). Orders are not issued by workcamp leaders, rather the group discusses and guides, whilst individuals decide. If a participant has a particular interest, then this is often catered for by the workcamp.

The Location: Workcamps were once focused on developed countries in Europe, and the strongest movements are still in places like France, Italy and Germany. Nevertheless, these days workcamps take place all over the world. More than 90 countries worldwide have an established workcamp movement, and those that do not are visited by international workcamp organisations.

The People: Thousands of people from all over the world participate in workcamps each summer. The fact that their backgrounds, ages, religions, and nationalities are so different, is exactly what makes the workcamp such an interesting experience. Participants are able to view an entirely new culture both from their own perspective and from an international perspective. Wherever your travel, you will become part of an international community of volunteers who share your passion not only for travel, but also for learning about other cultures and enacting positive change in the world.

Although most workcamps tend to attract young participants, there are plenty of opportunities for older participants as well. Some workcamps are organised for professionals

A POSTCARD FROM rural France

American student Angelica Leone visited a renovation workcamp in rural France. Her rewarding experiences first appeared in *Transitions Abroad* magazine:

I was sent to St-Martin-Les Melle, a small village in central-western France. Our group of 10 from six countries and four mother tongues was assigned to reconstruct the ruins of an old lavoir, a stone building where villagers once congregated to wash their clothes. The council of St-Martin decided they wanted the lavoir reconstructed in the traditional style as an important part of their heritage. Equally as important, they wanted a group of international young people to come so they could get to know them.

Most nights (when we weren't too tired after mixing cement and building walls all day) we hung out with the villagers, playing volleyball or pétanque at the town hall, attending the fireworks show and dance on Bastille Day, or hosting an international meal at our castle. What an introduction this experience was to French culture! For the first time, I ate escargot and bantered with paysans. I knew our presence had been much appreciated when our tough 'boss', André the mason, tearfully videotaped our last morning together in St-Martin.

Volunteers live cooperatively; together we cooked, cleaned, and socialised with each other and with the locals. We had it made: villagers loaned enough bikes for all of us, drove us to the supermarket as we needed, brought snacks for our breaks and wine, beer and pinot for our dinners at the castle. We were constantly invited to this or that event and we were even interviewed for the local paper and the TV news. One member of the mayor's staff volunteered to help drive us and show us around the region. Thanks to Sam, we spent one weekend canoeing and another camping by the ocean.

The Turks at my camp could not speak a word of French while the Belgians could not speak English, but everyone helped each other out so we all understood what was going on. Thanks to the numerous challenges of living and working together – having to cooperate on so many different levels – we got to know and appreciate each other as individuals and as people from other countries. I felt so gratified to be 'out there' putting my language skills to good use and really getting to know French people, not just being another American student passing through. In St-Martin, I was the only person from the western hemisphere.

who have experience of the type of work to be done in the camp. Volunteers for Peace, for example, arranges mixed-age workcamps. There are also teen and family camps for those who wish to mix with people in a similar situation. Nevertheless, most people choose a camp based more on what they want to do than on the age group.

On all projects there will be one or more responsible people acting as leaders or coordinators for the work. Leaders live and work with the volunteers and are usually volunteers themselves, though they have been selected and trained by the hosting organisation.

Living Conditions: Every camp is different, but you should expect living conditions to be fairly basic. Volunteers may sleep in a school, a church, a private home, a community centre, and as the name suggests, often a tent. You will usually be required to bring a sleeping bag. This is not always the case however. Angelica Leone (see below) found herself in the lap of luxury in workcamp terms, when she volunteered in a small village in France:

My group lived in a 16th-century castle, now a retirement home. We had carpeted bedrooms, hot showers, a full kitchen, and even a microwave. However, volunteers sometimes live more rustically than this: our Irish comrade told us stories of camping in tents for weeks in the rain, bathing in lakes, cooking over a fire, and going door-to-door to ask villagers to use their shower.

Whatever the conditions, volunteers on a workcamp live cooperatively. They cook together, clean together and socialise with each other and the locals. The cost of food is almost always covered in the registration fee or by the camp, but it is usually up to participants to buy ingredients and prepare meals together.

Free Time: Participants spend their free time together, socialising and learning from each other's cultures. There are usually some activities outside the work programme, usually at weekends, such as visits to local sites of interest, sporting excursions such as kayaking and trekking, and discussions on particular topics.

Further Information

The vast majority of camps take place in the summer months, and camp details are normally published in March/April with most placements being made in April/May. Understandably, these organisations charge £4–£6 for a printed copy of their international programmes though a great deal of information is available online. It is necessary to pay a registration fee which includes board and lodging but not travel. Most of the organisations listed below place volunteers from their home countries abroad, but also receive foreign volunteers into domestic programmes. Within Europe, and to a lesser extent further afield, there is a massive effort to coordinate workcamp programmes. This means that the prospective volunteer may have to apply for workcamps in other countries through a partner organisation in their home country. This is not always the case however, so if you are unsure, contact the individual organisation to find out how best to apply. Potential participants from the UK should contact, in the first instance, the UK-based organisations listed below.

The organisations listed below represent merely a selection of what is available worldwide. Further workcamp organisations can be found at:

- www.volunt.net/iyvs/usr/ – A network of independent NGOs active in the field of youth voluntary service throughout eastern and central Europe. It is necessary to register in order to access the database of international workcamps.
- www.alliance-network.org – The Alliance of European Voluntary Service Organisations represents national organisations running summer workcamps.
- http://europa.eu/youth/volunteering_-_exchanges/work_camps/index_eu_en.html – A list of European workcamps.
- http://camps.sciint.org/ – The SCI's database of international workcamps.
- www.unesco.org/ccivs – The Coordinating Committee for International Voluntary Service lists more than 300 international workcamp member organisations.

Concordia

Location: UK projects and workcamps worldwide
Duration: 2–4 weeks
Season: Year round (but mostly June – September)
Prerequisites: Min. age 16–19 depending on project. No experience required

☎ 01273 422218
✉ info@concordia-iye.org.uk
🖥 www.concordia-iye.org.uk

Organisation: Concordia is a not-for-profit charity committed to international youth exchange
Description: The International Volunteer Programme offers young people the opportunity to join an international team working on community-based projects ranging from nature conservation, restoration and construction to more socially based schemes. There are two types of programme. The Standard Programme is Concordia's largest and includes workcamps in western, eastern and central Europe, North America, Japan and South Korea. The North South Programme includes workcamps in Africa, Asia and Latin America. There are also programmes available in the UK
Accommodation: Provided in a variety of lodgings, from a fully equipped hostel to a bare floor in a church hall, depending on project and location
Cost: UK projects cost £70. Standard and North South Programme fees are £110 but for the North South programme, the host organisation charges an additional fee of £80–£200 due to lack of funding. All prices include food, accommodation and project costs

Service Civil International (SCI)

Duration: 2–3 weeks
Location: Worldwide
Season: May – October
Prerequisites: Ages 18–70. 16–17-year-olds can be

✉ ivssouth@ivs-gb.org.uk; ivsnorth@ivs-gb.org.uk; scotland@ivs-gb.org.uk; info@sciint.org
🖥 www.ivs-gb.org.uk; www.sciint.org

placed on some workcamps. No specific skills or qualifications required
Organisation: International organisation working for peace, tolerance and justice, and coordinating voluntary projects for people of all ages and backgrounds. The UK branch of SCI is called International Voluntary Service
Description: SCI's short-term voluntary work projects (workcamps) give people from different countries the opportunity to live and work together on a project with the aim of breaking down barriers between people and increasing international understanding. SCI offers concrete support to local non-profit organisations that work on human rights, international solidarity, social inclusion, anti-racism, women's issues, refugees, sustainable development and other social issues. More than 5000 volunteers participate in SCI work projects every year. Lists of projects are available online from late March each year
Accommodation: Ranges from mattresses in a school hall, to camping, and dormitories in a youth hostel or residential centre. There will be at least basic washing and cooking facilities
Cost: £90 for UK projects and £185 for overseas projects, including membership, board and lodging and project costs. A few projects may require an additional fee upon arrival

INTERNATIONAL WORKCAMPS UK

UNA Exchange – International Volunteer Projects

Duration: 2–4 weeks
Location: More than 70 countries worldwide
Season: Year round (with most projects June – September)
Prerequisites: Min. age 18, enthusiasm, flexibility and an open-minded attitude

☎ 029 2022 3088
✆ info@unaexchange.org
💻 www.unaexchange.org

Organisation: Non-religious, non-governmental, charitable organisation dedicated to promoting intercultural understanding and cultural exchange

Description: UNA's workcamps (called IVPs) take place all over the world and could involve anything from planting trees in Tanzania to organising activities for youth groups in Turkey; from renovating castles in the Czech Republic to maintaining national parks or clearing beaches in Italy. Projects fall into the following categories: environmental, construction, renovation, archaeology, working with children, cultural, festivals, teaching and study. Volunteer projects aim to support community development initiatives, promote cultural exchange and provide an opportunity to gain a unique perspective on the host country. Participants work up to eight hours per day with free evenings and weekends

Accommodation: Provided by the host organisation in basic lodgings such as tents, local schools, village halls, hostels and youth centres. Meals are prepared communally by the group

Cost: £110–£150. North South projects require an additional fee and training costs. Fees include food, accommodation, membership and project costs

A POSTCARD FROM Indonesia

Lindsey Moss volunteered with UNA Exchange on an Earthquake Relief Project in Indonesia:

Together with two other volunteers from the UK, two from Korea and four from Indonesia, I spent two weeks working in a village in Java. We were working to clear the ruins caused by the earthquake where 98 people in the village had died. Out of 171 houses, 168 had been either totally destroyed or partially damaged.

We were involved in clearing the school area of the ruins so that the field around the school could be ploughed and used for farming – a large part of the villagers' income. The local people were not able to assist us with this as they had so much of their own clearing up to do around their own homes. We also built a water tank, which the locals were able to help us with.

We would start work at 9am every day, clearing ruins. Sometimes the children of the village would come and try to help us. We worked in the open most of the day, so it was really hot, but it didn't seem to get us down. The work was hard at times, but we would try to sing and joke about to keep our spirits up. We had a lot of fun together while we worked.

After work we would sometimes play with the children, either playing football or trying to talk to them. I tried to teach one of the children a few chords on a guitar that he had. We would also sit with the family that lived near to us and talk over coffee. Lots of local people would come and join us in the evenings.

The night before we left, the community put on a show for us with all the local children singing and dancing. All in all it was a great experience, and one that I would definitely repeat. I felt really sad when the time came to say goodbye.

INTERNATIONAL WORKCAMPS UK

Youth Action for Peace

Duration: 1–4 weeks
Location: Europe, Middle East, Africa, Asia, USA
Season: Year round
Prerequisites: Min. age 18 (though some projects are specifically for teenagers). No particular skills required
Organisation: An international movement which works towards a society of justice, peace and human solidarity

☎ 08701 657927
🖱 action@yap-uk.org
💻 www.yap-uk.org

Description: Volunteers are needed to take part in voluntary work projects (workcamps) organised by YAP in the UK and through its sister organisations in more than 50 countries. The work undertaken may consist of tasks such as restoration, working with disadvantaged children and teenagers, environmental work, artistic and cultural events, etc. Participants work about 35 hours per week alongside volunteers from different countries and locals
Accommodation: Varies according to project ranging from very basic (tents) to quite comfortable (hotels) and occasional homestays with families. Generally lodging is provided in public buildings such as schools and community centres, with basic cooking and showering facilities
Cost: All volunteers pay a placement fee of either £120 or £160. This includes membership of YAP UK, food, accommodation, and the social programme. Any additional fees are indicated in the project description online

ORGANISATIONS WORLDWIDE

Action Reconciliation Service for Peace (ARSP)

Duration: Min. 2 weeks
Location: Belarus, Belgium, Czech Republic, France, Germany, Great Britain, Israel, the Netherlands, Norway, Poland, Russia and Slovakia
Season: June – September

☎ 020 8880 7526
🖱 grossbritannien@asf-ev.de
💻 www.asf-ev.de

Prerequisites: Min. age 18 (or 16 for youth camps)
Organisation: ARSP is a multi-denominational organisation founded by advocates of the protestant resistance against the National Socialist regime. Still supported by the churches of Germany, ARSP, conscious of the fact that the results of the Nazi past can only be overcome through intensive dialogue, works for a better understanding between cultures and generations
Description: Volunteers for the 'Sommerlager' programme help with the maintenance of Jewish cemeteries and memorial centres, work in social facilities and involve themselves in projects that support intercultural experiences. In addition there is discussion concerning historical and current issues. Groups work for five or six hours a day, with plenty of free time to explore the area
Accommodation: Provided in simple lodgings such as tents or bunkhouses
Cost: Participation fees are €130 (or €100 for students/unemployed). This covers accommodation, food, insurance and project costs

Ajude

Duration: 2 weeks
Location: Mozambique
Season: August – March
Prerequisites: No experience required
Organisation: The Youth Association for the

☎ +258 1 312854
🖱 ajude@tvcabo.co.org
💻 www.ajude.org.mz

Development of Voluntary Service In Mozambique was
developed as a reaction to the civil war and is dedicated to promoting solidarity, rebuilding
social cooperation and creating economic stability so as to provide people with access to
healthcare, sanitation and education
Description: Ajude organises 20 workcamps each year. Each camp is made up of
around 20 national and international volunteers, who are stationed at development
projects in communities across the country. The camps range in focus from construction
work, to nature conservation and AIDS awareness. There is also plenty of free time for
volunteers to explore the local area and participate in group activities and excursions
Accommodation: Varies according to project but usually in campsites with basic facilities,
shared dormitories or bunkhouses
Cost: Approx. US$220 including board and lodging and local transportation. Flights are
not included

Amis De Chevreaux-Chatel

Duration: 3 weeks
Location: Chevreaux,
Franche-Comté, France
Season: July/August
Prerequisites: Age 16–25.

☎ +33 3 84 85 95 77
🖱 accjura@free.fr
💻 http://accjura.free.fr/chantiers/chantiers_ang.htm

No experience required
Organisation: The association organises two international annual workcamps to help
restore the medieval castle of Chevreux
Description: Every summer, young people from all over the world come together to
help restore Chevreaux castle. The work involves clearing debris, reconstruction of ruins,
stoneworking, carpentry and archaeology. Volunteers are expected to work around six
hours a day under the supervision of trained professionals (masons, carpenters and
archaeologists). After work local recreation facilities are provided including a swimming
pool, volleyball, badminton, football and organised walks. Excursions to sites of interest in
the area are organised at weekends
Accommodation: Provided in shared tents with camp-beds on site, with washing,
laundry and cooking facilities
Cost: Registration and insurance costs €55

Apare

Duration: 2 or 3 weeks
Location: Provence/Mediterranean, France
Season: July – October
Prerequisites: Min. age 18. No upper limit. No prior experience required

☎ +33 (0)490 85 51 15
🖱 apare@apare-gec.org
💻 www.apare-gec.org

Organisation: An association for regional participation that organises workcamps dedicated to the restoration of historic buildings and heritage sites in Provence and the Cévennes
Description: Hands-on holiday-makers come from all over the world to workcamps that seek to strike a balance between practical restoration and heritage work (usually carried out in the mornings) and the discovery of the region through cultural and sporting events. The work, directed by technical advisers, includes dry stone walling, restoring a Romanesque chapel or a medieval village in the Var, or re-paving the streets of a Corsican village. Activities are organised for the afternoons and evenings
Accommodation: Provided by the local camps. Usually basic – camping, public hostels, school lodging etc
Cost: €95 (2 weeks); €130 (3 weeks) including board and lodging, leisure expenses and insurance

Association Alpes de Lumière

Duration: Min. 2 weeks
Location: Provence, France
Season: April – September
Prerequisites: Age 18+. Good physical condition. French or English language

☎ +33 492 75 22 01
💻 http://alpes-de-lumiere.org

Organisation: Environmental development association of Haute-Provence
Description: Around 150 participants from all over the world dedicate themselves to the restoration of historic buildings and the development of historic sites throughout Provence. Specialised stone masons train participants in local building and restoration techniques. The working day lasts from 7.30am to 1.30pm, leaving volunteers free to join organised activities in the afternoons. The emphasis of the camps is on enriching the participants' awareness of the culture and customs of the area. Groups are made up of between 12 and 14 participants
Accommodation: Mostly provided on campsites, but varies between projects. Food provided
Cost: Approx €120 for a 2-week session

ATD Fourth World

Duration: Min. 2 weeks
Location: France, Belgium, Spain, Switzerland and the UK
Season: Summer months
Prerequisites: Min. age 18. No previous experience required

☎ 020 7703 3231
✉ atd@atd-uk.org
💻 www.atd-uk.org

Organisation: ATD Fourth World is an international organisation working with families who live in extreme poverty in city slums and deprived rural areas throughout the world
Description: ATD Fourth World regards the existence of poverty as a denial of basic human rights and works towards the eradication of poverty, learning from the poorest and working in partnership with them. ATD organises European Workcamps and Street Workshops throughout the summer. Workcamp participants take part in manual work during the day while the evenings are reserved for discussions and exchange of ideas about the eradication of extreme poverty. Street Workshops provide a concrete way to come together with the most underprivileged people through the sharing of skills (painting, crafts, computing, communication, sport, music, reading, etc) to invent with them paths towards the participation of everybody in tomorrow's world
Accommodation: Provided. Varies according to project location
Cost: There is a charge of £50 to cover accommodation and food

Bangladesh Work Camps Association

Duration: 12–15 days
Location: Throughout Bangladesh
Season: October – March
Prerequisites: Aged 18–35. No special qualifications or experience required

☎ +880 2 935 8206
✉ bwca@bangla.net
💻 www.mybwca.org

Organisation: Voluntary youth organisation that helps communities, NGOs and others to learn how to cope with natural hazards by conducting local, national and international workcamps
Description: Young people from around the world are invited to attend workcamps which focus on social welfare, rural development, community and organisational development, healthcare, blood donation, environmental conservation, mobilising resources, relief and rehabilitation work after natural disasters and many other activities. Participants are offered the opportunity to integrate with a new society, culture, tradition and lifestyle, to exchange ideas at an international level, and to work together as a team for the greater good. Specific examples of camps include planting trees, construction work and organising temporary eye clinics for cataract patients
Accommodation: Usually provided in fairly basic dorm-rooms or bunkhouses with communal cooking facilities
Cost: US$200 registration fee per camp. Includes food, lodging and in country transportation

Conservation Volunteers Greece (CVG)

Duration: 1 – 3 weeks
Location: Remote locations in Greece
Season: July – August
Prerequisites: Ages 18–30, fairly good
English
Organisation: CVG is a non-profit NGO

☎ +30 10 62 31 120
🖱 cvgpeep@otenet.gr
💻 www.cvgpeep.gr/eng/enindex.htm

promoting conservation work and intercultural exchanges between young people from all over the world
Description: Participating in a CVG volunteer project offers a short-term opportunity to live and work in a group, visit new places and offer your free time for a worthy cause. Under the guidance of experts, volunteers participate in activities such as: working in protected areas, laying footpaths and installing signposts, planting trees and clearing undergrowth. Work can also include restoring traditional buildings, assisting in cultural centres, working with children and the elderly and participating in festivals and cultural events. During free time, local excursions are organised, allowing participants to get to know the area, its history and the surrounding natural environment
Accommodation: Provided by the hosting community in schools, youth centres, gyms or tents. Living conditions are modest but efficient
Cost: Participation fees vary according to the individual project

The Emmaus International Summer Volunteer Programme

Duration: 3–4 weeks
Location: Italy, Bosnia, France
Season: June – September
Prerequisites: Min. age 18
Organisation: International movement
dedicated to eradicating the roots of

☎ +33 (0)148 93 29 50
🖱 contact@emmaus-international.org
💻 www.emmaus-international.org

poverty and misery. The movement is made up of 350 communities, work cooperatives and volunteer groups worldwide
Description: Emmaus invites volunteers each summer to help out with work rag-picking and recycling materials to raise money for the poor. Participants work 35–40 hours per week, living among an Emmaus community, where they will meet new people from all over the world and discover the economic, political, cultural and social values of the community. The work is mainly composed of salvage, sorting, repairing and selling items. There are repair workshops for items such as furniture and participants learn a range of new skills at training and information sessions. During free time, the communities organise activities to help participants discover the region
Accommodation: Board and lodging is provided within the community
Cost: No participation costs. Volunteers must cover their own travel, medica
personal costs. Meals, housing and accident insurance are provided free of c
Emmaus

Etudes et Chantiers (UNAREC)

Duration: 2–3 weeks
Location: Throughout France and via partner organisations worldwide
Season: Mainly in the summer months
Prerequisites: Ages 14–16 (adolescent workcamps); Min. age 18 (adult workcamps). Any nationality. No experience required

☎ +33 (0)1 453 89626
🖱 unarec@wanadoo.fr
💻 www.unarec.org/welcome.htm

Organisation: UNAREC was founded in 1962 by several youth movements and is dedicated to non-violence, humanism, international cooperation and exchanges
Description: About 800 volunteers each year are needed for workcamps to help with a variety of work including restoring a village bread oven, cleaning riverbanks, organising a festival and working with school children in France. Overseas the range of projects is even wider. Around 10–15 participants are placed together in each camp and everyone participates in daily life from shopping to preparing meals and cleaning. Leisure activities are also arranged which involve discovering the region and meeting with local people. Workcamps are led by a team of two or three people who are trained and experienced
Accommodation: Provided. Often very basic and organised according to what is available, such as a school or gym. It is most likely that participants will be camping, using a big tent for the kitchen and living space
Cost: €140–€420 worldwide or €115 in France. Includes full board and lodging and insurance

EstYES: International Youth Association Estonia

Duration: 2–3 weeks
Location: Throughout Estonia
Season: June – September
Prerequisites: Min. age 18, or 20 for camps working with children, or aged 15–17 for teenage camps. No maximum age limit. Participants should be motivated, flexible and open to new experiences. No special skills required

☎ +372 6013309
🖱 estyes@estyes.ee
💻 http://estyes.ee

Organisation: Non-profit, non-political NGO dedicated to promoting youth and cultural exchanges
Description: EstYES workcamps concentrate on local development within Estonia. They provide an excellent and alternative method of getting to know Estonia and are a great opportunity to participate in a project that is of benefit to the local population. Around 300 volunteers are invited each year to work on a variety of urban and rural projects including construction and manual work, nature conservation work, social work and cultural work. These activities can contribute to the regeneration of particular areas and can support the work of local communities and NGOs. Participants work five to seven hours per day for five or six days a week, with plenty of free time to socialise and explore the area
Accommodation: Provided. Varies according to individual project but may be in farm houses, local guesthouses, bunkhouses or tents
Cost: A small contribution is required to cover admin costs, food and accommodation. This is usually around €65

Gençtur – International Voluntary Workcamps in Turkey

Duration: 2 weeks
Location: Throughout Turkey
Season: Summer months
Prerequisites: Min. age 18. No experience required
Organisation: Non-profit Turkish NGO

☎ +90 212 249 25 15
🖱 workcamps.in@genctur.com
💻 www.genctur.com/indexe.htm

Description: Gençtur organises international voluntary workcamps in small villages and towns involving mainly manual work such as constructing schools, village centres, healthcare houses, teachers' lodgings, digging water trenches, landscaping projects, environmental development projects or social work like teaching English to children or teenagers, organising social activities for disabled people, etc. Gençtur encourages the participants to have contact with the locals for cultural exchange and uses all occasions to create an international, intercultural atmosphere. The language of the camp is English
Accommodation: Provided in schools or village centres, sleeping on the floor or mattresses, or in dorms. Meals are provided by local families who cook for participants in their own homes
Cost: There is a small registration fee of €50 which includes board and lodging. At an additional cost of €60 participants can have an extra 3 days in Istanbul with organised activities

Greenway International Workcamps

Duration: 14 days per camp (participants can stay for 1 or more camps)
Location: Thailand, Vietnam, China
Season: Year round
Prerequisites: Min. age 18. No specific skills required

☎ +66 (74) 473 506
🖱 info@greenwaythailand.org
💻 www.pitayasuwan.org

Organisation: Non-profit operation dedicated to alternative ways of thinking about environmental care, small-scale economic development and sustainable growth
Description: Greenway short-term camps are all created with the intention of bringing participants together with local populations in an informal atmosphere that promotes cultural exchange. There are different types of workcamp: **Environmental** – clearing riversides, setting up recycling centres, environmental teaching in schools; **Agricultural** – harvesting and planting organic fruit and vegetables; **Social Work** – organising sporting events, setting up after-school centres; **Arts and Education** – teaching English, organising festivals, performing plays, crafts projects. All of the camps have an educational component
Accommodation: Living conditions vary depending on the programme but may include Greenway centres (dorms), temples or community buildings, or homestays with local families
Cost: Approx. US$170 per camp including board and lodging

International Bouworde-IBO

Location: Throughout Europe
Duration: 3 weeks
Season: June – September
Prerequisites: Min. age 18, reasonable level of fitness, flexible

☎ +31 24 322 6074
🖰 info@bouworde.nl
💻 www.bouworde.nl

Organisation: Established in 1953 to provide volunteers to assist with construction projects for people who need help
Description: Internationale Bouworde (or International Building Companions) gives volunteers the opportunity to assist in socially useful building projects in Europe, constructing and renovating orphanages, houses, hospitals, churches, social centres and so on. IBO has contributed to more than 5,500 projects worldwide including more than 354,000 volunteers of more than 70 nationalities. Volunteers work for eight hours per day, five days per week, with weekends free to explore the local area
Accommodation: Volunteers lodge on-site in simple accommodation or tents. Meals are generally prepared by the groups themselves
Cost: Approx. €100–€140 contribution is required to go towards insurance, board and lodging

Involvement Volunteers Association

Duration: 1–3 weeks
Location: More than 20 countries including Australia, Bolivia, China, Egypt, Fiji, Korea, Latvia, Mongolia, Namibia, Peru, Samoa, Togo and Venezuela
Season: Year round

☎ +61 3 9646 9392
🖰 ivworldwide@volunteering.org.au
💻 www.volunteering.org.au

Prerequisites: Anyone can volunteer, preferably with knowledge and experience but also possible without. Min. age 18 (unless they have parental agreement)
Organisation: Registered not-for-profit NGO
Description: IVA offers a cost-effective way for people of all ages to gain practical experience while helping others as a real volunteer and meeting the local people, and experiencing their culture. Current projects include eye-care camps in Bangladesh, environmental and social service camps in Colombia, sea-turtle protection in Greece, youth festival work in Mongolia, renovation in Spain, working with HIV/AIDS widows and orphans in Togo, assisting disabled people to harvest wheat in Lebanon, and renovation and heritage workcamps in the Czech Republic
Accommodation: Provided in basic but clean and safe lodgings. Varies from project to project
Cost: Fees are negotiated with volunteers on an individual basis. Fees include food, accommodation, admin costs and in-country transportation

Just Works

Duration: 1 week
Location: Different locations within the USA each year
Season: February – August
Prerequisites: Min. age 14/16/18 depending on project

☎ +1 617 868 6600
🖱 justworks@uusc.org
💻 www.uusc.org/info/workcamps.html

Organisation: Just Works camps are run by the Unitarian Universalist Service Committee, a nonsectarian organisation that promotes human rights and social justice worldwide

Description: The camps are short-term projects that help volunteers examine and understand the causes and damaging effects of injustice. Participants work directly with people in the communities they service, experiencing social justice struggles first-hand. While learning about human rights issues and promoting intercultural understanding and reconciliation, volunteers are taught advocacy skills to address issues of poverty, discrimination, and racism. In 2007 camps included Katrina Relief in New Orleans and working on the first burial site in the USA for 'unidentified' Native American ancestral remains

Accommodation: Varies from project to project. In the past it has been provided in camps and bunkhouses

Cost: US$300 including food and accommodation

KMC International Work Camps in the Czech Republic

Duration: 2–4 weeks
Location: Throughout the Czech Republic
Season: July – August
Prerequisites: Ages 18–30. No previous experience required

☎ +420 2222 20347
🖱 kmc@kmc.cz
💻 www.kmc.cz

Organisation: KMC is a travel service providing assistance with accommodation in youth hostels in the Czech Republic, package tours and acting as an intermediary for workcamps

Description: International volunteers take part in a range of service projects throughout the summer, which benefit the local community. These projects are designed to create international understanding while also providing a useful service. Current projects include working on an ecological project in a natural park, renovation and gardening in a centre for handicapped children, castle renovation work, social work, and animal conservation projects. British volunteers should apply through UNA Exchange (www.unaexchange.org)

Accommodation: Provided. Varies according to project but may include cottages, tents, local schools, and the grounds of a castle. Food is also provided for the group

Cost: A small contribution towards board and lodging is requested

NICE: Never-ending International Workcamps Exchange

Duration: 2–3 weeks or 1–3 days (weekend workcamps)

Location: Japan and some other countries in Asia

Season: February – November

Prerequisites: Min. age 18, motivated, open-minded, flexible. No experience required

 +81 3 3358 7140

 in@nice1.gr.jp

 http://nice1.gr.jp/e/indexe.html

Organisation: Non-profit NGO dedicated to organising workcamps and other voluntary projects in Japan and east Asia

Description: NICE invites volunteers annually to participate in more than 50 workcamps lasting two to three weeks and weekend workcamps lasting from one to three days. Each workcamp has a different focus but work can involve environmental projects, cultural projects, working with the disabled, social work, construction, working with the elderly, working with children and orphans, and renovation. Current projects include earthquake relief in Indonesia, teaching English in Mongolia, forest regeneration and running a cultural festival for children in Japan

Accommodation: Provided in basic but comfortable lodgings all with showers, communal kitchens and toilets

Cost: 10,000–27,000 Yen per workcamp to cover food and accommodation

OIKOS

Duration: 1–3 weeks

Location: Burkina Faso, Ecuador, France, Germany, Ghana, India, Kenya, Morocco, Mexico, Peru, Tanzania, Togo, Uganda

Season: Year round

Prerequisites: Min. age 18, flexibility. No specific qualifications required

+39 06 508 0280

oikos@oikos.org

www.oikos.org

Organisation: Association dedicated to the protection of the environment, humanitarian projects and the promotion of voluntary service in association with local NGOs around the world

Description: Oikos has organised workcamps around the world since 1979. Volunteers are invited to join in a range of environmental and humanitarian short-term projects with international volunteers. Current projects include learning about organic farming and agro-forestry in Ecuador, teaching English and social work in India, conservation work in Mexico, providing support for Palestinian refugee children, construction and renovation of community facilities in Tanzania, and caring for orphans in Uganda. There is plenty of free time for particpants to explore the local area

Accommodation: Varies according to camp. Often includes wooden huts, bunkhouses, tents, or homestays

Cost: Membership costs €80. Camp fees vary. Includes insurance, board and lodging

Philadelphia Yearly Meeting – International Volunteer Workcamp China

Duration: 4 weeks
Location: Changsa, China
Season: July – August
Prerequisites: Min. age 16

chinaworkcamp@pym.org
www.pym.org/workcamp/China/china.htm

Organisation: Quaker organisation that invites Quakers and non-Quakers to increase awareness of economic and cultural differences and inequalities
Description: The workcamp begins in Beijing for a few days of sightseeing, before participants travel to the Hunan province in rural central China. Here volunteers teach local children English and raise environmental awareness, experience life in rural China first-hand by living and working together with local college students, and learn about current social, political, environmental and economic issues in China. There are regular days off for participants to visit nearby towns and go hiking
Accommodation: Provided in dormitories with hot running water. Local food is provided and participants assist the cooks
Cost: US$2,400 including all food, accommodation and international travel

Pro International

Duration: 2–3 weeks
Location: Throughout Germany
Season: Easter; June – October
Prerequisites: Ages 16–26. No previous skills or experience required. Some German skills are required for some of the camps

☎ +49 (0)6421 65277
info@pro-international.de
www.pro-international.de

Organisation: Non-denominational and politically independent registered society with the aim of offering an international meeting place for young people
Description: Pro International holds 35–40 international workcamps each year. About 400 volunteers participate in these workcamps working as child-minders or manual workers, while others take part in activities connected with handicapped children, or the environment. The work (five to six hours daily) from Monday to Friday should encourage people to get to know each other by working towards a common goal and simultaneously providing a real service. Free time is spent together as a group, getting to know the country. Participants from the UK should apply to Pro International via Concordia (see entry)
Accommodation: Provided in simple lodgings such as youth hostels, schools, huts, tents and empty houses, all with self-catering equipment
Cost: Participation fee of approx €100, though this varies between projects. Food and accommodation are included

INTERNATIONAL WORKCAMPS

WORLDWIDE

Smile Society Workcamps

Duration: 2 weeks
Location: India
Season: Year round (begin on the 1st and 3rd Friday of every month)
Prerequisites: Min. age 16, basic English. No experience required

☎ +91 9830 686828
✉ info@smilengo.org
🖥 www.smilengo.org

Organisation: The Smile society is a volunteer organisation working for slum and street kids' welfare activities
Description: Smile organises international workcamps throughout the year. The work involved ranges from teaching English, to social work such as cleaning and food distribution, construction and reconstruction projects, art and craft projects, and healthcare. All of the workcamps are for the benefit of hungry and underprivileged children in India
Accommodation: Depends on project but is provided in halls, lodges, guesthouses, schools and with host families. Local meals are also provided
Cost: US$300 per person, including food and lodging, project material and in-country transportation

Voluntary Workcamps Association of Ghana (VOLU)

Duration: 3–4 weeks
Location: Ghana
Season: June – October/December – February
Prerequisites: Min. age 16, good health, willing to work hard and live in simple, modest conditions

☎ +233 21 663 486
✉ voluntaryworkcamp@yahoo.com
🖥 www.voluntaryworkcamps.org

Organisation: VOLU is a non-political, non-sectarian voluntary organisation dedicated to giving young people the opportunity to use their leisure time in the service of the community by participating in community development schemes. VOLU celebrated its 50th anniversary in 2006
Description: These workcamps are community-building projects in which a group of both Ghanaian and international volunteers come together to build a school, organise an HIV/AIDS awareness campaign, help replenish the local rainforest, or work on similar such projects. Volunteers live and learn together in simple conditions. They work voluntarily, mainly by manual labour, for the benefit of the community for around seven hours per day, Monday to Friday. Afternoons are free for trips, dancing, sports and leisure activities. On some weekends excursions are also planned
Accommodation: Provided in encampments, bunkhouses or with host families. Meals are also provided
Cost: US$200 per camp including board and lodging

Volunteers For Peace

Duration: 2–3 weeks
Location: 100 countries worldwide
Season: Year round (but mostly May – September)
Prerequisites: Min. age 18, motivated, flexible and
culturally sensitive. No special skills required. Teen camps
and family camps are also available

☎ +1 802 259 2759
🖱 vfp@vfp.org
💻 www.vfp.org

Organisation: VFP offers more than 3000 short-term voluntary service projects in
100 different countries. These programmes are an opportunity to complete meaningful
community service while living and interacting with an international group for two to three
weeks, providing a diverse cultural exchange with the other volunteers as well as the
local hosts. Work projects include: construction/renovation of low-income housing or
community buildings, historic preservation, archaeology, environmental education, wildlife
surveying, park maintenance, organic farming, social services, working with children,
the elderly, physically or mentally handicapped, refugees, minority groups, drug/alcohol
recovery, and AIDS education
Accommodation: Provided in a house, community centre, school or tents. Cooking and
cleaning responsibilities are shared among the group
Cost: US$250–$350 registration fee (includes meals and accommodation)

Workcamp Switzerland

Duration: 2–4 weeks
Location: Switzerland and around 30 countries
worldwide through partner organisations
Season: Year round (June – September is peak
season)
Prerequisites: Aged 18–30, motivated, moderate

☎ +41 (0)71 917 2486
🖱 info@workcamp.ch
💻 www.workcamp.ch

level of English, flexible, and able to get on well with other people. No experience required
Organisation: Non-profit group that aims to support social, cultural and ecological
projects via short voluntary workcamps
Description: Workcamp Switzerland invites volunteers to participate in socially,
ecologically or culturally relevant projects during their vacation time. Project examples
include improving existing hiking paths or laying new paths, assisting in the organisation
of holiday programmes for children, ongoing leisure activities with the disabled, renovation
work on an education centre, cleanup of nature reserves, playground construction, and
assisting in the planning, organisation and holiding of cultural events. Besides work there
is plenty of time for other activities such as trips, sports or games evenings
Accommodation: Provided in fairly simple lodgings such as a tent, barn or scout centre.
Meals or a budget for food are provided. Participants share in camp duties such as
cooking and cleaning
Cost: Registration fee for a workcamp in Switzerland is CHF100 (Swiss Francs). The fee
for a camp abroad is CHF150. Includes board and lodging. Insurance not included

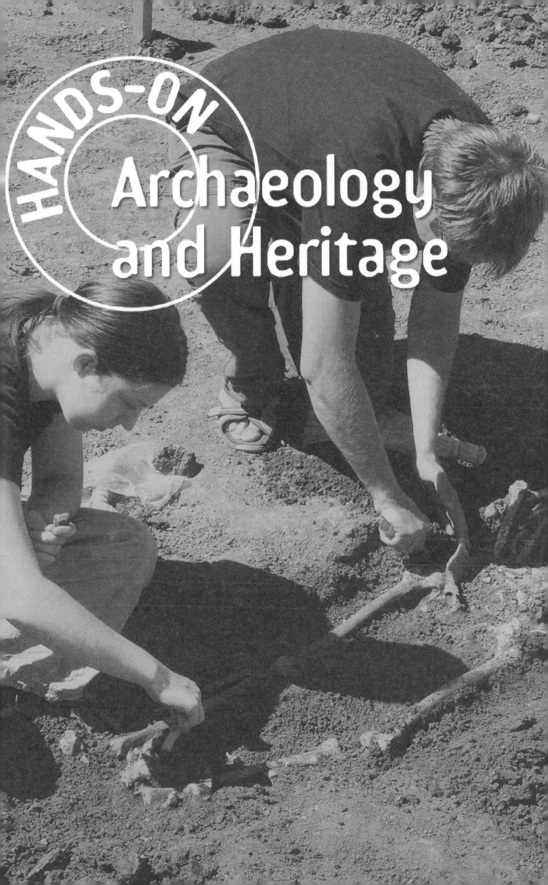

HANDS-ON
Archaeology and Heritage

WORKING ON A DIG

Each year, in the UK alone, more than 17,000 members of the public take part in archaeological digs, fieldwork, day schools, residential courses and study tours. The surge of British interest in archaeology is at least in part due to the enormous success of the television series *Time Team*. In fact, applications to study archaeology at university have increased three-fold since the TV show first hit our screens. But its not just the students who are getting their hands dirty. Each season there is high demand for places on the expanding number of training excavations and field schools worldwide as people of all ages and backgrounds swap their home comforts for knee-pads and a trowel in order to begin a first-hand exploration of the past.

Archaeology is the study of the material remains and environmental effects of past human activities from recent history to millions of years ago. Working a dig can be a fascinating way of indulging your interest and a fulfilling way to spend a week or so on a hands-on holiday. However, you should not allow yourself to indulge any Indiana Jones-style fantasies of unearthing vast chambers of forgotten riches. The work itself can be laborious. For example, it would not be uncommon to spend an entire dig working on the same square metre, delicately searching with a tiny pick and a brush. Nevertheless, digs and field schools do offer the possibility of uncovering something unexpected that may contribute to our understanding of the past, and that can be a thrilling experience. Ultimately digs offer the opportunity to personally contribute to the recovery and preservation of the past. When asked what he particularly enjoyed about working on a dig, Nic Clouston, a regular at excavations in the UK, answered:

I liken it to being like a small child on Christmas morning, wondering what is in the stocking or under the tree, but in this case in the trench or under the soil!

Generally digs can be divided into three types. Firstly there are research digs run mostly by university departments, with a preponderance of students from those departments. Secondly there are training digs, for which a fee is payable. And lastly there are digs run by local societies investigating the archaeology of their area – often the first stop for the beginner. Many a volunteer starts in their teens by attending a course at a local college, progressing to local or national digs and then spreading their wings to take part in digs abroad from Asia to Central America and from Malta to Israel. However, you don't have to have digging or archaeological qualifications and experience to take part in an excavation, as tuition, guidance and lectures are often given on-site to volunteers. Archaeology enthusiast Averil McHaffie, a retired school teacher, was put off attending a dig due to her lack of experience, but was reassured that this wouldn't be a problem:

I thought that it would be interesting to take part in a dig, but felt that it was only those who had been fully trained that could do it. But when I asked, I was told that I would be well supervised and not to worry that I hadn't done any archaeology before. As it turned out, the skills were taught as I went along. I was supervised and encouraged to ask questions. For example, I found stones which I thought were metal but it was explained that they were just iron stone. The explanations helped me to distinguish between what was valuable and what was not needed.

The Earthwatch Institute is an example of a reputable organisation that, for a price, sends unskilled and inexperienced volunteers to all corners of the globe, working alongside professional scientists in the field. Many other smaller organisations also offer such deals, but the experience can vary enormously depending on who you go with. Once you have done some courses and have experience, you are likely to get more interesting jobs and so feel more involved in a particular project.

Many digs specify that they are training digs, which means that there will be an element of tuition. Generally a structured training programme should provide tuition in a range of techniques and give participants the chance to try their hand at different aspects of the craft. Those with specific goals in mind should ask for a course outline listing the different skills that they can expect to learn.

Although there many training digs and excavations throughout Britain, archaeology is something that can be pursued all over the world. In many developing countries important research simply could not occur without the valuable input of volunteers, whose contribution is often the lifeblood of the organisation's revenue. Alternatively, projects that are organised in conjunction with an expedition company often have interesting excursions built into them and may offer more luxury than a small research project.

Almost all of the excavations and training digs listed below are residential. Those that aren't will be able to answer questions about finding accommodation local to the excavation site. However, the level of accommodation will vary enormously. Some organisations will ask participants to bring their own tent, whereas others will provide more comfortable board and lodging. The level of domestic provision usually, although not always, depends on the size of the fee payable for the course.

For insurance reasons, most digs will not accept volunteers aged under 18, unless supervised by an adult, although some digs offer non-excavation work that may be carried out by younger volunteers.

David Forster, a regular at the Vindolanda Roman Excavation in Northumberland lists his personal reasons for trying an archaeological dig, and for coming back year after year:

- Fulfilling a long-held dream to be involved in an excavation.
- Finding artefacts that haven't seen daylight for nearly 2000 years *[in 2006 David found a gold ring with intact intaglio. There have only been three or four rings found at Vindolanda and the last one was in the 70s]*.
- The trench banter which is usually highly entertaining, especially if you are working with people who also visit the site every year.
- Doing something useful as a holiday instead of just entertaining yourself – many of these projects could not exist without the help of volunteers.
- Meeting other like-minded people from almost all walks of life.
- Being made so welcome by the supervisors and being made to feel a bit special if you are an 'old hand'.
- Doing something completely different from normal everyday life.
- Working hard as a team in the fresh air.
- Spending a holiday with my sons and not being treated like a 'dad' but like a friend.
- Talking to the site visitors, showing them finds and letting them handle the artefacts, something which they cannot do in the museum.

What to Expect

Every project will differ in terms of the period under investigation and the type of artefacts that you can expect to find, but common to all digs is an element of hard toil. Excavation is certainly one of the most interesting and appealing elements of the work, but it is often very labour intensive, as Anthony Blake discovered during a summer dig near Le Mans, France: *'Archaeology is hard work. Applicants must be aware of what working from 8.30am to noon, and 2–6pm in baking heat means!'* Excavations can certainly be physically demanding. Hours are spent lifting excavated soil to the sorting area, kneeling down and digging with picks or bending over and shovelling. Remote sites may also involve hiking across difficult terrain, or carrying equipment up and down steep slopes, and work continues through driving rain and unbearable heat. This is not to say that participants need a super-human level of fitness, simply that they should make enquiries about the required fitness level if they have any concerns. Those with asthma should bear in mind that excavation sites can often be extremely dusty.

The work involved in an archaeological holiday is not restricted purely to excavation. A great deal of the work that volunteers help with takes place in the laboratory processing the finds and then archiving them. Among other aspects, archaeological fieldwork can also involve conservation, analysis, interpretation, education and record keeping. Alternatively, those who find archaeological work with a museum or heritage organisation may find themselves involved in setting up displays or public outreach programmes, or even becoming involved in community projects.

What to Bring to a Dig

Listed below are some of the main items to consider taking. Note that many of the organisations with entries in this book will supply their own recommended 'kit list' to potential volunteers. Most projects supply the heavy and technical equipment and safety gear required on site. Always check in advance.

- **Insurance:** Travel, medical and personal/life insurance are highly recommended. Even if the organisation or dig you are joining has its own insurance, it is better to have a personal policy as well.
- **Sleeping bag, tent, mat, torch:** Many digs are in remote areas and camping is the only accommodation option.
- **Medical and personal hygiene supplies:** A personal first aid kit is advisable and should include sunscreen, insect repellent and other items to deal with common skin complaints on a dig – blisters, cuts and scrapes.
- **Comfortable walking boots:** Flip-flops simply won't cut it, even if you are excavating in warm conditions. Sturdy shoes are required for working in the often rugged conditions of a dig.
- **Suitable clothing:** Waterproofs are essential, whatever the projected weather. A hat is also very useful if you want to avoid sunstroke. Generally clothing should be protective, but also comfortable. Tight or restrictive clothing will make excavation work difficult.
- **Trowel:** Some projects specify that you must bring your own excavation trowel. They will provide details.
- **Water bottle:** Dehydration is common on digs in hot climates. Try to drink water every few hours.
- **Zip-lock bags:** To keep sand and dust out of everything.
- **Kneeling pads and gardening gloves:** Recommended.

Finding a Dig

The digs listed below are a good starting point, but by no means offer a comprehensive guide to digs all over the world. Many digs are annual and require volunteers each year, whereas others may just last for a season and may not be advertised more than a few months in advance. It is therefore always worthwhile checking the organisations, publications and websites given here for current and on-going opportunities.

Useful Organisations, Publications And Websites

Archaeology Abroad
Tel. 020 8537 0849; arch.abroad@ucl.ac.uk; www.britarch.ac.uk/archabroad
Information about archaeological fieldwork opportunities outside the UK. Around 1000 placements are advertised annually for volunteers on a wide variety of projects, both online and in the publication *Archaeology Abroad.*

Council for British Archaeology
Tel. 01904 671417; info@britarch.ac.uk; www.britarch.ac.uk
The Council publishes *British Archaeology*, a bi-monthly full colour magazine, including announcements of forthcoming fieldwork opportunities on archaeological sites in Britain and costs £5 per issue.

French Ministry of Culture
Tel. +33 (1) 40557781; dapa@culture.gouv.fr; www.culture.fr/fouilles
In May each year, this government department publishes a list of summer excavations that accepts volunteers throughout France; searchable by region on the website.

Archaeological Institute of America
Tel. +1 617 353 9361; aia@aia.bu.edu; www.archaeological.org
The AIA is an excellent resource of amateur archaeological societies in the USA and also lists the requirements of over 200 archaeological excavations worldwide. A useful publication available from the AIA is the *Archaeological Fieldwork Opportunities Bulletin* (AFOB), which costs $19.95 from David Brown Books in the USA and £14.95 from Oxbow Books (www.oxbowbooks.com) in the UK.

Current Archaeology
Tel. 08456 447707; current@archaeology.co.uk; www.archaeology.co.uk
The magazine *Current Archaeology,* which deals with UK archaeology, and its sister magazine *Current World Archaeology,* which deals with the international archaeological scene, can be obtained by subscription from the website, which also lists the main digs in the UK plus a detailed description of the background, dig dates and contact details.

Websites
Archaeology Resources is a site mainly sourced from the UK but run from Canada (www.wordy.canadianwebs.com/page/arch.html) where you can find all matters relating to archaeology including dating methods, journals and publications, archaeology associations and archaeological sites and excavations and a database including the National Monument Record (Britain) and Sites and Monument Records (Britain). Other useful UK websites are:
www.archaeolink.com/archaeology_volunteer_opportunit.htm – lists international opportunities.
www.archaeological.org – the website of Society for American Archaeology.
http://archaeologic.com/fieldwork_directory.htm – directory of fieldwork opportunities.
www.pophaus.com/underwater/museums.html – Opportunities to participate in underwater excavations.

CULTURAL HERITAGE AND HISTORICAL RESTORATION

As well as archaeological fieldwork, this chapter also details a number of cultural heritage and historical restoration projects. A huge number of sites of cultural significance, such as buildings, monuments and structures are under threat from the ravages of nature, a lack of funding, and human neglect. For those with an interest in history or architecture, there can be no more satisfying way to spend your holiday time, than helping to restore or recreate sites of historical importance so that they may be appreciated by visitors, as well as the local community and its future generations.

In the UK, the National Trust runs a number of 'Working Holidays', that allow participants to restore historic structures, learn dry stone walling and preserve important trails. Other opportunities involve working on cathedral restoration at a 'Cathedral Camp', run by CSV, restoring Britain's neglected network of canals at a 'Canal Camp', and helping to recreate history by living as a Tudor in Suffolk's Kentwell Hall.

In France, the concept of the heritage preservation holiday is well established and there are a range of opportunities for the philanthropic holiday-maker. One of the most famous French organisations is Union Rempart, which employs individuals to help restore and maintain châteux, churches, villages and the old quarters of cities which are of unique cultural and historical value. Around a quarter of Rempart's volunteers are international. Another important French organisation is La Sabranenque, which provides a fascinating holiday experience for people of all ages and professions. Participants contribute to the restoration of sites, often dating from medieval times, learn traditional techniques such as stone-masonry and tiling from experienced technicians and live in the heart of typical Mediterranean towns.

If you fancy venturing a little further afield, there are plenty of opportunities worldwide for those whose interest lies in architecture, art history or historic preservation. One of the most exotic restoration holidays is run annually by the Cultural Restoration Tourism Project. The 12-day expedition focuses on a 300-year-old monastery in the Mustang region of Nepal. Participants work alongside a local crew, using traditional techniques to ensure that the treasures of the monastery are not lost for ever. The work is combined with guided tours, treks and community projects, offering a truly different holiday experience.

The work involved in a historical restoration programme will vary enormously depending on the project, so it is always best to contact the organisation directly for further information. None of the projects listed here require any specific skills or experience, although these are always welcomed, as participants work side-by-side with preservation specialists. Those who wish to find out more about the preservation of historic buildings should visit www.buildingconservation.com, which also features a huge range of building conservation masterclasses, workshops and seminars throughout the UK, to help potential participants learn more about preservation techniques for important historical structures.

Achill Island Field School

☎ +353 098 43564

✏ achill-fieldschool@iol.ie

💻 www.achill-fieldschool.com

Duration: Min. 3 days (introductory course); Min. 4 weeks (Field School)
Location: Achill Island in County Mayo, Ireland
Season: April – September
Prerequisites: Aged 18+. No experience required
Organisation: Accredited field school of National University of Ireland
Description: The field school is involved in a research excavation of a post-medieval deserted village on Achill Island. Since 1991, several hundred people from 21 countries have studied archaeology here and learnt about a much-neglected segment of Irish society. Many participants are students, but interested members of the public are welcome to take part. All training is provided. As well as the field school, there is a range of introductory courses, lasting from three days to two weeks
Accommodation: Provided in well-equipped, self-catering hostels and holiday houses, two minutes walk from the Archaeological Centre
Cost: Varies (see website). 2–week Bare Bones course costs €499

Bamburgh Research Project

Duration: 2–10 weeks
Location: Bamburgh Castle, Northumberland
Season: July – September
Prerequisites: Open to all
Organisation: Small group of dedicated professional field archaeologists

☎ 01904 769836

✏ paulgething@bamburghresearchproject.co.uk

💻 www.bamburghresearchproject.co.uk

Description: Research project centred around Bamburgh Castle with the aim of creating a long-term, field-based series of investigations to better understand Bamburgh's intricate and fascinating past. Each summer there are a number multi-period excavations and surveys in progress including an early medieval cemetery and a medieval port. The project provides an ideal environment for training in archaeological techniques under the guidance of professional field archaeologists. Participants work from 9am to 5pm for six days a week. Outside of work the project offers a rich and varied social life for the 100+ volunteers who visit each year
Accommodation: Fully equipped campsite
Cost: Approx. £120 per week including camping and all meals (£95 without)

ARCHAEOLOGY & HERITAGE

UK & IRELAND

Butser Ancient Farm

Duration: Min. 2 days
Location: Petersfield, UK
Prerequisites: Open to all
Season: Year round
Organisation: Replica of a British Iron Age farm

☎ 023 9259 8838
💻 www.butser.org.uk

Description: Butser farm is a museum and open-air laboratory carrying out research into the Iron Age and Roman periods using the methods and materials available at that time. The farm has buildings, structures, animals and crops that would have existed at the time. There are year-round working weekends and 'practical experiences' workshops in which volunteers can learn basic archaeological excavation and recording techniques, assist in the construction of a Roman Villa with mosaic floors, contstruct a replica roundhouse and learn skills such as herb gathering, pottery and metal working
Accommodation: None provided, but the farm can advise on nearby accommodation
Cost: Practical workshops cost approximately £30–£50 per day

Canal Camps – Waterway Recovery Group

Duration: 1 week
Location: Throughout Britain
Season: March – August
Prerequisites: Open to anyone aged 18–70. No experience required
Organisation: Voluntary organisation, helping to restore derelict canals in Britain

 01923 711114
 enquiries@wrg.org.uk
💻 www.wrg.org.u

Description: A Canal Camp is an enjoyable week's outdoor holiday spent working on the canals, meeting new people and doing your bit for Britain's industrial heritage and the environment. Hundreds of volunteers take part in more than 20 camps each summer. Jobs on the camps can include restoring industrial archaeology, demolishing old brickwork, bricklaying and pouring concrete, driving a dumper truck, clearing silt, helping to run a waterways festival, cooking for other volunteers, clearing vegetation and trees. The working day is roughly 9am to 5pm with evenings free and social activities organised for those who want to take part
Accommodation: Provided in village halls, sports clubs etc. Electricity, showers, toilets and dry, draught-free sleeping areas guaranteed
Cost: £42 per camp. Includes food and accommodation

Castell Henllys Training Excavation

Duration: 1–4 weeks
Location: Pembrokeshire, west Wales
Season: July/August
Prerequisites: School/ university students and other interested people. No prior knowledge or experience required

☎ 01904 433902
✎ ppe101@york.ac.uk
💻 www.york.ac.uk/depts/arch/castellhenllys/web/

Organisation: Award-winning interpretive archaeology site run by York University
Description: An Iron Age inland promontory fort and adjacent Romano-British farmstead set in a beautiful location and surrounded by many other sites of interest. There are normally 30–40 people involved in the excavation. Participants learn about excavation and recording techniques, flotation and on-site environmental processing and benefit from being taught by experienced academic and field archaeologists. Participants work six days a week on a choice of sites
Accommodation: Provided at an excavation camp site with shower and toilet facilities
Cost: £170 per week (£120 if you stay 2 weeks or more) which covers camping, food, tuition and visits to other sites

Cathedral Camps

☎ 020 7643 1398
✎ cathedralcamps@csv.org.uk
💻 www.cathedralcamps.org.uk or www.csv.org.uk

Duration: 1 week
Location: Throughout the UK
Season: July – September
Prerequisites: Open to all. Most volunteers aged 17–25

Organisation: Cathedral Camps have been running residential breaks at cathedrals and churches throughout the UK for more than 20 years. The project is now run by the UK volunteering agency, CSV
Description: Experience the hidden history of some of Britain's oldest and most beautiful buildings. Religious buildings make up a huge part of Britain's architectural heritage and every year teams of young people from all over the world move in to help refresh and conserve these buildings. Cathedral Camps offers a challenging and different type of holiday and the chance to meet new people. The work involved varies from project to project but may involve restoring medieval stained glass, or delicate conservation work on a tomb that has been untouched for more than a hundred years. Volunteers are trained to tackle jobs throughout the building by experienced professionals. The working week begins on a Wednesday with Saturday afternoon and Sunday free to explore the local area .
Accommodation: Varies according to the project, but usually within the building that is being restored
Cost: Approx £85 per camp

Earthwatch Institute

Duration: 8/15 days (Hidden Kingdom); 14 days (Roman Fort)
Location: Yorkshire/South Shields
Season: June – September
Prerequisites: Ages 18–95. No experience necessary

☎ 01865 318838
✉ info@earthwatch.org.uk
💻 www.earthwatch.org/Europe

Organisation: International environmental charity offering volunteering opportunities on worldwide scientific research expeditions. All volunteer contributions go directly towards supporting the scientific research

Description: Earthwatch currently runs two UK-based archaeological expeditions.
Hidden Kingdom explores the mystery of the fifth to seventh century AD independent kingdom of Craven, which some believe to have existed in upland Yorkshire. Work is divided between surveying and excavation tasks in the Yorkshire Dales National Park.
Roman Fort on Tyne explores Arbeia, the site of a Roman garrison and harbour, a stone's throw from Hadrian's Wall. Participants are involved in stratigraphic excavation using a trowel and brush, recording techniques, site surveying, and sampling
Accommodation: Hidden Kingdom – provided in a traditional stone house with single and twin rooms, dining and sitting rooms and hot showers.
Roman Fort on Tyne – provided in a local guesthouse with shared bedrooms, hot showers and easy access to parks, beaches and pubs
Cost: £850–£1295 (including all tuition, food and accommodation)

A POSTCARD FROM the Roman Fort on Tyne

Retiree Jackie Ward spent a hands-on holiday at the Earthwatch Roman Fort on Tyne project:

I first became interested in archaeology while travelling around the world on holiday, and taking part in an excavation was something I had always fancied trying. I arrived at the excavation without any prior experience of an archaeological dig, but the professionals on site explained exactly how it was done. The staff were all very friendly and helpful and the work was not difficult. We had to scrape the earth away, take measurements and draw diagrams.

The group of volunteers was a mixed bag of mainly Americans, an Austrian, a Romanian, and me, the only Brit. We all got along very well together and I have kept in touch with the friends that I made. We were in a very busy area and there was plenty of time to explore the local vicinities of South Shields, Newcastle, and Edinburgh and there were plenty of local pubs to visit in the evening.

Although the work can get fairly repetitive, it was worth it in the end. The best moment on the dig came on the last day when we discovered an inscription on one of the stones, which was probably put there by one of the original builders. We must have been the first people to set eyes on it for around 1,800 years!

well Hall – Live As A Tudor

1–3 weeks

...tion: Nr. Long Melford, Suffolk
Season: June – July (also weekends at Easter and in September)
Prerequisites: Open to volunteers of all ages. No experience required

☎ 01787 310207
🖰 office@kentwell.co.uk
🖥 www.kentwell.co.uk

Organisation: A privately owned Tudor mansion in a tranquil parkland setting, famous for its annual re-creation of Tudor life

Description: During the summer re-creation, Kentwell aims to create an authentic representation of what life was like during the 16th century. Every summer a different year in history is chosen and volunteers are required to re-create that year as accurately as possible. Duties consist of demonstrating a range of activities, such as cooking or agricultural work, that would have been typical of the time, to up to 1,500 school-children who visit during the week, and the public, who visit at weekends. Applications are accepted in January and February each year

Accommodation: Campsite provided with meals and evening entertainment

Cost: None

Lindum Heritage – Summer Excavation

Duration: 1–4 weeks
Location: Sudbrooke, Lincolnshire
Season: July/August
Prerequisites: Open to all
Organisation: Lindum Heritage provides archaeology and history short breaks

☎ 01522 851388
🖰 info@lindumheritage.co.uk
🖥 www.lindumheritage.co.uk

Description: Get involved in the excavation of a Roman villa site. The summer excavation is open to everyone, even those who have never held a trowel before. Full training is provided by professional archaeologists. Participants gain basic recording and excavation techniques and also have the chance to participate in surveying, photography and pottery workshops. Workshops on different techniques run from Monday to Wednesday each week. This dig is extremely popular and early booking is strongly recommended

Accommodation: Not included in the price, but Lindum can advise or offer a special rate at a local 3–star hotel

Cost: £170 per week including daily transport from Lincoln and lunch

The National Trust - Working Holidays

Duration: 2–7 days
Location: England, Wales and Northern Ireland
Season: Year round
Prerequisites: Min. age 18 (special Youth Discovery programme runs for 16–18-year-olds). No specific skills are required. Every holiday has a trust warden who will explain how and why a job needs doing

☎ 0870 609 5383
🖰 volunteers@nationaltrust.org.uk
🖥 www.nationaltrust.org.uk/volunteering

Organisation: Charity, completely independent of the government, which protects and opens to the public more than 300 historic houses and gardens. The Trust also looks after industrial monuments, mills, forests, fens, beaches, farmland, islands, archaeological remains, castles and nature reserves

Description: Around 450 Working Holidays for the National Trust take place in more than 100 beautiful locations each year, all guaranteed to help participants escape the stresses and strain of everyday life. Participants can get involved in a huge range of projects, from herding goats, to painting a lighthouse; from dry-stone walling in the Lake District, to harvesting apples in Devon, and every holiday makes a real difference. Many of the holidays involve heritage preservation and there are also a number of archaeological digs, such as an excavation of an 18th century barn in Warwickshire and an Iron Age hill fort in Herefordshire.

Holidays are separated into different types based on the activity or the age of the group, for example there are Working Holidays specifically for younger, older or disabled volunteers. Other choices include Trust Active Holidays, which combine work with outdoor activities such as sailing, canoeing, pony trekking and walking, and Premium Holidays for those people who like to work hard during the day but prefer more luxurious surroundings in the evening. Work is usually from 9am-5pm with regular breaks and a picnic for lunch. Work is very rewarding, but can also be quite demanding. All volunteers get every evening and a full day off during the holiday to relax

Accommodation: For most holidays the accommodation is a National Trust basecamp – farmhouses, cottages or apartments that have been converted into volunteer accommodation. All have cooking facilities, dorms with bunk beds, lounge and toilet and shower facilities. All meals are included

Cost: From £75 per week including food and accommodation

40 Years of National Trust Working Holidays 1967–2007

In August 1967, the first working holiday volunteers spent a week restoring the tow path on the canal at Stratford-Upon-Avon. In the four decades that have passed since then, a huge portfolio of projects has been completed thanks to the help of volunteers, including the discovery of the existence of several nationally scarce species of wildlife at Orford Ness, the construction of five miles of footpaths at Cragside in Northumberland and the complete re-cobbling of Gunby Hall's courtyard.

In 2007, increasing numbers of people are leaving behind the stress and expense of travelling abroad for their holidays and are opting for an inexpensive break that delivers real conservation and heritage benefits.

ARCHAEOLOGY & HERITAGE

UK & IRELAND

North Pennines Archaeology

Duration: Min. 2 weeks
Location: North Pennines
Season: June – August
Prerequisites: Open to all over 18s – basic recording and excavating tuition carried out on site by field staff

☎ 01434 382 045
✆ info@nparchaeology.co.uk
💻 www.nparchaeology.co.uk

Organisation: Established archaeological contracting consultancy, part of the North Pennines Heritage Trust
Description: Based around Nenthead Mines, Nenthead Smelt Mill and Dilston Castle, the three-month summer field school has been set up to record and conserve valuable industrial remains in the North Pennines. It offers participants a mixture of archaeological recording and building conservation. Participants are trained in topographical surveying techniques, archaeological planning and excavation, environmental and finds processing techniques, building recording and historic building techniques, including drystone walling and lime mortar use. Participants work 8.30am-4.30pm, Monday to Friday, with weekends free
Accommodation: Self-catering bunkhouse on site with kitchen, recreation room, shower and toilet. Hotels nearby if you would prefer. See website
Cost: £110 per week (including accommodation and tuition, but not food). Membership of the trust is mandatory and costs £8

Poulton Research Project

Duration: Min. 2 days
Location: Near Chester
Season: July – August
Prerequisites: Open to all aged 16 or over
Organisation: A community landscape archaeology research project

☎ 07818 254989
✆ c.caroe@btinternet.com
💻 www.poultonproject.org

Description: A long-term investigation into the evolution of the historic, environmental and social landscape of Cheshire based on a medieval chapel associated with the lost Cistercian Abbey of Poulton. This investigation formed the basis of an episode of *Time Team* in 2006. There is also evidence for a Roman villa or farmstead here. Volunteers are welcome to join in the dig, under the guidance of professional archaeologists. Alternatively the project offers regular weekend courses in basic excavation techniques for participants of all ages
Accommodation: Not included. Campsite and youth hostel nearby and transport to and from the site is provided
Cost: Approx. £100 per week. Weekend courses cost £50 per day

Saveock Water Archaeology

Duration: Min 1 week
Location: Cornwall
Season: April – August
Prerequisites: No experience necessary.
Children 14+ welcome with parents
Organisation: Permanent archaeology centre

☎ 01872 560351
✍ jacqui@archaeologyonline.org
🖥 www.archaeologyonline.org

Description: Join a multi-period dig, now in its seventh season, studying a delightful sheltered river valley in Mid Cornwall. The site covers Mesolithic to 17th century pagan deposits and has a number of features that appear to be unique in British archaeology. During the season volunteers have the opportunity to dig in different areas of the site to broaden their excavation experience. The work week is Monday to Friday, leaving weekends free to explore the many ancient monuments in the county
Accommodation: Not included in price. Participants must make their own arrangements. Saveock holds a list of accommodation in the area
Cost: £170 per week

The Scottish Crannog Centre – International Fieldschool in Underwater Archaeology

Duration: 1–4 weeks
Location: Central Highlands, Scotland
Season: July – August
Prerequisites: Ages 18–60. Must have PADI rescue/
advanced qualification

☎ 01887 830583
✍ info@crannog.co.uk
🖥 www.crannog.co.uk

Organisation: run by the Scottish Trust for Underwater Archaeology which promotes the research and preservation of Scotland's underwater heritage
Description: Get involved in ongoing underwater excavations at the early Iron Age site of Oakbank Crannog, Loch Tay. A crannog is a type of ancient loch dwelling found throughout Scotland. Preservation of items at this 2,500-year-old site is outstanding due to the cold, peaty waters and there is even a butter dish with butter still in it. This is a unique opportunity to work on a submerged prehistoric settlement site. Training in underwater excavation techniques will be provided
Accommodation: Basic accommodation provided
Cost: Approx. £300 per week

Sedgeford Historical and Archaeological Research Project

Duration: 1 day courses or 1–6 weeks' excavation
Location: Sedgeford, Norfolk
Season: July – August
Prerequisites: All over 16s welcome regardless of experience. Those who wish to dig on site will need 3 weeks' relevant experience, or to attend the week-long basic excavation and recording technique course held in week one of the dig

☎ 01485 532 343
🖐 tanzee@supanet.com
💻 www.sharp.org.uk

Organisation: Long-term, multi-disciplinary local research project
Description: One of the largest archaeological projects in Britain set up to investigate the entire range of human settlement and land-use in a typical Norfolk parish from the earliest times to the present day. Up to 70 participants join the excavation team, digging, surveying, planning, and processing, sorting and cleaning finds. Volunteers work six days a week. This is a very friendly project and participants join in lectures, games evenings and a weekly party
Accommodation: Volunteers camp next to the excavation (included in subsistence cost)
Cost: £20 (1 day course); £130 per week plus £125 subsistence (optional)

Silchester Roman Town Field School

Duration: 1–6 weeks
Location: Near Reading
Season: July – August
Prerequisites: Open to all aged 16+ and suitable for beginners and those with some experience
Organisation: University of Reading

☎ 0118 931 8132
🖐 archaeology@rdg.ac.uk
💻 www.silchester.rdg.ac.uk

Description: The Town Life project is an ongoing excavation of one block of the Silchester Roman Town, due to continue until at least 2009. Each summer, students and volunteers work together to play an active part in uncovering the area's Roman and Iron Age history. Professional archaeologists lead the team in planning and section drawing, excavation, find-processing and site-maintenance tasks. Volunteers range from those in their teens to 'mature' participants and come from all over the world to take part. Work takes place six days a week, with a day off on Fridays
Accommodation: Basic campsite with access to toilets, water and nearby showers
Cost: £230 per week including camping, all food and facilities

Thistle Camps

Duration: 1 week
Location: Scotland – pick-up in Edinburgh
Season: April/September
Prerequisites: Open to all aged 18 or over
Organisation: Thistle Camps are organised by
the National Trust for Scotland – Scotland's leading
conservation organisation

☎ 0131–243 9360
🖰 thistlecamps@nts.org.uk
🖳 www.thistlecamps.org.uk

Description: Thistle Camps currently runs two archaeology-based week-long projects. The first centres on Ben Lomond, the slopes of which contain more than 200 archaeological features. Volunteers undertake survey plans of some sites, together with small-scale excavations. The second offers the opportunity to discover the history of the picturesque 16th century Brodie Castle. Volunteers undertake surveys in the grounds and excavate structures

Accommodation: Ben Lomond – dormitories provided at Glasgow University Field Station, situated in a clearing on the east shore of Loch Lomond.
Brodie Castle – dormitories at Findhorn Village Centre on the Moray Firth
Cost: £100 (including accommodation, food and transport to and from Edinburgh)

Upper Nene Archaeological Society – Summer Excavation

Duration: 1 week (Easter/September);
2/3 weeks (Summer)
Location: Northamptonshire
Season: April; August; September
Prerequisites: Over 16s
Organisation: Local archaeological
society with museum and research facility

☎ 01604–870312
🖰 unas@friendship-taylor.freeserve.co.uk
🖳 www.unas.org.uk

Description: UNAS oversees the long-term excavation of the Piddington Romano-British Villa and an underlying Iron Age settlement. There is also evidence of early Saxon activity on the site. Special interest holiday-makers are required to help with all aspects of the excavation process including processing finds, site drawing etc, to exacting scientific standards. Although not designated a 'training excavation', UNAS will take on beginners and guide them on basic excavation techniques. Lunches are provided on site and the summer dig boasts a lively, friendly atmosphere. Summer digs are open to all, but Easter and September digs are only available for members

Accommodation: Basic campsite with toilets and fresh water
Cost: £85 (2 weeks); £110 (3 weeks). Camping fees included. Food extra

The Vindolanda Trust

Duration: Min. 1 week. 2 weeks recommended

Location: Situated in the rolling hills of rural Northumberland with the dramatic whinsill crags of Hadrian's Wall two miles north

Season: April – September

Prerequisites: 16+ and physically fit. No previous experience necessary

☎ 01434 344277

✍ andrewbirley@vindolanda.com

💻 www.vindolanda.com

Organisation: Founded to excavate Roman remains in the area, the trust is now the UK's longest-running research excavation, entering its 37th year

Description: Each year around 350–400 volunteers work to uncover and explore one of the most important archaeological sites in northern Europe. Of the thousands of artefacts that have been uncovered on the site, the Vindolanda writing tablets, small wooden postcards written on with an ink pen, are the most sensational. Volunteers are a mixture of people from all walks of life and from all corners of the globe. According to assistant excavation director, Andrew Birley: *'Many volunteers come to Vindolanda with no previous experience of archaeology but leave with a good understanding of the discipline and a reinforced love of history and archaeology.'* More than 3000 people have benefited from the challenge of working on the dig and some 40% of the volunteers come back for more than one season

Accommodation: Not included in the price. There are numerous hostels, B&Bs and campsites in the area listed on the website

Cost: £50 excavation fee (for first 2 weeks, £10 per week thereafter); £15 membership fee. Accommodation not included

Volunteers help excavate one of the most important archaeological sites in northern Europe.

David Ingham, aged 28, first visited the Vindolanda Trust Roman Excavation on a school trip. He returned as an undergraduate to take part in a dig and has since been back four times, he says:

The excavation at Vindolanda is one of the best and most exciting around, and I would recommend it to anyone with an interest in Roman archaeology. The first time I attended, I already had basic excavation skills, but the people supervising the expedition can still offer useful advice to all but the most experienced excavators. There's nothing complicated about excavating and anyone can join in.

People arrive on site at Vindolanda at 9am and the working day is split into four blocks, with a morning and afternoon tea break either side of lunch. Each block lasts for about one and a half hours and the day finishes at about 4.30pm. The majority of time is spent excavating, but alternative wet-weather activities such as washing pottery or going for guided walks along Hadrian's Wall are sometimes provided.

The best moments during an excavation are when the outline of buildings emerge from what initially looks like a pile of rubble, and there is always a sense of apprehensive excitement when we find something that might be significant.

Archaeological excavation can be physically demanding and prospective volunteers should be prepared for more than a bit of light trowelling, despite the impression that is sometimes given on TV. In the evenings people are fairly exhausted, but there is plenty of scope for walking and exploring the Roman remains in the area and there are a number of nice pubs nearby.

People from all walks of life come to Vindolanda to work as volunteers – nurses, delivery drivers, teachers, postmen, plus a number of students and retired people. Everyone there has a shared interest in archaeology, so it's easy to make friends, and there is a fantastic sense of team spirit, especially in adverse weather!

ARCHAEOLOGY & HERITAGE

UK & IRELAND

Action Reconciliation Service for Peace (ARSP)

Duration: Min. 1 week
Location: Belarus, Belgium, Czech Republic, France, Germany, Great Britain, Israel, the Netherlands, Norway, Poland, Russia and Slovakia
Season: June – September
Prerequisites: Min. age 18 (or 16 for youth camps)

☎ 020 8880 7526
🖱 grossbritannien@asf-ev.de
💻 www.asf-ev.de

Organisation: ARSP is a multi-denominational organisation founded by advocates of the protestant resistance against the National Socialist regime. Still supported by the churches of Germany, ARSP, conscious of the fact that the results of the Nazi past can only be overcome through intensive dialogue, works for a better understanding between cultures and generations
Description: Volunteers for the 'Sommerlager' programme help with the maintenance of Jewish cemeteries and memorial centres, work in social facilities and involve themselves in projects that support intercultural experiences. In addition there is discussion concerning historical and current issues. Groups work for five to six hours a day, with plenty of free time to explore the area
Accommodation: Provided in simple lodgings such as tents or bunkhouses
Cost: Participation fees are €130 (or €100 for students/unemployed). This covers accommodation, food, insurance and project costs

ArchaeoSpain

Duration: 2–6 weeks
Location: Burgos, Valladolid, Soria (Spain); Rome (Italy)
Season: June – September
Prerequisites: Over 18. No experience required

☎ +1 866 932 0008
🖱 info@archaeospain.com
💻 www.archaeospain.com

Organisation: Non-profit organisation providing an opportunity for people of all nationalities to participate in archaeological projects in Spain and Italy
Description: Current excavations include the Roman theatre of Clunia in Burgos, the Iron Age/Roman Necropolis of Pintia in Valladolid, the multi-period excavation of the city of Tiermes in Soria, and an artificial Roman hill in Rome. ArchaeoSpain teams of six to 10 people join local crews to help excavate the sites. There is also some lab work and artefact restoration. Training is given in basic excavation techniques from leading archaeologists. Free excursions to cultural sites are provided at weekends
Accommodation: Provided in hostels or group houses
Cost: Approx. £1,180 (4 weeks)

Apare

Duration: 2 or 3 weeks
Location: Provence/Mediterranean, France
Season: July – October
Prerequisites: Min. age 18. No upper limit. No prior experience required
Organisation: An association for regional participation that organises workcamps dedicated to the restoration of historic buildings and heritage sites in Provence and the Cévennes
Description: Volunteers come from all over the world to workcamps that seek to strike a balance between practical restoration and heritage work (usually carried out in the mornings) and the discovery of the region through cultural and sporting events. The work, directed by technical advisers, includes drystone walling, restoring a Romanesque chapel or a medieval village in the Var, or re-paving the streets of a Corsican village
Accommodation: Provided by the local camps. Usually basic – camping, public hostels, school lodging etc
Cost: €95 (2 weeks); €130 (3 weeks) including board and lodging, leisure expenses and insurance

☎ +33 (0)490 85 51 15
🖱 apare@apare-gec.org
💻 www.apare-gec.org

Amis de Chevreaux-Chatel

Duration: 3 weeks
Location: Chevreaux, Franche-Comté, France
Season: July/August
Prerequisites: Ages 16–25. No experience required
Organisation: The association organises two international annual workcamps to help restore the medieval castle of Chevreux
Description: Every summer, young people from all over the world come together to help restore Chevreaux castle. The work involves clearing debris, reconstruction of ruins, stoneworking, carpentry and archaeology. Volunteers are expected to work around six hours a day under the supervision of trained professionals (masons, carpenters and archaeologists). After work local recreation facilities are provided including a swimming pool, volleyball, badminton, football and organised walks. Excursions to sites of interest in the area are organised at weekends
Accommodation: Provided in shared tents with camp-beds on site, with washing, laundry and cooking facilities
Cost: Registration and insurance cost of €55

☎ +33 3 84 85 95 77
🖱 accjura@free.fr
💻 http://accjura.free.fr/chantiers/chantiers_ang.htm

Anglo-American Project in Pompeii

Duration: 4–6 weeks
Location: Southern Italy
on the Bay of Naples
Season: July/August
Prerequisites:
Particularly suitable for

☎ 01274 233 536
✍ archschi-pompeii@bradford.ac.uk
💻 www.brad.ac.uk/acad/archsci/field_proj/anampomp

students of archaeology and anthropology but applications are encouraged from people
of all backgrounds
Organisation: University of Bradford/University of Oxford
Description: The Pompeii project integrates a field school providing high-quality training
in modern archaeological practice with a major international research project. The buried
Roman city of Pompeii is one of Italy's major tourist attractions. AAPP has been studying
a complete block of the city since 1994 and is currently focusing on the House of the
Surgeon. The field school provides structured practical training with close supervision and
includes guided visits and seminars. The working language of the project is English, but
the team is international
Accommodation: Provided at a campsite 300 metres from the ancient city, with toilets,
showers, washing machines, café/bar, shop and internet point. All meals are served on site
Cost: US$3850 all in fee (6 weeks excluding flights)

Association Alpes de Lumière

Duration: Min. 2 weeks
Location: Provence, France
Season: April – September
Prerequisites: Age 18+. Good physical
condition. French or English language

☎ +33 492 75 22 01
💻 http://alpes-de-lumiere.org

Organisation: Environmental development association of Haute-Provence
Description: Around 150 participants from all over the world dedicate themselves to
the restoration of historic buildings and the development of historic sites throughout
Provence. Specialised stone masons train participants in local building and restoration
techniques. The working day lasts from 7.30am to 1.30pm, leaving volunteers free to join
organised activities in the afternoons. The emphasis of the camps is on enriching the
participants' awareness of the culture and customs of the area. Groups are made up of
between 12 and 14 participants
Accommodation: Mostly provided on campsites, but varies between projects. Food
provided
Cost: Approx €120 for a 2-week session

CHAM – Medieval History Volunteer Projects

Duration: 2–4 weeks
Location: France and French territories
Season: July – August
Prerequisites: Applicants must be aged over 16, be enthusiastic and have a good knowledge of French
Organisation: CHAM is an NGO dedicated to the conservation and restoration of medieval buildings around France
Description: More than 600 volunteers per year participate in summer workcamps for the restoration of monuments, châteaux, bridges and abbeys. CHAM has contributed to the restoration of more than 50 French historical sites. Work can involve masonry, stone-cutting, site clearing, archaeological surveys and excavations. All projects are led by trained and experienced CHAM officers. Volunteers enjoy time off to explore the local area
Accommodation: Usually provided in campsites with showers, toilets and basic cooking facilities
Cost: €30 membership plus a €15 fee for non-French applicants and approximately €12 per day, depending on the individual camp

☎ +33 1 43 35 15 51
🖱 cham@cham.asso.fr
💻 www.cham.asso.fr

Club du Vieux Manoir

Duration: 15 days
Location: Hautes Alpes, Aisne, Oise, Indre (France)
Season: June – September
Prerequisites: Min. age 14–17. No experience necessary. Some French language ability required
Organisation: Non-profit making association dedicated to the rescue and restoration of endangered monuments and historical sites
Description: Each year 4,000 volunteers contribute to the preservation of France's heritage and at the same time acquire manual and technical skills as well as some knowledge of archaeology and history. Apart from working on a site, club members may take part in research, publication or committee work. The work involves masonry and general restoration work, archaeological excavations, mapping and cultural interpretation, mostly on castles, villas and forts. The teams are mostly international, although the working language is French (the website is only in French)
Accommodation: Basic camping facilities provided
Cost: Membership costs €14 and each chantier (camp) requires a contribution of €14 per day for food and accommodation

☎ +33 (0)3 44 72 33 98
🖱 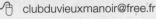 clubduvieuxmanoir@free.fr
💻  http://clubduvieuxmanoir.asso.fr

Earthwatch Institute – Early Man in Spain

Duration: 14 days
Location: Murcia, Spain
Season: July – September
Prerequisites: Ages 18–95. No experience necessary

 01865 318831
 info@earthwatch.org.uk
 www.earthwatch.org

Organisation: Earthwatch is an international environmental charity which offers volunteering opportunities on scientific research expeditions around the world. All volunteer contributions go directly towards supporting the scientific research

Description: Human remains thought to be 1.2 million years old have been found in the Cueva Victoria in Murcia. These are some of the oldest in western Europe and may provide information about when humans first migrated from Africa to Europe. The cave consists of six large rooms and more than 2km of galleries. Participants are trained to excavate the sediment, removing fossils and artefacts, and map the remains. Work takes place in the morning and early evening. The hottest hours of the day are reserved for lunch, siestas and refreshing swims. The team usually visits the nearby beach after a day's work

Accommodation: Volunteers share spacious rooms in a large house with gardens and a pool

Cost: £995 including all board and lodging

Open Houses Network

Duration: 2 or 3 weeks (building weeks); as long as you like (open houses)
Location: eastern regions of Germany
Season: May – October for building weeks. Open houses run all year round
Prerequisites: Open to all

+49 3643 502390
info@openhouses.de
www.openhouses.de

Organisation: Formed in the mid-80s, when a group of young people voluntarily undertook to restore village churches in danger of decay, the network currently runs six historic buildings in the eastern part of Germany

Description: Originally it was intended that anybody could help out with restoration work in return for board and lodging, and this policy continues today. Anybody can walk into an 'Open House' and stay for as long as they are prepared to work there. However the project has grown to include building weeks, art workshops, workcamps and practical training for students. Building weeks allow participants to gain real restoration experience, working under the guidance of trained professionals

Accommodation: Basic lodgings provided in exchange for work. Meals are prepared by the group and are a part of community life

Cost: A contribution of €25–€40 per week depending on individual means

Projects Abroad – Archaeology in Romania

Duration: Min. 3 weeks
Location: Bordusani, Bunloc, Sibiu, Poiana Brasov, Avrig, Harsova, Brasov Highway (Romania)
Season: Year round
Prerequisites: Open to all

☎ 01903 708300
✒ info@projects-abroad.co.uk
💻 www.archaeology-romania.org

Organisation: Projects Abroad organises volunteering projects in 20 countries around the world
Description: Romania's rich archaeological history is only just starting to be discovered and fully researched. This project allows participants a first-hand insight into Romanian history from the Neolithic Gumelnita culture, through ancient Dacians and Romans and continuing with medieval times in Transylvania. The main focus of the project is the mysterious Dacian civilization, the role of witchcraft and the country's fortified Saxon churches. There are currently eight projects in Romania, with more in the pipeline. Each team is run by professional archaeologists and volunteers learn excavation and artefact reconstruction techniques
Accommodation: Provided with a host family
Cost: £1,195 for 1 month (excluding flights)

A POSTCARD FROM Romania

Linda Vonken joined Projects Abroad for an archaeological field trip to Romania:

Many things tempt visitors to Romania, including lower prices, good food, very drinkable local wines, mountain villages, and of course, the legend of Dracula. Yet I came to Romania to unearth traces of the rich history this country holds.

My first field trip was to Avrig. With its once glorious baroque and English gardens, the Brukenthal summer palace is an almost magical and fairytale-like environment. We spent around two weeks excavating these gardens and on the fourth day, as we were scraping dirt away with our trowels, we struck stone. We proceeded to unearth a pavement which wasn't visible on any of the historical maps. Although it was only a pavement, the feeling you get from finding something unexpected is amazing.

Another highlight was a trip to the Apusenia mountains in order to find a traditional blacksmith who could assist in the making of an ancient weapon, the Dacian falx. This was an amazing trip. Far from the lights and cosmopolitan atmosphere of the capital Bucharest, time seems to have stood still. Peasants still work the fields with hoes and live in ramshackle villages with rutted dirt streets right out of a Tolstoy novel. Farmers ride horse-drawn wagons along the roads. Even though no electricity, gas, running water or English language may sound scary and very primitive, my mountain experience was one of the most interesting periods of my life. In fact, the whole experience was incredible, thanks to the Romanian hospitality, the archaeology programme and all the wonderful people I met along the way.

Responsible Travel – Archaeology Holidays

Duration: 9–15 days
Location: Albania, Poland, Romania
Season: June – September
Prerequisites: Open to all
Organisation: Brighton-based online eco-travel agent marketing more than 270 tour operators

☎ 01273 600030
✍ amelia@responsibletravel.com
🖥 www.responsibletravel.com

Description: Responsible Travel currently offers three short-term, hands-on archeological holidays in Europe. Participants are not tourists, they are working as field assistants helping world-renowned scientists. In Albania work involves protecting the World Heritage Site, Butrint National Park, which, according to legend, was founded after the fall of Troy. In Poland participants work as part of the first comprehensive survey and excavation of one of the most impressive burial grounds in Europe. The burials cover at least 2,000 years of local history – from the late Bronze Age to the Middle Ages. In Romania participants help to excavate the Roman fort of Halmyris, which includes one of the best-preserved tombs of early martyred Christians in Europe. Activities are organised during free time

Accommodation: Host family, B&B, hotel, motel
Sample Cost: 2 weeks excavating a Roman Danube fort in Romania £1095 (excluding flights)

A POSTCARD FROM Albania

Italian Federico Spinucci travelled to Albania for Responsible Travel's Archaeology Conservation Project in 2006:

This was my first experience on an archaeological project, although it was something I had always fancied trying. I chose Albania as a destination as although it is quite close to Italy, it still seems in many ways quite far away and mysterious. I thought that the project would be a very good opportunity to learn about Albania's unique history.

The project was split into two parts. First of all we travelled to Saranda in southern Albania to help with the organisation of the local archaeological park that had been created to preserve the ancient Roman town of Butrint. This was extremely interesting and when we left, the villagers of Butrint organised a massive feast to say thank you for all the work we had done. Then we moved on to Melani in the centre of Albania. Here we lived in, and helped to restore, an 18th century monastery that had been badly damaged during the atheist campaign carried out by the communist regime.

We worked incredibly hard on both projects, starting early in the morning and working through until 5pm. But I learnt an awful lot about Albanian culture, British culture (I was the only Italian in an all-British team!), and about the various techniques of organising an archaeological site, restoring ancient walls, and preparing sites of interest to receive visitors. The whole experience taught me a great deal and I made some fantastic friends. I am looking forward to my new British friends coming to visit me in Rome.

La Sabranenque

Duration: Min. 2 weeks (summer projects); 1 week (April, May, October)
Location: Provence, France
Season: April – October
Prerequisites: Aged 18+ and in good health. No experience required

☎ +33 (0)4 66 50 05 05
🖱 info@sabranenque.com
💻 www.sabranenque.com

Organisation: A non-profit organisation in southern France, dedicated to revitalising historic villages and preserving traditional, environmentally friendly building techniques
Description: Participants of all ages and professions, from all over the world contribute to the restoration of sites, often dating to medieval times, learn traditional building techniques from experienced technicians and live in the heart of typical Mediterranean towns. The work involves stone masonry, stone cutting, tiling, paving and drystone walling. Between June and September the two-week Summer Projects take place. Participants work in the mornings and have the afternoons free to explore. In April, May and October one-week visits combine restoration work with either organised cultural outings, hikes or architectural visits, depending on which course you select. The project offers a warm community feeling
Accommodation: Provided in stone houses in the village of Saint Victor la Coste. Meals are home-cooked and shared between the entire team
Cost: US$710 for a 2-week summer project. US$565 (1 week visits)

A POSTCARD FROM rural France

Linda Handiak volunteered at La Sabranenque, helping to breathe life into crumbling stones:

Volunteers are picked up at Avignon train station, which proved to be a bonus because it gave me the chance to experience the exuberance of the city's famous arts festival. I stowed my bags in a locker at the train station and caught a few street performances. By the time I made my way back, other volunteers had arrived: an American archaeology professor, a Canadian museum curator, a Dutch sculptor and a Finnish architect. It made for lively conversation on the drive past rows of ancient stone walls and brilliant sunflowers.

Supper was served on a terrace in the shade of fruit trees. That night, we were lodged by twos in stone huts overlooking a Van Gogh landscape of vineyards and cypresses.

Our workdays began early, at 8am, and broke off before the afternoon heat blanketed the village. We helped carry water and equipment up to an 11th-century castle, negotiating a winding path designed to slow down invading armies. Small teams of supervised volunteers may be involved in consolidating castle structures, or in restoring village paths, ramparts and chapels. The enthusiastic staff breathes fresh life into crumbling stones – and into tired volunteers. Mr Gignoux, Director of La Sabranenque, exhorts workers grappling with dry stone walling to listen to the stones and let them find their natural place. If you are successful, the rewards are great. 'Now', beams Gignoux, 'the walls are smiling'.

In the afternoons we could participate in more specialised workshops. Pascal, a master stonecutter, taught us the difference between shaping stones to fill walls and chiselling them to support arches and windows. He cut with the care and attention of a surgeon, feeling for the pulse of the stone.

Continued

Respect for the local environment permeated everything the staff undertook, from cutting stone to cutting vegetables. We took turns helping in the kitchen, where we were taught to recognise and select appropriate herbs from the garden, create artwork out of radishes and mashed potatoes, and appreciate the virtues of fresh, organic food.

Opportunities for authentic contact with the locals come more easily than if you were travelling alone. The owner of one general store offered this encouraging perspective. Tourists, he explained, came mostly to take pleasure and formed few attachments. 'La Sabranenquers' on the other hand came to give something to the village.

Union Rempart

Duration: 2 or 3 weeks
Location: Throughout France
Season: Spring/summer
Prerequisites: Min. age 18. No upper age limit. No prior experience required
Organisation: A network of organisations promoting

☎ +33 1 42 71 96 55
🖱 monpert@rempart.com
💻 www.rempart.com

heritage preservation and running more than 200 heritage chantiers (workcamps) in France
Description: Volunteers are employed each year to restore and maintain châteux, churches, villages and the old quarters of cities which are of unique cultural and historical value. Workcamps also undertake a limited number of archaeological digs throughout France. Volunteers work around 35 hours per week on restoration activities and one or two days are devoted to cultural and leisure activities such as hiking, swimming and sightseeing. 25% of Rempart's volunteers come from outside France
Accommodation: Takes various forms according to the individual chantier. It ranges from A (most luxurious) to F (tent, cold water) on the website
Cost: Varies between chantiers but is around €5–€8 per day

Underwater Archaeology Project

Duration: 1, 2 or 3 weeks
Location: Sicily
Season: May – September
Prerequisites: Min. age 18
Organisation: The Institute for Underwater Activities (IAS)

☎ +39 335 451533
🖱 marcello@infcom.it
💻 www.infcom.it/subarcheo

Description: Train in underwater excavation techniques while taking part in important surveys of classic, Roman and medieval archaeology. Participants dive every day as part of a team, working in the areas of graphic survey, photography, air-lift excavations, drawing and mapping. All equipment is supplied to participants, who are under the direct supervision of field archaeologists and receive regular health checks from the on-site doctor
Accommodation: Provided in apartments for two to four people
Cost: Participation, room and board €680 (1 week), €980 (2 weeks), or €1,300 for 3 weeks

ARCHAEOLOGICAL DIGS IN ISRAEL

Israel merits its own special section here because it possesses the largest density of rich and varied archaeological sites in the world and the country's passion for uncovering and preserving its heritage is reflected in the vast number of ongoing excavations at any one time. Each university in Israel houses a strong archaeology department or institute, involved in research, excavation, conservation and training. Due to the region's Biblical links, Israeli archaeology often attracts a lot of international attention, and despite the ongoing troubles in Israel, volunteers from around the world remain keen to gain first-hand experience at some of the most important archaeological sites in the world.

Hundreds of sites, from all periods of recorded history, dot the Israeli landscape and excavation continues at a relatively rapid pace. Nevertheless, it is conducted according to extremely high standards, and those seeking to gain experience on a dig, will usually receive exceptional training in Israel. Many archaeologists enlist volunteer help on their digs, and although the work is often difficult and tedious, and carried out under the scorching Middle-Eastern sun, there is never a shortage of eager workers.

Due to the fact that the majority of archaeological digs in Israel are conducted under the guidance of universities and academic institutions, the fees for participation in a dig tend to bo fairly low, and usually include a programme of voluntary lectures. The main cost is therefore accommodation, which ranges from sleeping bags in the field, to rooms in hostels or kibbutzim, to high-spec hotels near a site. Each expedition has its own accommodation arrangements and the majority also provide food for volunteers. Recreational facilities such as swimming pools, beaches and sports equipment may be available and most expeditions organise sightseeing and field trips to sites in the area and to neighbouring museums.

Because of the heat, the work schedule at an excavation tends to begin at dawn and end around noon. There is normally a rest period after lunch, when the sun is at its strongest, followed by cleaning and sorting of pottery and other finds, and then lectures. Some sites erect screen netting that provides a degree of shade, but it is vital that volunteers provide themselves with suitable comfortable working clothes, strong shoes, a hat, sunglasses and skin protection. Participants also need to drink water continuously in order to prevent dehydration.

Security in Israel

The traditional summer dig has been one of the bedrocks of archaeological training in the Middle East and despite the on-going violence in Israel in recent years, the authorities are trying to keep that tradition alive, and to do it safely and with sound scientific objectives that provide a genuine archaeological experience for interested parties. The majority of the digs are still going ahead, and excavation leaders believe the risk to volunteers to be relatively small. Some issue their own protective guidelines, which should lead to a trouble-free trip if followed sensibly. Currently the Foreign and Commonwealth Office advises against travelling to the West Bank, the Gaza strip or within 2km of Israel's border with Lebanon. Always check the advice of the Foreign Office before travelling. However, more than 150,000 British tourists visit Israel each year without incident.

A selection of digs worth applying to is listed below, however an up-to-date list of digs that accept volunteers is compiled by the Israeli Ministry of Foreign Affairs each year and can be viewed at www.mfa.gov.il. Other useful sources of information include the Israel Antiquities Authority (www.antiquities.org.il) and the Institute of Archaeology at the Hebrew University of Jerusalem (see below).

ISRAEL ARCHAEOLOGY & HERITAGE

Bethsaida

Duration: Min. 1 week
Season: May – July
Prerequisites: Min. age 18

☎ +1 402 554 4986
🖱 rarav@mail.unomaha.edu
💻 www.unomaha.edu/bethsaida

Description: Bethsaida, situated on the north sea of Galilee was founded in the 10th century BC as the capital city of the biblical kingdom of Geshur. It is one of the most frequently mentioned towns in the New Testament and Jesus was purported to perform many miracles here. The past four seasons of excavations have focused heavily on the Iron Age City Gate complex (one of the biggest and best preserved in the region) and its link to a previously excavated palace. Participants work at the excavation from 5.30am-12.30pm, Monday to Friday. Weekend tours are organised throughout the season
Accommodation: Ginosar Inn (www.ginosar.co.il)
Cost: US$467–$673 per week according to type of accommodation (dorm, double room, or single room)

Ein Gedi

Duration: Min. 1 week
Season: January
Prerequisites: Min. age 18

🖱 gideonhadas@yahoo.com
💻 http://planetnana.co.il/ghadas/callforvolunteers.htm

Description: Ein Geddi is an oasis on the western shore of the Dead Sea. Archaeological excavations here have revealed a Chacolithic Temple, an Iron Age settlement and a Roman-Byzantine period village. Current excavations focus on a site 200 metres north-west of the Byzantine synagogue and village. The expedition continues to search for a Hasmonean or Herodian palace believed to be located in the area. Fieldwork is conducted Monday to Thursday, 7am – 2pm, with evening lectures
Accommodation: Ein Gedi Youth Hostel
Cost: US$30 registration fee. Hostel costs $250 per week

Hebrew University of Jerusalem – Institute of Archaeology

Duration: 1–4 weeks
Location: Projects throughout Israel
Season: June – September
Prerequisites: Min. age 18. No experience required

☎ +972 2 588 2403
🖥 www.hum.huji.ac.il/archaeology

Organisation: The oldest university department of archaeology in Israel. Works in cooperation with the Israel Antiquities Authority
Description: Research activity of the institute is based on the archaeological excavations carried out at an average of 15 sites each year. Each project is linked through the above website, and as well as taking students from universities all over the world, the various projects also take inexperienced, enthusiastic volunteers. The work includes all aspects including survey, excavation, lab work and archiving
Accommodation: Usually in a kibbutz, but may vary
Cost: Approx €600 per week but cost varies depending on the project

Hippos (Sussita) Excavation Project

Duration: 1–4 weeks (full season preferred)
Season: July
Prerequisites: Min. age 16

☎ +972 4 8249392
🖂 hippos@research.haifa.ac.il
🖥 http://hippos.haifa.ac.il

Description: The ancient walled city of Hippos-Sussita is located on the eastern shore of Tiberias Lake. The site, one of two cities of the Decapolis located in Israel, is situated on top of a flat, diamond-shaped mountain, 350 metres above the Sea of Galilee. Current excavations include a Roman temple, the Hellenistic Compound and Roman fortifications. Volunteers are required to work from 5am-12pm, Sunday to Thursday. The work is rewarding but demanding
Accommodation: Youth hostel and flats provided at Kibbutz Ein-Gev. Two to four people per room. All rooms are air conditioned
Cost: US$100 registration fee plus $410 per week for room and board

Ramat-Rahel

Duration: 2–4 weeks
Season: July – August
Prerequisites: Min. age 14
Description: Ramat Rahel in Jerusalem has just been re-opened for excavation after a 40–year break. Work will continue with exposing remnants of a king's palace from the First Temple period as well as exploring the stratigraphic continuity of layers from the Persian, Hellenistic, Roman and Byzantine periods. Participants work from 5.30am-12.45pm, Monday to Friday. Afternoons include pottery washing, followed by academic lectures and weekly summary tours of the site
Accommodation: Hostel or 4–star hotel with pool, sauna and jacuzzi
Cost: Weekly fee for hostel (without private bathrooms), 2 persons per room US$460. Hotel, 2 persons per room, $550. Includes participation in the dig, room and board, lectures, insurance, flights within Israel and social activities

omertelaviv@gmail.com or
excavations@ramat-rache.org.il

www.tau.ac.il/humanities/
archaeology/projects/ramat_rachel/

Tel Bet Yerah Research and Excavation Project

Duration: 2–6 weeks
Season: June – July
Prerequisites: Min. age 18. No experience required
Description: Tel Bet Yerah is the site of a large fortified Early Bronze Age town situated at the point where the Jordan River exits the Sea of Galilee. The site became a major regional centre and its fortifications, city gate, streets and houses reveal elements of advanced urban planning. The site was also occupied in the Persian, Hellenistic, Roman, Byzantine and Islamic periods. Tel Aviv University runs the excavation each year and welcomes volunteers who, in return for their hard work, are instructed in field techniques and welcome to participate in the lecture series and weekly field trips. Participants work Sunday to Thursday
Accommodation: Ohalo Manor Hostel. Shared rooms with full board
Cost: US$200 deposit, (of which $25 is a registration fee). Room and board from $600 (2 weeks) to $1600 (6 weeks)

☎ +972 3 640 5470

pazsarit@post.tau.ac.il

www.tau.ac.il/humanities/
archaeology/projects/betyerah/

Tel Dor Project

Duration: 2–5 weeks
Season: June – July
Prerequisites: Min. age 18
Description: Project devoted to investigating one of the largest coastal cities in ancient

☎ +1 206 543 2276

dor-proj@mscc.huji.ac.il or
bloch-smith@msn.com

www.hum.huji.ac.il/dor/

Israel. Current investigations include a large Hellenistic temple, early Roman industrial installations and hopefully exposing the Bronze Age city. Participants are engaged in excavation, digital registration of architecture and artefacts using advanced graphics software, on-site scientific sampling and site conservation. Volunteers will gain proficiency in these subjects, working closely with professional and academic staff. Participants stay at one of the best-rated seaside resorts in Israel and can enjoy diving and sailing trips in their recreation time

Accommodation: Nasholim Hotel. Shared, air conditioned rooms with en-suite showers and kitchenettes. Meals included

Cost: Half season, €1,400 (including board and lodging)

Tell es-Safi/Gath Archaeological Project

Duration: 2, 3 or 4 weeks
Season: July/August
Prerequisites: Min. age 18
Description: Tell es-Safi is identified by most scholars as the biblical city of Gath of the Philistines (the home

☎ +972 3 531 8299
🖱 maeira@mail.biu.ac.il
💻 www.dig-gath.org

of Goliath). It is one of the largest ancient ruin mounds and one of the most important archaeological sites in Israel. Excavation work runs from 6am–1pm, Sunday to Friday. Afternoons are filled with occasional tours, field trips and recreation time (there is a pool at the kibbutz). Lectures take place two evenings a week. Academic credit is available. Application deadline of 1 May each year

Accommodation: At the Kibbutz Revadim. Air-conditioned, shared rooms

Cost: US$350 per week (plus a $25 registration fee) or $1350 for full 4 weeks. Includes food, accommodation and travel from kibbutz to site

The Tel Rehov Excavations

Duration: 3–6 weeks
Season: July – August
Prerequisites: Min. age 18. No experience required
Description: This excavation is part of the

🖱 rehov@mscc.huji.ac.il
💻 www.rehov.org/volunteer/

continuing Beth-Shean Valley Archaeological Project. Previous excavations have revealed successive occupational layers from the late Bronze Age and Iron Age. Each year volunteers include men and women from all walks of life and from all over the world. Aside from digging, recreation is a large part of the Tel Rehov experience including parties and barbecues and swimming in the Sahne springs. Workdays are Monday to Friday, with lectures twice a week

Accommodation: Kibbutz Nir David in air-conditioned wooden cabins that accommodate up to five people. The kibbutz provides 3 meals a day, room and bedding

Cost: US$300 per week (including room and board)

The Yavneh-Yam Archaeological Project

Duration: 1–4 weeks (2 consecutive weeks preferred)
Season: July – August
Prerequisites: Min. age 14

ilansh@netvision.net.il
www.tau.ac.il/~yavneyam

Description: The coastal site of Yavneh-Yam was occupied from the late Bronze period until the Middle Ages. Current excavations deal with the late Iron Age, Persian, Hellenistic, Byzantine and Early Islamic periods. Participants work from 5am – 12pm every day with weekends free to relax, explore the area and swim in the Mediterranean. Excursions are organised

Accommodation: Air-conditioned dorm rooms for three to four people with en-suite bathroom

Cost: Registration fee of US$50. Room and board is between $400 (1 week) and $1,520 (full season). Also includes training, lectures and excursions

The Zeitah Excavations

Duration: 3–5 weeks
Season: June – July
Prerequisites: Min. age 18. No previous experience required. Must be physically fit and able to work in hot weather

+1 412 441 3304 Ex.2126
tappy@fyi.net
www.zeitah.net

Description: The town of Zeitah lies in the Beth Guvrin Valley. In 2005 an inscription bearing the oldest known example of the linear alphabet was found, and excavation efforts are now concentrating on the mound where this stone appeared. The first week is spent training volunteers. Thereafter, they are employed in a variety of tasks, from detailed excavation work to heavy hauling work. The working week runs from Monday to Friday and overnight field trips are organised

Accommodation: Kibbutz Gal-On. Hostel-style rooms with air conditioning
Cost: US$990–$1,450 (3–5 weeks) plus a registration fee of $25 (includes room and board)

Alutiiq Museum – Community Archaeology

Duration: 1 day – 6 weeks
Location: Kodiak, Alaska, USA
Season: July – August
Prerequisites: Min. age 14. All welcome

☎ +1 907 486 7004
🖱 Patrick@alutiiqmuseum.com
💻 www.alutiiqmuseum.com/education.htm

Organisation: Museum, funded by the non-profit organisation, the Alutiiq Heritage foundation, that preserves and shares the cultural traditions of the Alutiiq people through exhibits, educational programmes, publications and research

Description: Every summer the museum hosts an excavation at an archaeological site near the town of Kodiak. The site is Zaimka Mound, a prehistoric settlement on the eastern shore of Women's Bay. Participants assist museum archaeologists with every aspect of the excavation from digging and mapping to screening dirt. In the lab, participants assist with washing, sorting and labelling artefacts. Fieldwork lasts for four weeks, followod by two weeks of lab work. Participants are invited to volunteer as much time as they have available

Accommodation: No accommodation or meals provided. Motels, B&Bs and camping available in Kodiak

Cost: None (for those interested in academic credits, there is a charge of US$50 per credit for tuition)

Belize Valley Archaeology Reconnaissance Project

Duration: 2/4 weeks
Location: Cayo District, Belize
Season: June – August
Prerequisites: Age 18+ and physically fit. No experience required

🖱 archaeology@bvar.org
💻 www.bvar.org

Organisation: Ongoing investigation affiliated with the Belize Institute of Archaeology and the University of Mississippi

Description: The investigation focuses on the site of Baking Pot, one of the largest sites in the Belize Valley, which served as the capital to a small kingdom in the Classic period (AD250–830). Through excavations the team hopes to gain a better understanding of the physical and functional properties of Barking Pot's ancient court. There are two options for volunteers. The four–week option is designed for extensive exposure to archaeological methods and is tailored for students wishing to obtain academic credit. Nevertheless this option is suitable for enthusiastic non-students. The two–week option provides a basic introduction to field research techniques

Accommodation: Hotel facilities at weekends; more rustic facilities during the working week – usually camping

Cost: US$1,950 for 4 weeks, $975 for 2 weeks. Includes room and board

ARCHAEOLOGY & HERITAGE

WORLDWIDE

Caribbean Volunteer Expeditions

Duration: 1 week
Location: Throughout the Caribbean
Season: November – March
Prerequisites: Min. age 21; fairly physically fit
Organisation: Non-profit agency that organises hands-on holidays to help preserve the fragile cultural heritage of the Caribbean

☎ +1 607 962 7846
✆ ahershcve@aol.com
💻 www.cvexp.org

Description: CVE trips are made up of people who love history, and love the Caribbean but want to do more than lie on a beach. The expeditions contribute to the preservation of the cultural heritage of the Caribbean and are extremely varied in scope. Work may range from clearing vegetation around historic buildings to archaeological excavation, to computerising museum archives. Each programme includes site work for five to six hours per day, Monday to Friday, followed by a cultural or recreational activity in the early afternoon. Current projects include the Jamaica Jewish cemetery inventory trip, the Nevis Windmill conservation trip and the Bahamas archaeology project
Accommodation: Provided, often in beach-side hotels
Cost: Approx. US$500–$1000 including lodging, food and local transportation

Centre For The Study Of Eurasian Nomads

Duration: 3 weeks
Location: South central Mongolia
Season: June – August
Prerequisites: Min. age 19. No experience required
Organisation: Archaeologists from US and Mongolian research institutions

☎ +1 805 653 2607
✆ jkimball@csen.org
💻 www.csen.org

Description: The Baga Gazaryn Chuluu Survey offers a chance for archaeology enthusiasts with no experience to get involved in a full-coverage pedestrian survey of a remote section of the desert-steppe zone of the Middle Gobi province in Mongolia. The survey includes small-scale excavations of burial and habitation sites dated to the Bronze and early Iron Age. Finds so far include ancient petroglyphs and stone stelae erected by early Turkic nomads. Full training is provided by the on-site archaeologists. Participants have plenty of free time to explore the local area
Accommodation: Provided in basic campsites in remote locations and in lodges at the beginning and end of the session
Cost: US$1,400 ($1,250 for students)

Crow Canyon Archaeological Center

Duration: 1 week (adult research week/lab week);
3 weeks (for older teens)
Location: Colorado, USA
Season: June – September
Prerequisites: Min. age 18. No experience
necessary – special programmes are organised for
complete novices

☎ +1 800 422 8975
✒ travel@crowcanyon.org
💻 www.crowcanyon.org

Organisation: Centre dedicated to understanding and preserving the rich history of the
Pueblo Indians (the Anasazi). Programmes are run in consultation with American Indians
Description: The Mesa Verde region has one of the densest concentrations of well-
preserved archaeological sites in the world. Crow Canyon offers those with a passion for
archaeology the chance to work alongside professional archaeologists to unearth and
analyse Anasazi artefacts in the rugged landscape of the American South-West. Adult
research weeks include excavation work, laboratory processing, field trips to nearby sites,
and an evening programme several nights a week. There are also lab weeks in which
participants provide essential support at the end of the field season
Accommodation: Shared accommodation in Navajo-style log cabins with modern
facilities on a 170–acre campus
Cost: US$1,150 for a novice non-member for 1 week. Includes accommodation, meals,
permits and transport after your arrival

Cultural Restoration Tourism Project

Duration: 12 days
Location: Mustang region, Nepal
Season: April – June
Prerequisites: None required
Organisation: CRTP provides the opportunity for everyone
to get involved in the restoration of culturally significant
buildings

☎ +1 415 563 7221
 info@crtp.net
💻 www.crtp.net

Description: CRTP is currently focusing on the Chairro Gompa Restoration Project,
300-year-old monastery that was once the religious centre of the Takhali people of
Mustang. Economic hardships and the harsh weather of the area have taken their toll on
the structure and the treasures inside are at risk of being lost forever. CRTP's volunteer
tourism visits combine restoration work with guided tours, treks and community visits.
Participants work alongside a local crew, using traditional tools and techniques, ensuring
that the ancient works of master craftsmen and artists are not erased from existence. The
trip donation pays for an unforgettable holiday, helps buy materials for the project and
pays the wages of the local restoration staff
Accommodation: Provided in traditional housing for the area and shared with other
travellers. Meals are prepared by local staff
Cost: US$2,495 including food and accommodation

ARCHAEOLOGY & HERITAGE

WORLDWIDE

Earthwatch Institute

Duration: 7–14 days
Location: Peru, Micronesia, Easter Island (Chile), USA, Thailand, Mexico, Tanzania
Season: Year round
Prerequisites: Ages 18–95. No experience necessary

☎ 01865 318838
✉ info@earthwatch.org.uk
💻 www.earthwatch.org/Europe

Organisation: Earthwatch is an international environmental charity that offers volunteering opportunities on scientific research expeditions around the world. All volunteer contributions go directly towards supporting the scientific research

Description: Earthwatch runs a range of archaeological and heritage preservation holidays worldwide. Volunteers work as field assistants, helping scientists in their research on real archaeological and heritage projects and learning about the issues involved. Current projects include a study of Peru's Wari Empire, helping to preserve the Chuuk Lagoon's World War II submerged sites in Micronesia, excavating a mammoth graveyard in South Dakota, excavating sites of the magnificent Angkot civilisation in Thailand and uncovering megafauna fossils in central Mexico

Accommodation: Included in cost. Varies between projects – camp, hotels, lodges etc

Cost: £595–£1850 depending on project and duration (excluding flights)

A POSTCARD FROM Easter Island, Chile

63-year-old actor and small-business owner, John Gowans took part in Earthwatch's 'Easter Island Cultures' project, a 16-day archaeological expedition to find and document hitherto unknown primitive sites:

Easter Island is a place that I have been fascinated with for decades and this was a fantastic opportunity for me to go there not just as a tourist, but to actually get involved and do some hands-on investigation, and maybe in some small way contribute to a better understanding of the island and its culture.

Each day we were picked up after breakfast and driven to the work site. My team was assigned to walk the landscape in a prescribed grid, looking for man-made features. By using a GPS unit we would pick up where we had left off the day before and walk three or four abreast over a prescribed distance. When we found a feature we would plant a small flag. Another team would then measure, sketch, photograph and take GPS coordinates of the site.

But it wasn't all work. The first two days of the trip were spent on a tour of the most popular sites, and during the evenings we were treated to presentations by the staff of their past projects and the history of the island as they know it. The rest of our spare time was spent exploring the island and its only town, Hanga Roa. We also spent a lot of time eating! We had fresh fish almost every day and lots of local produce.

I made some really good friends on the trip and there are a handful that I know I will keep in touch with. The cross-section of participants was really interesting. There were people from all over America, Canada, and the UK, and their ages ranged from 29 to 83! But for me, the best part of the trip overall was when I discovered a fragment from a moai (the giant carved stone statues that Easter Island is famous for) that had never been documented. Although it was only a small discovery, it was exciting to know that I had played a part in contributing to a much larger research project.

Elderhostel Adventures in Lifelong Learning

Duration: 1 week
Location: Worldwide
Season: July/August
Prerequisites: Elderhostel programmes are only available to those aged 55 or over
Organisation: Elderhostel is a not-for-profit organisation dedicated to providing learning adventures for people aged 55 and over
Description: Elderhostel runs a range of archaeology and anthropology-based trips in collaboration with academic institutions. Participants accompany field archaeologists on expeditions to locate and record sites of interest. All trips include extracurricular social activities and excursions
Accommodation: Provided in a mixture of hotels, motels or conference centre facilities, depending on the project
Sample Cost: 1 week of archaeology and native American art in Colorado, US$839. Includes accommodation, meals, lectures and field trips

☎ +1 800 454 5768
✆ registration@elderhostel.org
💻 www.elderhostel.org

Friends of the Cumbres and Toltec Scenic Railroad

Duration: 1/2 weeks
Location: New Mexico, USA
Season: May, June, August
Prerequisites: Min. age 13, good physical fitness (all work is at high elevation in a remote area)
Organisation: Non-profit organisation with a specific public purpose: the historic preservation of the Cumbres and Toltec Scenic Railroad
Description: Hidden away in a corner of the southern Rocky Mountains is a precious historic artefact of the American West. Built in 1880, it is one of the finest examples of steam-era mountain railroading in America. The steam locomotives still labour up steep grades and along narrow shelves above yawning gorges for the benefit of visitors. Volunteers are invited to help work on the preservation and restoration of this historic railway. Participants' duties include painting, car lettering, track clearing, interior repairs to the carriages, landscaping, reconstruction, carpentry and electrical work. Some volunteers also help to document historic restoration work
Accommodation: Not provided. There are three campsites nearby as well as a range of motels and B&Bs
Cost: Participation fee: US$40 per week plus $15 (insurance). Lunch, snacks and drinks included in the fee. All other costs must be met by the volunteer

☎ +1 505 880 1311
✆ nanclark@cumbrestoltec.org
💻 www.cumbrestoltec.org

Hands Up Holidays

Duration: 4–15 days (also tailor-made options)
Location: Libya, Romania
Season: October – May (Libya); April – October (Romania)
Prerequisites: Min. age 18. No specific skills required, just enthusiasm but any skills you do have are matched with specific projects where possible
Organisation: Leading ethical tour operator working with local suppliers, NGOs, charities and little-known local projects. A minimum of 10% of profits go to further development projects
Description: Hands Up Holidays offers ethically and environmentally responsible holidays that blend sightseeing with fulfilling volunteering experiences. Approx. a third of the holiday is devoted to a meaningful 'taste' of environmental conservation volunteering and the rest of the time is spent sightseeing with local, English-speaking guides. In Libya you can help to restore the UNESCO World Heritage old town of Ghadhames. In Romania you can work alongside the local community of Viscri to restore Saxon buildings and develop their heritage as a sustainable tourism venture. All flights are carbon neutral
Accommodation: Ranges from camping to homestays or guesthouses/local hotels that are locally owned and managed where possible
Cost: From £400 for 4 days in Romania, or £550 for 9 days in Libya, through to £1,250 for 15 days in Libya

☎ 0800 7833554
✉ info@handsupholidays.com
💻 www.handsupholidays.com

Heritage Conservation Network

Duration: 1 or 2 weeks
Location: Worldwide
Season: Year round
Prerequisites: Open to all
Organisation: A non-profit organisation actively promoting the conservation of historic architecture and sites
Description: HCN organises a range of 'workshops' or volunteer vacations for people whose interest lies in architecture, art history or historic preservation. Participants with all levels of experience work side-by-side with community members under the guidance of a building conservation specialist to restore significant historic structures. Each workshop is unique, but all allow volunteers to get in touch with history, meet people from all over the world, experience new cultures and learn new skills. 2007 projects include post hurricane Katrina restoration in the Bay of St. Louis (USA), colonial building conservation in Ghana, and a conservation survey in the monastery of San Giovanni Battista in Italy
Accommodation: Usually at a B&B or small hotel with sustainable tourism goals. Some projects may be less luxurious eg bunk in a cabin
Cost: Fees range from US$300–$950 per week, depending on the project (includes lodging, insurance, training, materials, breakfast and lunch)

☎ +1 303 444 0128
✉ info@heritageconservation.net
💻 www.heritageconservation.net

Involvement Volunteers Association Inc

Duration: Min. 2 weeks
Location: More than 20 countries including Australia, Bolivia, China, Egypt, Fiji, Korea, Latvia, Mongolia, Namibia, Peru, Samoa, Togo and Venezuela

☎ +61 3 9646 9392
✆ ivworldwide@volunteering.org.au
💻 www.volunteering.org.au

Season: Year round
Prerequisites: Anyone can volunteer, preferably with knowledge and experience but also possible without. Min. age 18
Organisation: Registered not-for-profit NGO that aims to make volunteering readily available to those who wish to help around the world
Description: IVA offers a cost effective way for people of all ages to gain practical experience while helping others as a real volunteer and meeting the local people, and experiencing their culture. Current archaeological and heritage projects include historic town preservation and steam train operation in Australia, assisting at an ethnographic museum in Bolivia, working at a museum in Fiji, an archaeological project in Iceland, and excavation in Mexico, and historic building and boat restoration in New Zealand
Accommodation: Provided in basic but clean and safe lodgings
Cost: Fees are negotiated with volunteers on an individual basis. On average a 4–week placement costs around £800 including food, accommodation, administration costs and in-country transportation

Judith River Dinosaur Institute

Duration: 2 weeks
Location: Judith River, Montana, USA
Season: July – August
Prerequisites: Min. age 14. Experienced amateurs preferred

☎ +1 406 654 2323
✆ nmurphy@ttc-cmc.net
💻 www.montanadinodigs.com

Organisation: Collection and funding vehicle for the paleontology department of the Phipps Country Museum. The institute provides exploration, collection, preparation and curation services
Description: Findings of the stegosaurus are extremely rare in North America. This project represents an opportunity for volunteers to work on the first ever stegosaurus found in Montana. The work includes field exploration, recording and mapping finds, excavation and interpretation. This project is a serious excavation and participants must be willing to be trained and be dedicated to learning and working hard
Accommodation: Provided in campsites or arranged by the volunteer
Cost: Depends on the individual dig. Approx. US$895, not including accommodation or US$1,495, including accommodation

Maya Research Program

Duration: Min. 2 weeks
Location: Belize, Mexico, Peru
Season: May – July
Prerequisites: Min. age 18. No experience required

 +1 817 350 4986
 guderjan@mrpmail.com
 www.mayaresearchprogram.org

Organisation: US-based non-profit organisation that sponsors archaeological and ethnographic research in Central and South America
Description: Three programmes are currently run. The **Blue Creek Project** is an annual dig in an important Mayan site in Belize, which aims to understand the collapse of Mayan society. The **Yaxunah Ethnographic Program** is only available to participants who have previously taken part at Blue Creek. Participants are involved in an ethnographic study of a traditional Maya village in Yucatan, Mexico for two weeks. Proficiency in Spanish is required. Finally, there are several **Archaeology Programs in Peru** in which participants join an excavation of Moche living areas and a cemetery. This project has yielded some of the most exciting material to come from the Moche area. Participants are guided by professional archaeologists in each of the projects
Accommodation: Blue Creek – In cabanas at the MRP base station. Yaxunah – in an eco-tourist hotel run by the villagers. Peru – various options
Cost: Blue Creek and Yaxunuh – US$1,450 ($1,100 for students). Peru – US$1,500 (plus an optional third week for $1,000)

Nasca Project, Peru

Duration: Min. 4 weeks
Location: Nasca, Peru
Season: July – August
Prerequisites: Min. age 18. Basic experience required

 +39 030 377 3738
 animasalva@tin.it
 www.geocities.com/proyectonasca

Organisation: Run by the Italian Centre for Study and Research of Pre-Columbian Archaeology, a non-profit cultural association
Description: Excavations of the Cahuachi site have been ongoing for 25 years and in the last few years have concentrated on the restoration of Cahuachi's ceremonial centre. Participants are involved in a range of work including excavation of 5x5m sectors, drawing and mapping the site and preparation and cataloguing of artefacts. Participants work from Monday to midday Saturday, with Saturday afternoons and Sundays free for recreation and exploration of the local area
Accommodation: Provided at a campsite in the desert. Volunteers must bring their own tents
Cost: Approx. US$840 (excluding flights)

Passport in Time

Duration: Mostly 5 days. 2 or more projects can be strung together
Location: National forests and grasslands across the United States
Season: Year round
Prerequisites: Age 18+ but families and seniors encouraged
Organisation: PIT is a volunteer programme of the US Department of Agriculture Forest Service, which aims to preserve the nation's past with the help and support of members of the public
Description: Volunteers are required to work with professional historians and archaeologists on such diverse activities as archaeological excavation and survey, historic structure restoration, and analysis and curation of artefacts. Volunteers may select from a range of ongoing projects that are individually tailored to the needs of the resource. Some work sites are in towns or communities, but most are in woodland areas
Accommodation: In most cases volunteers camp near to the project areas in primitive campsites, bunkhouses and guard stations
Cost: No programme fees but volunteers must pay for their own food, lodging and transportation

☎ + 1 800 281 9176
🖱 pit@sricrm.com
💻 www.passportintime.com

A POSTCARD FROM Dog Canyon, New Mexico

Gail Carbanier spent a hands-on holiday volunteering with PIT in New Mexico searching for lost Apache battle sites in Dog Canyon:

Early the first day, our group started up the Dog Canyon trail. The first half mile was like climbing a ladder. I carried my metal detector and a full backpack. I was gasping for air and my legs felt like wet noodles when the trail finally levelled out.

Apache skirmishes with the U.S. Cavalry, emigrants, Mexicans and volunteer troops are documented from 1849 to 1880 in the Dog Canyon area. The fact that six significant encounters took place gave us hope that we would find either campsites or battle sites, or both.

After about 10 minutes – 'beep, beep, beep' – off went my detector. I was not off the trail more than 10 feet, still trying to catch my breath. Carefully scraping the sandy soil away, I uncovered a coin. My first find was an 1833 Mexcian Real – one of the earliest dated coins found in the area. If that coin could only talk!

Our group climbed up the canyon for four more days and we had great success finding both Apache and US Cavalry artefacts including several metal Apache arrow points, several 'tinklers' (tin or brass ornaments originally attached to clothing), brass Apache bracelets, and a military button. All told, we found enough artefacts to be pretty certain of the location of an Apache campsite and a potential 1880 US Cavalry skirmish line. Major sections of the canyon remain to be surveyed, and hopefully PIT volunteers will continue to be part of the adventure.

Responsible Travel – Archaeology Holidays

Duration: 14 days (Tanzania); 1–8 weeks (Caribbean)

Location: Tanzania, Netherlands Antilles (Caribbean)

Season: May – August (Tanzania); January – August (Caribbean)

 01273 600030

 amelia@responsibletravel.com

 www.responsibletravel.com

Prerequisites: Open to all

Organisation: Brighton-based online eco-travel agent marketing more than 270 tour operators

Description: The Early Man at Olduvai Gorge dig in Tanzania, takes place at a legendary 1.75 million year-old site with a rich record of discoveries. Teams excavate trenches in areas of concentrated artefacts and bone, sieve dirt for smaller artefacts and fossil, and wash, sort and record the finds. The Caribbean Archaeology Vacation takes place on St. Eustatius. The island is considered to have the densest concentration of colonial period sites in the Americas, and excavations here have been ongoing for more than 25 years. Volunteers tend to excavate from 7/8am to 12pm, followed by artefact processing and cataloguing from 2–4pm. Participants are then encouraged to immerse themselves in local culture, explore the national parks and enjoy spectacular diving

Accommodation: Included in the price – camping in the Serengeti and self-catering in the Caribbean

Sample Cost: Tanzania £1,350, excluding flights; Caribbean £234 (1 week) – £1091 (8 weeks), excluding flights

Royal Tyrrell Museum

Duration: Min. 15 days

Location: Alberta, Canada

Season: Year round

Prerequisites: Min. age 17. Seniors welcome. No specific skills required

☎ + 1 888 440 4240

🖱 tyrrell.info@gov.ab.ca

💻 www.tyrrellmuseum.com

Organisation: The only Canadian institution devoted exclusively to the study and exhibition of palaeontology

Description: The museum welcomes volunteers to participate in many areas of the museum's work, from welcoming visitors, to assisting with the museum's education and interpretive programmes. There is also work available in the preparation and collections department, cataloguing and caring for more than 120,000 specimens and fossil resources. Volunteer museum ambassadors provide information to guests on all aspects of palaeontology. Full training is provided

Accommodation: Volunteers organise their own board and lodging

Cost: None, but volunteers must arrange their own food and lodging (typically costs US$300–$600 for 3 weeks)

Sierra Club Outings

Duration: Mostly 1 week
Location: Throughout the USA, Puerto Rico, the Virgin Islands, Canada
Season: All year round
Prerequisites: Min. age 18. Seniors encouraged

☎ +1 415 977 5522
🖰 national.outings@sierraclub.org
🖥 www.sierraclub.org/outings

Organisation: The Sierra Club is a grassroots environmental organisation founded in 1892 to protect the planet's natural resources
Description: Offers a range of volunteer activities focused on archaeological digs. Sierra Club Outings projects are led by volunteers who plan and run all of the trips. All outings include at least one day with no activities scheduled in order to allow volunteers to explore the surrounding wilderness. The club stresses the importance of building a strong community as a group
Accommodation: Varies depending on location of project undertaken
Cost: Mostly between US$350 and $600

Western Belize Regional Cave Project

Duration: 4 weeks
Location: San Ignacio, Belize
Season: June – August
Prerequisites: Min. age 18. Prior archaeological, spelunking or caving experience preferred. Physical fitness required

 gwrobel@bvar.org
🖥 www.indiana.edu/~belize/

Organisation: Group of archaeologists studying the use of caves by the prehistoric Maya in Belize
Description: A four-week research programme providing an opportunity for participants to experience ancient Maya archaeology in a hands-on, educational, and exciting jungle setting in Belize. The project is designed to introduce participants to the fundamental approaches to the practice of speleoarchaeology and provide training in a variety of archaeological techniques. Investigations in the caves include extensive exploration, survey, mapping of rooms and artefacts, typing of pottery, data recording and excavation. The majority of the work week is spent deep within the jungle
Accommodation: Provided in comfortable campsites in the jungle during the week and at a resort hotel in San Ignacio at weekends
Cost: US$1,950 (including food and accommodation)

Wyoming Dinosaur Center – Dig for a Day Program

Duration: 1 day
Location: Warm Springs Ranch, Wyoming, USA
Season: Spring – Autumn
Prerequisites: Min. age 18. No experience required
Organisation: A museum and scientific research centre

☎ +1 307 864 2997
🖱 wdinoc@wyodino.org
💻 www.wyodino.org

Description: Volunteers help to discover, collect and document Jurassic period dinosaur fossils under the guidance of WDC technicians. The fossil-bearing beds overlook the picturesque red hills at the northern end of the Wind River Canyon and the two main excavation sites have yielded a large amount of well preserved material. All activities are designed to assist in current scientific research projects that provide valuable information concerning the environment in which dinosaurs lived 145 million years ago. The working day runs from 8am to 4pm. Once trained in the WDC's field methods, participants can earn volunteer status and participate in more delicate and critical work, without participation fees
Accommodation: Not provided. Contact the WDC for advice on suitable nearby lodgings
Cost: US$150 per person (including lunch)

HANDS-ON
Charity
Challenges

FUNDRAISING ADVENTURES

A large and growing number of charities in the UK offer adventurous group travel to individuals who are prepared to undertake some serious fundraising on their behalf. The range of trips now available is staggering. Participants can ride camels in Mongolia, cycle from Moscow to St. Petersburg or go white water rafting in Turkey. They can ski 24 peaks in 48 hours in Austria, drive Minis around Italy and sledge through the Arctic Circle. Then of course there are the old favourites: hiking the Inca trail, trekking to Everest base camp in Nepal, up Kilimanjaro, and along the Great Wall of China. And the best part is that these trips not only offer a rewarding holiday, but also raise a considerable amount of money for charity.

The charity challenge is an innovative and resourceful response to the growing demand for adventure holidays, underpinned by the need for charities to face up to an increasingly competitive funding environment. Around 15,000 people in the UK alone take a charity challenge each year raising millions of pounds for charity. The first operator to introduce the concept into the mainstream market was Classic Tours. Since 1991 it has raised £32 million for around 120 charities. They have since been imitated by a number of other operators and many charities also run their own challenges. Household names like Oxfam, the Youth Hostels Association and the Children's Society organise sponsored trips, as do many more obscure good causes.

These challenges have proved so popular precisely because they benefit both the individual and the charity. For the individual, challenges offer a life-changing experience that allows them to realise personal goals, to push their limits and discover hidden capabilities. They also find that they benefit in the long run from improved confidence and self esteem, as well as getting into the best physical shape of their lives. The challenge also allows participants to make a greater financial impression on an issue that means something to them, than their own financial resources would allow. Nobody can expect to change the world on a charity challenge, but you can certainly raise funds and awareness for your own personal choice of worthy cause. For the charity, the challenges bring its work into the public eye, helping to raise its profile and awareness of the work it does. Challenges are also a powerful way of motivating people to support its cause. Individuals have the ability to mobilise the generosity of people through their inspirational commitment and in doing so raise thousands of pounds for deserving causes. Erich Reich, founder of Classic Tours and the creator of the charity challenge concept explains the mutual benefits of the challenge:

Charity challenges are an effective method of raising money for charity because they appeal to such a wide spectrum of people, many of whom wouldn't normally get involved in fundraising. Often they are professional people, or those in their 40s or 50s who can use the challenge model to try something that they would never otherwise have tried, to travel to exotic places and to experience new cultures. As a result, charities are able to tap into a new source of valuable funds and spread their message to a wider audience, and participants are able to travel with a purpose and gain experiences that they never would as a conventional tourist.

How Does it Work?

The rapid expansion of the sector has led to a huge variety of choice to the prospective charity challenger. The concept of a charity challenge extends to any sacrifice of time and effort in return for fundraising. As well as more traditional challenges, in recent years, the idea of the volunteering challenge has also gained momentum. This combines the kind of short-term voluntary project described in earlier chapters with sponsorship. Nevertheless the challenges all have a lot in common.

Most charity challenges last no longer than a fortnight, and some are even short enough for participants to leave the office on a Thursday and have climbed Mount Olympus by the time they return on Monday morning. Even so, challenges are not an easy option. Participants must spend months training and fundraising before undertaking a physical challenge. Getting fit, raising thousands of pounds for charity, and then taking on a potentially gruelling challenge will all be extremely hard, but ultimately gratifying work.

Most challenges follow the same format. There are two ways to fund an expedition – self-funding and minimum sponsorship. Self-funders personally cover the full cost of the expedition (often including a small donation to the charity). The charity then receives every penny raised thereafter and although there is no minimum sponsorship requirement, participants are still encouraged to raise as much as they can for the charity.

With the minimum sponsorship option, participants pay an initial registration fee of £100–£500 to secure their place and the charity then sets a sponsorship target. This is often around £1,000 for a four-day trip, rising to as much as £3,000 for 10–day excursions. Depending on the nature of the challenge, participants then have between six and nine months to get in shape and meet their target. Most charities require participants to have raised 80% of their target 10 weeks before departure.

The charity or organisation in question then organises everything else, including flights, accommodation and logistical support on the ground. The only expenses that are not included are transfers to and from your departure airport, vaccinations, visas, personal equipment and spending money (although very little spending money will be required during the challenge).

While on the challenge, you are usually placed in groups of 15–20 people of different ages and backgrounds. The groups are usually led by a team of experienced guides as well as local guides and staff to help with cooking and setting up camp. Often because of the nature of the 'challenge', there is a certain amount of roughing it involved. Many of the host countries are developing countries with limited infrastructures and basic facilities. These are certainly not five-star holidays. You should expect modest accommodation, often camping and hostels, purely so that the cost of the trip is kept to a minimum and more money goes to the charity.

The Ethics Box: Saving the World or a Free Holiday?

While these events have proved a popular way of raising money for a favourite charity, some questions have been raised about exactly how ethical challenges are. Certainly the days when charities and organisations could be accused of misleading potential sponsors are long gone. When the charity challenge concept was in its infancy, there wasn't enough clarity about exactly where the money was going, but in response to this criticism, charities drew up their own code of conduct. Charities and tour operators must now be completely upfront about the full costs of the trip – which must be no more than 50% of the funds raised.

Nevertheless some critics still argue that the charity challenge is an inefficient way of fundraising for worthy causes. As much as half of the money raised by each sponsored traveller goes towards paying for their holiday (flight, accommodation, etc), something which family, friends and colleagues who support the fundraising might come to resent. The participant is in effect getting a free holiday (although the trips' promotional literature steers clear of the word 'holiday' – these are definitely 'challenges').

The charities themselves argue that while other fundraising activities might bring in more money, they do not offer the long-term benefits of challenge events, which attract a high number of young people and supply a dependable long-term income stream. Those who go on such holidays are often those who would not otherwise be donating, yet many first-time participants go on to undertake further challenges and sometimes become lifelong supporters of the charity. Charity challenges do appear to achieve the dual goals of raising money and raising awareness of the charity's purpose and achievements by engendering a sense of occasion.

It is also up to the participants to raise around £2,500. According to the charities, this is no mean feat and will take months of hard fundraising, via a range of different initiatives. Most of the challenges are also fairly gruelling and will involve months of training. This hardly sounds like a cheap cushy holiday. For those of you who have qualms about the way the trips are financed, there is an easy solution. You can simply pay the full cost yourself so that any funds you raise are pure profit for your chosen charity. According to Charity Challenge, around a third of their participants choose this option.

A final issue to consider before setting off on a charity challenge is the impact that such trips might have on the communities that they pass through. Hundreds of people trekking along the Inca Trail, for example, is not environmentally sustainable and potentially does little to benefit the host country. Tourism Concern's director Tricia Barnett highlighted this in a recent article in *The Observer*: *'There's a widespread awareness that tourism often impacts negatively on the host country. But somehow when people have put in so much hard work fundraising in aid of a good cause, they go out with a halo over their head and think none of that applies. My worry is that these challenges are in fact no different from any other form of tourism.'* However many of the charities and challenge organisations are now going out of their way to counter these concerns. Charity Challenge, for example, claims to use local guides, support teams and doctors as well as small family-run accommodation where possible. Potential charity challengers should therefore not be put off, but you should certainly ask some searching questions of the organisations that you intend to travel with.

Who Takes a Charity Challenge?

The chance to participate in a group activity which at the same time funds a good cause is welcomed by many different types of people, with the ages on each challenge ranging from 18 to those in their 60s (although the majority fall into the 30–50 age range). Charity challengers comprise people from a complete mix of professions, geographical locations, and backgrounds, so there is no standard profile. One of the great features of the challenge is the camaraderie that develops between otherwise disparate types of people, as Lee Levitt, writing in *The Independent* discovered:

At 18,000 feet, inner reserves and determination tend to go only so far when your head is pounding away and your muscles are giving out. Knowing that I couldn't have done it without the help of others was one of those fabled seminal moments that the tight-knit nature of the charity holiday group experience is, in some ways, primed to produce.

It may be partly for this reason that the charity challenge also appeals to singles. Around 90% of participants are travelling solo and, according to Charity Challenge, there is something about these trips that brings people together: *'On these challenges you see people at their worst and smelliest, so if you feel an affinity with them, that's a pretty good sign'.*

Participants need to be relatively fit and have an active sense of adventure. You should be willing to get involved and have a positive and flexible approach to travel. Nevertheless, having the backing of an organisation on a challenge also means that these trips appeal to those who are nervous of taking an adventurous trip on their own.

Another type of charity challenge is the Corporate Challenge, which has become extremely popular in recent years. Not only do corporate charity challenges play an important role in fundraising, but they also benefit the company taking part. Charity challenges work as team-building exercises, building bridges between departments and placing workers in new and stimulating situations.

How to Choose a Challenge

Once you have decided to take a charity challenge, there are many possibilities to consider. Thousands of charities are looking for your support, and as already established, the choice of challenges is endless. If you already have a charity in mind that you would like to support, this will make things easier. Listed in the directory below are some of the main UK charities that promote challenges as a significant arm of their fundraising activities. Some of these charities organise and run their own events, where as others work in partnership with a third party organisation such as Classic Tours or Charity Challenge.

In recent years there has been a growing tendency for charities to use an intermediary agency. This is because the smaller charities offering their own expeditions found that they were competing for a finite number of participants and over the years were forced to significantly lower their registration fees simply to fill the places. Intermediaries on the other hand often run open challenges in which the various participants may be supporting completely different charities. Not only does this mean that participants have a far greater choice, but also that smaller charities which could not afford to organise their own itinerary could offer fundraising expeditions to their supporters. So, whatever your preferred charity, it is possible to raise money for them via an open challenge, or by organising your own challenge.

Once you have decided on the charity, you may then have a choice of challenges available to you. When deciding which challenge to choose, there are a number of factors to consider. The first is the amount of time you are able to dedicate to the challenge. Challenges range from one day (marathons and hikes) right up to a month and beyond. However, the majority are targeted at long weekends, or periods of time that can easily fit into participants' annual leave (one to two weeks). Remember that the challenge time represents just a small percentage of the commitment that participants make. The second factor is therefore your own personal level of fitness, and the amount of time it will take to reach the required level. These challenges can be extremely difficult and your current level of fitness dictates whether realistically you can be ready in four to 12 months' time. Bear in mind that experts suggest a time frame of 18 months to two years for a person with no fitness regime to prepare for a marathon. And a challenge such as climbing Kilimanjaro will require a weekly training commitment of at least four hours a week over months. You should contact your doctor in order to discuss your plans and establish whether they are realistic.

Once you have established a time frame, you can think about your own personal goals and how best to achieve them. Participants are certainly not limited to the challenges provided by charities and third parties. Many people choose to set themselves a challenge that they organise entirely independently. Bear in mind that you should only consider this if you are an experienced traveller and confident of your abilities. Taking on an extreme challenge in a foreign environment can be fraught with difficulties and potential dangers. Using an experienced organisation helps to remove these obstacles. Whether or not you choose to go it alone, the charity that will benefit from your challenge will undoubtedly offer a great deal of support with both fundraising and training, providing materials and resources to help gain sponsorship and raise awareness.

Fundraising

One of the most important elements of the charity challenge, and also one of the most difficult, is raising funds. However, once you have resolved to meet a particular target, say £2,500, it is surprising how single-mindedly you can pursue it. Make sure you ask everyone you know to sponsor you, including friends, family, neighbours and work contacts. A very good place to start if you are in work, is your employer. Most companies are very willing to help their employees take on a worthwhile task (especially if they think they might get some publicity out of it!). Speak to your employers about potentially matching the money you raise, making a donation, or supporting you in fundraising or training.

Target organisations and companies with which you have some links, such as your old school or college, to ask for sponsorship. Local businesses are usually inundated with requests for donations and raffle prizes and are unlikely to give cash but some might donate some useful items of equipment. Keep track of all the individuals and businesses that have helped you and be sure to send them a thank you note later on describing the success of your fundraising trip.

Remember that charity challengers are able to collect donations from sponsors anywhere in the world, instantly and securely by using an online fundraising organisation such as JustGiving.com (tel. 0800 028 6183). These websites are approved by many charities. Participants simply set up their own online sponsorship fundraising page, which can be personalised with a message and photo and emailed to everyone you know. The charity gets an automatic 28% tax bonus (Gift Aid) from the Inland Revenue on donations made by UK taxpayers.

Another important aspect of fundraising is organising events. The ingenuity which charity challengers have demonstrated in organising money-making events is impressive. You may choose to shave your head, jump out of an aeroplane, organise a fancy dress pub crawl or a thousand other ways to raise money. Erich Reich, founder of Classic Tours, explains that fundraising is very personal: *'The key to fundraising is to concentrate on your individual skills and expertise. We have seen a huge variety of fundraising activities, but the most successful are the most individual and the most imaginative'.*

Publicise your plans and your need for funds wherever you can. Local papers and radio stations will usually carry details of your planned expedition, which may prompt a few local readers/listeners to support you. Consider possibilities for organising a fundraising event like a concert or a ceilidh, a quiz night, wine tasting or auction of promises. The organisation, Charity Challenge has a useful *A to Z of Fundraising Ideas* online (www.charitychallenge.com).

What to Take With You – Packing Check List

The exact items that you will need on a charity challenge will vary according to the type of challenge you are taking on. Always contact the charity or third party for further advice. Remember to road test all of your equipment thoroughly. Nothing should be used for the first time during an expedition. Also ensure that all of your equipment is covered by your insurance policy.

- Medium sized rucksack for luggage – on endurance challenges remember that pack weight is your priority
- Sleeping bag
- Hiking boots for trekking or mountaineering
- Water bottles
- Trainers or cycling shoes (for biking expeditions)
- Cycle helmet and gloves (for biking expeditions)
- Appropriate clothes for the type of challenge and climate – trekking socks, waterproofs, fleece, thermal underwear
- Small personal medical kit including antiseptic cream, plasters, knee support, pain killers, insect repellent, sting relief, immodium, re-hydration salts etc
- High-factor sun cream and lip salve
- Blister kit – compeed plasters are particularly effective
- Vaseline/talcum powder
- Toilet paper
- Matches
- Sun glasses, hat, neck scarf
- Strong torch
- Plastic bags/bin liners (to protect clothes from damp, for dirty washing etc)
- Passport (most countries require at least six months' validity from date of arrival)
- Camera

THE CHALLENGES

The number of overseas challenges is growing year on year, as is the number of people who take part. Although there is a charity challenge code of conduct in place, charities and organisations do not all operate in exactly the same way and it is sensible to match your own aim and goals with the policies of the charities and operators listed below. As previously mentioned, potential challengers have two choices. They can either register to take on a challenge with a charity or with an independent, third party challenge operator. Many charities do not run their own challenges but work in partnership with an operator. Other smaller charities may not even offer this option, in which case it will be necessary to attend an 'open challenge' with a third party operator, or to go it alone and organise your own challenge. Always vet your challenge operator carefully, making sure to speak to previous participants and question the organisation's policies on responsible tourism, cost effectiveness (ie how much of your fundraising target will actually go to the charity), and health and safety.

CHARITIES

Age Concern

Organisation: UK charity dedicated to promoting the well-being of all older people and helping to make later life a fulfilling and enjoyable experience
Example Challenges: Trek China, Trek Peru
Duration: 9–11 days
Minimum Sponsorship: £2,500

☎ 020 8765 7344
🖱 events@ace.org.uk
💻 www.ace.org.uk

The Anthony Nolan Trust

Organisation: Provides lifesaving donors for patients in need of a bone marrow transplant, taking back lives from leukaemia
Example Challenges: Trek the High Atlas Mountains, Morocco; Three Peaks Challenge (Ben Nevis, Scafell Pike, Mount Snowden); Mera Peak Trek, Nepal; Great Wall of China Trek; Everest Base Camp Trek, Nepal; Kilimanjaro Trek, Tanzania; Cross the Andes on Horseback, Chile and Argentina
Duration: 1–21 days
Minimum Sponsorship: £1,600–£4,200

☎ 020 7284 8284
🖱 challenge@anthonynolan.org.uk
💻 www.anthonynolan.org.uk

Breast Cancer Care

Organisation: Breast Cancer Care provides information, practical assistance and emotional support to anyone affected by breast cancer
Example Challenges: Trek India, Trek Peru, Trek China, Cycle London to Paris
Duration: 5–12 days
Minimum Sponsorship: £1,200–£3,000

☎ 020 7384 8397
🖱 treks@breastcancercare.org.uk
💻 www.breastcancercare.org.uk

Cancerbackup

Organisation: Leading cancer information charity dedicated to providing cancer patients and their families with up-to-date information, practical advice and support
Example Challenges: Milky Way Ski and Board Challenge – all the pistes in the Milky Way region (France/Italy) in two days; Esparon (South of France) to Notting Hill Cycle Ride; Mount Kenya Trek, Everest Base Camp Trek, Snowdonia Trek
Duration: 3–12 days
Minimum Sponsorship: £1,800–£3,000

☎ 020 7920 7212
💻 www.cancerbackup.org.uk

CHARITY CHALLENGES

CHARITIES

The Children's Society

Organisation: Leading national charity driven by the belief that every child deserves a good childhood. The society provides vital help and understanding for children who are unable to find the support they need elsewhere

☎ 0845 300 1128

✉ supporteraction@childrenssociety.org.uk

🖥 www.childrenssociety.org.uk

Example Challenges: Walk San Francisco or New York; Trek India, Kilimanjaro, Everest Base Camp (Nepal); Cycle London to Amsterdam; Project South Africa (combines a mountain trek with three days working with local people)

Duration: 5–12 days

Minimum Sponsorship: £1,450–£3,100

Fire Services National Benevolent Fund

Organisation: The FSNBF provides assistance to serving and retired UK Fire and Rescue Services personnel, their widow/ers and young dependents through the provision of sheltered accommodation, recuperative facilities, rehabilitation, therapy and financial support

☎ 01256 366566

✉ info@fsnbf.org.uk

🖥 www.fsnbf.org.uk

Example Challenges: One challenge is held each year. In 2007 the Peru challenge involves trekking the Inca Trail, white water rafting and mountain biking, and climbing a volcano

Duration: 12 days

Minimum Sponsorship: £2,650

Get Kids Going

Organisation: Charity which gives disabled children and young people the opportunity to participate in sports. It provides specially built sports wheelchairs and helps British disabled children to compete

☎ 020 7481 8110

✉ info@getkidsgoing.com

🖥 www.getkidsgoing.com/overseas_challenges.html

Example Challenges: Trek the Great Wall of China, Trek the Inca Trail, Trek Kilimanjaro, Trek Everest Base Camp, Cycle Vietnam, Cycle London to Paris

Duration: 5–19 days

Minimum Sponsorship: £999–£2,250

Great Ormond Street Hospital Children's Charity

Organisation: Great Ormond Street Hospital treats more than 100,000 patients each year – children who are suffering from the rarest, most complex and often life-threatening conditions. NHS funding cannot meet the hospital's ever-rising costs, which is where the charity steps in
Example Challenges: Paris to London Bike Ride, Kilimanjaro Trek, Great Wall of China Trek, Inca Trek
Duration: 6–11 days
Minimum Sponsorship: £1,150–£3,200

☎ 020 7239 30008
🖱 challenges@gosh.org
💻 www.gosh.org

Help the Aged

Organisation: Help the Aged works for disadvantaged older people in the UK and around the world, researching their needs, campaigning for their social and political rights and providing services which alleviate hardship and prevent deprivation
Example Challenges: Trek the Inca Trail, Trek India, Trek Cuba, Climb Kilimanjaro, Cycle the Sinai Desert
Duration: 10 days
Minimum Sponsorship: Approx. £2,800

☎ 020 7278 1114
🖱 treks@helptheaged.org.uk
💻 www.helptheaged.org.uk

Macmillan Cancer Support

Organisation: Macmillan Cancer Support improves the lives of people affected by cancer by providing practical, medical, emotional and financial support and working for better cancer care
Example Challenges: Cycle Peru, London to Paris, Vietnam, Mexico, Cambodia; Trek Great Wall of China, Kilimanjaro, Cambodia, Sahara, Inca Trail (Peru)
Duration: 4–14 days
Minimum Sponsorship: £2,000–£3,200

☎ 020 7840 7840
💻 www.macmillan.org.uk

Marie Curie Cancer Care

Organisation: Employing more than 2,700 nurses and doctors, Marie Curie Provides care to around 25,000 people with cancer every year. It also runs the Marie Curie Research Institute investigating the causes and treatments of cancer
Example Challenges: Trek the Great Wall of China, Inca Trail, Kilimanjaro, Morocco, Everest Base Camp; Long Weekend Lava Trek, Iceland; Brazilian Waterfalls Bike Challenge, Project Kenya (trekking combined with a community project)
Duration: 9–12 days
Minimum Sponsorship: approx. £3,250

☎ 0870 240 1021
💻 www.mariecurie.org.uk

MENCAP

Organisation: The UK's leading learning disability charity working with people with learning disabilities, their families and carers. Mencap fights for equal rights, campaigns for greater opportunities and challenges attitudes and prejudice

Example Challenges: Cycle to Rio, Brazil; Cycle the Rockies, Canada; Trek Vietnam; Trek Peru

Duration: 9–11 days

Minimum Sponsorship: £2,600–£ 2,950

☎ 020 7454 0454

🖥 www.mencap.org.uk

The Meningitis Trust

Organisation: The Meningitis Trust is an international charity with a strong community focus, fighting meningitis through the provision of support, education and awareness, and research

Example Challenges: London to Paris Cycle, Trek the Himilayas, Trek New Zealand, Great Wall of China Trek

Duration: 4–12 days

Minimum Sponsorship: £2,500–£3,500

☎ 01453 768000

🖱 events@meningitis-trust.org

🖥 www.meningitis-trust.org

Mental Health Foundation

Organisation: MHF provides information, carries out research, campaigns and works to improve services for anyone affected by mental health problems

Example Challenges: Cycle Cuba, London to Paris Bike Ride, Trek the Inca Trail, Trek the Sahara

Duration: 5–10 days

Minimum Sponsorship: £1,100–£2,650

☎ 020 7803 1101

🖱 mhf@mhf.org.uk

🖥 www.mhf.org.uk

National Deaf Children's Society

Organisation: UK charity solely dedicated to the support of all deaf children and young deaf people, their families and professionals working with them

Example Challenges: Cycle – Namibia Desert, Dead Sea to Red Sea, the Nile, Peru; Trek – Tibet, India, the Great Wall of China.

Project – Kilimanjaro Community Project (combines climbing Kilimanjaro with working on a local project)

Duration: 7–12 days

Minimum Sponsorship: £2,200–£3,750

☎ 0870 774 2444

🖱 ndcschallenges@ndcs.org.uk

🖥 www.ndcschallenges.org.uk

Oxfam Global Challenges

Organisation: Development, relief and campaigning organisation that works with others to find lasting solutions to poverty and suffering around the world

Example Challenges: Hike the Himilayas, Climb Kilimanjaro, Trek the Great Wall of China, Cycle Cambodia. All projects involve a visit to an Oxfam site in order to better understand the work it does and where the money goes

Duration: 9–11 days

Minimum Sponsorship: £2,725–£3,190

☎ 0870 333 2700

💻 www.oxfam.org.uk

A POSTCARD FROM Kilimanjaro

Sonya Grist spent her 64th birthday at the peak of Kilimanjaro to raise money for Oxfam:

As I met with the other 26 trekkers at London Heathrow to set off for the flight to Kilimanjaro, I kept thinking, perhaps I should have celebrated my 64th birthday in a more usual fashion. But no, in my wisdom, I had decided to trek to the top of the highest mountain in Africa – Mount Kilimanjaro.

After landing in Kenya, we flew onwards to Kilimanjaro airport in Tanzania, catching the first glimpses of the top of the mountain as we flew overhead. The first day, we trekked through lush rain forest where the birds and monkeys made themselves merry at our expense. Slowly we had a chance to find out everyone's story and reason for this major undertaking. And a motley crew we were, from an ex-MD of an airline company to IT experts, to two sisters training race and polo ponies, to an archaeologist, a vet, a dentist, a geologist and a call-centre clerk. We grew very close over the next few days.

The next day was the start of the real test: an eight-hour trek up into the barren desert where our overnight accommodation would be, at the foot of the final ascent in the Kibo huts at 4,700m – higher than any of us had ever been before. We were advised to walk very 'pole, pole' which is Swahili for 'slowly slowly'. We now had a full view of the steep slopes to the summit of Mount Kilimanjaro itself. It towered over us and we all speculated on whether we would be able to reach the top.

The snow-capped summit dominated our route and our thoughts. We had had to leave some members behind in the huts, resting and grappling with altitude sickness in the hope that they would be able to join us that night.

At 11pm we were ready to go. Ever so slowly, we shuffled our way forwards and upwards. The whole mountain looked like a scene out of Lord Of The Rings with the lights from all our head torches lighting up our path (about 100 of us were making the ascent that night). Our tour guide and the doctor moved up and down to check on us and our Tanzanian guides made sure we were safe and happy with the pace.

Seven hours passed. Limbs were growing weary, but the sky was growing light as we approached the very last part of the ascent. By this point, my asthma was starting to get the better of me. Very little oxygen was getting to my legs and they were growing unbelievably heavy. I was so near the top, but could I physically make it? Help came in the form of our tour guide, Claude and one of our African guides, pulling me, cajoling me, helping me. Just a few more heavy weary steps and then lo and behold – there I was: at the top of Kilimanjaro! And it was my birthday! My companions even managed a short rendition of the Beatles song 'when I'm 64'. I collapsed in a heap onto the bench at the sign for Gilman's Point. I had made it. I was photographed (I look about 80!!).

And then it was time for the descent.....

Royal National Institute for the Blind

Organisation: The UK's leading charity offering information, support and advice to over two million people with sight problems. RNIB also fights for equal rights and funds pioneering research for people with sight problems

Example Challenges: China Trek, Iceland Trek, Kenya Trek, London to Paris Cycle, Nile Cycle

Duration: 4–10 days

Minimum Sponsorship: £1,000–£2,500

☎ 0845 345 0054

 fundraising@rnib.org

 www.rnib.org.uk

A POSTCARD FROM Rajasthan, India

Paul Keyland, aged 44, is something of a charity challenge addict, having been on 16 in the last five years. In his latest undertaking, Paul cycled 425km in Rajasthan, India, for RNIB:

I take part in three or four overseas charity events every year. The benefits of the charity challenge model as I see them are a) you raise money for a worthy cause, b) you increase your health and fitness levels, c) you see parts of the world you wouldn't normally see and d) you meet fantastic people from all walks of life. The result is a win win situation for everybody.

Training for these events is of paramount importance if you want to get the most out of them. As my base fitness is fairly high, I usually start training nine weeks before the event. With biking I would normally train on roads incorporating plenty of inclines and I would try to cover 200–300 miles per week (reducing the distance in the last couple of weeks).

In Rajasthan we cycled solidly for five consecutive days, stopping off at basic but comfortable hotels and campsites along the way. Body management is very important for the endurance involved in these events. You really have to understand the effects of dehydration and lack of fuel, and make sure that you drink plenty and eat often while biking. For me the best moment of the challenge was getting on the bike for the first time and looking forward to the challenge ahead and the friendships that I knew were about to be created through the adversity of the challenge.

The camaraderie and the friendships that build up are what make charity challenges unique. These events tend to attract fantastic people, and although my fellow challengers came from all walks of life with ages ranging from 20 to 60, we all helped each other out and shared in the sense of achievement.

I think people are wary of charity challenges because of fear of the unknown, but these events are so well organised, my advice is just to go for it. You won't regret it.

CHARITY CHALLENGES

CHARITIES

SCOPE

Organisation: Disability organisation in England and Wales whose focus is people with cerebral palsey. Their aim is that disabled people achieve equality in society and have the same human and civil rights as others
Example Challenges: Trek – China, Everest, Iceland, Kilimanjaro, Ladakh, Morocco, Peru, Venezuela; Cycle – London to Paris, Mexico; Ski – White Peaks (Austria), Utah
Duration: 3–19 days
Minimum Sponsorship: £1,400–£3,500

☎ 020 7619 7288
✎ events@scope.org.uk
💻 www.scope.org.uk

Whizz Kidz

Organisation: Whizz Kidz provides customised wheelchairs, tricycles and other specialised mobility equipment, wheelchair training, information and advice to change the lives of disabled children across the UK. It also works to raise awareness of the needs of these children
Example Challenges: Dog Sledding in Sweden, London to Paris Bike Ride, Trek the Himilayas, the Inca Trail, Kilimanjaro, Everest Base Camp and the Great Wall of China
Duration: 5–18 days
Minimum Sponsorship: £1,200–£2,750

☎ 020 7233 6600
✎ info@whizz-kidz.org.uk
💻 www.whizz-kidz.org.uk

Across The Divide

Locations: Africa, Asia, Australasia, Europe, Middle East, North America, South America
Activities: Trekking, cycling, multi-activity (climbing, mountain biking, orienteering, caving etc), community projects, dog sledding, extreme challenges (mountain climbing, three peaks etc)

☎ 01460 30456
🖥 www.acrossthedivide.com

Example Challenges: Dog sledding in Lapland as an open challenge, trekking in India for Concern Worldwide, community project work in Brazil for the Bobby Moore Fund
Organisation: ATD is an expedition company rather than a charity challenge company, so it treats all events as mini expeditions, with all the planning, equipment and support that expeditions require
Duration: 7–22 days
Minimum Sponsorship: At least double the cost of the challenge – approx. £1,000–£3,000
Charities: Any charity. Both dedicated and open challenges are run

Action For Charity

Locations: Varies. Currently Cuba, Peru, India, Egypt, Kenya, Jordan and Sicily
Activities: Trekking, cycling, mountain and triathlon events
Example Challenges: Hike the Himilayas for

☎ 0845 408 2698
🖱 events@actionforcharity.co.uk
🖥 www.actionforcharity.co.uk

The Big Issue; Desert Walk for Dogs for the Disabled; Women-only cycle ride through India for 'Women for Women' led by Professor Robert Winston
Organisation: AFC manages overseas adventure challenge events and UK-based events for both small and large national charities
Duration: 1–5 days
Minimum Sponsorship: £2,500 – £3,000
Charities: AFC manages challenges for specific charities including Samaritans, Barnardo's, Childline, Dreams Come True, Children in Crisis, British Heart Foundation, John Grooms, Action Medical Research, Haringey Mencap, Kith & Kids, Womankind Worldwide, Regain, Trinity Hospice and the British Dyslexia Assocation

CHARITY CHALLENGES

CHALLENGE OPERATORS

CARE Challenge

Locations: UK, Ireland, Spain (other overseas destinations are available in partnership with Charity Challenge)

☎ 020 7934 9470
✍ challenge@careinternational.org
🖳 www.carechallenge.org.uk

Activities: Mountain Challenges (three peaks); running, cycling, and multi-activity challenges, primarily for corporate teams. Individuals can enter for Spain and Adventure Race

Example Challenges: Three Peaks Challenge, Three Peaks Spain (which combines trekking and mountain biking)

Organisation: CARE Challenge is a fundraising arm of the third largest development agency worldwide, CARE International, which works in 70 countries with more than 48 million poor and marginalised people each year to find a way out of poverty

Duration: 1–3 days

Minimum Sponsorship: From £1,500–£6,000

Charities: All money raised goes to CARE International, whose mission is to create lasting and long-term change in the poorest communities, working with those communities to help them find sustainable ways of making a living

---

A POSTCARD FROM the mountains of Spain

Simon Ball, a 37–year-old designer, took part in the Spanish Three Peaks Challenge to raise money for Care International:

I had taken part in charity events in the past, including the UK Three Peaks Challenge and various road races but the Three Peaks Challenge in Spain attracted me because not only did it look extremely challenging, it was also being held in an area that I might otherwise not get to visit. Trekking and mountain biking three peaks in three days also appealed to my sporting sensibilities.

I first heard about the challenge from a colleague at the Simons Group, who also took part in the trip. We set to work straight away appealing for sponsorship from suppliers and sub-contractors that work with and for the company. We suggested a recommended amount for people to donate (in this case £250) as this helps to maximise potential for fundraising. I would normally do plenty of cycling, but to prepare for this challenge I had to increase my training volume several months before the challenge.

The challenge itself was a fantastic experience. Being in a beautiful natural environment, with a group of diverse, but in many ways like-minded people, and setting yourself a unique personal challenge is an experience you will never forget. During the challenge we stayed in a mountain refuge that was clean and functional, although I didn't enjoy the cold showers! But the accommodation and its remote location were a key part of the atmosphere of the challenge and the group.

The physical and mental exertion of the challenge are something you really have to try to prepare yourself for. But when you get there, you have to just give it 100%, no matter how hard it gets. It is important to remember that it is a challenge, not a trial and you should always try to enjoy yourself and feel good about what you are doing. Two moments from the experience really stand out in my mind. Firstly standing on top of the Alcazaba and taking in the view – I had tears in my eyes (it must have been the altitude!). And secondly racing off-road down from the top of Veleta. A truly unforgettable experience.

Charity Challenge

Locations: Africa, the Caribbean, Asia, Europe, the Americas and the Middle East

Activities: Trekking, mountain biking, mountain climbs, white water rafting, sailing, horse riding and community challenges

☎ 020 8557 0000

💻 www.charitychallenge.com

Example Challenges: Trek to the home of the Dalai Lama for ActionAid, Icelandic Lava Trek for any charity, Rajasthan Tiger Challenge for Diabetes UK

Organisation: Charity Challenge is an ethical travel company committed to working with charities to help raise money for deserving causes. CC operates more than 120 challenges each year and has so far raised around £15 million for more than 750 charities

Duration: 5–18 days

Minimum Sponsorship: £1,500 – £3,100

Charities: Any charity. Both dedicated and open challenges are run

Classic Tours

Locations: Africa, the Caribbean, Asia, Europe, the Americas and the Middle East

Activities: Trekking, running, cycle rides, horse riding, car rallies, husky sledding, motorbike trips

Example Challenges: Horse trekking in Inner Mongolia for the British Horse Society; husky

☎ 020 7619 0066

🖱 info@classictours.co.uk

💻 www.classictours.co.uk

sledding in Sweden for the Motor Neurone Disease Association; community project in Zambia for Aid International

Organisation: Travel operator dedicated to combining travel, a physical challenge and sponsorship to create a new format for charitable giving. Classic Tours was the first to bring the Charity Challenge model to a mass market. It has raised £30 million for more than 100 charities

Duration: 1–10 days

Minimum Sponsorship: £1,000 – £2,500

Charities: Any charity. Both dedicated and open challenges are run

A POSTCARD FROM Cuba

59-year-old voluntary worker, Liz Eaton, has taken part in several charity challenges. She suggested, developed and organised this Cycle Cuba challenge with Classic Tours to raise money for building new and improved facilities for Denman College:

The challenge was to spend five days cycling through Cuba. As this was my fourth cycling challenge, I knew exactly what was involved. About eight months before the challenge, I started to gradually build up my stamina through road and off-road distance cycle-rides. There are three main parts to a charity challenge – getting fit, raising the funds, and the challenge itself. For all three, the key quality that challengers need is determination.

continued

They need to have a strong commitment to the charity and the motivation to become both mentally and physically tough in order to undertake the challenge.

We were a group of 35, of which the majority were Women's Institute members, and we were all raising money for Denman College. Fortunately everyone gelled very well together and we all made it back to the UK in one piece!

Aside from raising money, we all gained a huge amount from the challenge. I enjoyed seeing and experiencing Cuba, meeting the Cuban team, working with our Classic Tours guide, and managing and caring for the other participants. But for me, the most rewarding part of the trip was seeing the satisfaction and achievement on each biker's face at the end of each day, and particularly at the end of the challenge.

Different Challenge

Locations: Galapagos Islands (Ecuador), the Sahara, Peru, Zambia, Kilimanjaro
Activities: Local community projects combined with more traditional physical challenges. Participants can choose Challenge 50/50 where approx. half the

☎ 02380 669903

 challenge@different-travel.com

💻 www.different-travel.com

time is spent hiking, cycling or mountain climbing etc, and half is spent on the project, or Challenge 100, where 100% of the time is dedicated to completing a demanding development project
Example Challenges: Galapagos Challenge – helping to restore and preserve the islands
Organisation: 'Direct Action' tour operator, committed to ethical and responsible travel, offering holidays that include an element of voluntary work, and charity challenges that involve local communities
Duration: 8–15 days
Minimum Sponsorship: Varies according to challenge. Approx. £2,000 with at least 50% going to the charity and a maximum of 50% going towards the costs of the challenge
Charities: Any charity. Both dedicated and open challenges

Discover Adventure

Locations: Worldwide
Activities: Trekking, cycling, horse trekking, multi-activity challenges, and community projects
Example Challenges: Vietnam to Cambodia Cycle Challenge for the Alzheimer's Society; Ice Cap Trek in Iceland as an open challenge; Arctic

☎ 01722 718444

 info@discoveradventure.com

💻 www.discoveradventure.com

Survival Challenge for the Round Table Children's Wish
Organisation: DA designs and operates fundraising challenges for charity groups and challenging trips for school and corporate groups
Duration: 3–22 days
Minimum Sponsorship: £500 – £3,250
Charities: Any charity. Bespoke and open challenges are run

CHARITY CHALLENGES

CHALLENGE OPERATORS

Do it for Charity

Locations: Worldwide
Activities: Trekking, running, cycle rides, horse riding, car rallies, husky sledding, community projects

☎ 0870 333 6633
🖱 enquiries@doitforcharity.com
💻 www.doitforcharity.com

Example Challenges: Dog Sledding in Sweden for the Motor Neurone Disease Association, the Champagne Run – driving through northern France for Penny Brohn Cancer Care; Rhino Cycle Namibia for Save the Rhino
Organisation: Doitforcharity.com is run by specialist charity events organiser: Skyline Events, but also lists challenges run by other organisers, to maximise choice
Duration: 1–20 days
Minimum Sponsorship: Approx. £2,000–£3,000
Charities: Any charity. Bespoke and open challenges

Global Adventure Challenges

Locations: Worldwide
Activities: Trekking, cycling, husky sledding, white-water rafting, multi-activity challenges, motorbike challenges

☎ 01244 676454
🖱 start@globaladv.org
💻 www.globaladv.org

Example Challenges: The Lapland Husky Trail for The Blue Cross; white-water rafting the Zambezi for Scope; riding through India on a Royal Enfield Bullet motorcycle as an open challenge
Organisation: Specialist charity challenge operator with a variety of challenge opportunities around the world, all year round
Duration: 5–18 days
Minimum Sponsorship: £1,600 – £2,995
Charities: Any charity. Bespoke and open challenges

Global Vision International

Locations: Worldwide
Activities: Bike rides and tailor-made challenges
Example Challenges: Charity bike ride from Guatemala to Honduras

☎ 0870 608 8898
🖱 info@gvi.co.uk
💻 www.gvi.co.uk

Organisation: GVI promotes sustainable development by supplying international volunteers, equipment, funding and training to governmental groups, charities, NGOs and communities around the world
Duration: Approx. 10 days for bike rides; any duration for tailor-made challanges
Minimum Sponsorship: £985
Charities: Global Vision International Charitable Trust; or any charity via a tailor-made open challenge

Great Walks of the World Charity Treks

Locations: Worldwide
Activities: Trekking, mountain biking, horse-riding, mountain climbing and watersports
Example Challenges: Horse Trek across the Andes for Teenage Cancer Trust; Malawi

☎ 01935 810820
💻 www.greatwalks.net/challenges/

Trek for the Farleigh Hospice, Saigon to Angkor Wat Cycle Challenge for Action Aid
Organisation: Great Walks specialises in organising customised fundraising challenge trips for a wide range of UK charities
Duration: 5–12 days
Minimum Sponsorship: Approx. £2,000 – £3,000
Charities: Any charity. Bespoke and open challenges are run

The Italian Job

Location: Across Europe from northern Italy to the UK
Duration: 10 days (October/November each year)
Organisation: Founded in 1990 with the aim of raising money for children in a fun way, the Italian Job organises an annual Mini rally through Europe

☎ 01273 418100
🖱 info@Italianjob.com
💻 www.italianjob.com

Description: Mini-owners aged 21 or over can take part in this 10–day fundraising rally that starts in Italy and follows a route that goes off the beaten track, over medieval bridges, through tiny villages and allows participants to explore cities such as Bologna, Turin and Venice. The itinerary varies each year. Teams stay in hotels along the route
Cost: Team entry fee (1 car and 2 persons) of £500. Participants also pay all accommodation costs along the way
Minimum Sponsorship: £1,500
Charities: NCH, The Children's Charity, which runs more than 500 projects for some of the UK's most vulnerable and excluded children and young people, and their families

A POSTCARD FROM Italy

Bev Wildeboer, company director and magistrate, on racing through Italy in a Mini in aid of NCH, The Children's Charity:

For 10 days, every October for the last ten years, I have transformed myself into a Jobber. Jobbers are a happy band of people who take part in The Italian Job, a charity event based on the film of the same name. Started in 1990 by Freddie St George when he was a student in Trento, Italy as a one-off fund-raiser for Children in Need, it has become an annual event, so far raising nearly £2 million for children's charities.

So what is it? The Italian job involves a group of nutters who get in their cars and drive to Italy, stay in wonderful places, do silly things and navigational rallies, and raise huge amounts for charities. Each team pledges to raise at least £1,500 and many manage much more. NCH is one of Britain's leading children's charities and financially it is extremely

continued

CHARITY CHALLENGES

CHALLENGE OPERATORS

247

efficient. For every £1 raised, it achieves four times that in matched funding. Every year we raise funds over 10 months through corporate sponsorship, quiz nights, and Italian wine tastings. The key to fundraising events is to make them fun and relevant.

So what do we do? A lot of driving. 3,500 miles in 10 days to be precise. Highlights include driving around the roof of the old Fiat factory in Turin (as featured in the film) pretending to be Michael Caine, with everyone shouting 'Try and find the exit next time!' We have also driven around the F1 circuits in Monza and Imola (scary at 50mph – never mind 200!). And we were also the first non-Ferrari people to be allowed access to Ferrari's test track in Maranello. Apart from taking part in driving stages, we stop off for wine and food tastings (parmesan cheese straight from the dairy, parma ham, fresh pasta – ahhh) and we stop off at car museums and sites of interest. The wonderful scenery, culture and history of northern Italy, make the perfect backdrop to the drive.

Every conceivable type of Mini joins in the challenge, and as the event is open to all the cars featured in the films, we have all sorts of other cars. Last year there was even a Fiat Gulia done up as an Italian police car, and back in 2003 a London taxi made the journey (and yes, the meter was running the whole time). But the best thing is the friends we make. Jobbers, like Mini-owners, come from all walks of life and all ages, from students to grandparents and teachers to firefighters, all enjoying the stunning scenery, lovely food, and fantastic company.

'Jobbers' stop to admire the view of the Alps on the French/Italian border.

Responsible Travel

Locations: Worldwide
Activities: Trekking, cycling, canoeing, community challenges, conservation challenges
Example Challenges: Charity trek and rhino tracking in India; Zambezi charity canoe and community project; charity jungle trek in Mexico

☎ 01273 600030
🖱 amelia@responsibletravel.com
💻 www.responsibletravel.com

Organisation: Brighton-based online eco-travel agent which markets more than 270 tour operators
Duration: 6–17 days
Minimum Sponsorship: £1,500–£3,200
Charities: All challenges are open events for any charity

Tall Stories

Locations: UK and Europe
Activities: Trekking, mountain biking, multisport challenges, adventure races, ski and snowboard challenges
Example Challenges: London to Paris cycle ride for the Stroke Association; Camino de Santiago (the Pilgrim's Way) as an open event; White Peaks Challenge for Scope

☎ 020 8939 8739
🖱 info@tallstories.co.uk
💻 www.tallstories.co.uk

Organisation: Tall Stories specialises in charity fund-raising events, corporate events and group events in the UK and Europe
Duration: 2–10 days
Minimum Sponsorship: Approx. £1,000–£3,500
Charities: Any charity. Both dedicated and open challenges are run

Ultimate Travel Company

Locations: Africa, Asia, Australasia, Europe, Middle East, North America, South America
Activities: Trekking, biking, desert expeditions, jungle expeditions, mountain climbing, 5–peaks challenge

☎ 020 7386 4680
🖱 events@theultimatetravelcompany.co.uk
💻 http://utc-charity-challenges.co.uk/

Example Challenges: Kenya Rift Valley Trek for Mind; Iceland Trekking Challenge for RNIB, Rajasthan Bike Challenge for the National Hospital for Neurology and Neurosurgery Development Foundation
Organisation: UTC is a long-established travel company with a department solely dedicated to organising overseas challenges for a wide variety of UK charities, both large and small
Duration: 5–20 days
Minimum Sponsorship: £1,000 – £3,000
Charities: Any charity. Both dedicated and open challenges are run

VSO Challenges Worldwide

Locations: Currently Peru, China, Kilimanjaro, the UK and India

☎ 020 8780 7289

💻 http://www.vso.org.uk/news/treks_landing.asp

Activities: Trekking, cycling and mountain climbing.
Combined with visits to VSO projects to see the work they do first hand

Example Challenges: Three Peaks Challenge, UK; Macchu Picchu Challenge, Peru; Himalayas Challenge, India

Organisation: VSO is an international development charity sending skilled professional volunteers to work for two years in 34 countries, where they pass on their expertise to local people. Their long-term involvement with development projects positions them ideally to provide challenges worldwide

Duration: 9–12 days

Minimum Sponsorship: Approx. £3,000

Charities: All money raised goes to help fund crucial VSO projects throughout the world

World Expeditions

Locations: Worldwide

Activities: Trekking, cycling, mountain climbing

Example Challenges: Climb Mount Sinai for Whizz Kidz; cycle Sri Lanka for Cancer Research UK; trek in Darjeeling for the Bobby Moore Fund

☎ 020 8870 2600

 challenge_events@worldexpeditions.co.uk

💻 www.worldexpeditions.com

Organisation: One of the original adventure travel companies covering all continents and offering a range of charity challenges

Duration: 5–15 days

Minimum Sponsorship: Approx. £2,000 – £3,000

Charities: Any charity. Bespoke and open challenges

YHA Challenges

Locations: China, Peru, Kilimanjaro, Iceland

Activities: Trekking and mountain ascent

Example Challenges: The Iceland Icecap Trek; the Atlas Mountain Challenge, Morocco; trekking the Grand Canyon

☎ 01629 592638

events@yha.org.uk

💻 www.yha.org.uk

Organisation: YHA operates a network of more than 200 youth hostels across England and Wales

Duration: 5–18 days

Minimum Sponsorship: Approx. £2,500

Charities: YHA raises money for Breaks 4 Kids, a charity that gives disadvantaged children the opportunity to take part in residential educational breaks where they can learn and develop new skills

HANDS-ON
Agriculture

GETTING BACK TO THE LAND

An agricultural working holiday allows you to get off the beaten track, to the rural heart of a country, to work closely with local people and to spend virtually nothing in the process. While the idea of swapping your holidays for a hoe, hard agricultural labour and nights spent under canvas or in basic farm accommodation may sound like sheer madness, many people find that a working holiday spent outside, surrounded by the fruits of mother nature can be one of the most gratifying ways of escaping the reality of the daily grind. Lazy beach holidays are all very well, but how many of us really feel like we've got away from it all, especially with the modern temptations of email and the BlackBerry to suck us back into the working world?

Agricultural working holidays offer the opportunity for real engagement with the physical world. The raw satisfaction that can be gained from scything the meadows, picking grapes that will be made into fine wines, ploughing the fields, and helping to restore farm ecosystems that have been ravaged by intensive agriculture make all the other petty satisfactions of daily life, such as concluding a successful meeting or finishing an essay look artificial and preposterous. Regular participants of holidays on farms attest to the fact that physical exercise in the great outdoors, complete with the opportunity to immerse yourself in a different culture and work that has, in some cases, remained unchanged for centuries, are all elements that make for the most invigorating break possible. They guarantee that there will be nothing further from your mind than the daily irritations and hassles of your normal life.

Whether you are earning a wage, or volunteering on an organic farm or environmental generation project, there are huge advantages to a hands-on holiday that gets back to nature. Workers are usually rewarded with free, or at least subsidised room and board in rustic and often unusual accommodation. Meals are usually provided and are eaten communally, often with much of the food on your plate having been grown right there on the farm. Workers are also able to enjoy the benefits of being in beautiful and sometimes wild surroundings, whilst having the reassurance that they have a safe place to stay and a secure social network around them. However, the most fulfilling aspect of such a working break is the chance of participating in a project with local people in a rural setting and getting right to the grassroots of a country. Agricultural holiday-makers will be exposed to an experience that they would be extremely hard pressed to find as an independent traveller.

This chapter details all of the agricultural opportunities available to the working-holiday maker, from short paid agricultural working holidays (mostly limited to the harvest season) to a range of voluntary positions that will allow you to get a in depth look at a new culture from the ground up.

VOLUNTARY AGRICULTURAL WORK

Organic farms and permaculture and sustainable agriculture projects are rapidly appearing all over the world as people become increasingly aware of the damage that intensive farming has done to the environment. Organic produce is one of the fastest growing retail sectors in the food industry, and a general public distrust of agri-economics has developed.

The issue of genetically modified foods has split political opinion in the wider community. Large numbers of critics are concerned about both the health and environmental dangers of these products, many of which are still in the developmental stage, as well as with the ethical problems and ramifications of seed patenting, especially in the developing world. Concurrently, growing awareness of the genetic hot potato has led to increased demand for organically produced foods. Organic farming systems have been designed to produce food with care for human health, the environment and animal welfare. The use of genetically engineered crops is not compatible with this aim. This position is shared by the organic movement worldwide. Organic foods in the UK are regulated by the Soil Association and by EC law. Their method of production provides a safe and sustainable alternative to modern, intensive farming methods, most notably by avoiding artificial chemicals, pesticides and fertilisers (more than 25,000 tonnes of these agrichemicals are used in Britain every year). Organic agriculture also emphasises the importance of animal welfare; reduces dependence on non-renewable resources; and relies on a scientific understanding of ecology and soil science, while at the same time depending on traditional methods of crop rotation to ensure fertility and weed and pest control. In this way it aims to produce safe, nutritious and unpolluted food, and to remove the pressures which modern agriculture places on the natural environment: the pollution of wildlife, soil and the water system with man-made chemicals, and the clearing of rare or unique habitats for cultivation, for example.

Without recourse to machinery, pesticides and other labour-saving techniques the need for manual workers on these farms and projects is acute, yet very few of them can afford to employ the required workforce. For potential volunteers these issues have opened up a range of new experiences all over the world. Whether you are a traveller on a tight budget, you want to do your bit for the environment or you simply want to learn more about the aims of these projects and the issues involved, there are thousands of farms all over the world to cater for your needs. The experience can vary greatly from an agritourism farmstay, where you simply chip in to the daily farm schedule, to working six hours a day on an organic farm in return for board and lodging, to working full time on a voluntary agricultural project.

The beauty of these projects is that anybody who has time to spare (anything from a few days up to a few months), is relatively healthy (although your fitness levels will soon increase!) and doesn't mind getting a bit muddy is free to arrange work on farms throughout the world. This kind of working holiday is an environmentally conscious route to seeing a country from a grassroots perspective and offers an enjoyable and unpretentious eco-experience.

Agritourism

Whereas in the UK the 'farmstay' is usually a fairly luxurious concept designed for city-based families with children who have never seen a live duck before, in many countries agritourism allows tourists to gain a real taste of farm life by participating in the daily round of activities of a working farm. In Scandinavia, New Zealand, Holland, Germany and Italy in particular rural tourism is gaining in popularity and offers the chance not only of having a relatively inexpensive and interesting holiday, but also of learning a little about hay-baling, cheese-making and so on. The extent to which you muck in with the farm duties is entirely up to you, so agritourism could provide a fairly leisurely working holiday, or a week of back-breaking labour, depending on your own tastes. Finding a good base for your farmstay will be the subject of a little internet research. Below are some useful links and ideas.

- **Costa Rica:** Actuar: Community-based rural tourism (www.actuarcostarica.com). A range of initiatives run by community associations that own private ecological reserves. These communities combine tourism services with the opportunity to share the campesino way of life. Two examples of member communities are Montana Verde and Tesoro Verde, both of which allow visitors the chance to meet people who live in harmony with their surroundings and to join them in projects from organic gardening to reforestation
- **Guatemala:** Comunidad Nueva Alianza (www.comunidadnuevaalianza.org). A collective of families that owns a fair-trade organic coffee and macadamia nut plantation. Guests can stay at the eco-lodge, managed and run by the community's women's collective and take tours of the plantation with an opportunity to help growers and learn about medicial and edible herbs and plants of the forest.
- **Peru:** Granja Porcon, (information can be found at http://www.perutravels.net/peru-travel-guide/tours-cajamarca-experiential-granja-porcon.htm). Guests can enjoy hiking and camping at this working farm, and if they wish to, participate in milking the cows, and work in the biological gardens, or with the sheep and alpaca.
- **Italy:** The Touring Club of Italy (www.tourismclubofitaly.com) publishes *Agriturismo: The Guide to Farm Holidays in Italy* (£9.95); Long Travel (tel. 01694 722367; www.long-travel.co.uk) offers around 25 agritourist properties in Italy; www.agriturismo.net – complete guide to farmhouse accommodation in Italy. Quinta da Comeda (www.quintadacomenda.com) is an agri-organic lodging which helps the local community with employment, recycling and eco-preservation techniques. Guests can take part in grape harvesting, fruit picking, or help around this fully organic farm.
- **Denmark:** www.ecoholiday.dk. Network of farm accommodation in Denmark.
- **Sweden:** www.niome-jusegard.com. Small family farm in Gotland. Guests are encouraged to muck in with farmyard duties .
- **Holland:** www.dutch-farmholidays.com/uk/. List of farmstays in Holland.
- **New Zealand:** www.truenz.co.nz/farmstays. Detailed farmstay accommodation guide for New Zealand.
- **Poland:** www.poland.eceat.org; www.agritourism.pl. Two very useful farmstay directories for Poland.
- **South Africa:** www.farmstay.co.za. Portal for agricultural and eco-tourism in South Africa.
- **Germany:** www.landtourismus.de. Farmstays throughout Germany.

Asociación Anai – Finca Lomas

Duration: Min. 1 week
Location: Costa Rica
Season: Year round
Prerequisites: Min. age 18, good physical condition
Organisation: An intermediary NGO seeking to
nurture locally based transformational processes
leading to self-sufficient grassroots organisations focusing on sustainability

☎ +506 224 3570
✍ volunteers@racsa.co.cr
🖥 www.anaicr.org

Description: This unique farm and nature reserve was the first of ANAI's projects in agro-ecosystem development. Before ANAI took it on, the farm had been abandoned for a number of years, but thanks to the efforts of volunteers, one of the most diverse collections of perennial crops in the humid lowland tropics is in the process of redevelopment. Volunteers are invited to experience life in a truly rural area, to learn about more than 150 plant species on the farm, including tropical fruit, nuts and spices and to live in a communal environment with like-minded volunteers. The work involves caring for plant species and the surrounding rainforest, seed collection, data recording and maintenance. Finca Lomas benefits the local community by providing a nursery of tropical fruit trees whose seeds can be distributed to farms in the region, helping farmers to diversify their production
Accommodation: Provided in basic but clean lodgings (there is no electricity, phones or roads)
Cost: Registration fee of US$160 plus US$3 per day for accommodation

Biodynamic Agricultural Association

Duration: Min. 1 week
Location: Throughout the UK and some overseas
Season: Year round
Organisation: Registered charity founded in the
UK in 1929 to promote biodynamic farming and gardening

✍ office@biodynamic.org.uk
🖥 www.biodynamic.org.uk

Description: Biodynamic agriculture is the oldest consciously organic approach to farming and gardening and is also one of the most sustainable. It is based on the principles established by the philosopher and social reformer, Dr. Rudolph Steiner. Biodynamic farms aim to become self-sufficient in compost, manures and animal feeds and all external inputs are kept to a minimum. Workers are often required to volunteer their services on biodynamic farms and the BDAA's website keeps an up-to-date listing of opportunities in the UK and overseas
Accommodation: Varies from camping, to lodges and bunkhouses
Cost: No participation fees. Participants are responsible for their own travel costs

AGRICULTURE

VOLUNTARY WORK

Bullocks Permaculture Homestead

Duration: 1–14 days
Location: Orcas Island, USA
Season: Year round
Prerequisites: Open to all
Organisation: Centre offering permaculture
courses, workshops, and internships to help develop and implement practical solutions
for sustainable living

info@permacultureportal.com
http://permacultureportal.com

Description: The permaculture homestead has been demonstrating sustainable living
techniques for more than 25 years. Interested parties are invited to visit for short periods
throughout the growing season and help with a variety of projects such as organic
gardening, pruning, irrigation mursery management, pond construction, mushroom
propagation, bee keeping, solar hot water systems, natural building, carpentry and so
on. These projects are all very hands-on and visitors are expected to jump into farm life
straight away and join in with all chores and activities. The centre also offers a range of
residential permaculture design courses year round
Accommodation: Space for a tent is provided. Meals are prepared together as a group
Cost: A small per person per day donation is requested to help cover the costs of food
and propane

Citizens Network For Foreign Affairs

Duration: Min. 16 days (placements are
usually 3 weeks)
Location: Ukraine, Moldova and Belarus
Season: Year round
Prerequisites: Volunteers should have
at least five years' experience in their

☎ +1 888 872 2632 or 202 296 3920
info@cnfa.org
www.cnfa.org

fields. Required specialities include farmers, cooperative specialists, food processing
professionals, agribusiness executives and agricultural organisation leaders. Seniors are
encouraged to apply
Organisation: Dedicated to increasing and sustaining rural incomes in less developed
areas of the world by empowering farmers and rural entrepreneurs
Description: CNFA sends around 80 volunteers each year for short-term placements to
work on long-term projects that seek to develop private farmer associations, cooperative,
private agribusinesses, women's and young farmers' groups and other organisations
Accommodation: Provided either with a host family in the village where participants
work or in a regional hotel or apartment
Cost: There are no participation fees. All costs for volunteers are covered, including
airfares, food, accommodation and transportation

AGRICULTURE

VOLUNTARY WORK

Rica Vacations With Farmer
's Project

...ion: Min. 1 week
Location: Northern Zone of Costa Rica
Season: Year round
Prerequisites: Min. age 18. No experience
required

☎ +506 460 5106 or +506 354 6047
✍ info@costaricaruraltours.com
💻 www.costaricaruraltours.com

Organisation: Group of farming families
that has independently organised itself to complement agricultural activity with rural
tourism
Description: Working-holiday makers are invited to lodge with local farming communities
and contribute to their sustainable development by carrying out a variety of agricultural
and community work. The programme is made up of a network of rural communities and
volunteers are matched with projects depending on their individual interests and skills
Accommodation: Provided in the houses of local farming families. Basic and clean, with
meals provided
Cost: US$150 per person per week, including food and accommodation

Ecoforest Education for Sustainability

Duration: Min. 1 week
Location: Southern Spain
Season: Year round
Prerequisites: Participants must live a vegan raw food
lifestyle whilst visiting. No drugs, smoking or alcohol on
site. No experience required

☎ +34 661079 950
✍ ef@ecoforest.org
💻 www.ecoforest.org

Organisation: Charitable, non-profit organisation set up to provide education about
living and working in simple, natural, sustainable and healthy ways
Description: Ecoforest has created a unique ecological project on a small fruit farm
in Spain. Their mission is to demonstrate that food can be produced by families and
communities all around the world without destroying the natural environment, making
people more economically self-reliant and offering a positive alternative to globalisation
trends. The project runs a working visitor programme where work contributed subsidises
keep. As well as learning about the project and contributing to its future, visitors also have
time for relaxing, swimming and socialising
Accommodation: Provided in tents or a bunkhouse
Cost: €5–€15 per day to help contribute towards food and accommodation

AGRICULTURE

VOLUNTARY WORK

Farm Sanctuary Internships

Duration: Min. 1 month
Location: New York or California, USA
Season: Year round (positions begin on the first day of each month)
Prerequisites: Min. age 16, strong commitment to animal rights. Participants must follow vegan principles while on site
Organisation: Farm animal protection and education organisation dedicated to combating the abuses of industrialised farming
Description: Farm sanctuary owns two farms which house more than 1,000 rescued cows, chickens, turkeys, geese, sheep, goats, rabbits, pigs and ducks. Volunteers are invited to help out with general farm chores such as cleaning barns, and animal care and feeding, as well as leading educational tours and helping with administrative tasks. All participants work 40 hours per week and may be required to be on call at the animal shelter
Accommodation: Provided on site in shared houses with bathroom and kitchen facilities
Cost: No participation fees. Housing is provided at no charge, but volunteers are responsible for all other costs

☎ +1 607 583 2225
🖱 intern@farmsanctuary.org
💻 www.farmsanctuary.org

Farm Helpers in New Zealand (FHINZ)

Duration: Min. 3 days
Location: Throughout New Zealand
Season: Year round
Prerequisites: No farm experience required
Organisation: Voluntary group of more than 190 farms throughout New Zealand that offer free farmstays to visitors in exchange for labour
Description: FhiNZ began in 1994, with the Grady family deciding to offer free board and lodging on their farm to visitors in exchange for help around the farm. The idea was to treat visitors like one of the family so that they could experience the real Kiwi farming way of life. Today the concept has spread to more than 190 farms. Participants are expected to work an average of four to six hours per day, depending on the specific needs of the farm. The work will vary according to season, and may include cooking, housework and gardening as well as farm work. Most farms will collect visitors from the nearest town at no cost, and return them after the stay
Accommodation: Board and lodging is provided in the family home in return for daily farm work dependent on season and type of farm
Cost: Participants buy a booklet (valid for 1 year) from FHiNZ for NZ$25, which lists all of the member farms and must be presented as proof of membership upon arrival at a farm. There are no further participation costs

🖱 info@fhinz.co.nz
💻 www.fhinz.co.nz

Hands Up Holidays

Duration: 11–17 days (also tailor-made options)
Location: Brazil, New Zealand, Peru, Vietnam
Season: Year round
Prerequisites: Min. age 18. No specific skills required, just enthusiasm but agricultural or horticultural skills you do have are matched with specific projects where possible

☎ 0800 7833554
🖱 info@handsupholidays.com
💻 www.handsupholidays.com

Organisation: Leading ethical tour operator working with local suppliers, NGOs, charities and little-known local projects. A minimum of 10% of profits go to further development projects

Description: Hands Up Holidays offers ethically and environmentally responsible holidays that blend sightseeing with fulfilling volunteering experiences. Approx. a third of the holiday is devoted to a meaningful 'taste' of environmental conservation volunteering and the rest of the time is spent sightseeing with local, English-speaking guides. Current projects include working alongside cocoa farmers and helping to conserve native Jacaranda forests in Brazil, organic farming on a Maori trust in New Zealand, assisting a farming community in the Andes (Peru), and an organic gardening project with victims of Agent Orange in Vietnam. All flights are carbon neutral

Accommodation: Ranges from homestays to 5–star hotels and ecolodges that are locally owned and managed where possible

Cost: From £750 for 11 days in India, through to £2,300 for 15 days in the Galapagos and Ecuador. Average price (excluding flights) for 2 weeks is £1,600

Volunteers help victims of Agent Orange with the organic garden at the Friendship Village near Hanoi, Vietnam.

AGRICULTURE

VOLUNTARY WORK

Global Service Corps: Sustainable Agriculture Program

Duration: Min. 2 weeks
Location: Arusha region, Tanzania
Season: Year round
Prerequisites: Min. age 18. No agricultural experience required

☎ +1 415 788 366
🖰 gsc@igc.org
💻 www.globalservicecorps.org

Organisation: Non-profit international volunteer organisation providing service-learning opportunities for people worldwide
Description: The sustainable agriculture programme offers participants opportunities to learn about organic farming method, to work with Tanzanian community groups, farmers and non-governmental organisations to initiate small-scale organic agriculture projects. Participants first learn and then educate community members about sustainable small-scale farming – specifically biointensive agriculture (a specialised form of organic agriculture). Volunteers and locals then work together to create organic farming plots
Accommodation: Provided in a homestay with local families. Meals provided
Cost: US$2,325 (2 weeks); US$2,815 (4 weeks). Fees include airport pick-up and project transportation, accommodation, meals, excursions and support

Volunteer Farm Of Shenandoah

Duration: Min. 1 day
Location: Virginia, USA
Season: Year round
Prerequisites: Open to all. Under 18s must present a liability waiver signed by their parents

☎ +1 540 459 3478
🖰 bob.blair@volunteerfarm.org
💻 www.volunteerfarm.org

Organisation: Non-profit, charitable operational arm of the World Foundation for Children, working through the Blue Ridge Area Food Bank
Description: The volunteer farm helps to feed around 129,000 hungry, homeless or deprived people each year in 25 counties in the northern mountains of Virginia. Volunteers are invited to help with this worthwhile project either in the office – database entry, mailings and volunteer recruitment, or in the fields helping to provide fresh food for those in need through plow work, planting and harvesting
Accommodation: No accommodation provided
Cost: There is no participation fee. Volunteers must cover all their own expenses

Sunseed Desert Technology

Duration: Min. 2 weeks if possible
Location: Almeria, Spain
Season: Year round
Prerequisites: Open to all ages and interests.
Children, families and senior visitors welcome. Under
16s must be accompanied by an adult

☎ +34 950 525 770
✎ sunseedspain@arrakis.es
🖥 www.sunseed.org.uk

Organisation: A UK registered charity that aims to develop, demonstrate and
communicate accessible, low-tech methods of living sustainably in a semi-arid environment
Description: Around 250 volunteers per year take the opportunity to spend time working in
a beautiful rural location, helping to demonstrate a sustainable lifestyle using methods that
have the least detrimental environmental impact. Short-term volunteers work a minimum of
24–hours per week, six days per week on a variety of projects including organic gardening,
dryland management, garden produce preservation, irrigation line clearing, sowing and
transplanting seedlings, turning compost heaps, tree maintenance, hoeing and weeding,
and other non-agricultural projects such as general maintenance, publicity and education
Accommodation: Individual or shared basic rooms are provided on-site. There is a toilet
and shower block at the main house. Staff and volunteers eat together and share cooking
duties. All food is vegetarian; some is organic
Cost: A contribution of £65–£118 per week depending on status and season is
requested, to cover food and accommodation

Task Brasil – Ecotour: The Organic Farming Experience

Duration: 5/9 days
Location: Brazil
Season: April, June, October, August
Prerequisites: Min. age 18. No experience required
Organisation: UK registered charity set up to operate
a network of services for street children in Brazil

☎ 020 7735 5545
✎ info@taskbrasil.org.uk
🖥 www.taskbrasil.org.uk

Description: Task Brasil's Epsom College Farm is the home of teenage boys who would
otherwise remain on the streets trapped in a circle of violence and crime. The project aims
to establish a sustainable programme of living for these children based on organic farming
and the ecotour allows participants a holiday combined with the opportunity to invest
time and energy into a worthwhile project. The farm aims to become sustainable within
five years and all funds raised through the ecotour are injected back into the project.
Participants work on the farm on projects such as organic vegetable garden construction,
fruit tree planting, fence construction and compost making. Five days are spent working
on the farm, with a three-day tour of Rio and other sites included. A shorter five-day tour,
just visiting the farm, is also available
Accommodation: Provided in 2/4-star hotels, pousadas, and accommodation at the
farm. All meals are provided
Cost: £495 (standard package); £295 (budget package)

AGRICULTURE

VOLUNTARY WORK

COMMUNITIES

Many communities (previously referred to as communes) welcome foreign visitors who share their values. Sometimes a small charge is made for a short stay or the opportunity given to work in exchange for hospitality. The details and possible fees must be established on a case-by-case basis.

Rob Abblett from Leicester is someone who has taken dozens of breaks in communities around the world:

I've visited, worked and had many varied experiences in more than 30 communes around the world. I like them because they are so varied and full of interesting people, usually with alternative ideas, beliefs, but also because I almost always find someone that I can really connect with, for sometimes I need to be with like-minded folk.

Before arranging a longish stay in a community, consider whether or not you will find such an environment congenial. Some are very radical or esoteric in their practices so find out as much as you can before planning to stay for any period of time. Most communards are non-smoking vegetarians and living conditions may be primitive by some people's standards.

Shorter stays in more distant places can be readily arranged. Many communities are engaged in special projects which may coincide with your interests. For example the long-established Corrymeela Community in County Antrim works for reconciliation between Protestants and Catholics in Northern Ireland.

Many well-known communes in the world welcome visitors. For example Stifelsen Stjärnsund is located among the forests, lakes and hills of central Sweden. Founded in 1984, the community aims to encourage personal, social and spiritual development in an ecologically sustainable environment. It operates an international working guest programme throughout the year, but is at its busiest between May and September when most of the community's courses are offered. Carpenters, builders, trained gardeners and cooks are especially welcome. First-time working guests pay SEK500 (about £38) for their first week of work and if the arrangement suits both sides it can be continued with a negotiable contribution according to hours worked and length of stay. Enquiries should be made well in advance of a proposed summer visit.

In Denmark the Svanholm Community consists of 120 people including lots of children. Numbers are swelled in the summer when more volunteers (EU nationals only) arrive to help with the harvest of the organic produce. Guests work 30 to 40 hours a week for food, lodging and (if no other income is available) pocket money.

One of the most famous utopian communities is Auroville near Pondicherry in the South Indian state of Tamil Nadu, whose ambition is nothing less than 'to realise human unity'. Volunteers participate in a variety of activities to reclaim land and produce food and are charged anything from $5 to $20+ a day for board and lodging according to their contribution.

Contacts and Resources
• Diggers and Dreamers: *The Guide to Communal Living* published by Edge of Time, BCM Edge, London WC1N 3XX (tel. 0800 083 0451; www.edgeoftime.co.uk). The 2006/7 edition (£6.50) contains updated listing of communities in the UK. *Eurotopia: Directory of Intentional Communities and Ecovillages in Europe*, (www.eurotopia.de).

AGRICULTURE

VOLUNTARY WORK

English version provides a comprehensive listing of 336 international communities in 23 countries (mainly Europe and the UK). It can be ordered from Edge of Time for £12.50.

- Communities, 138 Twin Oaks Road, Louisa, VA 23093, USA (tel. +1 540 894 5798; http://directory.ic.org). Publish *Communities Directory: A Guide to Co-operative Living* (2005); price US$24 plus $4 US postage or $8 overseas by surface post. It lists about 600 communities in the US and about 100 abroad including 'ecovillages, rural land trusts, co-housing groups, kibbutzim, student co-ops, organic farms, monasteries, urban artist collectives, rural communes and Catholic Worker houses'. Much of the information is available on their website.
- Global Ecovillage Network (GEN), based at ZEGG Community in Germany and at Findhorn in Scotland (info@gen-europe.org/ www.gen-europe.org). GEN functions as the umbrella organisation for a wide range of communities and ecovillages all over the world, many of whom welcome guest and volunteers. (American contact: ecovillage@ thefarm.org; Australiasia information: http://genoa.ecovillage.org).
- Auroville, Bharat Nivas, Tamil Nadu 605101, India (tel. +91 413 622121; www.auroville.org).
- Stifelsen Stjärnsund, Bruksallén 16, 77071 Stjärnsund, Sweden (tel. +46 225 80001; www.frid.nu). Community that welcomes working guests.
- Svanholm Community, Visitors Group, Svanholm Allé 2, 4050 Skibby, Denmark (tel. +45 4756 6670; www.svanholm.dk).

WWOOF – WORLDWIDE OPPORTUNITIES ON ORGANIC FARMS

The WWOOF movement allows people from all walks of life to work on a farm in exchange for bed and board throughout the world. Not only is WWOOFing a cheap way to travel, it also offers good physical exercise in beautiful countryside, an education in organic farming and much else besides, and most importantly a great opportunity to meet people and make new friends. Founded in 1971, WWOOF began in the UK as a useful way for city folk to get out into the countryside for the weekend and learn about the burgeoning organic movement. These days the movement has partners all over the world and provides access to a far greater diversity of experience. Many WWOOF hosts offer health and healing centres, pottery and arts, restoring buildings, eco-villages, centres for the environment, brewing and food production and so on. As such the movement has gained enormously in popularity and appeals to a diverse group of people, from backpackers looking to escape the endless round of bunkbeds and hostels, to women travelling on their own who find it to be a safer option, to high-flyers searching for a truly different holiday experience.

With growing fears of genetically modified foods, the organic farming movement is attracting more and more of a following around the world, from Toulouse to Turkey (to Prince Charles' Highgrove). It has been predicted that within five or 10 years, one in six farms will have gone organic. Organic farms everywhere are extremely keen to take on volunteers as without the use of chemicals and heavy machinery, farm work becomes incredibly labour intensive.

WWOOF stands for World Wide Opportunities on Organic Farms, changed from Willing Workers on Organic Farms, with an eye to the sensitivities of immigration officers around

WWOOF volunteers work on organic farms in exchange for bed and board around the world.

the world who always bridle at the word 'work'. (If the topic arises at immigration, avoid the word 'working'; it is preferable to present yourself as a student of organic farming who is planning an educational farm visit or a cultural exchange).

WWOOF has a global website (www.wwoof.org) with links to both the national organisations in the countries that have a WWOOF co-ordinator and to those which do not, known as WWOOF Independents. Each national group has its own aims, system, fees and rules but most expect applicants to have gained some experience on an organic farm in their own country first. WWOOF is an exchange: in return for your help on organic farms, gardens and homesteads, you receive meals, a place to sleep and a practical insight into organic growing. The work-for-keep exchange is a simple one that can be immensely satisfying. Visitors are expected to work around six hours per day in return for free accommodation and can stay from a few days to many months depending on whether or not they click with the owners and, of course, how much work needs to be done. Mike Tunnicliffe joined the long-established WWOOF New Zealand to avoid work permit hassles and his experience is typical of WWOOFers' in other countries:

My second choice of farm was a marvellous experience. For 15 days I earned no money but neither did I spend any, and I enjoyed life on the farm as part of the family. There is a wide variety of WWOOF farms and I thoroughly recommend the scheme to anyone who isn't desperate to earn money.

Before arranging a stay on an organic farm, consider whether or not you will find such an environment congenial. Many organic farmers are non-smoking vegetarians and living

Julie Russell spent an extended hands-on holiday WWOOFing in Italy:

I've just returned from WWOOFing in Italy and I'd like to share with everyone the wonderful experiences I had with three of the most friendly and hospitable WWOOF farms. Having studied Italian at university, I thought it time to go to rural Italy to get a taste of the culture, the language, and of course life on an organic farm.

My first stop was in the Apennine mountain range, famous for its porcini mushrooms. It was a beautiful spot, so high up on a mountain that we were often above the clouds. Needless to say, it was sunny nearly all the time. Graziamaria, who has 28 cats, cultivates calendula, which she dries and sells for medicinal uses. She also has herb and vegetable gardens, fruit and nut trees, geese, hens and dogs. During my time there, there were usually four or five WWOOFers so we all pitched in to do the work together: from picking pears to weeding, sowing seeds, collecting and cleaning walnuts, picking calendula and digging potatoes.

We also spent our free days together going to Pisa, the Cinque Terre (a coastal walk which passes through five towns) and a traditional food festival celebrating the mushroom season. Grazia also spent quite a bit of time explaining the biodynamic techniques she uses, which was fascinating. We all had a great time and enjoyed Grazia's cooking!

My next stop was with Laura and Filippo in Tuscany. Since all the outside work was finished for the year, my work was exclusively in their agriturismo (rural bed and breakfast). Laura, Filippo and all their family really looked after me. Laura and I had a great time going round all the local markets and making things in the kitchen together. And then, when they went on holiday, another WWOOFer and I looked after the B&B ourselves, which was great fun.

The house was in a beautiful setting looking over the hilly landscape in the Chianti region. Filippo makes his own wine from the vines they have and produces his own olive oil, too. The olive harvest was not very abundant in Italy this year but I did manage to get one day helping Filippo and his father picking them – I couldn't go to Italy during the olive season and not pick any!

Anyway, at my third and final farm, I did get to help with the raccolta delle olive (the olive harvest). This time, still in Tuscany, I was at a proper working farm near the sea. They were brand new hosts and I was their first WWOOFer so I had to make a good impression!

At first, it was all olive picking, mainly with someone who gave me some interesting Italian history lessons while we were working. On the farm they had goats, a horse, a donkey and chickens, and a huge vegetable garden with everything from broccoli and onions to cabbage, fennel and all different kinds of lettuce. Friday was the busiest day of the week. We would spend the entire morning harvesting, washing and preparing the vegetables ready to be packed up in the afternoon for an organic box scheme. Then in the evening I went along to a nearby coastal town to deliver the boxes. That gave me a great sense of satisfaction, seeing the end result of all the hard work and eating the delicious vegetables straight from the earth. I really loved this place and again was made to feel one of the family.

My stay in Italy was brilliant. I got to do so many new things at the farms that I can hopefully use in the future, and I met so many like-minded people. I'd recommend WWOOFing in Italy to anyone who wants to experience organic farming in another country.

conditions may be primitive by some people's standards. Although positive experiences are typical, Craig Ashworth expressed reservations about WWOOF, based on his experiences in New Zealand, and claims that a proportion of WWOOF hosts are 'quite wacky'. However, part of the beauty of the WWOOF arrangement is its flexibility. As it is an entirely voluntary arrangement you are always free to move on, and if one placement is not working out, you can simply up sticks to another. WWOOF does not regulate the various hosts so the opportunities available can vary enormously in terms of the type of work you're expected to do, the friendliness of the hosts and their organic credentials. For example Armin Birrer, who has spent time on organic farms in many countries, claims that the weirdest job he ever did was to spend a day in New Zealand picking worms out of a pile of rabbit dung to be used to soften the soil around some melon plants. With such a loose network of individuals around the world, the system is bound to be hit and miss. Kathryn Good described WWOOFFing as 'a lucky dip way to travel' in a recent article in *The Independent*: *'True, you could turn up at Cold Comfort Farm but equally, pick right next time and you could find yourself, as I did, sitting on a veranda looking out over a vineyard, knocking back wine and eating steak hot off the barbie – all in return for a few hours of good, old-fashioned hard work'.* Bear in mind that the plush sounding WWOOF hosts, such as a Byron Bay beach house where WWOOFers have access to a spa and pool in exchange for two hours work per day, tend to get booked up well in advance.

How to WWOOF

If you want to WWOOF in countries that have their own WWOOF organisation like the UK, Italy or Korea, it is necessary to join the national WWOOF organisation before you can obtain addresses of these properties. This usually costs €15 or €20 per year. The present list of countries with their own WWOOF co-ordinators is detailed in the box below.

To obtain the addresses of properties in all the other countries, It is necessary to join WWOOF International. In the UK this can be done by sending £15 for Internet access, or £20 for a printed booklet, to WWOOF International c/o WWOOF UK, PO Box 2675, Lewes, East Sussex BN7 1RB (hello@wwoof.org.uk).

An alternative list of WWOOF opportunities in the USA can be found at www. organicvolunteers.com and in Ireland at www.planorganic.com.

Contact Details and Membership Fees for National WWOOF Organisations

UK: hello@wwoof.org.uk; www.wwoof.org.uk. Membership £15 plus IRC
Australia: Tel. 61 03 5155 0218; wwoof@wwoof.com.au; www.wwoof.com.au. Membership AUD$55
Austria: Tel. 43 (0)316 464951; wwoof.welcome@utanet.at; www.wwoof.welcome. at.tf. Membership €20
Bulgaria: wwoofbulgaria@hotmail.com; www.geocities.com/wwoofbulgaria. Membership free
Canada: Tel. +1 250 354 4417; wwoofcan@shaw.ca; www.wwoof.ca. Membership CD$35
China: support@wwoofchina.org; www.wwoofchina.org. Membership US$40
Costa Rica: wwoofcostarica@yahoo.com; www.wwoofcostarica.com
Czech Republic: Tel. +42 (0) 776 22 60 14; www.wwoof.ecn.cz. Membership €15
Denmark: Tel. +45 9893 8607; info@wwoof.dk; www.wwoof.dk

Germany: info@wwoof.de; www.wwoof.de. Membership €18 + 2xIRC
Ghana: Tel. +233 21 716091; kingzeeh@yahoo.co.uk. Membership US$25 + 3xIRC
Hawaii: www.wwoofhawaii.org
Italy: info@wwoof.it; www.wwoof.it. Membership €25
Japan: info@wwoofjapan.com; www.wwoofjapan.com. Membership US$40
Korea: Tel. +82 2 723 4458; wwoofkorea@yahoo.co.kr; www.wwoofkorea.com. Membership US$30
Mexico: wwoofmexico@yahoo.com; www.wwoofmexico.com. Membership US$20
Nepal: Tel. +977 1 01 4363418; fdregmi@wlink.com.np; www.wwoofnepal.org. Membership US$40
New Zealand: Tel. +64 3 544 9890; support@wwoof.co.nz; www.wwoof.co.nz. Membership NZ$45
Slovenia: pgostan@volja.net; www.wwoofslovenia.cjb.net. Membership €10
Sweden: jandi@spray.se; www.wwoof.se. Membership €20
Switzerland: wwoof@gmx.ch; www.dataway.ch/~reini/wwoof/. Membership 20 Swiss Francs
Turkey: Tel. +90 (0) 212 252 5255; info@tatuta.org; www.tatuta.org
Uganda: Tel. +256 346856; bob_kasule@yahoo.com. Membership £20
USA: Tel. +1 831 425 3276; info@wwoofusa.org; www.wwoofusa.org

PAID AGRICULTURAL WORK

AGRICULTURE PAID WORK

If you are looking for a satisfying job that is limited in duration, allows you to work outside, pays reasonably well, often with free accommodation, and at the same time will expand your cultural horizons by flinging you into a hard-working environment with people from all over the world, then fruit and vegetable harvesting may well be for you. Historically, agricultural harvests have employed the greatest numbers of casual workers, who have traditionally travelled hundreds of miles to gather in the fruits of the land, from the tiny blueberry to the mighty watermelon. Unlike much paid work, fruit picking is extremely flexible and hence fits nicely into the average person's holiday time. Farms often take casual labour on for as little as a day, and harvests of a particular fruit rarely last longer than four or five weeks. Spending a week to a month of your holiday time fruit picking is a great way to earn money, get fit, explore a new culture, and make new friends.

Fruit picking is by no means easy. Past participants agree that the job entails more than a few negative aspects: early starts for back-breaking work, nine hour days, with very few days off, and the weather, which is too cold and damp in the early autumn mornings and too hot at midday. Accommodation may consist of a space in a barn for a sleeping bag, and the sanitation arrangements of a cold-water tap. Nevertheless, there are more than enough positive features of the fruit-picking experience to compensate for a few weeks' discomfort.

Part of the appeal of fruit picking is the ability to raise a fair amount of money in a short space of time. Most fruit-picking work is paid at piece rates, so while you may start off barely scraping minimum wage, as you get more experienced your pay will rapidly increase. Admittedly the wage is rarely much more than those legal limits set by the Agricultural Wage Boards of any given country, but there is little opportunity to spend your earnings on an isolated farm and most people are able to save several hundred pounds in say, a 10–day grape harvest in France.

Equally appealing is the opportunity to experience something different. There are few more authentic ways of experiencing an alien culture than working in the most rural areas. The grape harvest, or vendange, in France for example, lures many for the pure romance of participating in an ancient ritual. While mechanisation may have completely replaced casual labour in some areas such as Cognac, the finest Grand Cru chateaux are unlikely to ever completely do away with hand-picking.

There is also a tremendous community spirit among fruit pickers, from the North African migrants and the huge numbers of Eastern Europeans looking for a western wage, to western working-holidaymakers. When thrust into such a hard-working environment, living together at close quarters with a large group of young people, it is almost impossible not to make friends. Many of the larger farms, especially in Australasia, offer communal excursions for workers on their days off, barbecue areas, and shared sporting facilities. There is often a work-hard, play-hard party atmosphere in fruit-picking camps. During vendange season, the free wine provided after a hard day's work, often makes for sparkling and convivial evening company. Keep in mind however, that an early start, and tiring work are not ideal companions for a hangover.

What to Expect

If your experience of farm work is limited to family excursions to the local PYO orchard, then the reality of a fruit-picking holiday may be something of a rude awakening. Physical fitness is a definite prerequisite; some farms only hire those aged 25 or under, and having a little experience is likely to make the whole business more enjoyable. Without either, you are likely to find the first few days gruelling. If you are part of a large team you may be expected to work at the same speed as the most experienced picker, which can be both exhausting and discouraging. Try not to become disheartened. More experienced pickers will be happy to help you and it is a good idea to study their technique closely. After a week or so your confidence and indeed your earnings will have increased.

Finding Fruit Picking Jobs

Had this book been written 10 years ago, then the availability of harvest work would have been much greater. In 2007 however, the number of fruit-picking jobs has been greatly reduced by the vast numbers of Romanians, Poles, Albanians etc now roaming every corner of Europe, trying to earn the money that their own struggling economies cannot provide. As a result of the new competition for jobs, wages have been dropping for some time. Nevertheless, the jobs are still there for the taking and there are several organisations detailed below that will help you to find a one to four-week working break, as well as details of some of the main farms that employ seasonal workers on a regular basis. In Australia and New Zealand, there is not such a ready supply of cheap seasonal labour, and as such the harvests still rely heavily on travellers and working-holidaymakers.

There is no need to restrict yourself to the organisations and farms detailed below however. While on a short-term working adventure, it would be nice to have set up employment in advance, but many agricultural jobs are best found in situ through word of mouth. Asking around is a key technique to finding such work. In rural areas people are far more likely to know their neighbours' labour requirements and are often more sympathetic and helpful in their attitudes than city dwellers. Jobs available may be increased by later or better harvests, by the farmer underestimating the number of pickers required, or by workers with other commitments leaving before the harvest is over.

FRUIT PICKING IN THE UK

The principal fruit growing areas of Britain are: the Vale of Evesham over to the Wye and Usk Valleys; most of Kent; Lincolnshire and East Anglia, especially the Fens around Wisbech; and north of the Tay Estuary (Blairgowrie, Forfar). Harvest types and times vary between regions, so raspberries may ripen two weeks later in Scotland than in the South of England. Fruit-picking work lasts all summer, throughout the UK. Strawberries and gooseberries are among the first fruits to ripen in southern Britain, usually in June. The final harvests of the season are the apple harvest, running from August until mid-October and traditionally offering more lucrative work, and the grape harvest of the small vineyards in the south of England, which usually begins in September and runs until mid-November.

Many of the fruit farms listed below take on over a hundred pickers at a time for anything from a day up to a few months. All of those listed below also offer accommodation, often free of charge or heavily subsidised. Remember that the following list is only a small selection of what is available. There is intensive agricultural activity in most parts of Britain so always check with the Jobcentre (www.jobcentreplus.gov.uk) or Farmers' Union in the areas where you are interested in finding farm work. The internet is another good source of work. Fruitfuljobs.com (tel. 0870 0727 0050; info@fruitfuljobs.com) is a web-based agency which helps people find jobs with accommodation on UK farms. Other useful international websites include www.pickingjobs.com; www.seasonworkers.com and www.farmhands.co.uk.

Any citizen of the 27 EU countries is free to undertake fruit-picking work, and since the EU enlarged in 2004, seasonal farm-workers are an incredibly diverse bunch. Whereas there was once a shortage of seasonal workers to cope with the huge short-term demand, this is no longer the case and it is always a good idea to apply for work well in advance. Those citizens from the newest EU member states (with the exception of Cyprus and Malta) are obliged to register with the Home Office under the Worker Registration Scheme. For further details visit www.workingintheuk.gov.uk.

Citizens from outside the EU and the Commonwealth can only gain such work if they are a student who is over 18 and in full-time education. They must apply through the Seasonal Agricultural Workers Scheme (SAWS) which will remain in place until 2010. Farm camps under this scheme are authorised by the Home Office. Non-EU nationals who are accepted on the scheme are issued special Work Cards. Places on the scheme are limited and fill up very quickly, so it is necessary to apply in November for the following summer. Recruitment for farm camps is handled by SAWS operators, including Concordia (tel. 01273 422293; www.concordia-iye.org.uk)

Citizens of Commonwealth countries including Australia, New Zealand, Canada and South Africa between the ages of 17 and 30 are free to work in the UK under what was previously known as the Working Holiday-Maker Scheme. Further details can be found at www.workingintheuk.gov.uk. Canadian students, graduates and young people should contact the Student Work Abroad Programme (www.swap.ca) and Australians and New Zealanders should contact International Exchange Programmes, a non-profit organisation specialising in sending young Australians and New Zealanders on working holidays overseas (www.iep.org.au or www.iep.co.nz).

Wages

Pay varies according to the fruit and the difficulty involved in the picking process. Many farmers pay piecework rates, which means that you are paid according to the quantity that you pick. This method can be very satisfactory when a harvest is at its peak but when fruit is scarce earning more than the minimum can be much more difficult. However, even when you are paid on a piecework basis the amount you earn for each hour worked must average the wages set out in the Agricultural Wages Order. Many farmers calculate wages by a combination of piecework and hourly rates of pay. For the 2006/2007 period the minimum rate for standard workers is £5.74 per hour. However, these rates vary and are subject to change, so it is worth checking with the Agricultural Wages Board before starting work (tel. 020 7238 6523). The Department for Environment, Food and Rural Affairs (DEFRA) also has a helpline for employees who want to know more about the Agricultural Wages Order (tel. 0845 000 0134; www.defra.gov.uk).

THE FARMS

Allanhill Farm

Location: Near St. Andrews, Scotland
Season: May – August
Picking: Strawberries
Accommodation: In self-catering mobile homes with good facilities
Duration of Work: Min. 4 weeks
Working Hours: 8 hours per day, 6 days a week
Pay: Piecework rates

dot@allanhill.co.uk
www.allanhill.co.uk

S.H.M. Broomfield & Son

Location: Worcestershire
Season: June – October
Picking: Apples, pears, plums, cherries, raspberries
Accommodation: Room/mobile home for £3.50 per night. Camping places for £1.50 per night
Duration of Work: Min. 2 weeks
Working Hours: 6 days per week, Monday to Saturday
Pay: £5.30–£8.00 per hour

☎ 01543 674871
phodsonwalker@farming.me.uk

Cairntradlin

Location: Aberdeenshire, Scotland
Season: June – July
Picking: Strawberries
Accommodation: In caravans or mobile homes
Duration of Work: Min. 4 weeks
Pay: Piecework rates

info@cairntradlin.co.uk
w.cairntradlin.co.uk

Chandler & Dunn Ltd

Location: Near Canterbury, Kent
Season: June – September
Picking: Strawberries, gooseberries, plums, apples, pears
Accommodation: Campsite close by
Duration of Work: Min. 3 weeks
Working Hours: 8am-5pm, Monday to Friday
Pay: Piecework rates

☎ 01304 812262
🖱 jobs@chandleranddunn.co.uk
💻 www.chandleranddunn.co.uk

Charlton Orchards

☎ 01823 412959
🖱 sally@charlton-orchards.co.uk
💻 www.charltonorchards.com

Location: Taunton, Somerset
Season: August – October
Picking: Apples, pears, plums
Accommodation: Campsite available at no charge
Duration of Work: Min. 1 week
Working Hours: Approx. 8 hours per day, Monday to Friday
Pay: Agricultural Wage Board rates

S.H. Chesson

Location: Sevenoaks, Kent
Season: June – October
Picking: Strawberries, apples, pears

☎ 01732 780496

Accommodation: Campsite with kitchen, showers, laundry, TV room, canteen etc at £11.20 per week
Duration of Work: Min. 4 weeks
Working Hours: Vary. Day off alternate Sat/Sun
Pay: Piecework rates in the region of £200–£250 per week

C. Francis

Location: Spalding, Lincolnshire
Season: June – October
Picking: Soft fruit
Accommodation: Hostel with showers, cooking and sporting facilities: £30 per week
Duration of Work: Min. 4 weeks
Working Hours: 8 hours a day, 5 days a week
Pay: Piecework rates

☎ 01775 723953
🖱 cecilfrancis@aol.com

AGRICULTURE

PAID WORK

Fridaybridge International Farm Camp

Location: Wisbech, Cambridgeshire
Season: April – November
Picking: Strawberries, apples, broccoli, potatoes
Accommodation: Basic, with breakfast and dinner provided at weekly charge
Duration of Work: Min. 3 weeks
Working Hours: 5–6 days per week
Pay: As set by Agricultural Wages Board

☎ 01945 860255

Harold Corrigall

Location: Perthshire
Season: June – August
Picking: Raspberries
Accommodation: Available at £4 per day
Duration of Work: Min. 4 weeks
Working Hours: 6am-3pm, 6 days a week
Pay: Approx £40–£60 per day

☎ 01764 684532
🖱 haroldcorrigall@btconnect.com

Hayles Fruit Farm Ltd

Location: Cotswolds, Gloucestershire
Season: August – September
Picking: Apples, pears, plums and nuts
Accommodation: Campsite available at no charge
Duration of Work: 3–5 weeks
Working Hours: 8am–4pm
Pay: Piecework rates (approx. £30–£50 per day)

☎ 01242 602123
🖱 jobs@hayles-fruit-farm.co.uk
💻 www.hayles-fruit-farm.co.uk

Hill Farm Orchards

Location: Hampshire
Season: September – April
Picking and packing: Apples and pears
Accommodation: Provided for a small fee
Duration of Work: Min. 4 weeks
Working Hours: 8am–4.30pm, Monday to Friday
Pay: As set by Agricultural Wages Board

☎ 01489 878616
🖱 hifol@eur-isp.com

S & P Hodson-walker

Location: Staffordshire
Season: June – September
Picking: Strawberries and raspberries
Accommodation: Available at approx. £25 per week
Duration of Work: Min. 4 weeks
Pay: Piecework rates

☎ 01299 851592
🖱 colin@broomfieldsfarmshop.co.uk
💻 www.broomfieldsfarmshop.co.uk

International Farm Camp

Location: Tiptree, Essex
Season: June – July
Picking: Various fruit
Accommodation: Caravan site at small weekly charge
Duration of Work: Min. 4 weeks
Working Hours: 6am-3pm Monday to Friday
Pay: Piecework rates

☎ 01621 815496
🖱 ifc@tiptree.com

Laurel Tree Fruit Farm

Location: East Sussex
Season: August – September
Picking: Apples and pears
Accommodation: Limited camping permitted
Duration of Work: approx. 20 days
Working Hours: 6 hours per day
Pay: National minimum wage

☎ 01892 661637
or 01892 654011
mobile 077 6898 0308

F.W. Mansfield & Son

Location: Kent
Season: May – November
Picking: Apples, pears, strawberries, plums, cherries
Accommodation: In caravans with communal kitchen, washing facilities
Duration of Work: Min. 2 weeks
Working Hours: Variable
Pay: National minimum wage or piecework rates

☎ 01227 731441

D.A. Newling & Son

Location: Wisbech, Cambridgeshire
Season: August – September
Picking: Apples and pears
Accommodation: Shared caravans; showers and laundry facilities: £18 per week
Duration of Work: Min. 4 weeks
Working Hours: 8 hours per day with some overtime
Pay: Piecework rates. Approx £50 per day

☎ 01945 870749
🖱 p9ear@aol.com

E. Oldroyd And Sons Ltd

Location: Near Leeds, Yorkshire
Season: January – March; May – September
Picking: Strawberries, rhubarb and vegetables
Accommodation: Available
Duration of Work: Min. 4 weeks
Working Hours: Up to 8 hours per day
Pay: Piecework or hourly rates

☎ 0113 282 2245
🖱 eoldroyd@btconnect.com

Peter Marshall & Co

Location: Perthshire
Season: June – August
Picking: Raspberries
Accommodation: Available at £3 per night
Duration of Work: Min. 4 weeks
Pay: Piecework rates

☎ 01828 632227
or 07916 259298
🖱 donna@petermarshallfarms.com
💻 www.petermarshallfarms.com

Prices Fruit Farm

Location: Portadown, Northern Ireland
Season: September – October
Picking: Apples
Accommodation: Self-catering caravans. Electricity and gas charged at £5 per week
Duration of Work: Min. 4 weeks
Pay: Piecework rates

☎ 07711 725752
🖱 andrew@burnedearth.co.uk

S&A Produce Ltd

Location: Hereford
Season: April – September
Picking: Soft fruit and vegetables
Accommodation: Caravans and facilities approx. £30 per week
Duration of Work: Min. 4 weeks
Working Hours: 8 hours per day, 48 hours per week
Pay: Piecework rates

 01432 880235
 pickingjobs@sagroup.co.uk
www.sagroup.co.uk

Salmans Ltd

Location: Near Tunbridge Wells, Kent
Season: August – November
Picking: Raspberries and blackberries
Accommodation: Caravans and mobile homes with full self-catering facilities £3.75 per day
Duration of Work: Min. 4 weeks
Pay: Piecework rates

jobs@salmons.co.uk
www.salmons.co.uk

Paul Williamson Ltd

Location: Near Bury St. Edmunds, Suffolk
Season: May – October
Picking: Strawberries, raspberries, apples, pears
Accommodation: Campsite with showers, toilet, kitchen
Duration of Work: Min. 3 weeks
Working Hours: 8am–4pm, Monday to Friday
Pay: Agricultural Wage Board rates

 01284 386333
 paul@williamsongrowers.co.uk
www.thepoly.co.uk/paulw

Withers Fruit Farm

Location: Ledbury, Herefordshire
Season: March – October
Picking: Strawberries. Other farm work available
Accommodation: In shared caravans
Duration of Work: Min. 4 weeks
Working Hours: 6 full days per week
Pay: Hourly or piecework rates

 01531 635504
 withersfruitfarm@farmline.co.uk
http://members.farmline.com/withers/

FRUIT PICKING WORLDWIDE

Farmers from Norway to Tasmania (with the notable exception of developing countries) are unable to bring in their harvests without assistance from outside their local community. Finding out where jobs occur is simply a matter of doing some research. Listed below are some of the farms worldwide that take on seasonal staff, but it is beyond the scope of this book to list them all. If you have limited time then it is far better to organise a job in advance than simply to turn up. Listed below are some useful organisations that can help you do this.

Apart from the organisations listed below, there are a number of websites that can help you to find a fruit-picking holiday abroad. Some of these are country specific such as the New Zealand site: www.seasonalwork.co.nz, but others cover the entire globe: www.seasonworkers.com; www.pickingjobs.com; www.anyworkanywhere.com.

EU members are free to find work in any of the other EU member states. For other citizens it is more complicated, and it is advised that you contact the appropriate embassy for immigration regulations. British citizens looking for a fruit-picking holiday in Australia and New Zealand will be required to obtain a Working Holiday visa. Further information about this is included in *Practicalities and Red Tape*.

Vineyard Vacations – Working and Volunteering the Grape Harvest

There has always been a sense of romance about the notion of picking grapes that will eventually end up as some of the finest wines the world has to offer. The vendange conjures up images of rolling hills, breathtaking landscapes and fair French maidens stomping the grapes with their bare feet in huge wooden barrels. For wine-lovers the benefits of experiencing this ancient ritual first-hand far outweigh the hard work, the early starts and the often ferocious September sun.

Grape picking was once the staple of the student backpacker funding their travels and the jobs were as plentiful as the grapes themselves. The pay wasn't great and work conditions were sometimes gruelling, but the benefits included free board and lodging, a chance to meet locals, learn the language, and indulge in the celebrations that go along with the harvest season. With the expansion of the EU, and greater mobility of workers from poorer countries, there is now much more competition for grape-picking work and it can be challenging to find a job. Those looking to work the vendange in France can approach the office of the *Agence National pour l'Emploi* in the region where they hope to find work. If your French is up to it, the ANPE website (www.anpe.fr) matches potential pickers with individual French vineyards. Alternatively there are agencies that can, for a fee do the grunt work for you, and crucially, speak English. One of the most popular is the Dutch organisation *Apellation Controlée* (see below), which helps young people to organise much coveted grape-picking work in France. Each year up to 500 people avoid the scramble for a job by paying the £85 fee to this agency. Another agency arranging grape-picking jobs in the Champagne and Beaujolais regions of France is *Jeunesse et Réconstruction* (www.volontariat.org/2/jr_29.html).

If, for you, grape picking is all about the experience and not so much about the often slim remuneration, then volunteering may be a far more productive option. The concept of vineyard vacations is now so popular that some wineries actually charge people for back-breaking work among the vines, so choose carefully where you volunteer. A good starting point for finding vendange volunteering work in France is the local tourist office in the region you wish to visit. For example, in Champagne, several local wine-growers organise grape-picking days where guests start with a hearty breakfast and are rewarded with a substantial lunch after a morning's picking, followed by a tour of the wine cellars and lessons in wine tasting. Such a day will set you back €30–€50 and further information can be found at www.tourisme-en-champagne.com. Alternatively many WWOOF (see above) hosts offer grape picking work on organic farms. These are not paid, but in return for six hours work a day, you will receive free board and lodging. The majority of the organic vineyard WWOOF hosts are to be found in Australia. Visit www.wwoof.com.au for more details.

Alternatively hotels and villas across Europe can often arrange grape picking as part of your stay. For example Baronnie de Bourgade (www.baronnie-de-bourgade.com) offers wine tours of the Languedoc region that include a day's work picking grapes. Perfect Places (www.perfectplaces.com) also arranges grape picking excursions for guests in some of its villas, without a fee. In Croatia there are also several grape-picking opportunities attached to holiday properties. Try, for example www.croatianvacation.co.uk and www.hotel-kastel-motovun.hr.

Some holiday companies specialising in wine tours can also arrange holidays that include a grape-picking element. Activities Abroad (www.activitiesabroad.com/wine) has teamed up with the Newcastle Wine School to create the Rhone Valley, France Tour, a six-day wine tasting tour, which includes a day's grape picking. For the wine enthusiast, such tours, which only include a short period of actual 'work' can be ideal, giving an insight into methods of wine production without the days of back-breaking labour.

Appellation Controlée – Vendange Programme

Organisation: Agency that organises grape-picking jobs in France for an application fee of £85
Location: Beaujolais and Maconais regions, nr. Lyon, France
Season: September – October
Picking: Grapes
Accommodation: Clean, basic: campsites, dorms, annexes etc. All meals provided
Duration of Work: 7–18 days (one full harvest)
Working Hours: 8 hours per day, 7 days a week
Pay: Approx. €50 (net) per working day

☎ +31 505492434
✉ info@apcon.nl
🖥 www.grapepicking.co.uk

A POSTCARD FROM the vineyards of France

Dutch student, Danielle Thomas, used Appellation Controllee to find a working holiday picking grapes in France:

I set off for France to work on the vendange, primarily to make a bit of money to fund further travels and also to have a different kind of holiday and meet new people. It worked out well, in 11 days I made around €650 which was enough to fund further travels in the UK and I met all sorts of people. Many of the workers were locals or friends of the family that I stayed with, and there were three other people from Holland. The ages of the workers varied from 19 (me – I was the youngest), through to about 60!

The work was very hard. We worked from 8am to 6pm with two hours for lunch and short breaks every 45 minutes. But it was also enjoyable because of the team I was working with and the hospitality of our hosts. Meals were provided and both lunch and dinner were very impressive – five course meals including soup and bread, salad and vegetables, meat or fish, a variety of cheeses and finally a dessert. Local wine or their own wine was also served with each meal.

The only downside was sleeping in a tent. Pickers who had worked at the farm before were allowed to stay in the farmhouse with the family, but first-time pickers like me brought their own tents and slept in the garden. By the end of the day my back usually hurt and I woke up freezing cold every morning!

When we weren't working, I was able to improve my French by spending time with the other workers and talking about anything and everything. We often went for a drink and sometimes we went to different towns to look around. Dinners were very social and fun often lasting a few hours!

I would advise anyone thinking of working the vendange to bring waterproofs and wellies as the weather can change at any moment. Also bring rubber washing up gloves as in the mornings the grapes are wet and your hands get soaked. And most importantly, don't expect the French to be able to speak English – bring a phrase book!

AGRICULTURE

PAID WORK

279

Agricultural Labour Pool – Canada

Organisation: Recruitment and job-seeking assistance service for seasonal workers looking for agricultural employment in Canada
Location: Throughout Canada
Season: Year round
Work: Seasonal harvesting work, as well as a range of other agricultural positions

☎ +1 604 855 9261
or 604 855 7281
💻 www.agri-labourpool.com

Cherry Growers' Association Canada

Organisation: Pooled resources of a number of cherry growers in the area that can help put seasonal workers in touch with employers. See website
Location: Okanagan/Kootenay, Canada
Season: June – August
Picking: Cherries
Accommodation: Most growers have free on-site camping facilities
Duration of Work: 2–4 weeks
Working Hours: 5am–1pm
Pay: Above minimum wage, with incentives

☎ +1 250 763 9790
 info@bccherry.com
💻 www.bccherry.com

Outback International

Organisation: Australia-wide rural employment agency providing on-going support and back-up during your time working in Australia
Location: Rural areas throughout Australia
Season: Year round
Work: Outback has seasonal harvesting jobs as well as positions for farmers, tractor drivers and cotton workers
Accommodation: Usually included
Duration of Work: Min. 2 weeks
Working Hours: 8–12 hours a day over a 5 or 7 day week

☎ +61 74927 4300
 admin@outbackinternational.com
💻 www.outbackinternational.com

AGRICULTURE

PAID WORK

Landdienst-Zentralstelle

Organisation: Non-profit, publicly subsidised organisation which places 3,000 Swiss and 500 foreign farmers' assistants on family farms each year
Location: Throughout Switzerland
Season: April – October
Work: Farmers' assistants. Must have knowledge of French or German and be aged 18–25
Accommodation: Free board and lodging
Duration of Work: Min. 3 weeks
Pay: Set monthly figure. See website

☎ +52 264 0030
🖱 admin@landdienst.ch
💻 www.landdienst.ch

THE FARMS

Anjou Myrtilles

Location: Loire, France
Season: May – August
Picking and Packing: Blueberries, raspberries, strawberries, redcurrants, blackcurrants, blackberries
Accommodation: On campsites nearby
Duration of Work: Negotiable
Pay: Piecework rates

🖱 travail_saisonnier@anjoumyrtilles.fr
💻 www.anjoumyrtilles.fr

Ballybin Fruit Farm

Location: Co. Meath, Republic of Ireland
Season: September – October
Picking: Apples
Accommodation: Free in self-catering caravans with washing facilities on site
Duration of Work: Min. 4 weeks
Working Hours: Long. 6 days per week
Pay: Piecework rates. Expect to earn £30–£40 per day – more with experience

☎ +353 1825 6344
🖱 michael.mackle@mackleapple.com

Birkholm Frugt & Baer

Location: Faaborg, Denmark
Season: June – July
Picking: Strawberries
Accommodation: Space for tents, use of washing and cooking facilities
Duration of Work: Min. 2 weeks
Pay: Piecework Rates

☎ +45 6260 2262
🖱 birkholm@strawberrypicking.dk
💻 www.strawberrypicking.dk

Cobradah Orchards

Location: Yarra Valley, Victoria, Australia
Season: November – January
Picking: Cherries
Accommodation: Campsite with kitchen and washing facilities provided
Duration of Work: Negotiable
Pay: Piecework rates and award wages

info@cobradahorchards.com.au
www.cobradahorchards.com.au

Corboy Fresh Fruit

Location: Victoria, Australia
Season: November – June
Picking: Apricots, apples, peaches, nectarines, plums, pears
Accommodation: Nearby campsite, with free bus service
Duration of Work: Min. 2 weeks
Pay: Piecework rates. See website

+61 (0)3 5855 2727
coraliec@corboys.com.au
www.corboys.com.au

RJ Cornish

Location: On the border of Victoria and NSW, Australia
Season: January – April
Picking: Apples, pears and peaches
Accommodation: Campsite and caravans available for small fee
Duration of Work: Negotiable
Working Hours: 7.30am–4pm, 6 days per week
Pay: Piecework rates

+61 (0)3 58 72 2055
jobs@rjcornish.com
www.rjcornish.com

Hawkes Bay

Location: Hawkes Bay, New Zealand
Season: January – May
Picking: Apples
Accommodation: Living complexes at a minimal charge, with transport to and from the orchards
Duration of Work: Min. 4 weeks
Pay: Piecework rates. Generally NZ$100–200 per day

+64 (0)6 873 1061
employment@mrapplenz.biz
www.mrapplenz.co.nz

Koogie Downs

Location: Sunshine Coast, Queensland, Australia
Season: March – November
Picking/Packing: Strawberries
Accommodation: Shared rooms with toilets and showers
Duration of Work: Negotiable
Pay: Hourly rate

☎ +61 (0)7 45459100
🖱 brsdaniels@iprimus.com.au
💻 www.koogiedowns.com

Molyneux

Location: Cromwell, New Zealand
Season: December – February
Picking and Packing: Cherries
Accommodation: Hostel
Duration of Work: Negotiable
Pay: Piecework rates

🖱 admin@molyneux.co.nz
💻 www.orchardfresh.co.nz

Plunkett Orchards

Location: 2 hours north of Melbourne, Victoria, Australia
Season: December – April
Picking/Grading: Apples, pears and peaches
Accommodation: Board and lodging available in hostel, huts, caravans or camping. Full facilities. AUS$12 per night
Duration of Work: Min. 2 weeks
Working Hours: 6.30am–2pm, 6 days a week
Pay: Piecework rates

☎ + 61 3 5829 0015
🖱 info@plunkettorchards.com.au
💻 www.plunkettorchards.com.au

P. Pullar & Co.

Location: Victoria, Australia
Season: January – April
Picking: Peaches, pears, apples, plums, cherries
Accommodation: Basic rooms with meals at AUS$111 per week, or caravans for AUS$50 per week
Duration of Work: Negotiable
Pay: Piecework rates

🖱 picking@ppullar.com
💻 www.ppullar.com

Silvan Estate Raspberries

Location: Victoria, Australia
Season: December – April
Picking: Raspberries
Accommodation: Campsite with shared kitchen/shower facilities. Some caravans available on-site. Small fee
Duration of Work: Min. 3 weeks
Pay: Piecework rates based on market price and crop condition

☎ +61 (0)3 9737 9105
🖰 sylvan@raspberries.com.au
💻 www.raspberries.com.au

Torrens Valley Orchards

Location: Adelaide, Australia
Season: Work all year round but most jobs from December – March
Picking and Packing: Cherries, pears
Accommodation: Hostel style with dorms, bathroom, kitchen
Duration of Work: Negotiable
Working Hours: 7.30am–4pm
Pay: Piecework rates. Typical day's gross earnings – AUS$80

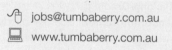

☎ +61 (0)8 8389 1405
🖰 tvo@oils.net.au
💻 www.tvo.com.au

Tumbarumba Blueberries

Location: Snowy Mountains, NSW, Australia
Season: December – March
Picking and Packing: Blueberries
Accommodation: Caravan park nearby
Duration of Work: Min. 2 weeks
Pay: Piecework rates. Currently AUS$3 per kg

🖰 jobs@tumbaberry.com.au
💻 www.tumbaberry.com.au

Turnbull Brothers Orchards

Location: Victoria, Australia
Season: November – April
Picking: Cherries, pears, peaches, plums, apples
Accommodation: Shared rooms with communal kitchen/dining/washing areas
Duration of Work: Negotiable
Working Hours: Monday to Thursday, 7.30am-4.30pm; Friday 7.30am-1pm
Pay: Piecework rates

☎ +61 (0)3 5829 0002
🖰 turnbros@mcmedia.com.au
💻 www.turnbullorchards.com

HANDS-ON Teaching and Summer Camps

VOLUNTEER TEACHING HOLIDAYS

One billion people speak or are trying to speak English around the world and those of us who speak it as a first language tend to take for granted how universally dominant it has become. English is the language of business, popular music, the internet and air traffic control. For better or worse it has become the language of the global culture we seem to be creating for the 21st century.

There are areas of the world where the boom in English language learning seems to know no bounds, from Ecuador to Slovenia, and from Ghana to Vietnam. English has been called a 'barometer of Western influence' and there are only a handful of countries in the world that have rejected Western influence outright (like Bhutan and North Korea) and therefore have no need for English teachers. The kind of people who want to learn English are just as numerous as the places in which they live. Some people of course simply learn for pleasure, but for many more people around the world, fluent English offers them the chance for a better future, and an opportunity to escape poverty.

An increasing number of working travellers are finding that English teaching offers fantastic opportunities for prolonged travels all over the world. But at first glance, teaching English is not something that can be easily achieved during a hands-on holiday. For the majority of teaching work worldwide, it is necessary to sign a contract for at least three months and probably nine, and to have some kind of specialist TEFL qualification. However, this chapter examines a range of short-term teaching opportunities that can make a difference to people's lives and provide a rewarding experience for the participant. It is unlikely that you will find paid work for a short-term teaching placement as the most rewarding work is often in deprived rural and urban areas where schools simply cannot afford to pay. Those looking to make a little money from teaching should consider working at a summer camp (see below).

Anyone who can speak English fluently and has a lively, positive personality can take part in a hands-on English-teaching holiday. While having a TEFL qualification is a prerequisite to finding long-term paid work, it is not expected for short-term voluntary positions. This is largely because volunteers are usually not expected to take their own class or explain the technicalities of grammar. In the vast majority of cases, their role is to provide support to local teachers, take on small conversational English groups, provide a model for correct pronunciation, and to motivate children and adults by building their confidence in every day conversational language skills. In rural and deprived areas, the role of the volunteer may go beyond simple language skills. Some schools are so under-resourced that an enthusiastic volunteer can provide help in many other areas that interest them, such as sports, art, drama, music, computing, and extra-curricular activities. This was certainly the experience of Andrew Kitching, who volunteered at schools in Ambato, Ecuador with Voluntarios de Occidente. He taught not only English, but also computing and sports to primary school children, and found the experience extremely rewarding:

Every morning, when the volunteers arrived at the schools, we were bombarded with hugs, toothless grins, flowers, fruit and shouts of 'Good morning teacher.' It's a pleasant way to start the day, and the reason behind it is simple: classes are fun, and they provide the children with something seriously lacking around here; opportunity. Living and working in a relatively poor community is not mentally or physically easy; but I've come out of it with good friends, good memories, and a lot to think about.

Not all of the voluntary teaching positions below are in the Third World. Nor do they all involve working with children. VaughnTown for example is a new and exciting project in which volunteers are provided with five nights of 4–star hotel accommodation in return for talking in English to Spanish businessmen. Vaughn Systems, the language school behind this innovative programme has converted an abandoned town in the heart of the Spanish countryside into a living English education project. Volunteers visit for one week and their role is to help Spaniards practise their conversational English. Although participants work long hours, they are also able to make new friends, benefit from excellent facilities and enjoy a virtually free holiday in a stunning location.

The Ethics Box: Can Short-Term Teaching Projects Really Make a Difference?

There is some debate about the validity of teaching children for just a short period of time. It may be the case that some organisations sending a rotating stock of teachers on short placements to the same school are thinking about their profits rather than the welfare of the children. Children may well find it disruptive to have to start again with a new teacher every few weeks and responsible travel authorities suggest that a month is really the minimum time frame in which an individual teacher can have a positive impact.

However, most of the projects listed below are specifically designed for amateur teachers and classroom assistants. Having taken on board the criticism that short-term teaching placements for those without a teaching background may be more beneficial to the volunteer than the child, the majority of placement organisations do not require volunteers to take on their own class. More often than not, volunteers are working with small groups, helping the children to try out their English conversation skills and build up confidence. In many developing countries, children have very little access to native speakers of English, and therefore they have little opportunity to practise their pronunciation. Volunteers often find that there is such a dearth of native English speakers (especially in rural areas) that local teachers are just as keen to talk to them and practise their English conversation skills.

Sometimes volunteers will take on their own classes, but this tends to happen at a very basic level (i.e. in primary schools), and only where there is a real shortage of qualified teachers. It is very unlikely that volunteers would be taking jobs away from local teachers. It is, of course, infinitely preferable for children in developing countries to receive some English instruction (which will improve their chances of going on to further education or finding a job in later life) than none at all. Where volunteers do take on their own class, it is important that they are following a formal teaching plan or curriculum, otherwise the high turnover of teachers could be extremely disruptive. Most of the placement agencies will ensure that a formal plan is in place, that volunteers work to a syllabus, and that local teachers help to plan the lessons, but it never hurts to ask.

Placement organisations are also far more hands-on in the support and back-up that they offer volunteer teachers than they once were. Projects Abroad for example ensures that volunteers receive a comprehensive briefing about teaching English before they leave the country. Volunteers also receive teaching guides packed with ideas, games, advice and guidelines, as well as being under the constant supervision of local staff.

Of course there are still some unethical projects out there, but it is up to the volunteer to ask the right questions and talk to former participants to ensure that their hands-on teaching holiday has the maximum beneficial impact on the host community.

WORKING AT SUMMER CAMPS

An alternative to a teaching placement is to join one of the temporary English and activity summer camps that take place across the world. Such is the desperation of parents across Europe to occupy their children in the long summer holiday, recent years have seen a boom in American-style summer camps. The American camps themselves are not included here, as employees are required for too long a period for a hands-on holiday. Across the UK and Europe however, a large number of short-term residential summer camps for children and teenagers combine sports and outdoor activities such as horse-riding and archery with English tuition. Not only do they create short-term opportunities for teaching English, but they also provide a range of opportunities for camp counsellors, monitors, group leaders, activity instructors, and sports coaches.

Teachers, lifeguards and specialist sports instructors will obviously need the appropriate qualifications but for many of these jobs, applicants will simply require an outgoing personality, the ability to get along with children, and a responsible attitude (for camps in the UK all applicants intending to work with children will also need a criminal records bureau check). The more general positions often involve organising team games, discos and excursions, and being responsible for the welfare of your group.

Summer camps generally last from one to four weeks and are structured in such a way that children get the most that they possibly can from such a short period. Hence, the ethical considerations surrounding short-term teaching placements do not really apply to summer camps: the language-learning programme is specifically designed for a short duration.

Teaching English as a Foreign Language (TEFL) Qualifications

While this chapter focuses mainly on amateur and conversational English teaching, a few of the language course and summer camp organisers will require or simply prefer their teachers to have obtained a TEFL qualification. Whether or not you need one for your holiday, TEFL qualifications are an extremely useful string to add to your bow, and will certainly improve your confidence and versatility as a short-term teacher. A vast number of TEFL courses and qualifications are on offer, varying widely in length, location and cost.

One of the most widely recognised and required certificates is the Cambridge CELTA (Certificate in English Language Teaching to Adults). These courses can be taken full or part-time at more than 250 approved centres in the UK and overseas. For more information and to find a centre, see www.cambridgeesol.org/teaching. The other major certificate, carrying equal recognition to the CELTA is the Trinity Certificate in TESOL (www.trinitycollege.co.uk). Both of these certificate courses provide a rigorous introduction to teaching English in just one month full-time, or part-time over a number of months. Both courses cost around £800–£1,000.

Alternatively, there are many cheaper introductory courses on offer. Some of these are residential courses that take place over a weekend or four to five days, and while they may not enable you to get a job anywhere in the world, they will certainly give you confidence, and some of the most important teaching skills. Introductory courses can cost anywhere between £180 and £450, not including accommodation. A number of the organisations below also require potential teachers to take their own TEFL or orientation course, introducing them to a particular curriculum or method of teaching.

A useful directory of the courses on offer is contained in Susan Griffith's excellent *Teaching English Abroad* (Vacation Work, £14.95), which also contains useful information for those wishing to combine more lengthy travels with English teaching worldwide.

SHORT–TERM ENGLISH TEACHING WORLDWIDE

Alliance Abroad Group

☎ +1 (512) 457 8062 or
toll-free in US 1 866 6 ABROAD

🖱 outbound@allianceabroad.com

🖥 www.allianceabroad.com

Duration: From 1 month (Argentina, Spain); from 3 weeks (China); from 2 weeks (Costa Rica, Ecuador, Peru)
Location: Argentina, China, Costa Rica, Ecuador, Peru, Spain
Prerequisites: Min. age 18. Intermediate level of Spanish
Organisation: Offers customised international volunteer programmes for students and graduates
Description: Participants can volunteer as English teachers, teaching very basic English to students. Teaching may take place in a formal classroom setting or informally after school
Accommodation: Provided with a local family
Cost: From $400 a week, including accommodation and meals. Excludes airfares

Dakshinayan

☎ +91 (124) 221 9090

🖱 info@dakshinayan.org

🖥 www. dakshinayan.org

Duration: Min. 4 weeks
Location: India
Prerequisites: Min. age 18; socially sensitive and willing to work in remote locations. No formal teacher training needed
Organisation: Non-profit, non-religious organisation providing basic education to tribal and rural communities
Description: Volunteers work with a registered trust engaged in providing education assistance to tribes in the Rajamhal Hills and the surrounding plains. Education is of primary level and volunteers are expected to assist in teaching English or arts and crafts, sports, poetry or singing. Volunteers normally work four to six hours a day, six days a week
Accommodation: Living conditions on most projects are very basic
Cost: US$300 per month including food and accommodation. Volunteers are expected to cover all expenses to and from the project

---

A POSTCARD FROM India

Geoffroy Groleau arranged to work for a month with Dakshinayan. Although he ended up thinking that his enjoyment took precedence over his usefulness, he still enjoyed his time there enormously:

The project provides an opportunity to acquire a better understanding of the myths and realities surrounding poverty in the developing world, and specifically about the realities of rural India. The tribal people of these villages do not need or want fancy houses or televisions, but simply an education for their children and basic healthcare in order to improve the life they have been leading in relative isolation for centuries. It was interesting for me to see that they lead a quiet and simple life based on the rhythm of harvests and seasons, in marked contrast to most westerners. The primary role for volunteers is to

A POSTCARD FROM India *Continued*

teach English for a few hours every day to the kids attending the three Dakshinayan-run schools. I should also mention the numerous unforgettable football games with enthusiastic kids at the end of sunny afternoons. One should be aware that Dakshinayan is an Indian NGO fully run by local people, which in my view is another positive aspect. But it also means that volunteers will have to adapt to Indian ways.

Volunteers should expect to learn more from the people than they will ever be able to teach. Remember that the villagers know much more about their needs than we do, and they have learned long ago to use effectively the resources around them. On the other hand, the contact with the outside world that the volunteers provide is a valuable way for the villagers to begin to understand the world that surrounds them. In my experience, the hardest things were to adapt to the rather slow rhythm of life and to the fact that as a volunteer you will not manage to change significantly the life of the villagers other than by putting your brick in a collective work that has been going on for many years.

Dragonfly

☎ +66 (0) 44 281073
🖥 www.thai-dragonfly.com

Duration: Min. 4 weeks
Location: Thailand
Prerequisites: Candidates should be in good physical health and most projects require a high level of spoken and written English. No specific skills are required as training is provided for all projects
Organisation: Provides governmental and non-governmental projects with volunteers, financial support and training
Description: 50 to 70 volunteers are recruited annually to teach English in government-run schools in the most rural and traditional areas of Thailand
Accommodation: Depends on placement but includes volunteer houses or homestays
Cost: 4 weeks £585, includes accommodation and meals and airport pick-up but excludes airfares

Fox Language Academy

☎ (591) 4644 0688
 foxlaacademy@yahoo.com
🖥 www.foxacademysucre.com

Duration: No minimum or maximum length of time
Location: Sucre, Bolivia
Prerequisites: Some Spanish language skills are useful but not essential
Organisation: Non-profit-making institution dedicated to teaching English and Spanish. Founded in 1982, primarily as an English language school
Description: Fox requires people to teach English to small classes of local children or adults in the evenings or afternoons. Volunteers can work alongside professional language teachers or those with experience can take on a class of their own. Lessons are planned by qualified teachers working to a syllabus and the role of volunteers is to improve pronunciation and make lessons more fun
Accommodation: Sometimes provided. If not help is given to find lodgings at a reasonable price
Cost: There are no participation fees. Volunteers cover all of their personal expense

Go Differently

Duration: 1–4 weeks
Location: Thailand
Season: Year round
Prerequisites: Min. age 18, enthusiastic, willing to work with local people; normal fitness, respectful of Thai culture. No experience required

☎ 01799 521950
🖱 info@godifferently.com
🖥 www.godifferently.com

Organisation: Tour operator specialising in ethical holidays and volunteering trips based on appreciation and respect of the local environment and people
Description: Go Differently offers a homestay programme teaching English in a hill tribe village. Participants learn about the traditional way of life of the Karen people, while teaching English to their children and also helping with other village tasks such as farming. In addition to your teaching assistance, your payment for project fees and lodgings will also help to support this village on a financial basis
Accommodation: Very basic lodgings provided within the bamboo house of a local family
Cost: £320 per week for the first 2 weeks; £250 per week for additional weeks

Global Crossroad

Duration: Min. 1 month
Location: China
Prerequisites: Native English speakers. No special qualifications needed but some sort of ESL, teaching experience, or experience with children is usually expected
Organisation: International volunteer organisation committed to providing meaningful volunteer opportunities abroad

☎ +1 (972) 252 4191, or in UK 020–8263 6095
🖱 info@globalcrossroad.com; ukinfo@globalcrossroad.com
🖥 www.globalcrossroad.com

Description: See and experience China during your summer vacation or career break while teaching simple and conversational English to public and private school children for 22–30 hours a week
Facilities/Support: Help obtaining visa, services and support of field staff
Accommodation: Provided with a local family
Benefits: Up to RMB2,000 a month for a native English speaker; RMB3,000–4,000 a month for a native English speaker with a degree in English, and TEFL or TESOL training

Global Vision International

Duration: From 2 weeks in Latvia; other projects min. 4 weeks
Location: Worldwide
Prerequisites: No experience necessary
Organisation: GVI promotes sustainable development, supplying international volunteers, equipment, funding and

☎ 0870 608 8898
 info@gvi.co.uk
 www.gvi.co.uk

training to government groups, charities, NGOs and communities around the world
Description: Current short-term teaching projects include teaching children in Costa Rica, Nicaragua, Peru, Guatemala, Ecuador, and Nepal, teaching communities in Honduras, South Africa, Ghana, India and Sri Lanka, teaching English to Buddhist monks in Laos
Accommodation: Included in price. Varies according to project
Sample Cost: Teaching monks in Laos from £1,100 (4 weeks). All prices include food, accommodation, full training, airport pick-up and drop-off, in-country orientation, back-up and insurance

---

A POSTCARD FROM Guatemala

Although nervous when first signing up with Global Vision International, Vishna Shah will never forget his experience in Guatemala:

From the moment I arrived in Guatemala, I was made to feel very welcome. With so many anxieties about travelling on my own, such as not speaking the language and never having taught before, it was simply amazing how homely I was made to feel.

I had always wanted to teach in a rural school where I knew the work was genuine and the impact on the children was a real one. This is exactly what the project in Santa Maria was. The children, some of the poorest in the world, lived such a different lifestyle from the one I am used to, based around farming and selling produce at the markets. During my time in Guatemala, we moved into a new school and we introduced a balanced diet for the kids.

The first week was terrifying but once the initial period was over, I never wanted to leave. I created an unbreakable bond with these special children and their keen approach to learning made me want to teach them forever.

I had an amazing summer, and I was extremely reluctant to leave at the end of it, having learnt so much about myself and the world around me, having discovered the truly colourful Mayan culture, and having made friends with some wonderful people.

Hands Up Holidays

Duration: 15 days (also tailor-made options)
Location: Thailand
Season: Year round
Prerequisites: Min. age 18. No specific skills required, just enthusiasm. However, if you have teaching skills, or an ESL qualification, these will be beneficial

☎ 0800 7833554
✍ info@handsupholidays.com
🖱 www.handsupholidays.com

Organisation: Leading ethical tour operator working with a local Thai supplier and education provider. A minimum of 10% of profits go to further development projects
Description: Hands Up Holidays offers ethically and environmentally responsible holidays that blend sightseeing with fulfilling volunteering experiences. Approx. a third of the holiday is devoted to a meaningful 'taste' of environmental conservation volunteering and the rest of the time is spent sightseeing with local, English-speaking guides. Participants on the 'Smiles of Siam' holiday help to teach English in the province of Nakom Rachasima, Thailand. All flights are carbon neutral
Accommodation: 4 to 5–star hotels
Cost: £1,450 for 15 days

Horizon Cosmopolite

Duration: From 2 weeks
Location: 25 countries worldwide
Prerequisites: Min. age 18. No previous
experience necessary. Mandatory one-day
pre-departure training

☎ +1 514 935 8436
🖱 info@horizoncosmopolite.com
💻 www.horizoncosmopolite.com

Organisation: Cultural exchange organisation
offering international education programmes in more than 30 countries working with local
NGOs and community organisations
Description: HC offers more than 40 programmes throughout the year that are designed
to meet individual needs. Teaching projects take place mainly in rural areas where pupils
and teachers alike face a shortage of resources
Accommodation: Provided and arrangements made for meals
Cost: Registration and participation fees apply but vary according to project and destination.
Sample Cost: 1 month teaching in a village in the Amazon rainforest: Approx US$900

Madventurer

Duration: Min. 2 weeks
Location: Fiji, Ghana, Guatemala, India, Kenya,
Peru, Tanzania, Thailand, Uganda
Prerequisites: No special skills or experience
required
Organisation: Madventurer combines volunteer
projects and adventures with assistance for rural
community development

☎ 0845 121 1996 or
0191 269 9495
🖱 team@madventurer.com
💻 www.madventurer.com;
www.careerbreaker.com

Description: Madventurer offers rural and urban projects in which volunteers work
as part of a team alongside local communities in developing countries. As a teacher,
volunteers play an important role in reducing class sizes and injecting enthusiasm and a
fresh style of teaching into schools. Volunteers mostly help full-time teachers with basic
literacy, maths and various other subjects. The schools are particularly keen for volunteers
to help with conversational English
Accommodation: Provided in local homestays or a shared group house
Cost: From £800 including food, accommodation and support

Mar De Jade

Duration: 3 weeks
Location: Puerto Vallarta, Mexico
Prerequisites: No specific skills or experience
required. Some Spanish language proficiency is helpful,
but not required

 info@mardejade.com
 www.mardejade.com

Organisation: Retreat centre in a fishing village on the Pacific Coast of Mexico, which
offers volunteer opportunities

Description: Mar de Jade is a socially responsible resort on Mexico's Pacific coast. The resort offers its guests volunteering opportunities within the local community including conversational English teaching to local children. Any home-based skills, such as sewing and embroidery and weaving, ceramics and other crafts that volunteers can teach are also welcome

Accommodation: Provided in a shared guesthouse

Cost: US$1,400. Price includes accommodation, 3 buffet meals a day and local transport. Airfares and Spanish classes are not included

Muang District Non Formal Education Service

Duration: Min. 2 weeks
Location: Thailand
Prerequisites: Graduates, native English-speakers, willing to live in developing world conditions. Under Thai law volunteers need a non-immigrant work visa (arranged by the school)

☎ +66 07563 2746
✆ volunteerthailand@yahoo.com
🖥 www.volunteerthailand.com

Organisation: Part of the Thai Ministry of Education. Provides educational access to underprivileged segments of the population eg hill tribes and Thai Muslims

Description: NFE provides language and other classes at local village centres. English-speaking volunteers are required to teach for three to six hours a day in economically disadvantaged areas. Class sizes vary from 10–50 students

Accommodation: Simple housing, homestay or in bungalows

Cost: There are no participant fees but volunteers must pay their own way (approx. $15 a day for accommodation, food, transport)

Original Volunteers

Duration: Min. 1 week
Location: Argentina, Brazil, Bolivia, Costa Rica, Ecuador, Ghana, Guatemala, Honduras, India, Mexico, Nepal, Kenya, Peru, Tanzania
Prerequisites: Min. age 18. No experience required

☎ 0800 3457582
 contact@originalvolunteers.org.uk
 www.originalvolunteers.org.uk

Organisation: Places volunteers with grassroots organisations around the world. Includes supported volunteer placements and more independent voluntary experiences away from the tourist trail

Description: Original Volunteers was formed in 2006 by a number of former volunteers who came together to provide a network of grassroots organisations willing to take volunteers at a very low cost. Various volunteering opportunities to teach conversational English are available year round. 24–hour back-up support is provided on-site and from the UK

Accommodation: Varies from homestays to hostels

Cost: One-off placement fee of £295 plus £15–£36 a week for board and lodging

Peace Villages Foundation

Duration: Min. 1 week
Location: Venezuela
Prerequisites: Min. age 18; enthusiasm; desire to spend time living in a different culture. Senior volunteers welcome
Organisation: PVF helps communities to achieve sustainable development, social justice and peace
Description: PVF carries out many types of project including working in the Tucusito school for children with special needs, living with Pemon Indians, teaching English, and taking education to children not served by a school system in a mobile school
Accommodation: Four types of accommodation are provided: camping, guest rooms, co-operative living, and host family
Cost: From $718 for 1 week full-board and $473 self-catering. Price includes accommodation and food. Airfare not included

☎ +58 (289) 416 0718
🖱 mail@peacevillages.org
💻 www.peacevillages.org

Personal Overseas Development

Duration: Min. 1 week
Location: Nepal, Peru, Tanzania, Thailand
Prerequisites: Min. age 18. No specific skills are required
Organisation: Volunteer placement agency providing a link between small organisations in less developed countries and UK volunteers
Description: POD offers a range of short-term projects and summer mini-gaps including summer English camps. Volunteers work with local teachers for 10 hours (six hours in Nepal) a week. Their role is to focus on improving children's speaking and listening skills
Accommodation: Provided free of charge for the first two weeks (£50 per week thereafter) in homestays, schools and local hotels
Sample Cost: 2 weeks teaching at an English camp in Thailand costs £695

☎ 01242–250901
🖱 info@thepodsite.co.uk
💻 www.thepodsite.co.uk

Projects Abroad

Duration: Min. 1 month
Location: Argentina, Bolivia, Cambodia, Chile, China, Costa Rica, Ethiopia, Ghana, India, Mexico, Moldova, Mongolia, Morocco, Nepal, Peru, Romania, Senegal, South Africa, Swaziland, Thailand
Prerequisites: Open to all volunteers
Organisation: Projects Abroad organises volunteering projects in 20 countries around the world
Description: Projects Abroad placements are in primary, secondary and special schools as well as universities that have a genuine need for conversational English practice. Volunteers take conversational English lessons for approx. 18 hours per week, very rarely taking their own class. They also receive a great deal of support from their supervisor and Projects Abroad local staff. As well as teaching English, most schools welcome volunteers who want to get involved in other aspects of school life and help with sports, drama and music or extra-curricular activities
Accommodation: Varies according to project. Included in price
Sample Cost: 1 month's teaching in Moldova – £995 including food, accommodation, insurance and teaching materials and support

☎ 01903 708300
✉ info@projects-abroad.co.uk
🖥 www.projects-abroad.co.uk

Projects Abroad volunteer teaching at a primary school in Mahachai, Thailand.

Real Gap Experience

Duration: 2 weeks – 6 months
Location: Over 40 countries worldwide
Prerequisites: Generally no qualifications or previous teaching experience are needed, just a passion to do something worthwhile and make a difference
Organisation: The leading independent gap year specialists, offering the most comprehensive range of gap year opportunities

 01892 516164
info@realgap.co.uk
www.realgap.co.uk

Description: Teaching abroad is a great way to experience the culture of a country. The majority of placements on offer are teaching English, while other subjects such as maths, IT, sports and science are also required. Many placements are in Third World countries where people are eager to learn and improve their situation. Participants can choose between paid work placements and rewarding volunteer projects. **Paid placements** are available teaching English to school children in China and Japan. **Volunteer teaching projects** are available all over the world including Central and South America, Africa, Eastern Europe, Thailand, Nepal, Sri Lanka, India and Mongolia. For the older traveller, Gap Year for Grown Ups (www.gapyearforgrownups.co.uk) is the leading specialist in career breaks and volunteer work, with hundreds of teaching projects around the world
Accommodation: Varies depending on programme – ranges from homestays, volunteer houses, tented camps, huts and hostels
Cost: From £399 including accommodation, meals, airport pick-up, orientation, volunteer placement and tuition

The Real Nepal Experience

Duration: Min. 2 weeks
Location: Nepal
Prerequisites: Min. age 18. No specific skills/ experience required
Organisation: Real Nepal aims to create an opportunity for Nepali youth to work together with

 +977 (1) 460 0210
info@realnepal.org
www.realnepal.org

international participants so that both can have a better understanding of their respective cultures
Description: Teaching English to Tibetan children. Volunteers work around three to five hours per day on the project and have the rest of the time free for sightseeing and travel. Excursions are also organised, including rafting, trekking and jungle safaris
Accommodation: Provided in a family home or hotel (on request)
Cost: £400 for 2 weeks or £550 for 4 weeks. Price includes airport transfers, 2 days orientation, accommodation and main meals

Rural Community Development Programme

Duration: Min. 2 weeks
Location: Nepal, India, Sri Lanka, Tibet
Prerequisites: Min. age 18. Volunteers should have
excellent English writing and speaking skills
Organisation: A non-profit organisation empowering
local communities through education

☎ +977 (1) 278305
✆ rcdpn@mail.com.np
💻 www.rcdpnepal.com

Description: RCDP takes on volunteers to teach English to children of all ages.
Volunteers work around three hours a day, six days a week in both public and private
boarding schools. Courses are taught in collaboration with local teachers, following a
fixed curriculum, but volunteers are invited to develop their own projects
Accommodation: Provided with host families
Cost: From US$725 for 2 weeks including accommodation, food, local transport and orientation

Rural Organisation for Social Elevation

Duration: No minimum or maximum time frame
Location: India
Season: Year round
Prerequisites: None
Organisation: Non-profit charitable
organisation founded in 1981

☎ +91 5963 241081
✆ ilverma_rosekanda@yahoo.co.in
💻 www.rosekanda.info

Description: Provides volunteers with the opportunity of experiencing rural Indian life
while providing education, teaching English to local children and also helping to improve
local conditions
Accommodation: Provided in a family home
Cost: Application/registration fee of £45. Volunteers pay their own travel costs and about
£4.50 (350 rupees) a day towards board and lodging costs, administration, telephone,
internet and school expenses

Smile Society Workcamps

Duration: 2 weeks
Location: India
Prerequisites: Min. age 16, basic English. No
experience required
Organisation: The Smile Society is a volunteer
organisation working for slum and street kids' welfare activities

☎ +91 9830 686828
✆ info@smilengo.org
💻 www.smilengo.org

Description: Smile organises international workcamps throughout the year. The work
involved in some specialised workcamps concentrates on teaching English 1
of underprivileged children in India
Accommodation: Depends on project but is provided in halls, lodges, gues
schools and with host families. Local meals are also provided
Cost: US$300 per person, including food and lodging, materials and transpo

STAESA – Students Travel And Exposure South Africa

Duration: Min. 2 weeks
Location: South Africa, Ghana, Togo, Benin, Nigeria, Cameroon, Mali, Tanzania, Malawi, Senegal, Zambia, Uganda, The Gambia, Lesotho, Botswana, Namibia
Season: Year round
Prerequisites: Min. age 18. No previous experience necessary
Organisation: A registered NGO promoting and enhancing cultural exchanges to more than 50 communities in Africa
Description: A great opportunity for students and professionals to gain hands-on experience and to see and understand more about African culture, while making a difference to the lives of many people by working as volunteer teachers
Accommodation: Provided in host family lodging, or at independent accommodation
Cost: 3 weeks US$895; 2–week mini adventure US$650

☎ +27 (11) 910 4095
🖰 info@staesa.org
💻 www.staesa.org

Starfish Ventures

Duration: Min. 4 weeks
Location: Thailand
Prerequisites: Ages 18–55; fluent in English. No previous experience necessary
Organisation: British company specialising in supporting development projects in partnership with Thai organisations
Description: Volunteers work in groups at a number of primary schools in Surin Province near the Cambodian border. Participants work four to six hours a day, four to five days a week, and are provided with a full briefing kit (a checklist of what to take and day-to-day activities)
Accommodation: Provided in basic, functional facilities
Cost: £1,095 (4 weeks) including a TEFL training weekend, accommodation, in-country transport and insurance. Airfares and food not included

☎ 0800 197 4817
🖰 enquiries@starfishventures.co.uk
💻 www.starfishventures.co.uk

Teach Peru

Duration: Min. 1 week
Location: Huarez and Lima, Peru
Prerequisites: Native English speakers, no experience required
Organisation: Small volunteer placement agency working with Peruvian English teachers to provide short-term voluntary teaching placements

☎ 0113 275 8960
🖰 jeremykeates@teachperu.com
💻 www.teachperu.com

Description: Volunteer teachers put their skills as a native English speaker to good use in Peruvian schools and universities, making a real difference in the classroom and helping students to practise their language skills. All programme coordinators are local Peruvians
Accommodation: Provided with local families or in the Teach Peru hostel
Cost: One-off placement fee of US$650. Family homestays cost US$30 per month in Huarez (free in Lima). The Teach Peru hostel costs US$100 per month (or US$190 including food)

UNIPAL

Duration: 4–5 weeks
Location: West Bank, Gaza Strip, Lebanon
Prerequisites: Min. age 20. Native English speakers,
based in the UK. Previous teaching experience or
TEFL/TESL qualifications an advantage. Background reading on situation in Middle East is essential

 info@unipal.org.uk
www.unipal.org.uk

Organisation: Registered charity that provides English language teaching in Palestinian refugee camps. Additional teaching with older students or with women's groups can be arranged
Description: Volunteers are required to teach children aged 12–15 from mid-July. The work involves teaching English, with an emphasis on art, craft, games, music and drama
Accommodation: Depends on project but is provided along with meals
Cost: About £500 to cover airfare, insurance, food and accommodation

Vaughantown

Duration: 6 days (Sunday – Friday)
Location: Puerta de Gredos, Avila, Spain
Prerequisites: Min. age 18; native English
speakers. Not available to non-EU citizens. No
experience required

☎ +34 (91) 748 5950
 anglos@vaughantown.com
 www.vaughantown.com

Organisation: Vaughan Systems has
transformed an abandoned Spanish village into a
permanent English language school stocked with native English speakers
Description: VaughnTown is a volunteer programme where participants exchange conversation for room and board in the heart of the Spanish countryside. The role of the volunteer is not to know or teach grammar, but to talk to Spanish professionals as they would a good friend, thereby immersing them in conversational English. Volunteers should help them towards greater confidence in their ability to communicate in English by exposing them to a wealth of rich speech and accents. Participants will be involved in games and group dynamic exercises, among many other activities, all to help the Spanish participants practise their language skills. The majority of classes are one-on-one, and volunteers work eight hour days
Accommodation: Provided in 4–star hotel accommodation with private rooms, en-suite bathroom (with jacuzzi), television and phone
Cost: There are no participation fees. Volunteers are responsible for their own costs. Accommodation and in-country transport are provided free of charge

Voluntarios de Occidente

Duration: Min. 1 month
Location: Ambato, Ecuador
Prerequisites: Min. age 18. No experience required

voccidente@hotmail.com
www.voluntariosdeoccidente.org

Organisation: Small independent
organisation recruiting volunteers to teach in an economically deprived area of Ecuador
Description: VDO takes on volunteers to teach English, information technology and sports in five rural primary schools in the outskirts of Ambato. Without volunteers, the children would have no opportunity to learn English (a prerequisite for secondary education). Volunteers are provided with two days' initial training
Accommodation: Provided in a VDO home or with local family with a shared bathroom
Cost: From $175 a month including in-country transportation, training, food and accommodation

SUMMER CAMPS – UK AND IRELAND

Active Training and Education

Duration: 7–10 days (Easter and summer holidays)
Location: Various parts of UK
Prerequisites: Min. age 17. Interview not necessary. Applicants must complete a one-week residential training course

☎ 0845 456 1205
liz@ate.org.uk
www.ate.org.uk

Organisation: A not-for-profit educational trust
providing creative summer camps and residential holidays for children aged eight to 16
Description: Volunteer monitors are required to lead groups of children, live as a member of the group and take part in the activities of a 'Superweek'. Children play games, explore, build dens in the woods, sing songs around the campfire and get away from it all. There are also specialist camps for activities such as creative writing, young inventors, and arts and crafts. During all these activities, monitors are responsible for keeping the group happy, safe and well behaved
Accommodation: Provided in dorms in country mansions and castles
Benefits: Free board and lodging, travel costs and a 'small financial thank you'

Alexanders International School

Duration: Min. 2 weeks (June – August)
Location: Suffolk
Prerequisites: Min. age 23. RSA cert. TEFL or better (for English teachers); professional coaches or undergraduate sports teachers (for sports assistants)

☎ 01394 411633
alexanders@skola.co.uk
www.skola.co.uk/alexanders

Organisation: An international summer school for 11–17-year-olds from all over the world
Description: Qualified ELT teachers are required for the summer short courses. Classes consist of a maximum of 15 students with all levels from beginners to advanced. Residential sports assistants are also required to run the sporting activities
Accommodation: Provided on-site at no cost
Benefits: £330–£350 a week for teaching and £185–£250 for sports assistants, plus free board and lodging

Aardmore Language Schools

Duration: Min. 1 week (July/August)
Location: Throughout the UK
Prerequisites: Candidates should hold a CELTYL, CELTA, CTEFLA, TESOL and/or PGCE, and relevant experience (for teaching positions); NPLQ qualification (lifeguards); and have experience in activity holidays

☎ 01628 826699
✆ info@theardmoregroup.com
🖥 www.ardmore-language-schools.com

Organisation: Aardmore offers summer junior vacation courses in English to overseas students at residential and homestay centres located throughout Britain
Description: Aardmore recruits short-term residential sports leaders, lifeguards, site assistants and EFL teachers during the summer to help run language and activity courses for students from overseas. Key duties include: pastoral care of students, meal duties and assisting with the day-to-day running of the centre
Accommodation: Provided mainly in schools and colleges
Benefits: Competitive salary and free board and lodging

Concord College

Duration: 3 or 4 weeks
Location: Shropshire
Prerequisites: RSA Cert. TEFL (EFL teachers) and experience required
Organisation: An independent, international school for students from all over the world. During July and August the college provides short, intensive science and English courses for students aged 8–18

☎ 01694 731631
✆ summercourse@concordcollegeuk.com
🖥 www.concordsummerschool.com

Description: Science, EFL and art teachers and outdoor education tutors are required to teach a maximum of 12 students per class. Teachers must also accompany students on excursions, supervise meals and deal with students' problems and complaints. The college has excellent facilities
Accommodation: Provided in a single university hall-style bedroom
Benefits: Teachers receive a competitive wage, accommodation, three meals a day, laundry and expenses

Discovery Summer

Duration: 2–5 weeks (July – mid August)
Location: Radley, Shrewsbury, Uppingham, Woldingham
Prerequisites: Teachers require a minimum first degree, plus CELTA, Trinity TESOL or PGCE. Lifeguards and sports coaches require appropriate qualifications and experience. All positions require a CRB check

☎ 020 7937 1199
🖰 mary@discoverysummer.co.uk; info@discoverysumer.co.uk
💻 www.discoverysummer.co.uk

Organisation: Discovery specialises in junior summer courses for overseas students
Description: Discovery runs intensive English tuition plus a full multi-activity programme for nine to 16-year-olds. EFL teachers, activity leaders, sports coaches and social directors are employed for short term contracts to work 15–22½ hours, five days a week
Accommodation: Provided at one of the four discovery colleges with full board
Benefits: From £310 a week, depending on qualifications and experience plus food, accommodation and a discretionary end of contract bonus

EJO – English Language Holiday Courses

Duration: From 2 weeks (Easter and summer holidays)
Location: Around the UK
Prerequisites: Enthusiasm and flexibility; interview; CRB check. For teaching positions CELTA, Cert. TESOL or equivalent qualifications required

☎ 01428 751933
🖰 steve@ejo.co.uk
💻 www.ejo.co.uk

Organisation: An accredited established school with 35 centres that arranges short-term English language holiday courses for young people from abroad
Description: EJO aims to introduce students to the social and cultural life of the UK and give them an enjoyable stay. EFL teachers and activiy leaders are required to work six day weeks. Teachers take on single nationality classes of 15–30 students. Activity leaders supervise sports, tournaments, workshops and excursions
Accommodation: Available in a residential school owned by the organisation
Benefits: £190–£252 per week plus full-board accommodation

ELAC Study Vacations

Duration: Min. 1 week
Location: Eastbourne, London, Mayfield, Nottingham, Camarthen
Prerequisites: EFL qualifications and experience required plus enthusiasm and flexibility

☎ 01323 506205
🖰 info@elac.co.uk
💻 www.elac.co.uk

Organisation: ELAC has been organising and teaching English language courses for young people from all over the world for more than 20 years

Description: EFL tutors are required to teach foreign students aged 13 to 17 for five to eight hours a day. Courses combine classroom tuition with cultural excursions, project work and sports
Accommodation: Provided at the college
Benefits: £9–£11 an hour plus board and accommodation

International Quest

Duration: Min. 2 weeks
Location: 30 vacation study centres throughout UK and Ireland
Prerequisites: Native speaker; team player; able to confidently organise indoor games and activities and referee various sports

☎ 01202 296868
🖱 activity@internationalquest.net
💻 www.internationalquest.net

Organisation: A leading provider of vocational summer English programmes for overseas students aged 11–18 from June to August
Description: International Quest centres take on activity leaders to live on campus and be available when required to help with any aspect of the recreational and social programme. Activity leaders help to organise activities, accompany students on excursions and help to ensure that all aspects of the programme run smoothly and efficiently
Accommodation: Provided on campus in one of the IQ centres
Benefits: Competitive salary plus room and board

King's School of English: Summer Camps

Duration: Min. 2 weeks
Location: Near London, Bath and Reading
Prerequisites: CRB check; CELTA, TESOL or PGCE qualification. Native speaker competence in English. Experience and knowledge of contemporary life and culture in the UK. All applicants must be

☎ 01202 293535
🖱 info@kingsschool.uk.com
💻 www.kingsgroup.co.uk

enthusiastic, versatile and enjoy working with young people. Interview necessary
Organisation: A well-established accredited private school offering English for overseas students. Short residential summer camps are run from July – August
Description: EFL teachers and activity leaders are required for short-term residential contracts each summer. Students are provided with a hectic programme of English lessons, excursions and activities each day. Participants work five to six days per week
Accommodation: Provided in boarding school accommodation
Benefits: Approx. £200–£350 a week plus full board and lodging

Project International

Duration: 2–5 weeks
Location: Kent, Hertfordshire, Somerset, Dorset, Wales, Devon, Liverpool, West Midlands, Powys
Prerequisites: Vibrant, energetic, competent, native English speakers. TEFL and PGCE qualifications an advantage but not essential
Organisation: Leading UK youth tour operator providing an educational, recreational, social and cultural experience to students from different countries
Description: Summer staff are required to teach English, supervise sports and activities, help out with social events and escort excursions at residential summer schools across the UK. Participants work as part of a close-knit team
Accommodation: Provided at residential centres
Benefits: £190–£350 a week (depending on experience) plus full board

☎ 020 7916 2522
✆ recruitment@projectinternational.uk.com
💻 www.projectinternational.uk.com

Super Camps Ltd

Duration: 4 days – 4 weeks
Location: South and central England
Prerequisites: Min. age 18; enthusiastic; energetic; 2 days' SC training. Relevant sports coaching qualifications or childcare/teaching experience, or first aid skills
Organisation: SC runs multi-activity half-term, Christmas, Easter and summer day camps for children age 4–13
Description: Positions available with SC include group leaders, lifeguards, trampolinists, sports coaches, and art and performing arts leaders. Activity instructors are the main point of contact for children and their role is to lead children in the timetabled activities ensuring maximum participation. Camps run Monday to Friday during school holidays
Accommodation: Only provided at some camps but SC can help participants to find suitable lodgings
Benefits: From £225 per week

☎ 01235 832222
✆ employment@supercamps.co.uk
💻 www.supercamps.co.uk

The Abbey College

Duration: Min. 2 weeks
Location: Malvern, Worcestershire
Prerequisites: EFL teachers must be fully qualified. Activities staff must be enthusiastic about sports and good communicators
Organisation: A 70–acre residential campus with students from more than 30 nations that runs a comprehensive summer school for students aged 8–18
Description: Qualified EFL teachers and activities staff are required for a minimum of two weeks during the summer. EFL teachers provide a lively, informative environment for learning English, and activity staff are required to provide sports and leisure pursuits in safe, secure surroundings as well as participating in excursion programmes
Accommodation: Provided on-site for those who take on residential duties
Benefits: EFL teachers: £230–£350 per week; activity staff: £140–£275

☎ 01684 892300
✍ jobs@abbeycollege.co.uk
💻 www.abbeycollege.co.uk/jobs.htm

EUROPE

ACLE

Duration: Min. 2 weeks
Location: Italy
Prerequisites: Between 20 and 30 years of age; love of working with children; native English speaker. Italian language skills are not required. Successful applicants must attend a four–day TEFL orientation course
Organisation: Programme recognised by the Italian Ministry of Education to use drama in education. English lessons are combined with games, songs, sports and drama to make English interesting and accessible to children
Description: Each year ACLE sends English-speaking counsellors to around 50 camps in Italy. Camps are located all over Italy from the Dolomites to Sicily and are either city based or residential. Previous camps have been held in Rome, Milan, Sicily, Bologna, Pisa, Siena and Naples. Teachers work 40+ hours a week
Accommodation: Provided with meals either at the residential camp or in a hotel
Benefits: Participants receive €190 to €230 per week plus board and lodging

☎ +39 (184) 506070
✍ info@acle.org
💻 www.acle.org

Anglo-Polish Universities Association Assisted Teaching Project (APASS)

Duration: 4 weeks

Location: Poland

Prerequisites: Good command of written and spoken English; college education or higher. Teaching experience is not essential

Organisation: Self-supporting fraternity of students, graduates, teachers and persons willing to teach English in Poland, working in conjunction with the Polish Ministry of Education

Description: APASS camps involve three weeks of teaching plus a week-long tour of Poland. English language instructors teach in the summer language camps, held in education/leisure centres in Poland. English staff organise and run morning lessons and afternoon activities as well as taking part in evening activities and weekend trips

Accommodation: Dormitory-style accommodation

Cost: Approx. £130 including a year's membership of APASS and return travel by coach

Benefits: Generous pocket money plus free board and lodging and leisure activities plus a free tour of Poland

Application Procedure: For a comprehensive information pack send a 45p stamped A4 size SAE, plus £3 postal order to APASS (North) 93, Victoria Road, Leeds LS6 1DR

☎ 0113 275 8121

💻 http://virtualdebris.co.uk/apass (unofficial website)

A POSTCARD FROM Bydgoszcz, Poland

Having recently graduated from university, Lianne Slavin jumped at the chance to put off making any life or career decisions and set off to teach English in Poland with APASS:

I found out about APASS summer camps by complete chance. My mum had been sent an email at the school where she works, requesting volunteers to go and teach English in Bydgoszcz for three weeks. The cost of the project seemed incredibly reasonable and I was really interested in working with people.

Being a complete teaching novice, I was unsure how to prepare for the trip. I made a paper version of Articulate, wrote some crib sheets for myself reminding me of the definitions of an adverb and so on, and I bought some sweets to use as prizes. Then I packed my bags and left for London.

From London, I met up with 17 other volunteers, and together we got a 23 hour coach to the summer school in Bydgoszcz. The day after we arrived we were assigned a class to teach with our teaching pair. Although some people had come with friends, most had come alone and were paired up by the team leader. The team leader took interests and personalities into account, but also mixed those with some teaching experience with first-time teachers.

We stayed in the school for three weeks and we were treated extremely well by our host and even taken for (free) trips at the weekend, before an all-expenses paid tour around Zakopane, Warsaw, Krakow and Auschwitz at the end of our stay. Most of the children displayed a great desire to learn and also great pride in their country (they were always keen to teach me a word or two of Polish!) I was quite sad when I left the school and I am pleased to say I still keep in touch with one of the children eight months later. All in all, it is an experience I would thoroughly recommend.

Bell International

Duration: 2 weeks
Location: Poland
Prerequisites: CELTA or Trinity TESOL and a first degree. Some teaching experience is preferred. Native speakers of English

☎ 945 281794
🖱 recruitment@elsbell.pl
💻 www.bellschools.pl/employment.php

Organisation: A member of Bell International, established in 1989. Runs English courses for general English and summer camps
Description: Bell runs summer camps for students aged seven to 18 for which short-term TEFL qualified teachers are required. The teaching is topic-based with a strong emphasis on students using their knowledge of English for practical as well as fun purposes
Accommodation: Provided in flats not far from the city centre that are well heated and comfortable, with a washing machine as standard
Benefits: Teachers receive a competitive wage based on experience, plus self-catering accommodation

DAD International UK-Romania

Duration: Min. 8 days
Location: Throughout Romania
Prerequisites: Min. age 17. No previous teaching or qualifications required

☎ +40 (788) 473523
🖱 camps@dad.ro
💻 www.dad.ro

Organisation: Non-profit charity organisation and official partner of the Romanian Ministry for Education & Research
Description: DAD International provides summer learning programmes at which volunteer tutors teach conversational English to Romanian students aged eight to 18 through informal classes, games and fun for four to six hours a day. There is no formal teaching structure and each volunteer brings their own style and ideas. Volunteers also supervise afternoon activities and excursions
Accommodation: Provided with full board at the camps in dormitory-style rooms
Cost: The cost is kept low at around £200 including insurance, 24–hour support and assistance, transfers to place of work, training, and internet access

English for Children – Summer Camp

Duration: 3 weeks in July
Location: Vienna, Austria
Prerequisites: Applicants must have experience of working with children aged 3–14, and of camps, be versatile, conscientious, oriented towards children and safety and have an outgoing personality. Experience in more than one subject area preferable

☎ +43 (01) 958 1972
🖱 office@englishforchildren.com
💻 www.englishforchildren.com

Organisation: An international school using learn-play programmes focusing on total immersion resulting in accent-free English
Description: Work in a total immersion summer camp, motivating children to speak English through different activities: sports, English language classes, arts & crafts, music, and to acquaint children with the different cultures of the English-speaking world through games and songs. To work during July, 8am-4pm Monday to Friday
Accommodation: Provided at the camp

English for Kids

Duration: 3 weeks
Location: Upper Austria
Prerequisites: CELTA or Trinity Cert. And some formal teaching experience. No German language skills required

☎ +43 (01) 667 4579
🖱 office@e4kids.co.at
💻 www.e4kids.co.at

Organisation: English-language organisation based in Vienna that has offered full immersion summer programmes since 1989
Description: Residential summer camps in a renovated 17th century building situated in 40 hectares of meadows and woods. Camps last for three weeks in August and teachers are required to work with students ranging from 10–15 years old. Teachers are required to create a full immersion experience and encourage active involvement of the children. They are also responsible for camp participants 24 hours per day
Accommodation: Provided on-site with full board
Benefits: Salary varies depending on qualifications, plus board and accommodation, and travel expenses within Austria

The Farm Fun

Duration: Min. 1 week
Location: Basque Country, Spain
Prerequisites: Min. age 18, outdoor skills, a creative nature and complete proficiency in English. EU citizens only
Organisation: Organises summer English camps in the Basque country

☎ +34 605 714390
🖱 tulio@thefarmfun.com
💻 www.thefarmfun.com

Description: The Farm Fun camps are activity camps for Spanish children aged eight to 15 that are entirely run in English. There is no formal English teaching (so no teaching experience is required) but groups communicate with each other in English. Native English speakers are required to monitor groups of around six to seven young people. Monitors usually have Spanish speaking assistants

Benefits: Competitive wage plus food and camping accommodation for the duration of the camp

Gençtur

Duration: 2 weeks
Location: Throughout Turkey
Season: Summer months
Prerequisites: Min. age 18. No experience required
Organisation: Non-governmental organisation based in Turkey

☎ +90 212 249 25 15
🖱 workcamps.in@genctur.com
💻 www.genctur.com/indexe.htm

Description: Gençtur organises international voluntary workcamps in small villages and towns. Some, but not all, of the camps specialise in teaching English to children or teenagers. No experience is necessary as the camps focus on conversational English.

Accommodation: Provided in schools or village centres, sleeping on the floor or mattresses, or in dorms. Meals are provided by local families

Cost: There is a small registration fee of €50 which includes board and lodging. At an additional cost of €60 participants can have an extra 3 days in Istanbul with organised activities

Lingue Senza Frontiere

Duration: 2 weeks
Location: Throughout Italy
Prerequisites: Min. age 20. Fluent English speakers with experience in teaching or working with children. Applicants should be able to lead sports, crafts or drama

☎ +39 (0184) 508650
🖱 info@linguesenzafrontiere.org
💻 www.linguesenzafrontiere.org

Organisation: Non-profit Italian cultural association that organises English-language summer camps in Italy

Description: The purpose of the camps is to immerse Italian children in an English-speaking environment and combine learning with other fun activities such as sports, drama, art, crafts, games and song. Counsellors are taken on to help teach English and supervise activities. At the end of the camp the children put on a show in English

Accommodation: Provided with meals. Varies according to camp from a flat to a private homestay

Benefits: Competitive salary, board and lodging, insurance, materials, 3–day orientation and travel to and from camps

Village Camps Inc

Duration: Min. 3 weeks
Location: Across Europe
Prerequisites: Min. age 21; relevant experience, qualifications; valid first aid and CPR certificate. A second language is desirable

☎ +41 (22) 990 9405
🖱 personnel@villagecamps.ch
💻 www.villagecamps.com

Organisation: Village Camps organises educational and activity camps for children from all over the world across Europe
Description: Village Camps operates residential and day camps in the summer and residential outdoor education camps in spring and autumn. Activities are provided for children aged from four to 18 years that are physically challenging and mentally stimulating. Monitors, TEFL teachers, counsellors, chefs and domestic assistants are required
Accommodation: Various types of full-board accommodation provided
Benefits: Generous allowance paid in local currency, full room and board, and accident and liability insurance

Young Austria

Duration: 1–2 weeks (July and August)
Location: Austria
Prerequisites: Min. age 18
Organisation: International summer English language camp for young people aged 9–17 in Alpine settings near Salzburg

☎ +43 (0662) 625758
🖱 office@youngaustria.at
💻 www.camps.at/en/

Description: YA provides summer camps that awaken children's enthusiasm for activity, sport, nature and international solidarity. YA takes on camp counsellors from around the world to supervise a range of activities including English language learning and outdoor activities
Accommodation: Provided in youth hotels with full board
Benefits: Remuneration plus free board and lodging

Bridges For Education Inc

Duration: 4 weeks
Location: Worldwide. 2007 camps took place in China, Turkey and Lithuania
Prerequisites: EFL qualifications (teachers). The team is prepared in basic ESL prior to departure
Organisation: Not-for-profit educational organisation promoting tolerance using English as a bridge
Description: Volunteers on the BFE project teach conversational English for three weeks and then travel for one week. There are places available for qualified teachers and unqualified teaching assistants to take three hours of classes in the morning and two hours of activities in the afternoon
Accommodation: Lodgings are provided in boarding schools and college dormitories. They may be fairly basic depending on the country
Cost: Approx. US$950 including board and lodging, pre-departure training and weekend activities. All travel and accommodation for the final week is provided

☎ +1 (716) 839 0180
🖱 jbc@bridges4edu.org
🖥 www.bridges4edu.org

Svezhy Veter Travel Agency

Duration: 2–3 weeks
Location: Izhevsk, Russia
Prerequisites: Min. age 18, relative experience, positive references. A TEFL certificate and a little Russian is useful but not madatory
Organisation: Travel agents offering a series of Russia 'experiences'
Description: Volunteers are required at summer camps around Izhevsk to help out as sports instructors, language instructors, camp counsellors, and music, dance, arts and crafts instructors
Accommodation: Provided with local families in a homestay arrangement
Costs: €98 participation fee. Participants are also responsible for travel, visa and daily costs
Benefits: Full board accommodation is provided at all camps. Some camps also provide pocket money of €70–€150

☎ +7 (3412) 450037
🖱 sv@sv-agency.udm.ru; svezhyveter@gmail.com
🖥 www.sv-agency.udm.ru

SUMMER CAMPS: WORLDWIDE

TEACHING & SUMMER CAMPS

VESL Summer Schools

Duration: 4 or 5 weeks (July and August)
Location: Sri Lanka, India
Prerequisites: Min. age 18. Some experience useful, but any applicant with the right personality and the ability to make a difference is eligible

☎ 0845 094 3727
✏ info@vesl.org
💻 www.vesl.org

Organisation: Registered not-for-profit charity established to provide students from rural Asian communities with better educational possibilities
Description: VESL summer schools are conducted out of school hours or in school holidays and involve children and adults from the local community. From the teacher's point of view, the emphasis is on developing English language skills through games and spoken activities to help boost skills and confidence levels. Volunteers work four to six hours a day for five days a week
Accommodation: Volunteers are usually placed with a partner and live with a host family
Cost: Volunteers need to raise £850 towards the cost of their placement. This includes project set-up, food, accommodation, insurance and training

HANDS-ON

Sports, Holidays and Festivals

SPORTS AND ACTIVITIES

For sports enthusiasts, there is no better way to spend your holiday time than indulging your favourite sporting pursuit. Sporting holidays are of course widely available, but short breaks that combine a sporting interest with earning a little holiday money, or improving the lives of others are a little harder to come by. Some ideas are listed below.

Those whose passions lie on the snow slopes, and who return to the mountains at every opportunity will recognise just how expensive a hobby skiing and snowboarding can be. One way to improve your skills and lessen the financial impact is to spend a season working at a ski resort. Wages at resorts are low, but avid skiers see it as recompense enough to have access to the slopes during their time off. Those interested in ski season work will find everything they need to know in the book *Working in Ski Resorts* (Vacation Work; £11.95). Ski seasons of course last around five months and do not fit easily into the average person's holiday time. However, there is a way to combine a ski holiday with work – joining one of the operators which provide ski holidays to schools and youth groups. Listed below are several such companies, which take on reps, guides, couriers and even instructors for short periods of time (one to two weeks).

Equally, many specialist tour companies employ leaders for their clients, whether children or adults, on adventure sports holidays. Again, this employment usually lasts for the duration of the season, but listed below is some ad hoc work that allows participants to spend a holiday indulging their favourite sport abroad and earning a little money, or at least receiving free travel and accommodation. Any competent sailor, canoeist, diver, climber etc should have no difficulty marketing their skills abroad.

Alternatively you could consider taking one of the many organised sports coaching placements. Volunteer coaching in developing countries is one of the fastest growing areas of voluntourism and is proving extremely popular with participants of all ages and backgrounds. This is partly because coaching sports does not require the same conventional skills and language ability as teaching English or other subjects – the language of sport is universal. But more importantly, the growing number of coaching placements is testament to a growing recognition of the important role that sport plays in society, as the company Sportventurer explains: *'Sport can contribute to economic and social development, improving health and personal growth in people of all ages, particularly those of young people. Sport can also help build a culture of peace and tolerance by bringing people together on common ground, crossing national and other boundaries to promote understanding and mutual respect.'*

This might be slightly overstating the case, but it is clear that sport can help to build confidence in children who otherwise lead very difficult lives. It can also inspire them to succeed in other areas of their life, and improve their communication and leadership skills. Sports volunteer projects take a variety of different forms and cross a number of different sports. While football is one of the most popular coaching opportunities, it is also possible to coach anything from rugby and cricket, to swimming, athletics and even table tennis in developing countries. Whatever you choose, if you have a love of sports and some ability, your efforts will undoubtedly have a lasting and positive impact, and will benefit young people from some of the poorest parts of the world.

HF Holidays: Walk Leaders

Duration: 1 week at a time (2–30 weeks per year)
Location: Throughout the UK and Europe.
Some worldwide opportunities
Season: Year round
Prerequisites: Enthusiastic walker, enjoy
meeting new people, confident, social, able to
cope in an emergency situation, and good navigation skills

☎ 01768 890091
🖱 walkleaders@hfholidays.co.uk
💻 www.walkleaders.co.uk

Organisation: Non-profit organisation providing guided walking and special interest holidays
Description: HF has a panel of more than 900 voluntary walk leaders who travel the world guiding walks and ensuring that guests have a good time. Walk leaders cater for all levels of walker on week-long walking holidays. Applicants can choose where, how often and when they want to lead the holidays. In return they receive the opportunity to explore Britain and Europe for free, travelling expenses, accommodation and meals, discount holidays, regular training courses, and support and advice
Accommodation: Leaders are provided with full board single-room accommodation in either HF owned Country House hotels, or comfortable alternative
Application Procedure: Having registered online, applicants must attend a training session and if successful will be invited to lead a minimum of two walks per year. After leading UK walks, participants can also apply to lead walks in Europe and further afield

Freewheel Holidays: Hosts

Duration: Min. 4 weeks
Location: Throughout Europe
Season: July/August
Prerequisites: Excellent communication
skills, full/clean driving licence, good
knowledge of bicycle maintenance, good

☎ 01636 815636
🖱 info@freewheelholidays.com
💻 www.freewheelholidays.com

knowledge of language appropriate to the tour, flexible, reliable and enthusiastic.
Experience of a similar field is desirable
Organisation: Independent travel company organising high-quality gentle cycling holidays
Description: Freewheel hosts lead visitors on cycling holidays throughout Europe. In addition they represent the company on the ground and are responsible for meeting guests and transferring them to their hotels. Other duties include providing a welcome presentation, the safe transit of guests, their luggage and bicycles, liaison with hotel management, maintenance checks on bicycles and so on. Hosts work approximately 30–35 hours per week
Wages and Benefits: £200 per week plus accommodation and expenses. Couples are welcome to apply. They will receive one wage but free accommodation
Application Procedure: Hosts are appointed by the company directors following a successful interview at Freewheel offices in Nottinghamshire. Appointments are usually made in April. If accepted, hosts must undertake 5–7 days training (in May) during which they cycle the route and familiarise themselves with it

Ski-Plan: Peak Season Resort Reps

Duration: 1 week at a time for up to 5 weeks in total

Location: Austria, France, Italy and North America

Season: December – April

Prerequisites: Min. age 20; strong communication/customer service skills, conversational French, German or Italian

☎ 01273 810762
✍ overseasjobs@sts-skiplan.co.uk
🖥 www.skiplan.co.uk

Organisation: Dedicated schools ski specialist with more than 35 years of experience in school travel

Description: Peak season reps are required for a week at a time throughout the winter season, and especially during the school holidays to accompany supervised school groups on ski trips. Reps are responsible for the well-being of school groups while in resorts and act as a liaison between the company and school party leader

Wages and Benefits: £90–£110 per week dependent upon language/experience plus ski lift pass, insurance, full board accommodation, equipment hire and coach travel

Accommodation: Provided as part of the package

Application Procedure: Apply online or call Henri Stewart, overseas recruitment manager on the above number

Club Europe: Ski Resort Reps

Duration: 9 days

Location: Austria, France, Italy, Switzerland and Germany

Season: February half-term through to and including Easter

Prerequisites: Keen skiers with a friendly outgoing

☎ 020 8699 7788
 info@club-europe.co.uk
 www.club-europe.co.uk

personality and excellent organisational/communication skills; fluent in French, German or Italian; able to work under pressure

Organisation: Club Europe organises school ski package holidays to European destinations

Description: Resort reps are taken on each season to accompany school groups and assist with ski-hire, lift passes, the ski school and to arrange the evening entertainment

Wages and Benefits: £250 per nine-day tour including board and lodging, ski hire, lift pass

Accommodation: Provided as part of the package

Application Procedure: Call or visit the website for further information

Halsbury Travel: Ski Season Couriers

Duration: 1 week
Location: Austria, Canada, France, Italy, Switzerland, USA
Season: School holiday weeks – mainly Christmas/ New Year, February half-term and Easter
Prerequisites: Min. age 21; fluent French; previous ski rep experience and a good skiing standard preferred
Organisation: Family business that has been serving the travel needs of school and adult groups for the last 20 years
Description: Resort couriers and guides are taken on each year to help out with school groups during one week trips in the school holidays. Couriers act as a liaison between Halsbury, the school party leaders and local suppliers
Wages: Salary on application
Application Procedure: Check the website several months in advance of the ski season for updates on current vacancies

☎ 01159 404303
🖱 enquiries@halsbury.com
💻 www.halsbury.com

Interski Snowsport School: Ski Instructors

Duration: 1 week
Location: Aosta Valley, Italy
Season: February half term through to and including Easter
Prerequisites: BASI grade 3, national equivalent or above
Organisation: Market-leading organiser of school ski package holidays
Description: During each ski season, the Interski Snowsport School employs more than 600 part-time instructors. Legislation dictates that instructors can only work for one week per season. Instructors work six days per week with four hours of instruction per day
Wages and Benefits: £200 for one week plus concessionary scheme for partners, return executive coach travel, six-day lift pass, half board accommodation, insurance and uniform
Accommodation: Provided at a 2 or 3-star hotel. Breakfast is provided at the hotel, evening meals at a local restaurant
Application Procedure: Apply online from the season before you intend to work

☎ 01623 456333
🖱 email@interslo.co.uk
💻 www.interski.co.uk

Equity Ski: Peak Season Reps

Duration: 1 week
Location: France, Austria, Italy
Season: Christmas and New Year, February half-term and Easter

 recruitment@equity.co.uk
 www.equity.co.uk/employment/

Prerequisites: Min. age 21; mature and sensible attitude. French, German or Italian language skills an advantage
Organisation: Direct sell tour operator organising educational tours, sports tours, ski holidays and weekend breaks
Description: Christmas, New Year, February half-term and Easter are the busiest weeks of the season and extra staff are required to accompany school groups on their ski trips. Reps ensure all pre-booked services including ski-hire and lift passes are coordinated between the suppliers, party leaders and the school group. They also provide a varied après-ski programme, deal with problems that may arise, and are available to help with queries
Wages and Benefits: Salary on application plus return transport, full board accommodation, lift pass and ski equipment
Accommodation: Provided at the resort
Application Procedure: Email a CV and cover letter to Sue Lloyd at the above email address

Vitalise: Ski Guides

Duration: 1 week
Location: Austria, France, Canada, Italy, Finland
Season: February half-term and Easter only
Prerequisites: Communication skills, patience, understanding, enthusiasm and a

☎ 0845 330 0149
 volunteer@vitalise.org.uk
🖥 www.vitalise.org.uk

sense of humour. For beginner holidays guides must be strong intermediate skiers
Organisation: Vitalise is a national charity that provides holidays for visually impaired people
Description: Sighted guides are an essential part of Vitalise Holidays, making the difference between a visually impaired person having a much needed break or no holiday at all. Guides provide sighted assistance, and explain surroundings on a one-to-one basis. Guiding can be demanding, but first-time guides receive plenty of help and advice
Accommodation: Provided in hotels and inns. Guides are usually asked to share a room with a visually impaired person
Cost: Prices are subsidised for guides. Approx. £520 including flights and transfers and half board accommodation

Pavilion Tours: Watersports Instructors

Duration: Min. 1 week
Location: Greece and Spain
Season: May – October
Prerequisites: Min. age 18. Must have passed RYA sailing or windsurfing instructor courses or BCU Level 2 kayaking course

☎ 0870 241 0425
✉ info@paviliontours.com
🖥 www.paviliontours.co.uk

Organisation: Specialist activity tour operator for students
Description: Watersports instructors are required during the season to teach school groups and assist with evening entertainment. Participants work a seven-day week with negotiable hours
Wages: Participants receive £110 per week plus full board and lodging
Accommodation: Provided in comfortable shared accommodation
Application Procedure: Apply online from November

Cairnwell Mountain Sports: Activity Instructors

Duration: Min. 2 weeks
Location: Blairgowrie, Perthshire, Scotland
Season: January – September
Prerequisites: Min. age 18, must

☎ 01250 885255
✉ admin@cairnwellmountainsports.co.uk
🖥 www.cairnwellmountainsports.co.uk

have a nationally recognised qualification in coaching one of the activities on offer
Organisation: Multi-activity centre and hostel
Description: Cairnwell takes on activity instructors in the summer and winter for a range of activities including climbing, walking, watersports, canyoning, mountain biking, skiing etc
Wages: Approx. £240 per week
Accommodation: Provided at a cost of approx. £50 per week
Application Procedure: Applications should be made to Darren Morgan at Gulabin Lodge, Spittal of Glenshee, Blairgowrie, Perthshire PH10 7QE

Raasay Outdoor Centre: Activity Instructors

Duration: Min. 1 month
Location: Isle of Raasay, Scotland
Season: April – October
Prerequisites: Min. age 21. Senior instructors must have a full driving licence, experience in leading groups, first aid qualifications and a

☎ 01478 660266
🖱 info@raasay-house.co.uk
💻 www.raasay-house.co.uk

minimum of two national instruction qualifications. For junior instructors it is desirable that they hold an instructional award, but experience may be sufficient
Organisation: Outdoor centre located on a remote and peaceful Hebridean island
Description: The centre takes on junior and senior activity instructors for a range of sports including power boating, sailing, kayaking and canoeing
Wages: Competitive wage depending on experience and level of responsibility. Board, accommodation and activities provided
Application Procedure: Application forms can be found online. These should be emailed to staff@raasayoutdoorcentre.co.uk from February

Jubilee Sailing Trust

Duration: 5–29 days
Location: JST sails to a range of ever-changing destinations. Current trips include island hopping in the Canaries or Caribbean in the winter, or around the UK and Europe in the summer. There are two trans-Atlantic voyages per year

☎ 0870 443 5781
🖱 info@jst.org.uk
💻 www.jst.org.uk

Season: Year round
Prerequisites: Min. age 16. No sailing experience required
Organisation: Charity that aims to promote the integration of people of all physical abilities through the challenge and adventure of tall-ship sailing holidays
Description: On each voyage up to 40 people, half of whom may be physically disabled, sail as the voyage crew. Everyone takes an active and equal part in the crewing of the yachts. Tasks include being part of a watch, helping to set the sails, helming the ship, assisting with onboard cleaning, and helping the cook in the galley. Each ship has a 10–strong permanent crew. Those of a competitive nature can take part in a tall ships race during the summer. Young people aged 16–25 are eligible for the 'Leadership at Sea' scheme, for which bursaries are available
Accommodation: There are individual bunks for crew members, although there are no separate cabins
Cost: £399–£1,249. Some funding is available for non-means tested grants, regardless of physical ability. Those qualified to work as ship's doctor or a watch leader receive a 50% discount on the brochure price

Gap Sports

Duration: Min. 4 weeks accommodated
Location: Costa Rica, Ghana, South Africa
Season: Year round
Organisation: Gap year provider that brands itself as 'the sports travel specialists'
Sports Available: Football, rugby, cricket, hockey, tennis, netball, basketball, golf, boxing, swimming
Description: Participants join teams of like-minded people to work on sports development projects, making a positive difference to developing communities. Participants usually work with children's teams who lack local support and funding
Accommodation: Varies according to project. Included in price
Cost: A 4–week project would cost £1,295 including food and accommodation

☎ 0870 837 9797
🖱 info@gapsports.com
💻 www.gapsports.com

Greenforce

Duration: Min. 4 weeks
Location: Brazil and Ecuador
Season: Year round
Prerequisites: Min. age 17; love of football. No previous experience or qualifications necessary
Organisation: Non-profit organisation working alongside local people on international conservation, community and sport volunteer projects
Sports Available: Football
Description: In Ecuador, participants work at schools in Quito providing coaching assistance to girls and boys aged five to 18. The 120 children involved in the scheme play in local, national and international tournaments and need regular training. In Brazil participants can combine coaching in communities with language lessons and training at a football academy
Accommodation: Included in price. Varies from project to project
Cost: £750 (4 weeks in Brazil); £990 (4 weeks in Ecuador). Price includes food, accommodation, transfers, and programme costs

☎ 020 7470 8888
🖱 greenforce@btinternet.com
💻 www.greenforce.org

i-to-i International Projects

Duration: Min. 2 weeks
Location: Argentina, Brazil, Costa Rica, Honduras, Kenya, Madagascar, Malaysia, South Africa, Sri Lanka, Dominican Republic, Ecuador, Ghana, Tanzania, Trinidad & Tobago
Prerequisites: Min. age 18. Some sporting ability required

☎ 0870 333 2332
🖱 uk@i-to-i.com; usca@i-to-i.com
💻 www.i-to-i.com

Organisation: A founding member of the Year Out Group with Investors in People status, i-to-i is a TEFL training and volunteer travel organisation
Sports Available: General sports coaching, surfing, soccer, diving, cricket, baseball
Description: i-to-i sports coaching placements are designed for those with a love of sports and some ability to play an important part in the personal development of young people worldwide. It is intended that participants' coaching efforts will have a lasting and positive impact and will benefit young people from some of the poorest parts of the world
Accommodation: Included in price. Varies from project to project
Cost: Varies considerably. Example price: 2 weeks coaching football in Argentina – £645

Real Gap Experience: Real Sport Experience

Duration: 2 weeks – 6 months
Location: More than 40 countries worldwide
Season: Year round
Organisation: The sports travel specialists, offering the most comprehensive range of gap year sports opportunities in 18 countries

☎ 01892 516164
🖱 info@realgap.co.uk
💻 www.realgap.co.uk

Description: Real Gap Experience offers a variety of sporting programmes, ranging from volunteer coaching a sport to training in prestigious sports academies, ski and snowboard courses, scuba diving courses and sports adventure expeditions. The Sports Volunteering programme takes place in more than 10 countries for all sporting interests such as football, netball, athletics, cricket and rugby. RSE also offers sports training in prestigious academies abroad, learning to become a ski or snowboard instructor in New Zealand, scuba diving training in Honduras or Australia and sports adventure expeditions, for those who want to combine a variety of sports, volunteering and extreme activities
Accommodation: Varies depending on programme – ranges from homestays, volunteer houses, tented camps, huts and hostels
Cost: £699 for 4 weeks including all accommodation, meals, airport pickup, orientation, volunteer placement and tuition

Projects Abroad: Sports Coaching Opportunities

Duration: Min. 2 weeks (Ghana); Min. 1 month
(everywhere else)
Location: Bolivia, Cambodia, Costa Rica,
Ghana, India, Moldova, Mongolia, Peru, Romania,
Senegal, South Africa, Thailand
Season: Year round

☎ 01903 708300
✍ info@projects-abroad.co.uk
💻 www.projects-abroad.co.uk

Organisation: Projects Abroad organises volunteering projects in 20 countries worldwide
Sports Available: Football, rugby, cricket, volleyball, basketball, Thai boxing, tennis,
swimming, water sports, athletics, table tennis and badminton
Description: Participants coach children in developing countries in a range of sports
and make a real difference to their lives. Sport can provide children from disadvantaged
backgrounds with a platform for their development and also gives them essential skills for
the world outside sport
Accommodation: Varies according to project. Included in price
Cost: 2 weeks in Ghana: £995; 1 month elsewhere: £1,095 – £1,345. Price includes
accommodation, food and insurance

A POSTCARD FROM Ghana

**Football fan and AS-level student Alice Wonnacott spent two weeks at a
Sports Academy for underprivileged children in Ghana with Projects Abroad:**

Having booked the placement in a sports academy in Ghana, the summer term flew by and
before I could blink, I was standing in front of my somewhat tearful mother reminding me to
take good care of myself and not to talk to strangers.

Although I most definitely did take good care of myself, and hence obeyed one of my
mother's conditions, I broke the second within the first minute of arriving on Ghanaian
territory. The friendliness and openness of the Ghanaians is what first struck me about
Ghana. I think it is partly because of the reserved nature of the English and partly just
because of the wideness of the Ghanaians' smiles - I couldn't help but feel instantly at
home. The first thing I did was to change some money. I handed over a single £20 note and
a couple of minutes later received a thick wad of Ghanian Cedis. I quickly put them in my
money belt feeling richer than the Queen of Sheba.

I was met by perhaps the most friendly Ghanaian of them all - Annane (meaning 'God')
and was taken to my home for the next couple of weeks. I was living with a Ghanaian
couple called the Wolves and there were three other girl volunteers living there as well.

My first day was an introduction to Accra and there was a lot to see. All the main
sights were pointed out to me and the big landmarks, so that if I got lost I would have
some idea of where I was. I met all of the other volunteers that evening, all of whom
were keen to get to know the 'girl footballer' as I was known and they were keen to
relate their various stories, experiences and tips.

After arriving at my placement which was about 45 minutes out of Accra I met the
overall organiser of the project - Salim. Another member of the team, Salisu, was an ex-
professional footballer who had played for the Ghanaian national team. Every day Salisu
comes from one of the worst slum regions in Accra with a bus full of keen children, aged
between five and 12 and gives them the opportunity to get some fresh air away from the
bustling, polluted city centre. I cannot express in words the joy that I saw on the faces of
these children while playing football and having a good kick around. Every one of the children

comes from a family with problems, whether they are orphaned, or abused, I find it hard to stress just how worthwhile this project is. It gives them an invaluable opportunity to forget their family problems and to just play as children should. I was proud to be involved.

Looking back on my time in Ghana, not only had I acquired a very impressive feature on my CV as well as a once-in-a-lifetime experience, I had also improved my suntan! From going to Ghana and seeing such acute poverty contrasted with such happiness I will carry my memories with me forever.

Projects Abroad football coaching volunteers with a local school team, Cape Coast, Ghana.

Sportventurer

Duration: Min. 2/4 weeks
Location: Ghana, Uganda, Fiji, Tonga, Peru
Season: Year round
Prerequisites: Min. age 17. No experience or qualifications necessary

☎ 0845 121 1996
🖥 www.sportventurer.com

Organisation: Sportventurer is a specialist programme run by Madventurer, the development travel company that offers opportunities to take part in development projects and adventurous travel worldwide
Sports Available: Football, rugby, hockey, netball, swimming, cricket, basketball, athletics, waterpolo, tennis. More sports coming soon
Description: Participants coach and motivate young players and teach in schools
Accommodation: Varies according to project
Cost: 2–week projects start from £680 per person including food, accommodation and support

VOLUNTEER SPORTS COACHING

SPORTS, HOLIDAYS & FESTIVALS

Travellers Worldwide: Travellers Sports

Duration: Min. 2 weeks
Location: Australia, Bolivia, Brazil, China, Ghana, Guatemala, India, Kenya, New Zealand, Malawi, Malaysia, Russia, Samoa, South Africa, Sri Lanka, Zambia
Season: Year round

☎ 01903 502595
🖱 info@travellersworldwide.com
🖥 www.travellersworldwide.com

Prerequisites: Min. age 17; love of sports and some sporting ability
Organisation: One of the major providers of gap year-style placements sending participants from all over the world to all over the world
Sports Available: Athletics, Aussie rules football, badminton, baseball, basketball, cheerleading, cricket, football, golf, gymnastics, hockey, lacrosse, martial arts, netball, rugby union, rugby league, squash, swimming, tennis, rowing, volleyball, waterpolo, weight training
Description: Participants provide children around the world with the opportunity to receive professional coaching, nurturing raw talent that would otherwise go unnoticed. Participants help children and communities through developing and coaching a sport or variety of sports. There are also opportunities for participants to play themselves in local clubs and teams
Accommodation: Varies according to placement/country. Most participants live with local families or in school residences. A few live in hostels and guest houses
Cost: Prices start at £695 for 2–weeks including accommodation and airport pick-ups

ASSISTING GROUPS ON HOLIDAY

School/youth groups, the disadvantaged and the disabled all require assistance to take a short break and some of the opportunities for helping out are listed below. These opportunities offer a free or subsidised holiday, plus the chance to broaden your depth of experience, and either earn a little money, or make a huge difference to the holiday experience of others. The opportunities are divided into paid and voluntary work.

Tour managers, couriers, group leaders and reps are all taken on for short-term work contracts on educational tours. The work usually involves little more than accompanying a group throughout the tour, liaising between the tour operator (your employer) and the party leader, ensuring that visits and excursions run smoothly and organising the evening entertainment. These trips are often based around activities, language learning, concerts and culture or just sightseeing. However, educational travel is becoming increasingly diverse as teachers and group leaders embrace the philosophy of education through experience. World Challenge Expeditions for example, requires leaders on a per expedition basis to accompany school groups on such activities as climbing Mount Kilimanjaro, exploring the rainforests in Brazil, or sleeping under the stars in Mongolia.

Less dramatic, but potentially more rewarding are the voluntary opportunities to accompany disadvantaged children and disabled people of all ages on holiday. A number of charities offer disabled people the chance to have a memorable and fulfilling holiday. These holidays also offer the carer or family of that person a much needed break from the routine of caring. Volunteer helpers on these holidays are in huge demand to assist the permanent staff. As the 3H Fund puts it: *'Giving you time is probably the most valuable contribution anyone can make. By sparing just one week per year, you could make such a difference to so many lives. It is a personally rewarding experience that you will never forget'.*

Acorn Educational Exchanges: Group Leaders

Duration: 8 days at a time
Location: France, Germany, Spain and Italy
Season: April, July, October

☎ 0115 9404 303
🖱 rachel@halsbury.com
💻 www.aee.eu.com/jobs.asp

Prerequisites: Min. age 21, fluent French, German, Spanish or Italian, bright, positive personality and plenty of resourcefulness. Previous experience of accompanying groups of young people preferred
Organisation: Sister company of Halsbury Travel, specialising in work experience and language courses abroad for young people
Description: Group leaders are required to supervise groups of 16–18 year old students going abroad on eight–day work experience schemes. Leaders are required to offer advice and assistance, organise social activities and visit students at their work placement
Wages and Benefits: £165 per week, accommodation, full medical and travel insurance, return travel by air or coach and social activities
Accommodation: Half-board hotel accommodation provided
Application Procedure: Email Rachel at the address above for further details on how to apply

American Council for International Studies: Tour Managers

Duration: 9–15 days
Location: Throughout Europe
Season: Busiest periods are March/April and June/July

☎ 020 7590 7474
💻 www.acis.com

Prerequisites: Min. age 21, fluency in French, Italian, German or Spanish. Must have, or be studying for a university degree
Organisation: ACIS is the educational travel division of the American Institute of Foreign Study. It organises educational tours built on the belief that travel changes lives
Description: More than 100 short-term tour managers are taken on each year to lead American high school teachers and students in educational trips through Europe. Trips may visit one or several countries. All trip details and itineraries are pre-arranged. Tour managers meet groups on arrival, travel with them, act as commentators and guides, keep accounts and troubleshoot. Tour managers are vital to the success of trips and are given unequalled training and support
Wages and Benefits: Competitive daily salary provided plus accommodation, generous tips, insurance and back-up
Accommodation: Provided with the groups in 3 or 4-star hotels
Application Procedure: Check the website for application details from December onwards

ASSISTING GROUPS ON HOLIDAY

SPORTS, HOLIDAYS & FESTIVALS

Club Europe Holidays

Duration: 3–7 days
Location: Austria, France, Spain, Italy, Belgium, Netherlands, Germany, Czech Republic, Poland
Season: From Easter onwards
Prerequisites: Fluent language skills

☎ 020 8699 7788
✉ info@club-europe.co.uk
💻 www.club-europe.co.uk

and some knowledge of the host country; music experience and knowledge, good organisational skills
Organisation: Club Europe organises concert tours for youth ensembles to European destinations
Description: Concert tour managers are employed on a freelance basis, usually mainly during the spring and summer school holidays. The music tour manager's duties include reconfirming concert arrangements and liaising with local venue organisers, booking any excursions required by the client, carrying out on-the-spot publicity for concerts, and interpreting and communicating the client's needs at the accommodation. Tour managers are also responsible for discussing any changes to the itinerary with coach drivers and accompanying the group on all concerts and excursions
Wages and Benefits: Competitive rates of pay according to experience
Accommodation: Tour managers are provided with the same level of board and accommodation as the client
Application Procedure: Interested parties should request an application form from aferdita.f@club-europe.co.uk. All suitable candidates will be interviewed

Equity Travel: Educational Tour Reps

Duration: 3–8 days
Location: France, Germany, Italy and Spain
Season: Throughout the academic calendar
Prerequisites: Fluency in a second language

✉ recruitment@equity.co.uk
💻 www.equity.co.uk/employment/

(French, German, Spanish or Italian), full driving licence, personable and professional demeanour, ability to think on your feet. Previous experience of working within the travel industry or with school children preferred
Organisation: Equity Travel (Part of School Travel Group) is a direct sell tour operator organising educational tours, sports tours, ski holidays and weekend breaks
Description: Equity runs a range of study tours that include language, cuisine, history and sports. Second language speakers are employed on an ad hoc basis and are contacted when the tours arise. Main duties include accompanying the group throughout the tour, liaising with the party leader, ensuring pre-booked visits run smoothly, assisting the groups with interpreting, and taking part in evening entertainment
Wages and Benefits: Salary available on application plus full-board accommodation, transport, travel expenses, and medical insurance
Accommodation: Provided at the resort
Application Procedure: Email a CV and cover letter to Sue Lloyd at the above email address

World Challenge Expeditions: Expedition Leaders

Duration: 1–4 weeks
Location: UK and worldwide
Season: Mostly July/August but some
expeditions are available year round
Prerequisites: For UK expeditions
participants must have taken a training

☎ 08704 873173
🖰 leaderinfo@world-challenge.co.uk
💻 www.world-challenge.co.uk/leader.asp

course and be aged 21 or over. For overseas expeditions participants need training,
experience of working with 14–18-year-olds and should be aged 24 or over
Organisation: World Challenge runs expeditions and adventure activities in the UK
and overseas. All expeditions and activities are designed to enable education through
exploration and to raise motivation in young people through developing skills in
leadership, team building, and problem solving
Description: World Challenge expedition leaders ensure the safety and success of
individual expeditions and programmes and lead groups of young people to exciting
destinations. WC takes on leaders on a per expedition basis, but once you are on the
books you may be invited back
Wages and Benefits: Competitive rates of pay, rewarding developmental work, all
expenses paid travel and comprehensive back-up and support
Accommodation: Varies according to expedition
Application Procedure: World Challenge has a fairly rigorous selection procedure. All
potential leaders must pass a free Potential Leader Training and Assessment Course.
Recruitment begins in February for summer positions

Sport & Educational Travel: Couriers

Duration: 1 day – 1 week
Location: France, Germany, Belgium and Spain
Season: Year round
Prerequisites: Fluency in one or more languages relevant
to the destination

☎ 01502 567914
🖰 info@set-uk.com
💻 www.set-uk.com

Organisation: SET organises group travel for school
parties with students aged between 11 and 17 years old
Description: SET runs a range of school trips and holidays from visits to Disneyland
to World War I and II tours. Couriers are needed to accompany the groups, to provide
factual information during the trip in both English and the local language as well as
managing checking-in procedures, and visits throughout the trip. Full training is provided
Wages and Benefits: Couriers receive from £100 for a day trip. On longer trips
wages are from £100 for the first day and from £60 for each subsequent day. Travel,
accommodation and food are provided
Accommodation: Varies according to trip but always provided
Application Procedure: Applications are accepted at any time in writing to Mr G.
Bishop, managing director, 3 Dukes Head Street, Lowestoft, Suffolk NR32 1JY

ASSISTING GROUPS ON HOLIDAY

SPORTS, HOLIDAYS & FESTIVALS

The 3H Fund: Holiday Volunteers

Duration: 1 week
Location: Throughout the UK and Europe
Season: May – September
Prerequisites: A caring nature, motivation and the ability to cooperate as a team member. No experience required

☎ 01892 547474
✉ info@3hfund.org.uk
💻 www.3hfund.org.uk

Organisation: Charity that makes it possible for disabled people, children and adults, to have memorable and fulfilling holidays and giving a period of respite to their carers
Description: Each year, the 3H Fund plans a range of subsidised group holidays for physically disabled people and recruits around 90 volunteer carers to provide help and support. Each holiday has two experienced leaders and a nurse who advise volunteers. Participants are matched with a guest depending on their level of experience. Practical training is given during each holiday to ensure an enjoyable holiday for all
Accommodation: Provided in venues such as holiday centres and hotels
Cost: Volunteers are requested to provide a financial contribution towards board and lodging. Advice can be given on raising sponsorship

Badaguish Outdoor Centre: Holiday Volunteers

Duration: 1–4 weeks
Location: Aviemore, UK
Season: April – October
Prerequisites: Must enjoy the outdoors and take part in all activities offered. No qualifications required
Organisation: Centre run by the Speyside Trust

☎ 01479 861285
✉ info@badaguish.org
💻 www.badaguish.org

specialising in outdoor recreation holidays for children and adults with learning and multiple disabilities
Description: Visitors to the centre enjoy various adventure activities and 24–hour respite care in a spectacular setting. Volunteers are required as assistants to the group leaders to help in all aspects of the camp such as direct care, activities on and off-site, general upkeep of centre facilities, and domestic duties. Volunteers work five days per week
Benefits: £30 pocket money per week, full board and accommodation
Accommodation: Provided on-site in caravans and chalets. Volunteers may have to share
Application Procedure: Apply online from January

BYV Adventure Camps: Holiday Volunteers

Duration: A weekend or a full week
Location: Residential centres and
campsites throughout the UK
Season: Weekend holidays run year round.
Week-long holidays only run in the summer
Prerequisites: Ages 17–40; CRB check. No
experience required. Experience of work with children preferred

☎ 0121 622 2888
🖰 adventurecamps@btconnect.com
💻 www.byadventurecamps.co.uk

Organisation: Charity running holidays for more than 200 of Birmingham's
disadvantaged children each year
Description: Around 140 volunteers are required each year to accompany children on
activity holidays. Holidays for younger children (aged five to 10) take place in a variety of
residential centres and volunteers help to supervise activities such as environmental trails,
arts and crafts, barbecues, walks, farm and safari park visits and swimming. Holidays for
older children are much more challenging. They provide new opportunities to allow the
children to discover the challenges of outdoor life such as raft building, gorge walking,
abseiling, mountain biking, caving, crabbing and rock climbing. Volunteers bring skills and
strengths which ensure a successful holiday for the children
Accommodation: Board and lodging provided at residential centres
Costs: Volunteers are asked to raise a minimum sponsorship of £25 to go towards food,
accommodation and treats for the kids
Application Procedure: Regular new volunteer weekends are run to help potential
applicants get a taste of an adventure camp. Download an application form online

Children's Country Holidays Fund (CCHF)

Duration: A weekend or a full week
Location: Stafford House, UK (www.
staffordhouse.org.uk)
Season: Activity weekends run year round.
Longer holidays run during the school holidays
Prerequisites: Min. age 18; UK residents only;

☎ 01273–847772
🖰 nyawa@childrensholidays.org.uk
💻 www.childrensholidays.org.uk

CRB check required. Participants must be able to relate to and motivate children and young
people, develop professional relationships and set clear boundaries with children, enjoy
working as part of a team, organised, energetic, and a positive role model for young children
Organisation: Charity established in 1884 dedicated to giving disadvantaged children
from London and the surrounding areas a range of holidays to help improve their lives and
achieve personal goals in a safe environment
Description: CCHF provides holidays in the countryside for children aged seven to 12 years,
who would otherwise have no chance of a holiday. Volunteers help children to learn to see
themselves in a new way, discover their strengths and skills through having fun. Volunteers
are also responsible, within a group, for the care and welfare of the children. Volunteers
choose the amount of weeks/weekends they volunteer. High quality training is provided
Accommodation: Board and lodging are provided at Stafford House
Application Procedure: Applications should be made between January and May.
Visit the website for further details

The Disaway Trust: Holiday Helpers

Duration: 8–14 days
Location: UK and Europe
Season: May – October
Prerequisites: Min. age 18. Helpers must be reasonably fit and strong. Every applicant is required to complete a medical form.

☎ 01903 830796
🖱 nickigreen@sunni.freeserve.co.uk
💻 www.disaway.co.uk

Organisation: Charity that organises group holidays with physically disabled people
Description: Disaway relies on voluntary help to provide disabled people with holidays. Each helper is asked to look after the needs of one disabled holidaymaker. It is the helper's responsibility to ensure that the holidaymaker gains the maximum enjoyment from the holiday. Inexperienced helpers are allocated with someone needing minimal care. Supervisors provide help, advice, guidance and support
Accommodation: Varies according to the type of holiday
Cost: Volunteers pay approximately half the cost of travel, accommodation, board and entertainment. The other half is fundraised by the trust
Application Procedure: Information about the year's holidays are available online from January. Applications should be made to Nicki Green, 51 Sunningdale Road, Worthing, West Sussex BN13 2NQ

Woodlarks Camp Site: Holiday Volunteers

Duration: 1 week
Location: Near Farnham, Surrey, UK
Season: May – September
Prerequisites: Min. age 16, police check. Participants must be prepared to get their hands dirty and join in

☎ 01252 716279
🖱 nickandsarah@woodlarks.org.uk
💻 www.woodlarks.org.uk

Organisation: The campsite is run by Woodlarks Camp Site Trust and provides a setting for people of all ages with disabilities to expand their capabilities and have fun.
Description: Volunteers are required to help out with general duties such as cleaning and preparing food, as well as working one-on-one with a disabled person looking after their needs and making sure they have a great time. The camps involve activities and excursions including archery, cricket, volleyball, trampolining and nature walks. Inexperienced helpers are provided with support and advice from those with more experience. Around seven or eight camps need helpers each year
Accommodation: Provided in tents on a site with full facilities and an indoor dining/leisure area. Volunteers help to prepare food for the group
Costs: Volunteers pay a registration fee of £16 plus a minimal camp fee to cover accommodation, food and outings. Total all inclusive cost is approx. £75 for the week
Application Procedure: Apply in January/February for the summer season to The Hon. Secretary/Warden, Nick and Sarah, Kathleen Marshall House, Woodlarks Campsite, Tilford Road, Farnham, Surrey GU10 3RN

Vitalise: Sighted Guides

Duration: 1 or 2 weeks
Location: Austria, France, Canada, Italy, Finland
Season: February half-term and Easter only
Prerequisites: Communication skills, patience, understanding, enthusiasm and a sense of humour
Organisation: Vitalise is a national charity that provides holidays for visually impaired people

☎ 0845 330 0149
✎ volunteer@vitalise.org.uk
💻 www.vitalise.org.uk

Description: Sighted guides are an essential part of Vitalise Holidays, making the difference between a visually impaired person having a much needed break or no holiday at all. Guides provide sighted assistance, and explain surroundings on a one-to-one basis. Guiding can be demanding, but first-time guides receive plenty of help and advice. Participants are expected to guide throughout the holiday from meeting the group until departure
Accommodation: Provided in hotels and inns
Cost: Depends on type, location and duration of holiday. Prices are subsidised for guides. From around £200 – £1,200. Accommodation and travel included

A Vitalise leader directs a walking group in the Yorkshire Dales.

WORKING FOR YOUR TICKET AT SUMMER FESTIVALS

Festival-going has been growing sharply in recent years, but at the time of writing, music industry insiders claim that the demand for tickets and new events is unprecedented. In the UK alone as many as 450 large and small festivals take place each year, yet even this doesn't satisfy the appetite of music lovers. Such was the demand for tickets to Glastonbury Festival in 2007, that organisers extended the festival's capacity from 150,000 to 177,500, the biggest legal attendance it has ever had. But even this failed to come close to satisfying demand: over double this number had pre-registered for tickets. Similarly T in the Park, Scotland's biggest annual music festival expanded from two days to three, with increased capacity. And the Irish festival, Oxegen, sold all of its tickets within an hour, with promoters claiming that they could have sold out three times over.

Away from the bigger rock festivals, there has also been a boom in smaller events. All Tomorrow's Parties, the line-up of which is curated each year by a different artist, moved from a small holiday camp in East Sussex, to Butlins in 2007, doubling capacity to 6,000. According to Paul Stokes, news editor of the *NME* (speaking in *The Guardian*), *'It is a total boom time for festivals. They are as much a part of the summer now [for young people] as going on a Club 18–30 holiday'*. In fact many young people are combining festivals with a holiday, by attending one of the thousands of festivals abroad such as Roskilde in Denmark and Benicasim in Spain.

As demand increases for all of these events, so too does the price. Top end festival tickets sell for around £150 for the weekend. It has also become increasingly difficult to obtain tickets due to vast competition from other desperate music fans, and a new breed of internet ticket tout, bulk buying tickets and selling them on at vastly inflated prices. While Glastonbury has gone some way to stamping out the touts, the rest of the festival circuit is slow to catch up and each year thousands of music fans are left disappointed, or forced to pay over the odds for their tickets.

There is an alternative. Each year hundreds of enterprising individuals gain entry to sold out festivals without paying a penny, by volunteering their services. Glastonbury godfather, Michael Eavis, has been at the forefront of encouraging people to get involved in the countless volunteering opportunities at festivals, stating:

Volunteers are vital to the running of the festivals. They help with lost children, picking up litter, stewarding on the gates and countless other things. Most of the doctors and nurses, social and welfare workers are also volunteers. All of these people have an essential role caring for the needs of the hundreds of thousands of people who flood through the gates.

Clearly volunteers are required to work quite hard, but in return, they receive ample time each day to enjoy the festival atmosphere and see their favourite bands. In the majority of cases, volunteers are also provided with a separate camping area (which tends to be far cleaner and less crowded than the public camping areas), warm showers and meal passes. Those of you who have spent a festival weekend wallowing in mud, unable to wash properly, and paying £5 for a sandwich, will see that working at a festival offers quite a good deal.

In the UK, many of the festivals rely on the charity Oxfam to provide a range of work in roles such as wristband exchange, stewarding, and general running of even. return, Oxfam receives a large donation from the event, helping to support its efforts in a wide range of charity projects. So by working at a UK festival, volunteers not only gain free entry and a comparatively luxurious experience, but they also help to raise money for charity.

Listed below are just some of the festival work opportunities around the world. All festivals require huge numbers of staff, so it is always worthwhile contacting the organisers directly to find out exactly what might be available. Remember that competition for festival jobs, whether paid or unpaid, is fierce and you are well advised to start investigating the possibilities up to nine months in advance.

MUSIC FESTIVALS IN THE UK

It is beyond the scope of this book to list all of the 450 or so music festivals that take place across the UK each summer. If you are interested in attending a specific festival and working behind the scenes, then it is always worth contacting the organisers directly, giving them plenty of notice. Generally staff for festivals are organised locally, so keep an eye on the local papers if you happen to live near a local site. Nevertheless, the organisations listed below work across a range of festivals and offer the chance to gain a free ticket, in exchange for a few shifts.

Oxfam

The Festivals: Oxfam's portfolio of festivals increases every year. In 2007 the charity provided stewarding services for Wychwood, Glastonbury, Cornbury, Latitude, The Glade, WOMAD, Summer Sundae, Green Man, Reading, Leeds, and End of the Road. Oxfam takes on around 4,000 volunteers each year spread across the festivals. For example, around 100 are taken on for the smaller Summer Sundae weekender in Leicester, whereas over 1,700 stewards are required for Glastonbury each year

☎ 0870 010 8553

📧 stewards@oxfam.org.uk

💻 www.oxfam.org.uk/stewards

The Work: Stewards are required to work three shifts of eight hours during the course of the festival. Usually each volunteer will work a morning shift, an afternoon/evening shift and a night shift. Volunteers are expected to arrive on the Wednesday or Thursday before the festival starts and most shifts end on the Sunday evening. Stewarding duties vary according to festival, but can involve working on the gates, directing traffic, checking tickets, meeting and greeting festival-goers, fielding questions about the site and giving directions. On-site stewarding is more of a safety role. Volunteers keep fire lanes clear of tents, staff fire towers, and watch out for fires, thefts and disturbances. Stewards are not involved in security work or crowd control.

At some festivals, stewards are also responsible for car parking, directing cars to their allocated parking space and guiding them in. Oxfam also takes on supervisors, whose role is to lead a team ranging from five to 35 people. Supervisors are selected from experienced former stewards

The Rewards: Oxfam stewards are provided with free entry to the festival, a separate place to camp (away from the public campsites), meal tickets, toilets and showers. Oxfam also provides transport to festivals where possible or necessary due to poor access by public transport. Participants can apply with their friends and ask to work the same shifts, and camp together. There are some opportunities for stewards to swap shifts among themselves to enable them to see their favourite bands

The Requirements: Participants must be 18 years old or over, fairly fit (able to stand for up to eight hours if required), and they should enjoy interacting with the public. They should bring their own tents and camping equipment (campervans are also acceptable), as well as suitable clothing for both extremes of weather

The Application Procedure: Oxfam begins recruiting for the summer season from 12 February each year for former stewards and from 12 March for new recruits. Applications are accepted up until the date of the festival, or until the target number of stewards have been recruited. Any application supported by a reliable referee will be considered. However, because of the level of demand for Glastonbury positions, preference is given to Oxfam supporters and former volunteers. Application forms can be found online (www. oxfam.org.uk/stewards)

Application forms should be accompanied by a deposit cheque. In 2007 the required deposit is £155, which is held in a holding account until the steward has completed all of their shifts. Assuming that all shifts are completed, the deposit is returned approximately one month after the festival has finished. Participants attending more than one festival only need pay the deposit once

Oxfam volunteers stewarding a busy Sunday morning yoga session at WOMAD.

Peppermint Bars

About: Peppermint Bars is a trading division of Peppermint Events Ltd, specialising in providing temporary cash bars for festivals and other large outdoor events

☎ 0845 226 7845

🖰 info@peppermintbars.co.uk

💻 www.peppermintbars.co.uk/jobs

The Festivals: Peppermint runs bars at a number of events including Bestival, Glad Festival, Lovebox, Secret Garden Festival, Kent Music Festival and many more

The Work: Volunteers are required to work two shifts of six to eight hours each per event. The responsibilities change from shift to shift but include: frontline bar staff, backline bar staff (making sure that drinks, cups, and bottles do not run out), building crew, litter pickers, and catering assistants (serving the bar crew)

The Rewards: Volunteer staff receive a free entry ticket, crew camping, plus a free meal and two free drinks per shift

The Requirements: Min. age 18. Experience is preferred, but not essential. Staff must bring photo ID, warm clothing and waterproofs and their own tent and bedding

The Application Procedure: Applicants fill out a form online at any time of the year. Peppermint will then contact them for voluntary work approximately two months (no later than one month) before the event to confirm availability

The Workers Beer Company

About: The Workers Beer Company is a fundraising arm of the labour and trade union movement, giving support to the campaigning and solidarity work of grassroots organisations. WBC raises money by running beer tents and bars at festivals

☎ 0207 720 0140

🖰 info@workersbeer.co.uk

💻 www.workersbeer.co.uk

The Festivals: In 2007 WBC sent bar staff to Latitude, The Tolpuddle Martyrs Festival (Dorset), Leeds, Reading, Glastonbury, and the Metro Weekender (Clapham Common)

The Work: Volunteers are required to serve drinks and tend bar for a six-hour shift each day. Team leaders are also required to manage teams of bar staff and keep records of the hours that each person has worked

The Rewards: WBC volunteers are provided with free entry to the event, two free drinks per person per shift, and when they are not working they can enjoy the music and atmosphere of the festival. They also have access to an enclosed, secure village area where WBC staff camp overnight. The village area has hot showers, a catering tent and a subsidised bar

The Requirements: Volunteers must be aged 18–27 and a member of PCS – the Public and Commercial Services Union (one of the UK's largest trade unions). Volunteers should bring their own tents and camping equipment

The Application Procedure: Download an application form at www.pcs.org.uk and email it to tracy@pcs.org.uk. The application period begins in February each year

Event Recycling

About: Network Recycling undertakes all aspects of event waste management, minimising the environmental impact of festivals and other events. It provides and services recycling points for litter control, carries out street cleaning, organises trade

☎ 0117 944 5883

✉ events@networkrecycling.co.uk

🖥 www.eventrecycling.co.uk

recycling and works to ensure that all disposables vended on-site are biodegradable

The Festivals: Event Recycling works at a variety of festivals from June to September. Keep an eye on the website for forthcoming events. ER have worked at many major festivals in the past including Glastonbury and Bestival (Isle of Wight)

The Work: Several voluntary positions are available including team leaders (a responsible position requiring confidence and previous experience), drivers, litter pickers and general crew. General work includes waste handling, and loading equipment. The work is hard, messy and often at anti-social hours

The Rewards: Festival entrance plus separate camping area with toilet and washing facilities, plus catering wherever possible

The Requirements: Volunteers must be 18 or over, be hard-working and motivated

The Application Procedure: Check the Work for us section of the website for regular updates and information on how to apply for individual events. Alternatively apply speculatively at any time at www.eventrecycling.co.uk/workForUs.html

Festive Lizards

The Festivals: Festive Lizards works with Glastonbury Festival

The Work: Working for Festive Lizards at Glastonbury varies from car park stewarding to working in the coach park, ensuring that people get off and on the buses safely.

☎ 0845 3987 151

✉ festivelizards@ukonline.co.uk

🖥 www.festivelizards.co.uk

Volunteers are required to work 25.5 hours in total, split into three 8.5 hour shifts over one week (Tuesday to Tuesday)

The Rewards: Festive Lizards workers gain free entry to the festival plus plenty of time to enjoy the music and atmosphere that Glastonbury has to offer. Volunteers camp in a separate enclosure

The Requirements: Volunteers must be honest, hard-working individuals aged 18 or over

The Application Procedure: Enquire online from January. Once your enquiry is received, you will be emailed an application form, which must be returned with four passport photos and a deposit of £200. The deposit is returned on completion of all three shifts

Samaritans – Festival Branch

The Festivals: Varies from year to year. Recent festivals have included HiFi, Download, T in the Park, Guildfest, Wickerman Festival, The Big Chill, V Festival, Carling Weekend and Bestival

☎ 020 8391 0754
✍ recruit@festivalsamaritans.org
💻 www.samaritans.org/~festival/index.html

The Work: Volunteers are trained to provide a non-judgmental listening service throughout the event and visitors can discuss anything that is getting them down, no matter how trivial. Samaritans finds that many people who would never consider phoning or visiting a local branch, seem more comfortable speaking to them at these events

The Rewards: Entrance to three festivals during the season, plus travel expenses

The Requirements: Anyone can apply to become a Samaritan with the Festival Branch, even if they have never been a Samaritan before. Volunteers are selected and trained. They are people of all ages, professions and beliefs. Volunteers must attend a preparation weekend in April, one in May, the AGM in November, and they must also work at three events during the season

The Application Procedure: Applications can be made throughout the year (to the telephone number or email above), but selections are made in December for the following festival season. The process of selection includes filling in a form and attending a selection weekend (usually in March)

Campsite Assistant Teams

The Festivals: Carling Weekend Reading; Carling Weekend Leeds

✍ cats@dcsiteservices.com
💻 www.dcsiteservices.com/CATs/

The Work: Volunteers are expected to work three shifts of eight hours each at any time between 4pm Wednesday and 4pm Monday. Typical duties of a volunteer include assisting festival goers with directions, helping them carry their belongings and pitch tents, reporting back on any problems in the campsites

The Rewards: In return for their efforts, all volunteers are provided with a festival pass, pack and uniform, a secure camping area, and access to the crew café, bar, toilets, and hot showers. Volunteers are welcome to enjoy the festival when off-duty

The Requirements: Volunteers must be 18 or over, be able to supply photo ID on arrival, be available to arrive at the festival on the Wednesday prior to the event. Whilst on duty they should wear a CAT uniform, report in every two hours to the area supervisor. A deposit is required

The Application Procedure: Volunteers should join the CAT mailing list online to inform them each year when the application goes online. Applications are usually online between February and March each year. Applications can be made online, via post or fax. Deposits need to be paid after the application and will be returned the following October

Environmental Health Monitors (Mean Fiddler)

The Festivals: Carling Weekend Leeds

The Work: Volunteers are required by Mean Fiddler to monitor sanitation at the Leeds festival. This may include inspecting campsites, toilet blocks, water points and hand-washing facilities

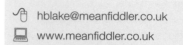

hblake@meanfiddler.co.uk

www.meanfiddler.co.uk

to check that they are working and that there is no build up of litter. Volunteers are not expected to do anything other than report back on these issues regularly. Volunteers work three eight–hour shifts or six four–hour shifts, reporting in every two hours

The Rewards: Volunteers receive free entrance to the festival and camping facilities in a separate area with toilets and hot showers

The Requirements: Volunteers must be 18 or over and able to provide a returnable deposit cheque for approx. £145.

The Application Procedure: Apply to Harmony Blake at the above email address from February

Vitalise: Sighted Guides

The Festivals: Varies each year. In 2007 Vitalise went to Glastonbury

The Work: Vitalise is a national charity that provides holidays for visually impaired people. Sighted guides provide assistance at festivals to the visually impaired and explain surroundings on a one-to-one basis.

☎ 0845 330 014

volunteer@vitalise.org.uk

www.vitalise.org.uk

Guiding can be demanding, but first-time guides receive plenty of help and advice. Participants are expected to guide throughout the festival from meeting the group until departure

The Rewards: Transfers from/to the festival. Guides do however have to pay a contribution towards the ticket cost

The Requirements: Communication skills, patience, understanding, enthusiasm and a sense of humour

The Application Procedure: Check the Vitalise website in January/February to see which festivals are available and for details on how to apply

Paid Festival Work

Opportunities for paid work at festivals do exist, but they are not so plentiful. Often stall-holders will require assistants to work on a shift basis, as will caterers and the many bars dotted around festival sites. However, paid work at a festival tends not to offer so much free time, and it can be extremely frustrating being within the festival grounds, but unable to enjoy the music. Nevertheless, those looking for paid short-term festival and events work, should investigate the following contractors and recruitment companies:

Peppermint Bars (www.peppermintbars.co.uk/jobs). As well as voluntary positions, Peppermint also directly employs skilled staff, 'as and when required' for weekend and evening work. Positions include bartenders, breakdown crew, cellar managers, cashiers, promotional work, and door ticket sales. Camping accommodation is provided at festivals only. Applicants must be over 18 and preferably have experience of bar work.

DC Site Services (www.dcsiteservices.com). DCSS provides services to a huge number of festivals each year including Glastonbury, Download, Wireless, T in the Park, Reading, Leeds, Latitude and The Big Chill. Paid staff are taken on per festival to work eight to 12 hour shifts every day of the festival. Most of the work is litter picking, safety stewarding and traffic management. Wages are set at the national minimum. Apply online from February.

Flair Events (www.eventstaffing.co.uk). Flair provides services to the V Festival and T in the Park among others. Staff are required on a per festival/event basis to work alongside permanent staff. To apply for a position email job@eventstaffing.co.uk, indicating which event is of interest.

Rock Steady (www.rocksteady.co.uk). Rock Steady supplies events services personnel to sports/music events and festivals such as Download. It recruits stewards for festivals and events to provide assistance and safety advice to the public. Stewards work fairly long hours during festivals and rates of pay are dependent on the event. Apply online at any time.

Ryan's Cleaning Services (www.ryanscleanup.ie/vacancies.html). RCS is Ireland's largest outdoor event cleaning company. Staff are provided for sporting events and major music festivals, including Oxegen and V festival. It employs 500+ litter pickers to work during the summer months. Staff must be over 18, self-motivated and hard working. Good rates of pay, free entry to events, secure campsite and transport provided. Apply online at any time.

SEP Events (www.sepevents.co.uk/jobs.asp). SEP specialises in event car parking, traffic management, admissions and ticket sales at outdoor events. Previous festivals include Bestival, Creamfields, Download, Isle of Wight, Rockness, T in the Park, V Festivals, and WOMAD. Staff are recruited on a per event basis or for the entire summer season. Apply online.

Cash and Traffic Management (www.cashandtrafficmanagement.com). CTM provides services to the events, sports, leisure and entertainment industry. Client festivals include the V Festival, and Reading. Pay rates range from £5.78–£10 per hour. Register your details online.

Literally hundreds of folk festivals take place across the UK from around April right through to October. A full UK folk festival calendar can be found at www.folkandroots. co.uk/festivals.html. Below are just a few that annually recruit for volunteer stewards:

Towersey Village Festival

Currently in its 43rd year, Towersey Village Festival annually recruits volunteer stewards to get involved in administration, ticket checking, traffic control, venue management, helping to keep the site clean and tidy, and looking after visitors. Regular volunteers return year after

Where: Towersey, near Thame, Oxfordshire
When: August
www.towerseyfestival.com

year, but the festival is always on the look out for new recruits. In return for their efforts, stewards receive a full weekend pass with camping. Volunteers must be aged 18 or over, reliable, committed to being part of a team, prepared to work around 16 hours before or during the festival and available from the Thursday before the August bank holiday weekend

Sidmouth Folk Week

Sidmouth, which takes place annually during the first week of August, recruits volunteer stewards each year to work behind the scenes in a range of roles including stage management, technical, cash handling, building

Where: Sidmouth, Devon
When: August
www.sidmouthfolkweek.co.uk

and maintenance, first aid (qualified only), management and administration. Stewards must be available to work five hours per day while at the festival in return for which they receive a full Folk Week season ticket plus free camping (worth £175). Stewards must be aged over 18. The application form can be found online from around March

Broadstairs Folk Week

Broadstairs Folk Week takes on an extensive volunteer workforce each year of around 150 people. Volunteers can choose from campsite duties, stage management, door staff, children's events, lottery,

Where: Broadstairs, Kent
When: August
www.broadstairsfolkweek.org.uk

technical team, administration, minibus driver, or any of the above. In return for 35 hours' work, volunteers receive entrance to all of the events and free camping. Participants must be over 18. Application forms can be downloaded as a pdf online. For further queries email workforce@broadstairsfolkweek.org.uk

Chester Folk Festival

Chester Folk Festival annually recruits stewards to help with checking tickets and regulating the campsite during the weekend. Stewards are asked to do 10–12 hours' duty throughout the weekend. Duties are on a rota basis on one of the venue doors or the campsite gate, plus other tasks which may arise. In return, helpers receive a free weekend ticket for the festival. Apply online at the above address, or email stewards@chesterfolk.org.uk for further details

Where: Chester
When: May
💻 www.chesterfolk.org.uk/stewards.htm

Priddy Folk Festival

A number of volunteer stewards provide back-up to the folk festival committee on the days of the festival. The main areas in which volunteers work are site crew team, venue team, festival office team, car parking team, camping team and first aid (must be a certified first aider). In return for four hour stints of duty, volunteers receive a full weekend ticket and free camping. For further information email stewards@priddyfolk.org

Where: Priddy, Somerset
When: July
💻 www.priddyfolk.org/web/stewards.htm

LITERARY FESTIVALS IN THE UK

Music festivals may not be to everyone's taste. If you like your culture a little more highbrow then volunteering your services at a literary festival might be for you. These festivals give members of the public the opportunity to quiz their favourite authors, attend workshops and generally broaden their literary horizons. The main literary festival seasons are spring to early summer, and the autumn. Information on how to work at the best known of these festivals is detailed below, but there are many other smaller festivals that require interested parties to volunteer their services.

Edinburgh International Book Festival

100 temporary staff are taken on during the festival (in August) to work in the box office. Staff are required to work 48 hours a week during the festival (18 days) and are paid at the rate of approx. £5.40 per hour. Interviews take place in May and June. To apply download the online application form and post it to: Box JA, 5A Charlotte Square, Edinburgh EH2 4DR

💻 www.edbookfest.co.uk

The Guardian Hay Festival

The Hay festival takes on around 150 volunteer festival stewards to make sure that authors and members of the public are safe and happy before,

(Hay on Wye, Wales)

www.hayfestival.com/wales/jobs.aspx

during and after each event. Shifts are for three to four hours per day and all festial events are stewarded by teams of between four and 10. Stewards receive free entry to any talk and accommodation at a local campsite. There are also paid positions available. Apply online from January onwards

The Times Cheltenham Festival Of Literature

Around 25 festival volunteers are taken on to look after authors and audience as well as helping

www.cheltenhamfestivals.com

to set up events, front of house duties, looking after the office and assisting the sound crew. Volunteers work for 10 days during the festival (in October). Applicants should be over 18, preferably graduates with an interest in literature, arts administration or events management. Volunteers receive free accommodation, travel expenses, food and drink and free entry to events. Visit the website from May for details of how to apply

The Sunday Times Oxford Literary Festival

Volunteer stewards are recruited annually for the Oxford Literary Festival held in March. Stewards

www.sundaytimes-oxfordliteraryfestival.co.uk

help to ensure that events run smoothly and in return gain free entrance to events. The days are split into three shifts and participants must be able to offer a minimum of three shifts over the week. Those interested should email their name and address and a covering letter to info@sundaytimes-oxfordliteraryfestival.co.uk at any time of the year. Festival organisers will be in touch when the recruitment process begins

There are thousands of festivals worldwide, but many choose to subcontract the work, or will only accept local volunteers. Listed below are various rock festivals that actively recruit volunteers or workers to help with a variety of tasks such as litter picking, entrance control, backstage tasks, traffic directing, and so on, usually in return for a festival ticket and a place to pitch your tent.

Big Day Out

About: BDO is an annual festival that tours Australia and New Zealand. It features seven or eight stages accommodating popular contemporary rock and electronic music from mainstream international and local acts

www.bigdayout.com

When: Approx 19 Jan – 4 Feb

Where: Australia and New Zealand (2007 locations were Auckland, Gold Coast, Sydney, Melbourne, Adelaide, Perth)

The Work: Volunteers are required to work a six-hour shift during the show to assist with crowd care, act as a mobile information source and keep an eye out for anyone needing assistance. Volunteers must be aged over 18 and having a first aid certificate is an advantage. Volunteers must be able to attend a training and information session before the event

How/When to Apply: Prospective volunteers will find all the information they need online. Each festival location has a separate volunteer coordinator to contact. Check the website from July

Coachella Valley Music And Arts Festival

About: Three-day festival approximately the same size as the Reading Festival with a tradition for booking some of the world's biggest bands. Coachella is located in a polo field in the middle of the desert, flanked by rows of palm trees

info@coachella.com

www.coachella.com

When: Approx. 27 – 29 April

Where: California, USA

The Work: Volunteers are required but are employed on an ad-hoc basis throughout the year and during the festival itself. Volunteers who work during the festival receive free entry

How/When to Apply: Keep an eye on the website for announcements from late November onwards

Exit Festival

About: This festival began life as an artistic antidote to the Milosevic regime and has grown into one of Europe's most vibrant musical celebrations. It takes place in the grounds of a citadel and attracts mainstream rock, indie and hip hop artists

💻 www.exitfest.org

When: Approx. 12–15 July

Where: Near to Novi Sad, Serbia

The Work: During the festival, Exit organisers employ around 1,500 workers and volunteers to work as bartenders, promoters, security, stewards and so on. Most of the volunteers are Serbian students, but a growing number of volunteers from all over Europe attends each year in return for a ticket

How/When to Apply: Those interested in volunteering should keep an eye on the website from March each year when further details about volunteering are made available

FIB – Festival Internacional de Benicassim

About: Europe's hottest summer music festival, set by the beach, boasting some of the biggest names in indie and electronic music

💻 www.fiberfib.com

When: Approx. 19–22 July

Where: Benicassim (Valencia), Spain

The Work: Volunteers are required for anything up to a month in July and August and particularly during the festival to work in a variety of roles. In return, volunteers receive entrance to the festival, insurance and meals during their shifts. Paid catering positions are also available

How/When to Apply: Those interested in volunteering should fill in the online application form (available only in Spanish – click on trabajo) at any time after January. Catering positions are advertised online one month before the festival begins

Hultsfred Festival

About: Hultfsred is the largest and longest running youth-oriented music festival in Sweden, with seven stages, set in a picturesque forest glade

🖱 info@rockparty.se
💻 www.rockparty.se

When: Approx. 14–16 June

Where: Hultsfred, Sweden

The Work: Non-profit organisation, Rockparty, takes on around 5,000 volunteers each year, with around 4,750 of them (Funktionärer) working only during the festival. In return for general duties around the site, volunteers receive a free ticket to the festival, a uniform, and free meals during the days they are working

How/When to Apply: Volunteers apply all year round to the above email address, but according to organisers, all volunteer places are taken by February. Volunteers should therefore send a CV and covering letter expressing their interest by January

Les Eurockeenes de Belfort

About: Situated among lakes and mountains in the east of France, Eurockeenes is a three-day festival, with four stages and capacity for around 90,000 people

www.eurockeennes.com

When: First weekend of July

Where: Franche-Comté region, France

The Work: Workers are required before, during and after the festival for paid roles including ticket sales (3 days), access control (3–5 days), electrical work (8–15 days), Building and taking down festival structures such as marquees and barriers (8–15 days), cleaning (3–15 days)

How/When to Apply: Information is available on the website from February/March onwards. It is likely that potential candidates will need to apply via the local employment agency (ANPE) in Belfort (tel. +33 (0)3 84 58 75 30) from early April

Roskilde Festival

About: Roskilde is the largest music festival in Northern Europe and has been running since 1971 (the same year as Glastonbury). It is a non-profit festival with a humanitarian focus

jobs@roskilde-festival.dk
www.roskilde-festival.dk

When: Approx. 5–8 July

Where: 35km from Copenhagan, Denmark

The Work: During the festival, Roskilde takes on around 60 volunteers from all over Europe at the annual Work Camp. According to organisers, 'Work Camp is a combination of volunteer work, cultural contact and a feeling of community'. Volunteers work for around 100 hours over 12 days in different areas of the festival. As a reward volunteers receive a ticket to the festival, a place to camp and three meals a day. There are also social events and a field trip organised

Other voluntary positions are available before, during and after the festival. As an example, humantohuman employs over 700 refuse collectors who help to raise money for various charities

How/When to Apply: Fill in a form on the website (in English) from around 26 March to 16 April each year

Pinkpop

About: Holland's most famous open-air festival, currently in its 38th year, presents more than 30 bands on three stages, across three days in May

info@pinkpop.nl
www.pinkpop.nl

When: Approx. 26 – 28 May

Where: Landgraaf, the Netherlands

The Work: According to organisers, Pinkpop takes on more than 1000 volunteers for the duration of the festival, for bar, backstage, catering, entrance and stewarding work. Some volunteers are provided via local venues, but others are recruited internationally. All volunteers work at least an eight hour shift on one day, with the rest of the time free to enjoy the festival

How/When to Apply: Information about volunteering appears on the website at least six months in advance of the festival

South by South West

About: SXSW is a festival that spreads itself across everything that is cutting edge in music, film and interactive media. There are performances, showcases, seminars, screenings and exhibitions over 50 separate venues in the city

vol@sxsw.com; tammy@sxsw.com
http://2007.sxsw.com/volunteer/

When: Approx 9–18 March

Where: Austin, Texas, USA

The Work: There are two types of volunteer. Conference crew operate throughout all 10 days of the festival and their responsibilities include registration, trade show conference access, staff transportation and hospitality. Music Production crews operate from Wednesday to Sunday during the music festival, from 6pm-2am each night. Volunteers must be aged 21 or over. In return for their work, volunteers receive free wrist passes

How/When to Apply: Prospective volunteers must create a record in the online volunteer database (see website above). Out-of-town volunteers must contact Tammy Bolton (see email address above) before submitting an application to confirm that they will be in Austin at the appropriate time. Applications must be submitted by the end of January

HANDS-ON Work Experience Abroad

FIND YOUR TRUE CALLING ON HOLIDAY

Work experience is the fastest growing sector in the world of youth travel today, according to the Global Work Experience Association. This is hardly a surprise. In today's career marketplace competition for the best jobs is at an all time high. An army of graduates is pouring out of the universities and standing out among them is becoming increasingly difficult. It is no longer sufficient to have good grades and a personable demeanour to get the job you want. Today's employers are looking for that little bit extra and how better to demonstrate motivation, initiative and maturity, along with the ability to adapt to challenging environments, than to take a work experience placement abroad?

Of course you could opt for a placement, or internship (as they are increasingly called) closer to home. But if you really want to stand out, an international internship offers not just fantastic experience, but also an adventure, a chance to gain in-depth knowledge of another culture and of yourself, an inexpensive way to improve foreign language proficiency, and preparation for an international career. As businesses become more globally focused, an understanding of different cultures is considered a huge asset, and experience of a *different* working culture will put you way ahead of the game.

However, it's not just the young who are enjoying international work experience. As mentioned previously, the hands-on holiday is a perfect opportunity to re-evaluate your options. At any stage in your career it is easy to feel trapped or to panic that you have chosen a path that's leading nowhere. The best way to alleviate these fears is to take on a work experience placement in your dream job that lasts just a short period of time. This way you don't have to take any momentous decisions such as resigning, before you have tried out the alternatives. Vocation Vocations (see below) has built a very successful business from the knowledge that people might not always be sure that they have taken the right path. Its huge range of work experience placements last from one to three days, so you don't even have to tell your boss. The advantages of taking a placement abroad are that you are still using your holiday time to go away, and there is not the same stigma surrounding work experience abroad as there might be if you were to take an unpaid placement in the UK.

For those already in work, sometimes a work experience placement abroad is simply an efficient way of getting it out of your system. This was what Rachael Muirhead found when she took on one of i-to-i's journalism placements in India:

I really wanted to give journalism a try, but it was never going to be an easy move to make. All my experience was in marketing. On my return I considered my options and decided to go back to marketing books. What I want from a job is creativity and I discovered that journalism is just one career I could choose. I'm glad I tried it out and now I know that marketing was definitely the right choice.

In other cases however, work experience on holiday could lead to a complete change of direction. The one thing to bear in mind is that you'll never know unless you give it a try.

Many of the opportunities listed in this book could be perceived as work experience. Any voluntary work in which an individual becomes immersed in a foreign culture can provide a

WORK EXPERIENCE

fantastic learning opportunity, and can also make a mediocre CV sparkle. The differences between volunteer work and work experience have diminished over the years as both universities and employers have noted the benefits of foreign immersion. Volunteering in a clinic in a developing country for example, provides a valuable service where funding and resources are short. However, it also provides fantastic work experience for a would-be healthcare professional, as due to necessity, the volunteer is likely to be given far more responsibility than they would at a hospital back home. The same could be said for a potential vet, or conservation worker who volunteers on a wildlife project abroad. Volunteers would be the first to tell you that they have learnt from their experience and that the rewards have outweighed the personal sacrifice. Cathleen Graham found a huge overlap between work experience and volunteering when she became a volunteer with the SCORE programme (Sports Coaches Outreach) in South Africa, while pursuing development studies at university:

An opportunity to gain some work experience overseas was a stepping stone towards my longer-term goals. Living and working locally in another culture, language and country for a year would develop some skills relevant to work areas I was interested in: intercultural communication, development project work, sports development. In terms of disadvantages, some people don't see this kind of opportunity as taking steps towards your future, but rather as sidelining it and I sometimes had to deal with people's judgements. I also had to look ahead to when I came back home and try ahead of time, for my peace of mind anyhow, to define the next steps for me and how I would build on this experience.

Nevertheless, the opportunities listed below are more targeted towards gaining experience in a specific field or line of work. Whether you choose to call your international experience work experience or volunteering, one thing is certain: you will end up with insight into another culture that you could never have achieved as a tourist.

Language Ability

Many of the opportunities included here have a language requirement. It is important to ask exactly what level of language ability the business or organisation requires from you and to be realistic about your own capabilities. Ideally if you are taking a work experience placement abroad, you should have a good command of the language – listening, reading, writing and speaking – and be willing to improve upon these skills during your placement.

Part of the appeal of taking a work placement abroad is that it allows you to improve on language skills. If you really want to make inroads in a language, or start from scratch, you should consider combining a work placement with a language course. Many language learning organisations such as Adelante Abroad and Eurolingua (see below) offer internships as part of a package. For example, you could spend two weeks learning at a language school, and then follow it up with a week or two working at a local company. Participants usually find that by putting into practice that which they have just learnt, the language becomes more firmly embedded.

There are placements available that do not have a language requirement, but according to the placement organisation, Global Experiences, participants may find that their tasks are more junior to their own experience level to compensate for the language barrier. In some cases, work experience placements abroad are available in English, especially within companies with close ties to the international marketplace.

Adelante Abroad

Duration: Min. 1 month
Location: Spain, Chile, Uruguay, Costa Rica
Season: Year round
Organisation: Small family-run US-based
business specialising in internships with a language
learning element

☎ +1 562 799 9133
🖱 info@adelanteabroad.com
💻 www.adelanteabroad.com

Type of Work: Placements are available in a huge range of fields including marketing and PR, business, social work, graphic design, IT, photography, film and video, tourism, accounting, law, engineering, journalism, architecture and construction, medical, working at a radio station, working in a winery (Chile)
Description: Adelante's placements combine two or three weeks' intensive language training with an unpaid work placement in an area of interest. Internships are for approximately four hours a day in either a local company or a larger international corporation. Participants gain real international work experience to add to their CV, plus the opportunity to improve a language and several excursions
Accommodation: Provided in shared apartments with other Adelante participants or locals
Cost: From US$1,650 for 1 month including intensive language classes, accommodation and excursions

African Conservation Experience: Game Ranger Guide Course

Duration: 2 weeks
Location: South Africa
Season: February – November
Prerequisites: Min. age 17. No experience required
Organisation: Specialises in volunteer placement
in, and providing financial support and information
exchange for conservation projects in southern Africa

☎ 0870 241 5816
🖱 info@conservationafrica.net
💻 www.conservationafrica.net

Description: This is an introductory course for those who may wish to make a career out of game-ranger guiding. Participants receive tuition in animal identification, ecology, the geology of southern Africa, habits of animals, basic 4x4 driving skills, handling firearms and interpreting wildlife sounds. On top of this they gain practical experience of tracking 'big 5' wildlife, sleeping out in the bushveld and conducting safaris. This course is particularly popular among working people on their annual leave. ACE also runs an advanced course
Recognition: Upon successful completion of the course and a practical and theoretical exam, participants receive a certificate accredited by The Field Guide Association of South Africa
Accommodation: Comfortable accommodation in a bush camp situated in a 'big 5' Game Reserve
Cost: £795 including full professional tuition, accommodation and meals

AVIVA Nature Guiding Course

Duration: 1 month
Location: Kruger National Park, South Africa
Season: Year round (all courses begin on the last day of each month)
Prerequisites: Min. age 18, good level of English. The off-road driving portion of the course requires a valid Photo-ID or international driver's licence
Organisation: Established volunteering company
Description: Participants on the nature guiding course spend 30% of their time in the classroom, and 70% of the time gaining practical hands-on experience, covering a wide range of activities such as wildlife recognition, off-road driving, tracking, bush survival skills, bush walks, day and night safari game drives and anti-poaching control. The course includes weekly exams and practical assessments
Recognition: Successful participants receive a course certificate endorsed by the Field Guides Association of Southern Africa (FGASA) and the Tourism and Hospitality and Sport Education Training Authority (THETA)
Accommodation: Participants live in a purpose-built bush camp overlooking the Kruger National Park
Cost: £1250 including airport collection, transfers, accommodation and meals

☎ +27 21 557 5996
✆ info@aviva-sa.com
💻 www.aviva-sa.com

C.E.I. (Centre d'Echanges Internationaux)

Duration: 2–4 weeks
Location: Brittany, France
Season: Year round
Prerequisites: Aged 17–20; a good knowledge of French
Organisation: Non-profit organisation that has been running international exchanges for young people since 1947
Type of Work: Placements can be arranged in shops, libraries, hotels, restaurants, and offices. Special placements in careers such as marketing and event management are available on request
Description: CEI offers work experience placements in Brittany for young people, the aim of which is to allow them to practise the language and make their first step into the business world. This is an efficient way to discover the French way of working, to become familiar with French techniques and methods and to improve professional competence
Accommodation: Full board accommodation is provided with host families
Cost: €690 (2 weeks) – €1,180 (4 weeks)

☎ +33 1 43 29 17 24
✆ france@cei4vents.com
💻 www.cei4vents.com

Cross Cultural Solutions: Intern Abroad

Duration: 3–12 weeks
Location: Costa Rica, India, Peru, Russia, Tanzania
Season: Year round
Organisation: A non-profit international volunteer organisation founded in 1995 and registered charity in the UK
Type of Work: Health, education and social services
Description: CCS Intern Abroad placements give participants the opportunity to work side-by-side with local people at a locally-designed and driven community initiative. Participants are assigned an experienced intern supervisor who will offer guidance. Placements are designed to be academically enriching, personally fulfilling and to meet the needs of the local community. Each placement is assigned according to the participant's preferred area of focus, taking skills, interests, objectives and the duration of the placement into account
Accommodation: CCS provides a comfortable shared house in a safe location for all participants. The accommodation is clean with basic amenities
Cost: £1,691 (3 weeks). After 3 weeks, additional weeks cost approx. £176 per week

☎ 0845 458 2781/2782
✒ infouk@crossculturalsolutions.org
🖥 www.crossculturalsolutions.org

Cultural Cube

Duration: Min. 1 month
Location: Armenia
Season: Year round
Prerequisites: Participants must be aged 18–35 and enrolled in full-time education
Organisation: Non-profit
Type of Work: Placements are available in a huge number of industries
Description: An opportunity for people to develop their professional careers while helping in Armenia. Applicants are placed in Armenian government agencies, reputable private companies, or other organisations. The internships are custom-designed to meet the applicants' training requirements. Participants gain professional skills and an insight into life and culture in Armenia
Accommodation: Accommodation is provided at an extra cost. Bed and breakfast accommodation is £35 per month; full board host family accommodation is £100 per month
Cost: Placement fees excluding travel costs start from £275. Most internships are unpaid

☎ 0870 742 6932
✒ info@culturalcube.co.uk
🖥 www.culturalcube.co.uk

Experiential Learning Ecuadorian Programs

Duration: Min. 4 weeks
Location: Rural and urban locations throughout Ecuador
Season: Year round
Prerequisites: Advanced level of Spanish required. Must be able to adapt to different cultures

 +593 2 254 3231
info@elep.org
www.elep.org

Organisation: ECEP is a private, cultural and educational organisation delivering practical programmes for those looking for experiences abroad who want to learn about Ecuadorian culture
Type of Work: Placements are available in a huge number of fields including architecture, computer science, economics, engineering, graphic design, journalism, law, marketing, medicine, media and social work
Description: ELEP seeks to supply internships according to the individual's requirements and profiles. This is an opportunity to gain real work experience, secure a professional job reference and to improve Spanish skills, while living among Ecuadorian people and learning about the culture
Accommodation: Provided as a homestay with a local family
Cost: Registration costs US$100. Placement fees are US$200. Costs include pre-trip information, orientation upon arrival and placement

Eurolingua

Duration: Depends on country and type of placement
Location: France, Germany, Italy and Spain
Season: Year round
Prerequisites: Min. age 18. Some language skills

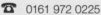 0161 972 0225
info@eurolingua.com
www.eurolingua.com/Work_Experience.htm

Organisation: International study abroad organisation with locations in many countries worldwide
Type of Work: Placements are available mainly in the hotel and catering industry but others can be found in shops, bars, tourism, engineering, sport, telecommunications, graphics and design
Description: A number of Eurolingua Centres are able to organise work experience placements in a variety of fields. Some of the work is paid. Some of the placements can be combined with a language course allowing you to improve the skills you have learnt within the workplace
Accommodation: Provided free of charge in hotels and homestays
Cost: From €750 according to location and length of stay

Global Crossroad

Duration: 2–12 weeks
Location: Bolivia, Brazil, Cambodia, Costa Rica, Ecuador, Ghana, Guatemala, Honduras, India, Kenya, Nepal, Peru, South Africa, Sri Lanka, Tanzania, Thailand, Togo, Tibet
Season: Year round

☎ 0800 310 1821 (UK);
   1 800 413 2008 (USA)
🖰 info@globalcrossroad.com
💻 www.globalcrossroad.com

Organisation: International volunteer organisation committed to providing meaningful opportunities abroad
Type of Work: GC says it can craft an internship project in nearly any area. Most past participants have joined placements in healthcare, journalism, women's issues, culture, sustainable development and business
Description: As part of the internship programme, participants are engaged in daily project activities. In most cases interns develop a proposal in a particular area of interest in collaboration with local supervisors and GC project staff. The director of the project acts as a supervisor for the intern
Accommodation: Provided with host families or a hostel near to the project with which the participant is involved
Cost: Varies according to project and duration, but a 2 week placement is approximately US$1,200

Global Experiences

Duration: Min. 4 weeks
Location: Italy, Australia, Spain, France
Season: Year round
Prerequisites: Ages 18–30

🖰 admin@globalexperiences.com
💻 www.globalexperiences.com

Organisation: International education programmes provider, specialising in international internships and work experience abroad
Type of Work: Fashion design, fashion merchandising, graphic design, culinary, marketing, law, advertising, PR, business, IT, website design, business administration, fine art/museum studies, finance, hospitality/tourism etc
Description: Professional international internships with GE provide an opportunity to gain invaluable practical work experience in a range of fields, and learn new foreign language skills. Special fashion internships are available in London, Milan, Florence, Paris and Sydney. These are designed to provide invaluable foot-in-the-door opportunities to one of the world's most competitive industries
Accommodation: Included in the programme fee. Generally rooms in shared apartments, homestays, or studios depending on the programme. GE attempts to provide accommodation close to the placement company
Cost: 95% of the internships are unpaid work experience. Sample fee in Australia is A$3990 for 4 weeks

Global Volunteer Projects

Duration: Min. 4 weeks
Location: Ghana, India, China, Mexico, Tanzania
Season: Year round
Organisation: Gap year-style placement agency offering projects with an equal focus on learning and giving
Type of Work: Medicine and journalism

☎ 0191 222 0404
🖰 info@globalvolunteerprojects.org
🖥 www.globalvolunteerprojects.org

Description: The journalism placements give participants the opportunity to write for an overseas newspaper. Some time is spent on a journalism course, learning the basics. This is followed by a secondment on a newspaper or magazine. Medical programmes involve shadowing doctors and spending time in specific departments that you're interested in. GVP's projects are designed to incorporate learning the local language and something about the local culture
Accommodation: Varies according to placement/country
Cost: £895 – £1,395 for 1 month placements

Globetrotters Education Consulting

Duration: Min. 1 week (Europe); Min. 4 weeks (NZ)
Location: Europe, New Zealand
Season: Year round
Prerequisites: Min. age 16. Some foreign language experience is required for some placements

☎ +1 416 565 4420
🖰 laura@globetrotterseducation.ca
🖥 www.globetrotterseducation.ca

Organisation: Private company established in 2003 to assist the young and young at heart to achieve their dream of pursuing education and work abroad
Type of Work: Huge range available. The most common placements are hospitality, business, museum work, IT, journalism, marketing, PR, engineering
Description: The type of work experience varies according to individual requirements and what is available at the time of application. All participants are placed in a screened company and receive a reference upon completion of the internship
Accommodation: Not included in price but homestay accommodation can be arranged for an additional fee
Cost: C$300 – C$5,000

Greenforce – Hollywood Film School

Duration: 3 weeks
Location: California State University, USA
Season: Year round
Organisation: Non-profit organisation working alongside local people on international conservation, community and sport volunteer projects

☎ 020 7470 8888
✆ greenforce@btinternet.com
💻 www.greenforce.org

Type of Work: Film production
Description: Short programme that introduces participants to the process of creating a short film. Movie professionals teach participants how to write a short screenplay and draw storyboards. Participants also learn basic camera skills, edit and add effects to the film. At the end of the programme, participants will present their movie showcase
Accommodation: Twin room accommodation in student residence or a homestay with an American family
Cost: £2,200 including airport transfers, accommodation, food, use of equipment, tours and excursions, activities and use of facilities

Institute Of Cultural Ecology: Internships

Duration: Min. 4 weeks
Location: Hawaii, Costa Rica, New Zealand, Fiji, Thailand, Nepal
Season: Year round

✆ ecology@mail.com
💻 www.cultural-ecology.com/ice.html

Organisation: ICE is committed to providing programmes matching the interests, academic goals and passions of participants while also contributing to environmental stewardship
Type of Work: Education, environmental conservation, social services/advocacy, information and media, museum and historical preservation, tourism, ecotourism, computer technology, art and culture, journalism, and religion. There are also custom placements in business, communications, photography, website design and other fields
Description: ICE placements teach important job skills while contributing to society and improving the environment. Interns are generally placed in socially and environmentally concerned fields. All positions are unpaid
Accommodation: Provided either in a homestay with a local family or shared dormitories
Cost: From US$1,895 for 4 weeks including accommodation, in-country support, placement fee and airport pick-up

International Student Placement Centre

Duration: Min. 1 week
Location: Throughout Australia
Season: Year round
Prerequisites: Min. age 16 (most participants are 18–30)
Organisation: ISPC is Australia's biggest independent internship provider, working on behalf of international students to organise professional internships and work experience placements within Australia

☎ +61 2 9279 0100
✉ info@ispc.com.au
🖥 www.ispc.com.au

Type of Work: ISPC deals with more than 2,000 companies in a huge variety of fields
Description: The internships are all in either multinational or medium to large, reputable Australian companies. All internships are custom designed for the individual, who is supervised by highly experienced staff. At the end of the placement, participants are provided with a reference. Most internships are unpaid
Accommodation: Not included in the fee. Homestays, shared houses, budget hotels and hostels can be arranged for an additional fee
Cost: A$1,300 (1–6 week placement)

Interspeak

Duration: 1–2 weeks (mini-placements);
Min 3 weeks (standard placements)
Location: France (Paris, Lille, St. Malo, Limoges), Spain (Madrid) or Germany (Munich, Regensburg)
Season: Year round
Prerequisites: Younger participants can take part in mini-placements only. Standard placements are for people aged 18 and over. Some knowledge of the language is required

☎ 01829 250973
✉ enquiries@interspeak.co.uk
🖥 www.interspeak.co.uk

Organisation: Interspeak has specialised in arranging work placements and internships in Europe since 1981
Type of Work: Popular choices include marketing, law, computing, travel, journalism, banking, shop work, restaurants, and working with children
Description: Interspeak provides short-term internships in Europe. Placements vary but Interspeak tries to match people exactly with their requirements
Accommodation: If required, Interspeak provides a choice of family accommodation as near as possible to the placement
Cost: Agency fee starts at £340

i-to-i International Projects

Duration: Min. 2 weeks
Location: Ecuador, Ghana, Honduras, India, China
Prerequisites: Min. age 18. No previous experience required

☎ 0870 333 2332
🖱 uk@i-to-i.com; usca@i-to-i.com
💻 www.i-to-i.com

Organisation: A founding member of the Year Out Group with Investors in People status, i-to-i is a TEFL training and volunteer travel organisation
Type of Work: Health, media, marketing, tourism
Description: The internship programme gives participants the opportunity to develop skills and gain experience in their chosen field, while exploring an exciting new destination. There are a range of options available from writing for a local newspaper in Ghana to working at a hospital in Ecuador, or even shooting a film in India
Accommodation: Included in price. Varies from project to project
Cost: Varies considerably. Example price: 4 weeks experience on a music magazine in Bangalore, India – £995

A POSTCARD FROM India

Rachael Muirhead left her marketing job to travel to India for a four–week journalism placement with i-to-i:

I really wanted to give journalism a try, but it was never going to be an easy move to make. Everywhere I asked, people were banging on about building up my portfolio and I decided that if I was seriously considering doing it, work experience was the only sensible way to go. But placements in the UK are very hard to come by and because I was working full time I didn't have the time to apply myself fully to looking for one. Also, after earning money for two years, I really didn't want to take on an unpaid placement in the UK. Doing it abroad had less of a stigma. I also wanted to travel but wanted to have some kind of structure to it. The i-to-i placement offered me an interesting experience, immersed in a foreign culture and the opportunity to prove that I had a demonstrable interest in journalism.

At first the work was a bit demoralising, compared to what I had been doing previously. I started off doing general admin and basic research. But work experience is always going to begin like this until your employers recognise what you are capable of. So I had to be prepared for that and be pro-active to counter it and progress quickly. Being eager and enthusiastic always gets you far. By the end of the placement I was writing features, editing and managing a project. Four weeks was certainly long enough for my managers to see what I could do and to give me some responsibility. I came away with some nice pieces to add to my portfolio and some great stories.

As well as the journalism experience, I also gained experience of working within a completely differing culture. Most of my time was spent in the office, but even there I was working with people very different to me which was both interesting and challenging.

I use the skills that I developed on my placement every day now, even though I decided not to pursue journalism as a career. In marketing I still need to write well and have an eye for design. It was also good to see how a newspaper and magazine work, because I pitch ideas to editors to get publicity for books. It was good to meet and understand people from other cultures too. I feel far more worldly now!

Learn Overseas

Duration: Min. 2 weeks
Location: Delhi, India
Season: January – April; August – December
Organisation: Learn Overseas is an India specialist with thorough local knowledge dedicated to providing rewarding and relevant placement opportunities

☎ 0161 226 5300
🖰 office@learnoverseas.co.uk
🖳 www.learnoverseas.co.uk

Type of Work: Medical, legal and hotel management placements
Description: Medical: This is a work shadowing experience. During the placement, participants visit three or four specialist hospitals with state of the art equipment. Here they shadow consultants and observe operations. They also visit rural clinics in poor communities, and cash-strapped state hospitals. This placement combines hands-on and observational work. Legal: This is a placement in a well-respected law firm in Delhi for those interested in a career in the legal profession. Participants shadow solicitors and help to research and prepare information. Hotel Management: Participants work in some of Delhi's best luxury hotels working alongside conference and events managers, HR and training teams, and kitchen and reception staff
Accommodation: Clean and safe lodging is provided for the duration of the placement. The type of accommodation and the standard can vary depending on the type of project.
Cost: A typical 2-week work experience placement costs £995 excluding airfares and insurance

People Tree Gap Year Placement

Duration: Min. 4 weeks
Location: Throughout India
Season: Year round
Organisation: Gap year placement company specialising in India, Nepal and Sri Lanka
Type of Work: Placements can be arranged

☎ 0207 402 5576
🖰 peopletree@gapyearinindia.com
🖳 www.gapyearinindia.com

in a huge number of industries ranging from law, engineering, medicine, IT, radio production, film production, advertising, sports management, PR, theatre management, marketing, retail, magazine/newspaper works, photography, leisure, travel, publishing and fashion
Description: Placements provide an invaluable opportunity to participate, contribute and learn, with access to all levels of management. People Tree has extensive contacts and can provide an inside track in a variety of industries
Accommodation: Accommodation is provided but varies according to the project and the area of India. All accommodation is clean, warm and comfortable
Cost: From £850 for a month placement excluding flights, visa and insurance

Projects Abroad: Summer Projects Abroad

Duration: 2–3 weeks
Location: See below
Season: July/August
Prerequisites: Ages 16–19; in full-time education or on a gap year
Organisation: Projects Abroad organises volunteering projects in 20 countries around the world

☎ 01903 708300
✉ info@projects-abroad.co.uk
💻 www.projects-abroad.co.uk

Placements Available: Placements include: journalism in Romania, medicine in India, photography in Romania, working with horses in Mongolia, medicine in Mongolia, veterinary in India, cookery in India, physiotherapy in Nepal, law in China
Description: The two week summer specials are specifically designed for the pre-university age group in full-time education in order to give them valuable work experience and develop a particular skill in two or three weeks. Participants are part of a small group of fellow students and receive a mixture of teaching, hands-on and observational work and weekend excursions
Accommodation: Varies according to project. Included in price
Cost: 2 week specials: £995 (plus £395 for an extra week). Price includes accommodation, food, insurance, placement and leisure activities

Projects Abroad

Duration: Min. 3 weeks
Location: Argentina, Bolivia, Cambodia, Chile, China, Costa Rica, Ethiopia, Ghana, India, Mexico, Moldova, Mongolia, Morocco, Nepal, Peru, Romania, Senegal, South Africa, Sri Lanka, Thailand
Season: Year round
Organisation: Projects Abroad organises volunteering projects in 20 countries around the world

☎ 01903 708300
✉ info@projects-abroad.co.uk
💻 www.projects-abroad.co.uk

Type of Work: Journalism, medicine, sports, veterinary medicine, animal care, IT, law, arts and crafts, and business (finance, advertising, marketing, PR, engineering, tourism)
Description: These projects are designed to set participants on the right track towards their ideal career. All placements give participants the opportunity to gain hands-on experience of their chosen career path in a new cultural setting, working within the local community
Accommodation: Mostly provided with local host families. In some places there are also hostels, flats and other types of accommodation
Cost: £1,045 – £1,495 (for 1 month)

A POSTCARD FROM Ghana

Law student, Danica Mullarkey, spent four weeks on a Projects Abroad human rights law placement in Ghana:

I tried not to have any expectations as to what my trip to Ghana would bring. Reflecting on it now, I can see that was the best mentality to set off with. Literature and TV images cannot compare to the culture shock you experience, in those first few hours, walking the streets of Africa in person!

Just a few days in, I was beginning to feel quite at home. My host family would go out of their way to include me in family gatherings, and at the same time allow me to have my own space when I needed it. Ghanaian people see a stranger in their country as a privilege, and appear to want to create the best impression of their country. Getting on a tro-tro (local mini-bus) you are greeted with 'good morning'; walking past schools children will wave and shout hello. I think it is fitting that the first word I learnt to say in Ghanaian was 'Akwaaba' - it means 'Welcome'. People greet you with this day-in-day-out.

The work placement provided me with a sense of purpose. Placed at The Commonwealth Human Rights Initiative, I was truly made to feel that being a law student from England was of some real value, and not just merely as a volunteer who had come to make the tea. I was able to get straight into making a difference, and got involved in looking into human rights abuses by the Ghanaian police, interviewing witnesses and documenting their testimonies, and researching material for the state of prison conditions. I was also able to attend human rights conferences, where I met parliamentarians to discuss the state of family-planning services across Ghana. Projects Abroad had listened to my requests and placed me with an organisation that truly furthered my interests in human rights law. The day-to-day experiences of being in Accra and the work I was doing had encouraged me to become far more adventurous than I ever would have imagined before I left England.

Real Gap Experience

Duration: 2 weeks – 6 months
Location: More than 40 countries worldwide
Organisation: The leading independent gap year specialists, offering the most comprehensive range of gap year opportunities

 01892 516164
 info@realgap.co.uk
www.realgap.co.uk

Description: Real Gap Experience offers paid work placements allowing participants to see the world and finance their trip as they go. Paid work placements abroad are an excellent way of making money go further while travelling. Real Gap offers opportunities for paid work in Australia, New Zealand, Canada, USA, South Africa, China and Japan. The placements are perfect for those that want to do fun jobs, interact with the locals and experience some of the culture. Packages include everything required for a working holiday including working visa processing, guaranteed job offers, the first few nights' accommodation, airport pick-ups and orientation
Accommodation: Varies depending on programme – ranges from homestays, volunteer houses, tented camps, huts and hostels
Cost: From £249

Smile: Internships

Duration: 2–12 weeks
Location: West Bengal, India
Season: Year round
Prerequisites: Ages 16–30, basic English. No experience required
Organisation: The Smile society is a volunteer organisation working for slum and street kids' welfare activities
Type of Work: Education, health, women's issues, rural development sector, yoga
Description: Smile organises internships designed for international students in a variety of sectors. During the placement volunteers receive tutorials from experts in the field twice a week, plus constant support from local staff
Accommodation: Depends on project but is provided in halls, lodges, guest houses, schools and with host families. Local meals are also provided
Cost: US$300 per person, including food and lodging, project material and in-country transportation

☎ +91 9830 686828
✉ info@smilengo.org
💻 www.smilengo.org

Subway Watersports

Duration:
Min. 4 weeks
Location: Roatan, Honduras
Season: Year round.
Internships start on the 1st and 15th of any month
Organisation: Small scuba diving and watersports operator offering in the east end of Roatan
Type of Work: Internship working in a dive shop while training towards a professional PADI Divemaster
Description: This internship offers participants the chance to learn how to run a small business operation focusing on adventure and diving in a resort atmosphere. There is also the chance to learn about all of the local marine life and understand the necessity of conservation and environmental education. There is also the option to pursue a choice of PADI diving certification courses
Accommodation: Provided in an apartment, shared with other interns. Lunches are also provided
Cost: US$1,100 (for 4 weeks)

✉ internship@subwaywatersports.com
💻 www.subwaywatersports.com/Courses/internship.htm

Travellers Worldwide

Duration: Min. 4 weeks
Location: Argentina, Australia, China. Ghana, India, Kenya, Malaysia, Russia, South Africa, Sri Lanka, Zambia

☎ 01903 502595

🖱 info@travellersworldwide.com

💻 www.travellersworldwide.com/work-experience.htm

Season: Year round
Prerequisites: Min. age 17. In some (but not all fields) participants need to be studying a related subject, or have some experience
Organisation: One of the major providers of gap year-style placements sending participants from all over the world to all over the world
Type of Work: Tourism, architecture, dive centre management, farming, hospitality, interior design, journalism, law, medical, PR, journalism, photography, TV/radio/multimedia, veterinary medicine, website design
Description: TW work placements are tailored to suit specific requirements to ensure that participants get the most from their experience. Participants work closely with professionals and gain hands-on experience of the industry
Accommodation: Varies according to placement/country. Most participants live with local families or in school residences. A few live in hostels and guest houses
Cost: Starts at £994 for 4 weeks including food, accommodation and full 24-hour support

Vocation Vacations: Dream Job Holidays

Duration: 1–3 days
Location: Throughout the USA (soon to be also in the UK)

🖱 info@vocationvacations.com

💻 www.vocationvacations.com

Season: Year round
Prerequisites: Min. age 18
Organisation: Business enabling participants to 'test-drive their dream job' and empowering them to 'turn their passions into their career'
Type of Work: Everything from actor and alpaca farmer, right through to wine sommelier and yoga studio owner
Description: Vocation Vacations offers hands-on dream job immersion experiences under the tutelage of expert mentors who are passionate about what they do. The short-term nature of these experiences means there is no need to leave your current job or even tell the boss. It allows you to see first-hand what your dream job is really like and satisfy your curiosity
Accommodation: Not included in the price. VV can make recommendations for local hotels
Cost: US$349 – US$1,999 per person

Index

INDEX OF ORGANISATIONS

A

A Pas de Loup (Volunteers for Nature)   50
The Abbey College   307
Achill Island Field School   188
ACLE   307
Acorn Educational Exchanges   329
Across The Divide   242
Action For Charity   242
Action Reconciliation for Peace   167, 200
Active Training And Education   302
Adarsh Community Development Trust   153
Adelante Abroad   355
African Conservation Experience   97, 335
African Impact   98, 147
Age Concern   235
Agricultural Labour Pool   280
Aidcamps International   118
Airline Ambassadors International   118
Ajude   168
Alexanders International School   302
Allanhill Farm   271
Alliance Abroad   88, 290, 139, 290
Alutiiq Museum   215
Amazon-Africa Aid Organisation   140
American Bear Association   80
American Council For International
   Studies: Tour Managers   329
American Hiking Society   80
Amerispan Unlimited   140
Arnis de Chevreaux-Chatel   168, 201
Amizade   119
Andean Bear Conservation Project   88
Anglo-American Project in Pompeii   202
Anglo-Polish Universities Association
   Assisted Teaching Project   308
Anjou Myrtilles   281
The Anthony Nolan Trust   235
Apare   169, 201
Appalachian Mountain Club   81
Appalachian Trail Conservancy   81
Appellation Controllée   279
ARCAS   89
ArchaeoSpain   200
Ardmore Language Schools   303
Asociación Anai – Finca Lomas   256
Assin Endwa Trust   148
Association Alpes de Lumiere   169, 202
ATD Fourth World   170

Atlantic Whale Foundation   73
Australian Koala Foundation   110
AVIVA Nature Guiding Course   356
AVIVA   98

B

Badaguish Outdoor Centre   332
Ballybin Fruit Farm   281
Bamburgh Research Project   188
Bangladesh Work Camps Association   170
Belize Valley Archaeological
   Reconnaissance Project   215
Bell International   309
Bethsaida   210
Big Day Out   347
Bike Aid   139
Biodynamic Agricultural Association   256
Biosphere Expeditions   51
Birkholm Frugt & Baer   281
Black Howler Monkey Project   90
Blue Ventures   99
Blue World: Adriatic Dolphin Project   74
Brathay Exploration Group Trust   50
Breast Cancer Care   235
Bridges For Education Inc   312
Broadstairs Folk Week   344
S.H.M Broomfield & Son   271
BTCV – Conservation Holidays   52
Bullocks Permaculture Homestead   257
Butser Ancient Farm   189
BYV Adventure Camps   333

C

C.E.I (Centre D'echanges Internationaux)   356
Cairntradlin   271
Cairnwell Mountain Sports   322
Campsite Assistant Teams   341
Canal Camps   66, 189
Cancerbackup   235
Cape Tribulation Tropical Research
   Station   109
Care Challenge   243
Caretta Research Project   82
Caribbean Conservation Corporation   89
Caribbean Volunteer Expeditions   216
Castell Henllys Training Excavation   190

Catalina Island Conservancy 82
Cathedral Camps 190
Centre for Alternative Technology 66
Centre for Rehabilitation of Wildlife 100
Centre for the Study of Eurasian
    Nomads 216
Cetacean Research and Rescue Unit 67
CHAM – Medieval History Projects 203
Chandler & Dunn Ltd 272
Charity Challenge 244
Charlton Orchards 272
Cheetah Conservation Fund 101
Cherry Growers' Association Canada 279
S.H Chesson 272
Childaid to Russia & The Republics 138
Children's Country Holidays Fund
    (CCHF) Holiday Volunteers 333
The Children's Society 236
Citizens Network For Foreign Affairs 257
Classic Tours 244
Club du Vieux Manoir 203
Club Europe Holidays 330
Club Europe: Ski Resort Reps 319
Coachella Valley Music and
    Arts Festival 347
Cobradah Orchards 282
The Colorado Trail Foundation 83
Community Challenge 119
Comunidad Inti Wara Yassi 90
Concord College 303
Concordia 120, 165
Conservation Project Utila Iguana 91
Conservation Volunteers Australia 110
Conservation Volunteers Greece 74, 171
Coral Cay Conservation 54
Corboy Fresh Fruit 282
Costa Rica Vacations With Farmer
    Families Project 258
Cross Cultural Solutions 120, 357
Crow Canyon Archaeological Centre 217
Cuba Solidarity Campaign:
    International Work Brigades 141
Cultural Cube 357
Cultural Restoration Tourism Project 217

D

DAD International UK-Romania 309
Dakshinayan 290
Delphis Mediterranean Whale and
    Dolphin Project 75
Different Challenge 245
Different Travel 55, 121

The Disaway Trust: Holiday Helpers 334
Discover Adventure 245
Discovery Summer 304
Do It For Charity 246
Dragonfly 153, 291

E

Earthwatch Insititute 56, 191, 204, 218
Eco-Centre Caput Insulae-Beli 75
Ecoforest Education For Sustainability 258
Ecovolunteer 55
Edinburgh International Book Festival 345
Ein Gedi 210
EJO – English Language Holiday
    Courses 304
El Porvenir 141
ELAC Study Vacations 304
Elderhostel Adventures in Lifelong
    Learning 219
Elephant Nature Park 105
The Emmaus International Summer
    Volunteer Programme 171
English For Children – Summer Camp 310
English For Kids 310
Enkosini Eco Experience 101
Environmental Health Monitors 342
Equity Ski: Peak Season Reps 321
Equity Travel: Educational Tour Reps 330
EstYES: International Youth
    Association Estonia 172
Etudes et Chantiers (UNAREC) 172
Eurolingua 358
Event Recycling 340
Exit Festival 348
Experiential Learning Ecuadorian
    Programs 358

F

The Farm Fun 310
Farm Helpers In New Zealand (FHINZ) 259
Farm Sanctuary Internships 259
Festive Lizards 340
Festival Internacional de Benicassim 348
Fire Services National Benevolent Fund 236
Fiskardo's Nautical Club 76
Foundation for Sustainable Development 122
Fox Language Academy 291
C. Francis 272
Freewheel Holidays: Hosts 318
Fridaybridge International Farm Camps 273
Friends of the Cumbres and Toltec
    Scenic Railroad 219

Friends of the Great Baikal Trail   76
Frontier   57
Fundacion Jatun Sacha   91

G

Gap Sports   324
Genctur   173, 311
Get Kids Going   236
Global Adventure Challenges   246
Global Citizens Network   122
Global Crossroad   57, 123, 292, 359
Global Eco-Spiritual Tours   105
Global Experiences   359
Global Routes   123
Global Service Corps   124, 261
Global Vision International 58, 125, 246, 292
Global Volunteer Network   59, 124
Global Volunteer Projects   360
Global Volunteers   126
Global Works   126
Globe Aware   127
Globetrotters Education Consulting   360
Go Differently   106, 154, 292
GoXplore   102, 148
Great Ormond Street Hospital   237
Great Walks of the World Charity Treks 247
Greenforce – Hollywood Film School   361
Greenforce   59, 324
Greenway International Workcamps   173
Groundwork   67
Grupo Lobo   77
The Guardian Hay Festival   346

H

Habitat for Humanity   127
Halsbury Travel: Ski Season Couriers 320
Hands Up Holidays 60, 128, 220, 260, 293
Harold Corrigall   273
Hawkes Bay   282
Hayles Fruit Farm Ltd   273
Hebrew University of Jerusalsm   211
Hebridean Whale and Dolphin Trust:
    Cetacean Research Project   68
Hellenic Ornithological Society   77
Hellenic Wildlife Hospital   78
Help the Aged   237
Heritage Conservation Network   129, 220
HF Holidays: Walk Leaders   318
Hill Farm Orchards   273
Hippos (Sussita) Excavation Project   211
Horizon Cosmopolite   294
Hultsfred Festival   348

I

i-to-i International Projects 61, 131, 325, 363
ICYE   130
Iko Poran Association   142
Imaginative Traveller   60, 130
Institute Of Cultural Ecology   361
International Bouworde-IBO   174
International Executive Service Corps 132
International Farm Camp   274
International Otter Survival Fund   69
International Quest   305
International Student Placement Centre 362
Interski Snowsport School   320
Interspeak   362
Involvement Volunteers
    Association   61, 132, 174, 221
Iracambi Atlantic Rainforest Research
    and Conservation Centre   92
The Italian Job   247
Iyok Ami Eco Reserve   92

J, K, L

Jubilee Sailing Trust   323
Judith River Dinosaur Institute   221
Just Works   175
Kentwell Hall – Live as a Tudor   192
Kings School of English   305
KMC International Work Camps in
    the Czech Republic   175
Kokee Resource Conservation Program   84
Koogie Downs   283
La Sabranenque   207
Landdienst-zentralstelle   281
Laurel Tree Fruit Farm   274
Learn Overseas   364
Les Eurockeenes De Belfort   349
Lindum Heritage   192
Lingue Senza Frontiere   311

M

M.E.E.R. E.V. Whale Behavioural
    Research Project   78
Macmillan Cancer Support   237
Madventurer   133, 294
F.W Mansfield & Son   274
Mar de Jade   142, 294
Marie Curie Cancer Support   237
Maya Research Program   222
MENCAP   238
The Meningitis Trust   238
Mental Health Foundation   238

Mercy Ships 133
Mingan Island Cetacean Research
Expeditions 84
Molyneux 283
The Monkey Sanctuary 69
Muang District Non Formal
Education Service 295
Munda Wanga Wildlife Park and
Sanctuary 102

N

Nasca Project, Peru 222
National Deaf Children's Society 238
The National Trust 70, 193
The Nature Corps 85
Naucrates Conservation Project 108
D.A. Newling & Son 275
New Zealand Trust for Conservation
Volunteers (NZTCV) 111
Nicaragua Solidarity Campaign 143
NICE: Never-ending International
Workcamps Exchange 176
North Pennines Archaeology 194

O

Ocean Spirits Leatherback Sea Turtle
Research and Education Programme 93
The Oceania Research Project 111
Oceanic Society Expeditions 93
OIKOS 176
E. Oldroyd And Sons Ltd 275
Open Houses Network 204
Operation Wallacea 61
Orangutan Health 108
Ores Foundation for Marine
Environment Research 85
Original Volunteers 94, 134, 295
Orphanage Outreach 143
Outback International 280
Oxfam Global Challenges 239
Oxfam 337

P

Passport in Time 223
Paul Williamson Ltd 276
Pavilion Tours 322
Peace Villages Foundation 144, 296
People and Places 135
People Tree Gap Year Placement 364
Peppermint Bars 339
Personal Overseas Development 62, 295

Peter Marshall & Co 275
Philadelphia Yearly Meeting – International
Volunteer Workcamp China 177
Pinkpop 349
Plunkett Orchards 283
Poulton Research Project 194
Pretoma – Sea Turtle Restoration
Program of Costa Rica 94
Pretoma – Shark Tagging Expeditions 95
Prices Fruit Farm 275
Priddy Folk Festival 345
Pro International 177
Project International 306
Projects Abroad 205, 297, 326, 365
Proyecto Karumbe 95
P. Pullar & Co. 283

Q, R

Quest 63, 135
Raasay Outdoor Centre 323
Ramat-rahel 212
Real Gap
Experience 64, 136, 298, 325, 366
The Real Nepal Experience 154, 298
Reality Kenya 103
Reef Check 64
Relief Riders International 156
Responsible Travel 65, 136, 249, 206
RJ Cornish 282
Roman Cat Sanctuary 79
Roskilde Festival 350
Royal National Institute For The Blind 240
Royal Society for the Protection of Birds 71
Royal Tyrrell Museum 224
Rural Community Development
Programme 299
Rural Organisation For Social
Elevation 155, 299

S

S & P Hodson-walker 274
S & A Produce Ltd 276
Saga Volunteer Travel Projects 149
Salmans Ltd 276
Samaritans – Festival Branch 341
The San Wild Wildlife Trust 103
Santa Martha Rescue Centers 96
Saveock Water Archaeology 195
SCOPE 241
The Scottish Crannog Centre 195
Sedgeford Research Project 196
Service Civil International 165

Shumba Experience 104
Sidmouth Folk Week 344
Sierra Club Outings 86, 225
Silchester Roman Town Field School 196
Silvan Estate Raspberries 284
Ski-plan: Peak Season Resort Reps 319
Smile Society Workcamps 178, 299
Smile: Internships 367
South By South West 350
Sport & Educational Travel: Couriers 331
Sportventurer 327
STAESA 150, 300
Starfish Ventures 300
Subway Watersports 367
Sunday Times Oxford Literary Festival 346
Sunseed Desert Technology 262
Super Camps Ltd 306
Svezhy Veter Travel Agency 313
Swiss Whale Society 65

T

Tall Stories 249
Task Brasil 146, 262
Teach Peru 300
Tel Bet Yerah Research and
    Excavation Project 212
Tel Dor Project 212
Tell Es-safi/Gath Project 213
The Tel Rehov Excavations 213
Tethys Research Institute 79
Thistle Camps 72, 197
The Times Cheltenham Festival
    of Literature 346
The 3H Fund: Holiday Volunteers 332
TOC H 138
Tolga Bat Hospital 112
Torrens Valley Orchards 284
Towersey Village Festival 344
Transformational Journeys 137
Travellers Worldwide 328, 368
Trees for Life – Work Weeks 72
Tumbarumba Blueberries 284
Turnbull Brothers Orchards 284

U, V

Ugunja Community Resource Centre 150
Ultimate Travel Company 249
UNA Exchange 166

Underwater Archaeology Project 208
Union Rempart 208
UNIPAL 301
United Planet 137
Upper Nene Archaeological Society 197
Vaughantown 301
VESL Summer Schools 313
Village Camps Inc 312
The Vindolanda Trust 198
Vitalise: Sighted Guides 335, 342
Vitalise: Ski Guides 321
Vocation Vacations: Dream Job Holidays 368
Voluntarios De Occidente 302
Voluntary Workcamps Association
    of Ghana (VOLU) 178
Volunteer Africa 151
Volunteer Bolivia 145
Volunteer Farm Of Shenandoah 261
Volunteer for Nature 86
Volunteers for Outdoor Colorado (VOC) 87
Volunteers for Peace 179
VSO Challenges Worldwide 250

W, X, Y, Z

Western Belize Regional Cave Project 225
Whizz Kidz 241
Wild Animal Rescue Foundation of
    Thailand (WAR) 109
The Wild Dolphin Project 96
Wildlife Trust of South and West Wales 73
Wind, Sand & Stars 152
Withers Fruit Farm 276
Wolf Education and Research Centre 87
Woodlarks Campsite 334
Workcamps Switzerland 179
The Workers Beer Company 339
World Challenge Expeditions:
    Expedition Leaders 331
World Expeditions 250
WWISA: Willing Workers in South Africa 152
WWOOF 267
Wyoming Dinosaur Centre – Dig for
    a Day Program 226
The Yavneh-Yam Project 214
YHA Challenges 250
Young Austria 312
Youth Action for Peace 167
The Zeitah Excavations 214

INDEX BY LOCATION

Worldwide
Airline Ambassadors International 118
Biosphere Expeditions 51
Bridges For Education Inc 312
BTCV – Conservation Holidays 52
Concordia 120, 165
Discover Adventure 245
Do It For Charity 246
Earthwatch Institute 56
Ecovolunteer 55
Elderhostel Adventures in Lifelong
  Learning 219
Etudes et Chantiers (UNAREC) 172
Frontier 57
Global Adventure Challenges 246
Global Vision International 58, 125, 246, 292
Global Volunteers 126
Great Walks of the World Charity Treks 247
Habitat for Humanity 127
Hands Up Holidays 128
Heritage Conservation Network 129, 220
Horizon Cosmopolite 294
i-to-i International Projects 61, 131
International Executive Service Corps 132
Involvement Volunteers Assoc. 61, 132, 174, 221
Projects Abroad 365
Real Gap Experience 64, 136, 298, 325, 366
Reef Check 64
Responsible Travel 65, 136, 249
Service Civil International 165
Svezhy Veter Travel Agency 313
UNA Exchange 166
United Planet 137
Vesl Summer Schools 313
Volunteers for Peace 179
World Challenge Expeditions 331
World Expeditions 250
WWOOF 267

Africa
A Pas de Loup (Volunteers for Nature) 50
Across The Divide 242
Action For Charity 242
African Conservation Experience 97, 355
African Impact 98, 147

Aidcamps International 118
Ajude 168
Alliance Abroad 290
Amizade 119
The Anthony Nolan Trust 235
Assin Endwa Trust 148
AVIVA 98, 356
AVIVA Nature Guiding Course
Blue Ventures 99
Brathay Exploration Group Trust 50
Cancerbackup 235
Centre for Rehabilitation of Wildlife 100
Charity Challenge 244
Cheetah Conservation Fund 101
The Children's Society 236
Classic Tours 244
Community Challenge 119
Cross Cultural Solutions 120, 357
Different Challenge 245
Different Travel 55, 121
Earthwatch Institute 218
Enkosini Eco Experience 101
Foundation for Sustainable Development 122
Gap Sports 324
Get Kids Going 236
Global Citizens Network 122
Global Crossroad 57, 123, 359
Global Routes 123
Global Service Corps 124, 261
Global Volunteer Network 59, 124
Global Volunteer Projects 360
GoXplore 102, 148
Great Ormond Street Hospital 237
Greenforce 59
Hands Up Holidays 60, 220
Help the Aged 237
i-to-i International Projects 325
ICYE 130
Imaginative Traveller 60, 130
Macmillan Cancer Support 237
Madventurer 133, 294
Marie Curie Cancer Support 237
Mental Health Foundation 238
Mercy Ships 133

Munda Wanga Wildlife Park 102
National Deaf Children's Society 238
OIKOS 176
Operation Wallacea 61
Original Volunteers 134, 295
Oxfam Global Challenges 239
People and Places 135
Personal Overseas Development 62, 295
Projects Abroad 297, 326, 365
Quest 63, 135
Reality Kenya 103
Responsible Travel 224
Royal National Institute For The Blind 240
Saga Volunteer Travel Projects 149
The San Wild Wildlife Trust 103
SCOPE 241
Shumba Experience 104
Sportventurer 327
STAESA 150, 300
Swiss Whale Society 65
Transformational Journeys 137
Travellers Worldwide 328, 368
Ugunja Community Resource Centre 150
Ultimate Travel Company 249
Voluntary Workcamps Assoc. Ghana 178
Volunteer Africa 151
VSO Challenges Worldwide 250
Whizz Kidz 241
Wind, Sand & Stars 152
WWISA: Willing Workers in South Africa 152
Yha Challenges 250
Youth Action for Peace 167

Asia and the South Pacific

Across The Divide 242
Aidcamps International 118
Age Concern 235
Alliance Abroad Group 290
The Anthony Nolan Trust 235
Bangladesh Work Camps Association 170
Breast Cancer Care 235
Cancerbackup 235
Centre for Study of Eurasian Nomads 216
Charity Challenge 244
Classic Tours 244
Community Challenge 119
Coral Cay Conservation 54
Cross Cultural Solutions 120
Cultural Restoration Tourism Project 217
Different Travel 121
Dragonfly 153, 291
Earthwatch Institute 218

Elephant Nature Park 105
Get Kids Going 236
Global Citizens Network 122
Global Crossroad 57, 123, 292, 359
Global Routes 123
Global Service Corps 124
Global Volunteer Network 59, 124
Global Volunteer Projects 360
Global Works 126
Globe Aware 127
Go Differently 106, 154, 292
Great Ormond Street Hospital 237
Greenforce 59
Greenway International Workcamps 173
Hands Up Holidays 60, 260, 293
i-to-i International Projects 325, 363
ICYE 130
Imaginative Traveller 60,130
Institute Of Cultural Ecology 361
Macmillan Cancer Support 237
Madventurer 133, 294
Marie Curie Cancer Support 237
MENCAP 238
The Meningitis Trust 238
Muang District Non Formal Education 295
National Deaf Children's Society 238
Naucrates Conservation Project 108
NICE: Never-ending International
   Workcamps Exchange 176
Operation Wallacea 61
Orangutan Health 108
Original Volunteers 134, 295
Oxfam Global Challenges 239
People and Places 135
Personal Overseas Development 62, 295
Philadelphia Yearly Meeting – International
   Volunteer Workcamp China 177
Projects Abroad 297, 326, 365
The Real Nepal Experience 154, 298
Royal National Institute For The Blind 240
Rural Community Development
   Programme 299
SCOPE 241
Sportventurer 327
Starfish Ventures 300
Travellers Worldwide 328, 368
Ultimate Travel Company 249
VSO Challenges Worldwide 250
Whizz Kidz 241
Wild Animal Rescue Foundation 109
Yha Challenges 250
Youth Action for Peace 167

India

Action For Charity	242
Adarsh Community Development Trust	153
Aidcamps International	118
Amizade	119
Brathay Exploration Group Trust	50
Breast Cancer Care	235
The Children's Society	236
Community Challenge	119
Cross Cultural Solutions	120, 357
Dakshinayan	290
Different Travel	121
Foundation for Sustainable Development	122
Global Crossroad	123, 359
Global Eco-Spiritual Tours	105
Global Volunteer Network	124
Global Volunteer Projects	360
Hands Up Holidays	60
Help the Aged	237
i-to-i International Projects	363
ICYE	130
Imaginative Traveller	130
Learn Overseas	364
Madventurer	133, 294
OIKOS	176
Original Volunteers	134, 295
People And Places	135
People Tree Gap Year Placement	364
Projects Abroad	297
Relief Riders International	156
Rural Community Development Programme	299
Rural Organisation for Social Elevation	155, 299
Smile: Internships	367
Smile Society Workcamps	178, 299
Travellers Worldwide	328, 368
VSO Challenges Worldwide	250

Australia/New Zealand

Across The Divide	242
Australian Koala Foundation	110
Big Day Out	347
Cape Tribulation Tropical Research	109
Cobradah Orchards	282
Conservation Volunteers Australia	110
Corboy Fresh Fruit	282
RJ Cornish	282
Farm Helpers In New Zealand (FHINZ)	259
Global Experiences	359
Global Volunteer Network	59, 124
Global Works	126
Globetrotters Education Consulting	360

Hands Up Holidays	60, 260
Hawkes Bay	282
ICYE	130
Institute Of Cultural Ecology	361
International Student Placement Centre	362
Koogie Downs	283
The Meningitis Trust	238
Molyneux	283
New Zealand Trust for Conservation Volunteers (NZTCV)	111
The Oceania Research Project	111
Outback International	280
Plunkett Orchards	283
P. Pullar & Co.	283
Silvan Estate Raspberries	284
Tolga Bat Hospital	112
Torrens Valley Orchards	284
Travellers Worldwide	328, 368
Tumbarumba Blueberries	284
Turnbull Brothers Orchards	284
Ultimate Travel Company	249

Central America and the Caribbean

A Pas de Loup (Volunteers for Nature)	50
Adelante Abroad	355
Alliance Abroad	88, 139
Amerispan Unlimited	140
Amizade	119
ARCAS	89
Asociación Anai – Finca Lomas	256
Belize Valley Archaeological Reconnaissance Project	215
Biosphere Expeditions	51
Caribbean Conservation Corporation	89
Caribbean Volunteer Expeditions	216
Charity Challenge	244
Classic Tours	244
Conservation Project Utila Iguana	91
Costa Rica Vacations With Farmer Families Project	258
Cross Cultural Solutions	120, 357
Cuba Solidarity Campaign	141
Earthwatch Institute	218
El Porvenir	141
Foundation for Sustainable Development	122
Gap Sports	324
Global Citizens Network	122
Global Crossroad	57, 123, 359
Global Routes	123
Global Volunteer Network	124
Global Volunteer Projects	360
Global Works	126

Globe Aware	127
Greenforce	59
Hands Up Holidays	60
i-to-i International Projects	325, 363
ICYE	130
Institute Of Cultural Ecology	361
Iyok Ami Eco Reserve	92
Jubilee Sailing Trust	323
Macmillan Cancer Support	237
Madventurer	133, 294
Mar de Jade	142, 294
Maya Research Program	222
Mercy Ships	133
Nicaragua Solidarity Campaign	143
Oceanic Society Expeditions	93
Ocean Spirits Leatherback Sea Turtle Research and Education Programme	93
OIKOS	176
Operation Wallacea	61
Original Volunteers	94, 134, 295
Orphanage Outreach	143
Pretoma – Sea Turtle Restoration Program of Costa Rica	94
Pretoma – Shark Tagging Expeditions	95
Projects Abroad	297, 326
Responsible Travel	224
SCOPE	241
Subway Watersports	367
Transformational Journeys	137
Travellers Worldwide: Travellers Sports	328
Western Belize Regional Cave Project	225
The Wild Dolphin Project	96

Europe

The 3H Fund: Holiday Volunteers	332
A Pas de Loup (Volunteers for Nature)	50
ACLE	307
Acorn Educational Exchanges	329
Across The Divide	242
Action For Charity	242
Action Reconciliation for Peace	167, 200
Adelante Abroad	355
Alliance Abroad	290
American Council For International Studies: Tour Managers	329
Amis de Chevreaux-Chatel	168, 201
Amizade	119
Anglo-American Project in Pompeii	202
APASS	308
Anjou Myrtilles	281
Apare	169, 201
Appellation Controllée	279

ArchaeoSpain	200
Association Alpes de Lumiere	169, 202
ATD Fourth World	170
Atlantic Whale Foundation	73
Bell International	309
Biosphere Expeditions	51
Blue World: Adriatic Dolphin Project	74
Brathay Exploration Group Trust	50
Breast Cancer Care	235
C.E.I (Centre d'Echanges Internationaux)	356
Cancerbackup	235
Care Challenge	243
CHAM – Medieval History Projects	203
Charity Challenge	244
Childaid to Russia & The Republics	138
The Children's Society	236
Citizens Network For Foreign Affairs	257
Classic Tours	244
Club du Vieux Manoir	203
Club Europe	319, 330
Conservation Volunteers Greece	74, 171
Cross Cultural Solutions	120, 357
DAD International UK-Romania	309
Delphis Whale and Dolphin Project	75
Different Travel	55
The Disaway Trust: Holiday Helpers	334
Earthwatch Institute	204
Eco-Centre Caput Insulae-Beli (ECCIB)	75
Ecoforest Education For Sustainability	258
The Emmaus International Programme	171
English For Children – Summer Camp	310
English For Kids	310
Equity Ski: Peak Season Reps	321
Equity Travel: Educational Tour Reps	330
EstYES	172
Etudes et Chantiers (UNAREC)	172
Les Eurockeenes De Belfort	349
Eurolingua	358
Exit Festival	348
The Farm Fun	310
Festival Internacional De Benicassim	348
Fiskardo's Nautical & Environment Club	76
Freewheel Holidays: Hosts	318
Friends of the Great Baikal Trail	76
Gençtur	311
Get Kids Going	236
Global Experiences	359
Global Volunteer Network	124
Global Works	126
Globe Aware	127
Globetrotters Education Consulting	360
Great Ormond Street Hospital	237

Grupo Lobo – The Iberian Wolf
   Recovery Centre 77
Halsbury Travel: Ski Season Couriers 320
Hands Up Holidays 220
Hellenic Ornithological Society 77
Hellenic Wildlife Hospital 78
HF Holidays: Walk Leaders 318
Hultsfred Festival 348
ICYE 130
International Bouworde-IBO 174
Interski Snowsport School 320
Interspeak 362
The Italian Job 247
Jubilee Sailing Trust 323
KMC International Work Camps 175
Landdienst-zentralstelle 281
Lingue Senza Frontiere 311
M.E.E.R. E.V. Whale Project 78
Macmillan Cancer Support 237
Marie Curie Cancer Support 237
The Meningitis Trust 238
Mental Health Foundation 238
OIKOS 176
Open Houses Network 204
Pavilion Tours: Watersports Instructors 322
Pinkpop 349
Pro International 177
Projects Abroad 205, 297, 326
Responsible Travel 206
Roman Cat Sanctuary 79
Roskilde Festival 350
Royal National Institute For The Blind 240
La Sabranenque 207
SCOPE 241
Ski-plan: Peak Season Resort Reps 319
Sport & Educational Travel: Couriers 331
Sunseed Desert Technology 262
Tall Stories 249
Tethys Research Institute 79
Ultimate Travel Company 249
Underwater Archaeology Project 208
Union Rempart 208
Vaughantown 301
Village Camps Inc 312
Vitalise: Sighted Guides 335
Vitalise: Ski Guides 321
Whizz Kidz 241
Workcamps Switzerland 179
YHA Challenges 250
Young Austria 312
Youth Action for Peace 167

UK and Ireland

The 3H Fund: Holiday Volunteers 332
The Abbey College 307
Achill Island Field School 188
Active Training And Education 302
Alexanders International School 302
Allanhill Farm 271
Amizade 119
The Anthony Nolan Trust 235
Ardmore Language Schools 303
ATD Fourth World 170
Badaguish Outdoor Centre 332
Ballybin Fruit Farm 281
Bamburgh Research Project 188
Biodynamic Agricultural Association 256
Birkholm Frugt & Baer 281
Broadstairs Folk Week 344
S.H.M Broomfield & Son 271
Butser Ancient Farm 189
BYV Adventure Camps 333
Cairntradlin 271
Cairnwell Mountain Sports 322
Campsite Assistant Teams 341
Canal Camps 66, 189
Cancerbackup 235
Care Challenge 243
Castell Henllys Training Excavation 190
Cathedral Camps 190
Centre for Alternative Technology 66
Cetacean Research and Rescue Unit 67
Chandler & Dunn Ltd 272
Charlton Orchards 272
S.H Chesson 272
Children's Country Holidays Fund 333
Concord College 303
Concordia 165
The Disaway Trust: Holiday Helpers 334
Discovery Summer 304
Earthwatch Insititute 191
Edinburgh International Book Festival 345
EJO – English Holiday Courses 304
Elac Study Vacations 304
Environmental Health Monitors 342
Event Recycling 340
Festive Lizards 340
C. Francis 272
Fridaybridge International Farm Camps 273
Global Works 126
Groundwork: Irish Wildlife Trust Volunteers 67
The Guardian Hay Festival 346
Harold Corrigall 273
Hayles Fruit Farm Ltd 273

Hebridean Whale and Dolphin Trust 68
HF Holidays: Walk Leaders 318
Hill Farm Orchards 273
S & P Hodson-Walker 274
International Farm Camp 274
International Otter Survival Fund 69
International Quest 305
Jubilee Sailing Trust 323
Kentwell Hall – Live as a Tudor 192
King' s School of English 305
Laurel Tree Fruit Farm 274
Lindum Heritage 192
F.W Mansfield & Son 274
Peter Marshall & Co 275
The Monkey Sanctuary 69
The National Trust 70, 193
D.A. Newling & Son 275
North Pennines Archaeology 194
E. Oldroyd And Sons Ltd 275
Oxfam 337
Peppermint Bars 339
Poulton Research Project 194
Prices Fruit Farm 275
Priddy Folk Festival 345
Project International 306
Raasay Outdoor Centre 323
Royal Society for the Protection of Birds 71
S&A Produce Ltd 276
Salmans Ltd 276
Samaritans – Festival Branch 341
Saveock Water Archaeology 195
The Scottish Crannog Centre 195
Sedgeford Archaeological Project 196
Sidmouth Folk Week 344
Silchester Roman Town Field School 196
The Sunday Times Oxford Literary
    Festival 346
Super Camps Ltd 306
Tall Stories 249
Thistle Camps 72, 197
The Times Cheltenham Festival 346
TOC H 138
Towersey Village Festival 344
Trees for Life – Work Weeks 72
Upper Nene Archaeological Society 197
The Vindolanda Trust 198
Vitalise: Sighted Guides 342
VSO Challenges Worldwide 250
Wildlife Trust of South and West Wales 73
Paul Williamson Ltd 276
Withers Fruit Farm 276
Woodlarks Campsite 334

The Workers Beer Company 339
World Challenge Expeditions 331

Middle East

Across The Divide 242
Action For Charity 242
Action Reconciliation for Peace (ARSP) 167
Bethsaida 210
Biosphere Expeditions 51
Charity Challenge 244
Classic Tours 244
Coral Cay Conservation 54
Cultural Cube 357
Ein Gedi 210
Genctur 173
Hands Up Holidays 60, 220
Hebrew University of Jerusalem 211
Hippos (Sussita) Excavation Project 211
National Deaf Children's Society 238
Operation Wallacea 61
Ramat-Rahel 212
Tel Bet Yerah Research Project 212
Tel Dor Project 212
The Tel Rehov Excavations 213
Tell Es-safi/Gath Project 213
Ultimate Travel Company 249
UNIPAL 301
The Yavneh-Yam Project 214
Youth Action for Peace 167
The Zeitah Excavations 214

North America

Across The Divide 242
Agricultural Labour Pool 280
Alutiiq Museum 215
American Bear Association 80
American Hiking Society 80
Amizade 119
Appalachian Mountain Club 81
Appalachian Trail Conservancy 81
Bike Aid 139
Bullocks Permaculture Homestead 257
Caretta Research Project 82
Catalina Island Conservancy 82
Charity Challenge 244
Cherry Growers' Association Canada 279
The Children's Society 236
Classic Tours 244
Coachella Valley Music & Arts Festival 347
The Colorado Trail Foundation 83
Crow Canyon Archaeological Centre 217

Earthwatch Institute 218
Farm Sanctuary Internships 259
Foundation for Sustainable Development 122
Friends of the Cumbres and Toltec
  Scenic Railroad 219
Global Citizens Network 122
Global Volunteer Network 59, 124
Greenforce – Hollywood Film School 361
Halsbury Travel: Ski Season Couriers 320
Institute Of Cultural Ecology 361
Judith River Dinosaur Institute 221
Just Works 175
Kokee Resource Conservation Program 84
MENCAP 238
Mingan Island Cetacean Expeditions 84
The Nature Corps 85
Ores Foundation for Marine Research 85
Passport in Time 223
Royal Tyrrell Museum 224
SCOPE 241
Sierra Club Outings 86, 225
Ski-plan: Peak Season Resort Reps 319
South By South West 350
Swiss Whale Society 65
Ultimate Travel Company 249
Vitalise: Ski Guides 321
Vocation Vacations: Dream Job Holidays 368
Volunteer Farm Of Shenandoah 261
Volunteer for Nature 86
Volunteers for Outdoor Colorado (VOC) 87
Wolf Education and Research Centre 87
Wyoming Dinosaur Centre 226
Youth Action for Peace 167

South America

Across The Divide 242
Action For Charity 242
Adelante Abroad 355
Age Concern 235
Alliance Abroad 88, 139, 290
Amazon-Africa Aid Organisation 140
Amerispan Unlimited 140
Amizade 119
Andean Bear Conservation Project 88
The Anthony Nolan Trust 235
Black Howler Monkey Project 90
Breast Cancer Care 235
Charity Challenge 244
Classic Tours 244
Comunidad Inti Wara Yassi 90
Coral Cay Conservation 54
Cross Cultural Solutions 120, 357

Different Challenge 245
Different Travel 55, 121
Earthwatch Institute 218
Experiental Learning Ecuadorian Program 358
Fire Services National Benevolent Fund 236
Fox Language Academy 291
Fundacion Jatun Sacha 91
Gap Sports 324
Get Kids Going 236
Global Citizens Network 122
Global Crossroad 123, 359
Global Routes 123
Global Volunteer Network 124
Global Works 126
Globe Aware 127
Great Ormond Street Hospital 237
Greenforce 59, 324
Hands Up Holidays 60, 260
Help the Aged 237
i-to-i International Projects 325, 363
ICYE 130
Iko Poran Association 142
Imaginative Traveller 60, 130
Iracambi Atlantic Rainforest Research 92
Macmillan Cancer Support 237
Madventurer 133, 294
Marie Curie Cancer Support 237
Maya Research Program 222
MENCAP 238
Mental Health Foundation 238
Nasca Project, Peru 222
National Deaf Children's Society 238
Oceanic Society Expeditions 93
OIKOS 176
Original Volunteers 94, 134, 295
Peace Villages Foundation 144, 296
Personal Overseas Development 62, 296
Projects Abroad 297, 365
Proyecto Karumbe 95
Quest 63, 135
Santa Martha Rescue Centers 96
SCOPE 241
Sportventurer 327
Task Brasil 146, 262
Teach Peru 300
Transformational Journeys 137
Travellers Worldwide 328, 368
Ultimate Travel Company 249
Voluntarios De Occidente 302
Volunteer Bolivia 145
VSO Challenges Worldwide 250
Whizz Kidz 241
YHA Challenges 250

If you liked this book, you might also enjoy:

GAP YEARS FOR GROWN UPS

"Informative and full of ideas and contacts"
The Times

Gap Years for Grown Ups
includes all the essential
information on the range of year
out opportunities available for
adults including:

- **Specialist gap year schemes
  that accept older participants**
- **Jobs and voluntary work
  around the world**
- **Working with animals and the
  environment**
- **Pursuing a hobby or a
  new project**
- **Planning the trip of a lifetime**

This book is the essential guide to
planning your career break.

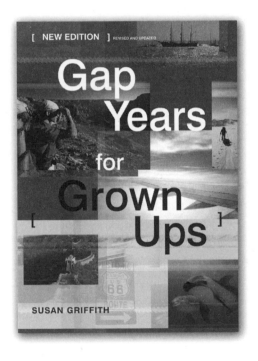

Author: Susan Griffith
Published: August 2006
ISBN: 978-1-85458-351-2

130068

THE INTERNATIONAL DIRECTORY OF VOLUNTARY WORK

"A comprehensive guide to voluntary work around the world"
Daily Telegraph

"An excellent source of information"
Daily Express

Now in its 10th edition, The International Directory of Voluntary Work is the most comprehensive and up-to-date guide of its kind. It covers all types of voluntary work around the world, both long and short-term; from studying whales off Hawaii to teaching English to Indian orphans, or from caring for seal pups in Cornwall to taking part in archaeological digs in France.

International Voluntary Work

Author: Victoria Pybus
Published: November 2006
ISBN: 978-1-85458-351-2